THE GLOBAL IMPACT AND LEGACY OF TRUTH COMMISSIONS

## SERIES ON TRANSITIONAL JUSTICE

The Series on *Transitional Justice* offers a platform for high-quality research within the rapidly growing field of transitional justice. The research is, of necessity inter-disciplinary in nature, drawing from disciplines such as law, political science, history, sociology, criminology, anthropology and psychology, as well as from various specialised fields of study such as human rights, victimology and peace studies. Furthermore, the research is international in outlook, drawing on the knowledge and experience of academics and other specialists in many different regions of the world.

The series is aimed at a variety of audiences who are either working or interested in fields such as crime and justice; human rights; humanitarian law and human security; conflict resolution and peace building. These audiences include academics, researchers, students, policy makers, practitioners, non-governmental organisations and the media.

All books published within the series are subject to a double-blind peer review by recognised authorities in the field.



**Published titles within this Series:**

10. Bas van Stokkom, Neelke Doorn and Paul van Tongeren (eds.), *Public Forgiveness in Post-Conflict Contexts* (2012), 978-1-78068-044-6
11. Ilse Derluyn, Cindy Mels, Stephan Parmentier and Wouter Vandenhole (eds.), *Re-Member. Rehabilitation, Reintegration and Reconciliation of War-Affected Children* (2012), 97894-000-0027-4
12. Anne-Marie de Brouwer, Charlotte Ku, Renée Römkens and Larissa van den Herik (eds.), *Sexual Violence as an International Crime: Interdisciplinary Approaches* (2012), 978-1-78068-002-6
13. Estelle Zinsstag and Martha Albertson Fineman (eds.), *Feminist Perspectives on Transitional Justice: From International and Criminal to Alternative Forms of Justice* (2013), 978-1-78068-142-9
14. Josep M. Tamarit Sumalla, *Historical Memory and Criminal Justice in Spain. A Case of Late Transitional Justice* (2013), 978-1-78068-143-6
15. Catherine Jenkins (ed.), Max du Plessis (ed.), *Law, Nation building and Transformation The South African experience in perspective* (2014), 978-1-78068-184-9
16. Susanne Buckley-Zistel and Stefanie Schäfer (eds.), *Memorials in Times of Transition* (2014), 978-1-78068-211-2
17. Nico Wouters (ed.), *Transitional Justice and Memory in Europe (1945–2013), 978-1-78068-214-3*
18. Agata Fijalkowski and Raluca Grosescu (eds.), *Transitional Criminal Justice in Post-Dictatorial and Post-Conflict Societies*, 978-1-78068-260-0
19. S. Elizabeth Bird and Fraser M. Ottanelli (eds.), *The Performance of Memory as Transitional Justice* 978-1-78068-262-4
20. Bo Viktor Nylund, *Child Soldiers and Transitional Justice*, 978-1-78068-394-2
21. Peter Malcontent (ed.), *Facing the Past: Amending Historical Injustices through Instruments of Transitional Justice*, 978-1-78068-403-1
22. Francesca Capone, *Reparations for Child Victims of Armed Conflict: State of the Field and Current Challenges*, 978-1-78068-438-3
23. Cheryl S. White, *Bridging Divides in Transitional Justice: The Extraordinary Chambers in the Courts of Cambodia*, 978-1-78068-440-6

**For previous volumes in the series, please visit http://tj.intersentia.com**

Series on Transitional Justice, Volume 24

# THE GLOBAL IMPACT AND LEGACY OF TRUTH COMMISSIONS

*Edited by*
Jeremy Sarkin

intersentia
Cambridge – Antwerp – Chicago

Intersentia Ltd
Sheraton House | Castle Park
Cambridge | CB3 0AX | United Kingdom
Tel.: +44 1223 370 170 | Fax: +44 1223 370 169
Email: mail@intersentia.co.uk
www.intersentia.com | www.intersentia.co.uk

*Distribution for the UK and Ireland:*
NBN International
Airport Business Centre, 10 Thornbury Road
Plymouth, PL6 7PP
United Kingdom
Tel.: +44 1752 202 301 | Fax: +44 1752 202 331
Email: orders@nbninternational.com

*Distribution for Europe and all other countries:*
Intersentia Publishing nv
Groenstraat 31
2640 Mortsel
Belgium
Tel.: +32 3 680 15 50 | Fax: +32 3 658 71 21
Email: mail@intersentia.be

*Distribution for the USA and Canada:*
Independent Publishers Group
Order Department
814 North Franklin Street
Chicago, IL 60610
USA
Tel.: +1 800 888 4741 (toll free) | Fax: +1 312 337 5985
Email: orders@ipgbook.com

This work is funded by national funds by the Portuguese Foundation for Science and Technology – Project UID/DIR/00714/2013.



Artwork on cover: Author Jan Jordaan, title 'Hurt', medium Linocut, 1999.
From the Universal Declaration of Human Rights – International Print Portfolio,
Article 5, published by Art for Humanity, South Africa, 1999.

ISBN 978-1-78068-794-0
D/2019/7849/41
NUR 828

GPRC Guaranteed Peer Reviewed Content

British Library Cataloguing in Publication Data. A catalogue record for this book is available from the British Library.

# ACKNOWLEDGEMENTS

This volume is the culmination of a process that began with a conference at NOVA University Lisbon, Portugal, in February 2018, when all the authors came together around the themes of the book. Draft chapters were presented. Chapters were then finalised and an internal review process occurred, to which all authors of the book and the editor contributed. A language review of the chapters was also carried out. Later, all the chapters were sent for double blind review by the editor of the TJ Series, after which the chapters were finalised.

There are many to thank for their assistance in this process. NOVA University assisted with support for the conference and the book. At the Law School, the research centre CEDIS and the organisation Jurisnova were very helpful in various ways. The funding agency FCT in Portugal assisted with funding.

Professor Chandra Sriram, who attended the conference and was involved in the book, passed away during the year. She was a major voice on transitional justice and her contributions to the field were very significant.

Jeremy Sarkin
Lisbon, November 2018

# CONTENTS

# LIST OF CONTRIBUTORS

**Susanne Buckley-Zistel** is Professor of Peace and Conflict Studies and Director of the Centre for Conflict Studies, Philipps University Marburg, Germany. She has held positions at King's College, London, the Peace Research Institute Frankfurt and the Free University, Berlin, and fellowships at the Research Center 'Governance in Areas of Limited Statehood' and at the Käte Hamburger Kolleg 'Global Cooperation Research'. Her research focuses on issues pertaining to peace and conflict, violence, gender and transitional justice, and she has co-edited volumes on *Gender in Transitional Justice* (Palgrave, 2012), *Transitional Justice Theories* (Routledge, 2014), *Memorials in Times of Transition* (Intersentia, 2014), *Spatializing Peace and Conflict* (Palgrave, 2016), *Gender, Violence, Refugees* (Berghan, 2017) and *Perpetrators and Perpetration of Mass Violence* (Routledge, 2018).

**Erin Daly** is Professor of Law at Delaware Law School and Co-Director of the Dignity Rights Project. She is the co-author, with Jeremy Sarkin, of *Reconciliation in Divided Societies: Finding Common Ground* (U. Penn, 2006, 2010) and the author of *Dignity Rights: Courts, Constitutions, and the Worth of the Human Person* (U. Penn, 2013). She is the co-editor, with James R. May, of *Encyclopedia of Human Rights and the Environment: Indivisibility, Dignity and Legality* (forthcoming, Edward Elgar) and many other books on environmental constitutionalism. She serves as the Director of the Global Network for Human Rights and the Environment, and as the US National Correspondent for the Centre international de droit comparé de l'environnement (CIDCE). She has served as the Vice President for Institutional Development at the Université de la Fondation Aristide in Haiti.

**Anita Ferrara** is a lecturer in Human Rights Law at the Irish Centre for Human Rights, National University of Ireland, Galway. She completed her PhD in Law at the School of Oriental and African Studies (SOAS), University of London, in 2012. She previously taught at SOAS on justice and reconciliation in post-conflict societies. Before her academic career, Anita worked for United Nations Agencies and NGOs in the field of human rights. She worked at the UN High Commissioner for Human Rights in Santiago, Chile and at the United Nations Development Programme in Gaborone, Botswana. Her research interests include transitional justice, human rights, the impact and legacy of truth commissions, and memory and law, with a particular focus on the Latin American region.

**Pádraig McAuliffe** is a graduate of University College Cork (BCL and PhD). After a brief period in the Legal Division of the Irish Department of Foreign Affairs, he became a lecturer at the University of Dundee in 2009. He became a Senior Lecturer in the School of Law and Social Justice at the University of Liverpool in 2013 and has been Associate Head of the Law School since 2017. He is the author of two books, *Transitional Justice and Rule of Law Reconstruction: A Contentious Relationship* (Routledge, 2013) and *Transformative Transitional Justice and the Malleability of Post-Conflict States* (Edward Elgar, 2017). His interests include transitional justice, the historic institutionalism of socio-economic rights and justice sector reform.

**Brianne McGonigle Leyh** is an Associate Professor at Utrecht University, Netherlands Institute of Human Rights. Her expertise includes human rights, rule of law, victims' rights and transitional justice. She also currently acts as Senior Counsel for the Public International Law & Policy Group and serves on the Advisory Board of the Netherlands Helsinki Committee. Previously she worked as Co-Counsel, Civil Party Lawyer at the Extraordinary Chambers in the Courts of Cambodia (ECCC). She won the International Association of Penal Law (AIDP), American Branch, Book of the Year Award in 2013. She has also been selected as a member of the Utrecht Young Academy. She received her PhD in law from Utrecht University, her Juris Doctorate, cum laude, and Master of Arts in International Relations from American University, and her Bachelor of Arts, cum laude, in the University Professors Program at Boston University.

**Luke Moffett** is a senior law lecturer at Queen's University Belfast, Northern Ireland. He previously worked as a research fellow on the Arts and Humanities Research Council (AHRC) funded project 'Amnesties, Prosecution and the Public Interest in the Northern Ireland Transition.' His PhD examined the role of victims within the International Criminal Court and their ability to participate and claim reparations. His book 'Justice for Victims before the International Criminal Court' was published in 2014. He is the co-editor of the *Research Handbook of Transitional Justice* (Edward Elgar, 2017). He is currently Principal Investigator on the AHRC funded 'Reparations, Responsibility and Victimhood in Transitional Societies' project in six jurisdictions, which explores victim identity and responsibility in reparation mechanisms and the obligations of non-state actors.

**Joana Rebelo Morais** is a PhD student of Comparative Politics at the Institute of Social Sciences, University of Lisbon. She holds an MA in Political Science from ISCTE-IUL. Her Master's thesis was entitled 'The Commission of the Black Book on the Fascist Regime: In Search of the Truth?' ('A Comissão do Livro Negro sobre o Regime Fascista: Em busca da verdade?'). It received an Honorary Mention in the 19th edition of the Mário Soares Foundation – EDP Foundation Award in 2017. Her research interests include democratisations, founding elections and truth commissions.

**Filipa Raimundo** is a research fellow at the Institute of Social Sciences, University of Lisbon, and Guest Assistant Professor in the Department of Political Science and Public Policy at ISCTE-IUL, Lisbon. She holds a PhD in Political and Social Sciences from the European University Institute, Florence. Her PhD dissertation on 'Post-Transitional Justice: Spain, Portugal and Poland Compared' received an Honorary Mention in the 2014 edition of the Portuguese Political Science Association PhD Dissertation Award. Her interests include democratisation, transitional justice, authoritarian legacies and political attitudes. Her research work has been published by journals such as *Democratization*, *South European Society and Politics*, and *Mediterranean Politics*, and in edited volumes by Palgrave/Macmillan and Columbia University Press.

**Jeremy Sarkin** is Distinguished Visiting Professor of Law at NOVA University Lisbon, Portugal. He has undergraduate and postgraduate law degrees from South Africa, a Master of Laws degree from Harvard Law School and a Doctor of Laws degree on comparative and international law. He is admitted to practice as attorney in the USA and South Africa. He was a member (2008–2014), and Chairperson-Rapporteur (2009–2012), of the United Nations Working Group on Enforced or Involuntary Disappearances. He served as an acting judge in 2002 and 2003 in the High Court in South Africa. He has published 17 books and more than 300 articles and book chapters. He is a member of a number of journal editorial boards and serves on the boards of a number of NGOs. He regularly assists the United Nations, the European Union, African institutions and others on constitutional, human rights and transitional justice issues.

**Elin Skaar** is a political scientist and senior researcher at the Chr. Michelsen Institute (CMI) in Bergen, Norway. Exploring the intersections between law and politics in Latin America and Africa, her research interests include human rights, transitional justice, and judicial reform. Currently, her main research focus is on Latin American truth commissions. She has for three decades published widely on democratisation processes and human rights. Her publications include *Judicial Independence and Human Rights in Latin America: Violations, Politics, and Prosecution* (Palgrave Macmillan, 2011), *After Violence: Transitional Justice, Peace, and Democracy* (Routledge, 2015, co-authored), and *Transitional Justice in Latin America: The Uneven Road from Impunity towards Accountability* (Routledge, 2016, co-edited). She holds a PhD in political science from the University of California, Los Angeles.

**Eric Wiebelhaus-Brahm** is Associate Professor of Political Science and Coordinator of the Middle Eastern Studies Program at the University of Arkansas at Little Rock. His research agenda focuses on transitional justice, human rights, post-conflict reconstruction, and democratisation. He critically examines the empirical and normative arguments used to justify the introduction of social and economic policies in societies emerging from periods of conflict and repression. Much of his work has focused on using social science research methods to evaluate transitional justice mechanisms. His research is driven by a normative desire to set more realistic policy expectations, particularly among victims and marginalised groups. He is the author of *Truth Commissions and Transitional Societies* (Routledge, 2010), as well as 11 book chapters and 17 peer-reviewed articles.

# INTRODUCTION

## Contextualising and Understanding the Global Role, Impact and Legacy of Truth Commissions

Jeremy SARKIN*



## 1. INTRODUCTION

Globally, truth commissions, often termed truth and reconciliation commissions, are popular options to deal with aspects of a country's violent past,[1] despite the extensive criticisms levelled against them.[2] Some claim that truth commissions are not the best choice. Call indicates that the major flaws of truth commission processes are that they often serve as 'second best' mechanisms to judicial

---

* My thanks for the helpful comments received from Eric Wiebelhaus-Brahm, Pádraig McAuliffe and the anonymous reviewers.

1 A. FERRARA, *Assessing the Long-Term Impact of Truth Commissions: The Chilean Truth And Reconciliation Commission in Historical Perspective*, Routledge, Abingdon and New York, 2015.

2 See on the criticisms J. SARKIN and T. DAVI, 'Examining the Criticisms Levelled Against Transitional Justice: Towards An Understanding of the State of the Field' (2017) 11(1) *Human Rights and International Legal Discourse* 7. See also S. NAUENBERG, 'Spreading the Truth: How Truth Commissions Address Human Rights Abuses in the World Society' (2015) 30(6) *International Sociology* 654.

punishment.[3] He argues that their reports are incomplete because in some cases only victims testify and because they lack funding. It has also been argued that truth commissions 'have recurrent, structural problems, ranging from limited resources to the politicization of the process to virtual impunity for a wide number of offenders'.[4] However, Martha Minow has argued that truth commissions 'are not a second best alternative to prosecutions … When the societal goals include restoring dignity to victims, offering a basis for individual healing, and also promoting reconciliation across a divided nation, a truth commission may be as or more powerful than prosecutions.'[5] It has also been said that truth commissions are no longer 'a political compromise [there has been a shift from them] being the "weaker alternative" to trials to a practice that is morally equal and complementary to the judicial option'.[6] These institutions play pivotal roles[7] in a number of respects, including truth recovery and aiding a society to repair the wounds that exist amongst victims and perpetrators and amongst divided groups.[8] This view is not accepted universally and some have doubts about the roles these institutions play.[9] However, the use and strength of truth commissions in regard to truth lies in creating complete records of human rights abuses, including the nature and extent of the crimes and the names and fates of the victims. While in some instances the reports issued by truth commissions include the identities of persons who gave the orders for human rights violations, as well as those who executed the orders, mostly such names have been omitted for political reasons.[10] However, truth commissions can play a multitude of roles in addressing past human rights violations.

---

3 C. Call, 'Is Transitional Justice Really Just?' (2004) 11(1) *The Brown Journal of World Affairs* 101.

4 A. Costi, 'Hybrid Tribunals as a Valid Alternative to International Tribunals for the Prosecution of International Crimes', paper presented at the Third Annual Victoria University Symposium on Human Rights, Wellington, 24 August, 2005, https://ssrn.com/abstract=2738183.

5 M. Minow, *Between Vengeance and Forgiveness: Facing History After Genocide*, Beacon Press, Boston, 1998, at 88–89.

6 M.B.J. Hirsch, 'Ideational Change and the Emergence of the International Norm of Truth and Reconciliation Commissions' (2014) 20(3) *European Journal of International Relations* 810.

7 J. Allen, 'Balancing Justice and Social Unity: Political Theory and the Idea of a Truth and Reconciliation Commission' (1999) 49 *The University of Toronto Law Journal* 315.

8 N. Dimitrijević, 'Justice beyond Blame: Moral Justification of (the Idea of) a Truth Commission' (2006) 50(3) *Journal of Conflict Resolution* 368.

9 D. Mendeloff, 'Truth-Seeking, Truth-Telling, and Post-Conflict Peacebuilding: Curb the Enthusiasm?' (2004) 6 *International Studies Review* 355.

10 H. Furtado, 'On Demons and Dreamers: Violence, Silence and the Politics of Impunity in the Brazilian Truth Commission' (2017) 48(4) *Security Dialogue* 316.

This volume emerges at a time when there is the confluence of two trends. The first trend is a growing critique of truth commissions as being unresponsive to the socio-economic needs of transitional societies as part of a growing body of critique about transitional justice as a whole. The second trend is the increasing use, salience, professionalism and ambitions of truth commissions. Thus, the book emerges at a time when truth commissions are being both doubted and reified like never before.

This introductory chapter examines a range of issues to contextualise the need for a book on the global impact and legacies of truth commissions. The book's purpose is to understand the role, impact and legacy of truth commissions over the last 50 years. It investigates what kind of impact and legacy previous truth commissions have left both for the societies in which they have taken place, and for future truth commissions around the world.

This chapter lays the groundwork for the rest of the book. It examines, firstly, why transitional justice processes are established in states. This is important to understand, as truth commissions are established in a transitional justice context. Understanding this context is important for appreciating the environment within which they work. The chapter provides an overview of some of the issues of importance when dealing with truth commissions. Another important subject explored is how a truth commission is defined. This is done because the debates about what is or is not a truth commission are important in understanding what institutions are classified as such, and why certain institutions that play similar roles are not defined as truth commissions. Also touched on is why the methodology behind defining a truth commission should be reconsidered. The chapter also examines what effect truth commissions have, because to understand truth commissions more fully, it is necessary to understand the many roles they play. The functions of truth commissions are briefly explored, as are their forms and the scope of their work.

The impact and legacies of past truth commissions are important issues to explore, as there is tremendous debate about whether truth commissions play a constructive role, and whether or not their effects have been positive. This chapter introduces the issues in the chapters concerning impact and legacy, i.e. what those terms mean, how they ought to be considered, and their relationship to one another. Also considered is what the legacy of truth commissions may be in particular states, putting forward a variety of contextual issues that need to be taken into account. These are important in the present global context as, while truth commissions continue to be created in large numbers, there is, in some parts of the world, an uncritical acceptance of what they do. There is little critical analysis of what these institutions achieve or sufficient understanding of the roles they have played or could play. There is often just an acceptance of their roles and the legacy roles that they play or might play in the future. In other parts of world where truth commissions are not usually created, there is much more scepticism about what they do. There is great mystery as to why countries in the global south rely on them so much. The fact that truth commissions as institutions have existed for half a century means that a more meaningful process for determining their impact and legacy is important. Therefore, it is time to make a solid accounting of what truth commissions do. To do this, it is necessary to go beyond the usual adages and determine more scientifically what their roles are and the extent to which they affect the democratic and human rights situations in the countries where they do their work. What is clear is that those who support and those that oppose the roles they play often overestimate or underestimate the contributions they can make.

However, it is important to note that the impact and legacy of these transitional justice mechanisms should not be measured in isolation.[11] This is because they are neither implemented nor work in seclusion. They cannot work separately from the range of other processes that exist in the country, be they in the public or private sector. For this reason, some societies have implemented a number of mechanisms in an attempt to redress a legacy of mass human rights abuses. However, it has more frequently been the case that a society will pursue one strategy and this will be reflected by one dominant transitional justice mechanism. This is ultimately a weakness, as for a society to deal with such problems it should utilise a combination of mechanisms that may achieve a broader range of objectives, such as accountability, peace and justice. Critically, in attempting to measure the role of truth commissions, it is problematic to do so in isolation, as truth commissions do not affect the situation on their own. They affect the situation, but as a part of a process. How that process unfolds is very much affected by how other aspects of the environment influence it. Thus, measuring the role of truth commissions individually is seemingly impossible. It is possible to arrive at some idea of the role they play individually, but since they work in a context where what happens in the country on a whole host of issues has an effect on the country, it is difficult to arrive at an objective exact individual role.[12] The question, therefore, is to find ways of measuring more objectively what truth commissions do and their roles, their impacts and their legacies in the short, medium and long term. Fundamentally, those who support them and those who oppose them often have a blinkered view of what they can or should do. They see their impact and legacy through either rose-tinted glasses or clouded ones.

---

11 G. Dancy, H. Kim and E. Wiebelhaus-Brahm, 'The Turn to Truth: Trends in Truth Commission Experimentation' (2010) 9(1) *Journal of Human Rights* 45, at 59.

12 C. Duggan, 'Editorial Note' (2010) 4 *International Journal of Transitional Justice* 315.

This chapter was used as the basis for the rest of the book to follow similar approaches. The chapter was sent to the other authors during the writing process for them to draw from it and ensure that all the issues, especially concerning impact and legacy, were taken up in a somewhat coherent fashion.

The first chapter of the book ('Is Anyone Listening? A Review of the Research on Attitudes Towards Truth Commissions' by Filipa Raimundo and Joana Rebelo Morais) reviews more than three dozen academic works, published between 1999 and 2017, that use public opinion data on truth commissions and truth revelation to understand the legacy and impact of these institutions. The chapter examines the samples and methods used in each of the publications, and studies their contribution to the understanding of citizens' attitudes and perceptions of this particular aspect of transitional justice. The chapter is structured around three topics: individual preferences, individual assessment, and the effects of truth commissions and truth revelation at the individual level. Regarding preferences, the chapter shows that support for truth revelation is usually significantly higher than support for truth commissions. Regarding assessment, the work reveals that better knowledge of a truth commission does not equal greater approval of its work. Finally, regarding effects, the chapter indicates there are often negative emotions associated with participation in truth commissions. The chapter also offers some considerations concerning the differences between post-authoritarian and post-conflict situations, as well as between victims and non-victims. The chapter concludes by recommending that scholars collecting this kind of data engage with each other more often in order to facilitate cross-country comparisons.

The second chapter ('Assessing the Long-Term Impact and Legacy of Truth Commissions' by Anita Ferrara) contends that despite the growing popularity of truth commissions, there is still little understanding of their longer-term effects and consequences. The chapter argues that investigating and understanding the long-term consequences of truth commissions is of fundamental importance to grasping the deeper social and political impact that these bodies seek to achieve in their respective societies. The chapter analyses the major challenges of undertaking this type of research, before suggesting a possible framework for evaluating the longer-term impact of truth commissions. It discusses how and to what extent truth commissions can support and interact with other transitional justice measures. The chapter concludes by arguing that truth commissions' long-term impact should be evaluated by their ability to change attitudes, beliefs and practices at the socio-political and institutional levels.

The third chapter ('The Global Textual Legacies of Truth Commissions: Narratives on Violence in the Reports of Sierra Leone, Liberia, Kenya and Beyond' by Susanne Buckley-Zistel) investigates texts – in the form of published reports – produced by truth commissions as part of their legacy. As presented elsewhere in this volume, the global legacy of truth commissions is often considered in terms of output, such as reparations and reforms, as well as less tangible societal aspects, such as the effect on the relationship between the conflicting parties and social change in a general sense. The present chapter, by contrast, is concerned with the global textual legacy of truth commission reports that depict the findings of the commissions based on individual statements and that are circulated widely to a global readership on the web. In truth commission hearings, individuals narrate what they have experienced and witnessed so that recounting these ordeals produces a cacophony of voices on violence. The truth commission reports, however, do not simply repeat these voices but interpret them. They offer particular narratives about the past, which are fixed in writing, printed on paper and made available as reports for future reference. In order to narrow the scope of the sake of the analysis, the chapter focuses on one particular form of violence – sexual violence – and on a limited number of commissions, namely Sierra Leone, Kenya and Liberia.

The fourth chapter ('The Implementation Record of Truth Commissions' Recommendations in Latin America' by Elin Skaar) argues that the body of recommendations made by state-sponsored truth commissions are theoretically neglected and empirically under-researched within the scholarly field of transitional justice. Yet, as this chapter argues, these recommendations form an important legacy of transitional justice. The truth commission recommendations have two main purposes: to seek to repair serious human rights violations of the past, and to prevent similar violations from happening again in the future. In Latin America alone, around 1,000 recommendations to governments have been made by truth commissions in their final reports over the past 30 years, spanning institutional and legal reforms, symbolic and material reparations, and a wide range of other measures. This chapter specifically analyses recommendations that deal with reparations to victims and their families, memorialisation, search for the disappeared, and human rights education. It shows that one important long-term effect of these truth commission recommendations is their contributions to the reconstruction of democracy and heightened societal consciousness around human rights.

The fifth chapter ('In the Aftermath of Truth: Implementing Truth Commissions' Recommendations on Reparations: Following Through for Victims' by Luke Moffett) notes that reparations and truth commissions are two key, but interrelated, pillars of transitional justice. Truth commissions often make recommendations on reparations to help further the commissions' goals of reconciliation and dealing with the past at the individual or community level. Reparations in turn can contribute to truth. The chapter therefore explores the connections between truth commissions and reparations by considering the scope of recommendations, the justifications for reparation and the processes that shape such measures. The chapter also considers the legacy and global impact of truth commissions and the challenges around implementing recommendations for reparations, including how victims and civil society partially or forcibly implement them. Following this, the chapter contrasts countries that have created reparation programmes without or before a truth commission and the shortcomings therein, highlighting the interconnected role of truth with reparations in addressing the legacies of mass atrocities.

The sixth chapter ('Truth Commissions and Social Justice: "Wishful Thinking or Not Very Thoughtful Wishing"?' by Brianne McGonigle Leyh) argues that post-conflict societies often design and implement transitional justice processes, such as trials, truth commissions or reparation programmes, in order to address past human rights and humanitarian law violations. These processes aim to make a clear break with past abusive practices in order to re-establish trust within and between society and the state. Transitional justice programming, however, has been criticised for being too focused on the past without addressing the root causes of the violence or social and economic concerns of the future. To address this gap, and prevent the reoccurrence of conflict, prominent scholars and practitioners have called for transitional justice processes to adopt 'social justice' as their ultimate objective, and to become transformative in result. Scholars have identified truth commissions as particularly well suited for delivering on social justice goals. In particular, their mandates, processes and outcomes provide the necessary space and flexibility to address social justice concerns. This chapter looks at the question of whether truth commissions have been able to live up to their transformative potential to bring about greater social justice. It looks at modest and potential contributions of truth commissions to the notion of social justice more generally, highlighting where truth commissions have, in limited circumstances, emphasised important social justice concerns, and where they should have emphasised these but have failed to do so. It notes the many challenges to any significant contribution to the lives and social justice concerns of affected communities. As a single policy instrument, truth commissions will inherently always play a modest role, in part because of their temporary nature and in part because of their weak political leverage. Yet, despite the fact that truth commissions have a restricted capacity to respond to the wide array of social justice needs, they are well placed to make a modest discursive contribution to a greater whole. The chapter concludes by calling for both more modesty when looking at the legacy of truth commissions and more collaboration between truth commissions' other transitional justice and post-conflict responses in order to better address social justice concerns.

The seventh chapter ('Transitioning Toward Dignity' by Erin Daly) maintains that most truth commissions are designed to help craft an inclusive society in which all citizens are engaged for the betterment of the communities that comprise the nation. Their success is difficult, if not impossible, to measure, but can be approximated by how well they catalyse change in the public and private spheres. This chapter argues that these transitional goals rest on a foundation of respect for human dignity, and that truth commissions can enhance their effectiveness by being more conscientious in respecting human dignity in their promotion of truth and reconciliation and if their pronouncements and reports more clearly explain how their recommendations relating to, for instance, amnesty, acknowledgement and the promotion of democracy are founded on human dignity and would promote a culture of respect for dignity. Just as the foundational documents of the international human rights era did, truth commissions can leave a lasting legacy by being explicit about the importance of human dignity to the establishment of the new post-transitional dispensation.

The eighth chapter ('Towards an Understanding of How Truth Commissions Can Use Their Amnesty Powers to Enhance Their Impact and Legacy' by Jeremy Sarkin) examines the legacy of truth commissions in relation to amnesty. In analysing the various range of mandates and powers of different truth commissions around the world, the chapter aims to establish that having the power to directly grant amnesty makes truth commissions more effective at revealing the past, bringing truth to victims, and creating a clearer narrative of what occurred during periods of conflict. The powers of truth commissions are reviewed because, while not always specifically articulated, a function of truth commissions the world over is to gain truth from perpetrators, but this is seldom achieved. While perpetrator testimony and cooperation is not usually achieved to any large degree, the ability of a truth commission to draw the truth out of perpetrators should be a factor in evaluating its success. This chapter contrasts the effectiveness of a truth commission amnesty process that directly grants amnesty with those that only had the power to recommend amnesty, in such countries as Grenada, Timor-Leste, Timor-Leste/Indonesia, Liberia, Kenya, and the Republic of Korea. A number of other processes that never came to fruition, or that are still working, are also briefly reviewed.

The ninth chapter ('Truth Commissions in Non-Transitional Contexts: Implications for their Impact and Legacy' by Eric Wiebelhaus-Brahm) notes that, in general, expectations about the impact of truth commissions assume that they are created in transitional contexts where social, political and economic institutions are undergoing significant upheaval. One of the global legacies of the truth commission model, however, has been that they are increasingly being employed in various contexts where little to no transformation is taking place. For example, truth commissions have been created in post-conflict scenarios, such as in Sri Lanka, where the government has decisively defeated an armed threat, so there is no real political transition. Truth commissions also have been created by firmly entrenched authoritarian regimes, such as in Bahrain and Morocco, to address histories of human rights violations. Finally, other truth commissions, such as Canada's Truth and Reconciliation Commission (TRC) and the Maine Wabanaki-State Child Welfare TRC in the USA, have been created in established democracies in order to address historical wrongs. This chapter probes conceptually and empirically whether and how scholars, activists and affected communities should adjust their expectations as to the impact of truth commissions in such contexts.

The tenth and final chapter ('Surrogacy and Resistance: Evolving Patterns in Unofficial Truth Commissions and Truth Projects' by Pádraig McAuliffe) argues that unofficial truth projects like testimony-gathering, books of the dead, memorials and exhumations are increasingly prevalent in transitional justice practice beyond the reach of the state. Some argue these bodies are a critical response to official truth commissions and their often-perceived disappointing legacies. Critics of truth commissions have argued that they might creatively re-appropriate the techniques of liberal-legalist transitional justice and challenge the state-bureaucratic model from which they were derived. The chapter notes reality has been somewhat different and argues that what can be seen is a somewhat ambivalent form of resistance that splits the difference between the idealised bottom-up model that could give meaningful effect to grassroots visions of truth on the one hand, and the more technocratic process of surrogacy where unofficial truth projects substitute for formal truth processes where the state proves unwilling or unable to institute them on the other.

## 1.1. WHY ARE TRANSITIONAL JUSTICE PROCESSES ESTABLISHED?

At the domestic level, states that emerge from a period of mass human rights abuses have to address a host of critical questions in determining whether and how to deal with the legacy of these abuses. Such questions include: what happened? Who carried out the abuses? Why were they carried out? Who were the victims? What types of violations were carried out? Should there be accountability or amnesty? And if so, to what extent should reparations be provided to victims and the wider society? Furthermore, other crucial issues ought to be taken into consideration. These include: how can national cohesion, nation-building and reconciliation be achieved? Will the accountability process raise the threat of further violence? What steps ought to be taken to prevent the recurrence of conflict?

At the national level, dealing with the past and achieving national reconciliation, building unity, and reconstructing the institutions necessary for stable political and economic systems are often seen to be in conflict with other issues, such as holding people accountable for their roles in human rights abuses in the past.[13] The needs of victims can diverge from those of society as a whole, especially on questions concerning what occurred and the need to prosecute those responsible, especially high-ranking members of the present and former security forces. These demands have to be balanced against the political reality of a new government, which may have inherited a fragile state and may have limited opportunity or less freedom of action than it would like to exercise state power. A critical question that is often asked is what balance ought to be sought between these goals, and how much emphasis ought to be placed on reconciliation?

Therefore, post-conflict states and states trying to move on from violence and conflict have several options through which they may address these issues.[14] For example, comprehensive accounts of the past are often sought as a useful tool to aid societies in their transitions from war or oppression to peace. However, atoning for the past can run counter to the aims of national reconciliation, unity and institutional reconstruction. Accordingly, post-conflict governments often choose policies based on the circumstances of their societies, taking into account the crimes committed, the effect that they have had, the political and economic situation, and the resources available to them. In so doing, they face choices including the prudence of granting amnesty, conducting criminal trials, or putting in place truth commissions. While criminal trials and truth commissions each facilitate the revelation of details of past abuses, they are not mutually exclusive.[15] Rather, the specifics of balancing differing mechanisms must be determined on a case-by-case basis. Moreover, the manner in which a nation deals with its past reverberates throughout its present and has critical effects for its future. Local and international observers, at least in part, often measure the success of a new state by its treatment of the past, including how victims and perpetrators are treated by each other and by society in general. While the redistribution of resources or retooling of the educational, health, housing or other welfare systems might be more important in the long run, as may be reconstruction tasks, reconciliation is almost as significant. Given that past abuse often prompts transition, the public often desires assurance that the sacrifices endured to change the regime were not in vain. A government that openly eschews impunity demonstrates its commitment to justice and the rule of law, whereas a more conciliatory, victim-oriented stance models empathy and forgiveness.

---

13 OHCHR, *Rule-of-Law Tools for Post-Conflict States: Truth Commissions*, United Nations, New York and Geneva, 2006.

14 E. Stanley, 'Truth Commissions and the Recognition of State Crime' (2005) 45 *British Journal of Criminology* 582.

15 B. Leebaw, 'The Irreconcilable Goals of Transitional Justice' (2008) 30 *Human Rights Quarterly* 95.

These matters of interest to states are also of academic interest. As an academic discipline, or field of study, transitional justice has come into being over the last 30 years as academia has taken a greater interest in understanding the past and dealing with it. Despite – and maybe because of – the massive developments in transitional justice over a very short period of time, the status and role of transitional justice is contested. Some claim that, due to its growing complexity and relevance, transitional justice has the characteristics of an evolving or emerging 'field'.[16]

Transitional justice has been defined as a 'set of practices, mechanisms and concerns that are aimed at confronting and dealing with the legacies of mass human rights violations'.[17] Whilst such a definition may seem to be somewhat imprecise, it is in fact a reflection of the number of divergent views as to how societies should endeavour to deal with large-scale human rights abuses and the multitude of methods that can be used to investigate the past. Thus, the academic field of transitional justice studies how truth, justice, reconciliation, reparations and institutional reform take place among other steps to avoid non-repetition of the same violations in the future. The main aspects of transitional justice therefore include dealing with matters relating to truth disclosure; but there are many others. Another critical role is in promoting or consolidating democracies and human rights principles.

The conceptual foundations of transitional justice imply that one can find its origin either as part of the human rights movement, or as an entirely new field.[18] On the one hand, transitional justice can be identified as a 'field' in that it:

> is clearly distinguishable from the field out of which it emerged, which is the field of human rights; 2) it implies a set of actors who have a set of common aims, and who are thus oriented toward one another in their practice; 3) it has developed a variety of institutions to advance those aims; and 4) it advances distinctive criteria of judgment and self-legitimation.[19]

Other scholars claim that transitional justice is not a field but rather a 'label or cloak that aims to rationalize a set of diverse bargains in relation to the past

---

16 See H. Weinstein, 'Editorial Note: The Myth of Closure, the Illusion of Reconciliation: Final Thoughts on Five Years as Co-Editor-in Chief' (2011) 5(1) *International Journal of Transitional Justice* 1.

17 H. van der Merwe, V. Baxter and A.R. Chapman (eds.), *Assessing the Impact of Transitional Justice: Challenges for Empirical Research*, United States Institute for Peace Press, Washington D.C., 2009, at vii.

18 C. Bell, 'Transitional Justice, Interdisciplinarity and the State of the "Field" or "Non-Field"' (2009) 3(1) *International Journal of Transitional Justice* 5.

19 P. Arthur, 'How Transitions Reshaped Human Rights: A Conceptual History of Transitional Justice' (2009) 31(2) *Human Rights Quarterly* 321, at 324.

as an integrated endeavour, so as to obscure the quite different normative, moral and political implications of the bargains.'[20]

Whilst the question of transitional justice has generally been raised in the aftermath of violent conflict, the concept is not limited to this context. Transitional justice continues to play an increasing role in post-conflict contexts, but it also plays a role in situations where a conflict is still ongoing.[21] Transitional justice also has an important role to play in emergencies,[22] although this has seldom been the case, and truth commissions are usually defined as dealing with the past alone and not current matters.

As a result, more focus has been applied to understanding why establishing a comprehensive account of the past is vital to successful transitions and ensuring that states do not erupt into violence again. While Correa, Guillerot and Magarrell note that truth commissions are usually implemented 'in contexts of transition, in which state institutions mandated to guarantee the rule of law are weak, corrupted, or non-existent, and victims are often focused on meeting their most basic daily needs',[23] there are other contexts in which truth commissions are established, including places where there has been conflict, violence and human rights abuse.

Transitional justice also overlaps with international justice, especially international criminal justice. Thus transitional justice is not only a domestic issue, as the international community deals with these issues as well. For this reason, there has been, over the last 25 years, a cascade of new international courts and internationalised courts coming into being. The formation of the ad hoc criminal tribunals for Rwanda and the former Yugoslavia, as well as the entering into force of the International Criminal Court, have brought about greater chances of accountability. So too have the hybrid breed of internationalised domestic courts in countries such as Sierra Leone, Cambodia and East Timor. At the same time, greater rights have been accorded to victims at the international, regional and domestic levels, both in theory and in practice.[24]

---

20 Bell, *supra* note 18, at 6.

21 A.L. Hinton, S.E. Bronner and N. Navarro (eds.), *Transitional Justice: Global Mechanisms and Local Realities after Genocide and Mass Violence*, Rutgers University Press, Piscataway, 2010, at 7.

22 G. Anders, 'Transitional Justice, States of Emergency and Business as Usual: Sierra Leone between 1999 and 2003' (2014) 45(3) *Development and Change* 524.

23 C. Correa, J. Guillerot and L. Magarrell, 'Reparations and Victim Participation: A Look at the Truth Commission Experience', in C. Ferstman, M. Goetz and A. Stephens (eds.), *Reparations for Victims of Genocide, War Crimes and Crimes against Humanity*, Brill, Leiden, 2009.

24 J. García-Godos, 'Victims' Rights and Distributive Justice: In Search of Actors' (2013) 14(3) *Human Rights Review* 241.

## 1.2. DEFINING WHAT A TRUTH COMMISSION IS

Truth commissions are just one mechanism to deal with the past. Other, similar mechanisms exist, including historical commissions, commissions of enquiry, tribunals and courts. The extensive nature of the truth-seeking processes that now exist reflects the extent to which truth is seen to be a vital issue in dealing with events from the past.[25]

There is not one accepted definition of what a truth commission is. Some, such as Barkan, define almost all commissions that examine truth as truth commissions. He states that:

> Truth commissions vary greatly: They range from international to local. Some are state-sponsored, while others are organized by civil society. Some attempt to uncover recent crimes, war crimes, and gross violations of human rights, while others are engaged in investigations of atrocities more than one hundred years old.[26]

This definition would therefore encompass hundreds of 'truth commissions'. Some include certain commissions that most others do not classify as such, for example commissions that investigated truth matters in Romania, Estonia, Lithuania and Latvia.[27] These mechanisms are not included in the accepted universe of truth commissions because they are deemed not to comply with the definition of what a truth commission is.[28] Some countries are deemed to have had many truth commissions. For example, in South Korea there have been approximately 20 truth commissions[29] to create national unity and gain a complete picture of the country's past. South Africa, during its transition, also had a number of truth commissions. They were established by the state and by political organisations, as well as by victims' groups.[30]

---

25 E. Daly, 'Truth Skepticism: An Inquiry Into the Value of Truth in Times of Transition' (2008) 2 *International Journal of Transitional Justice* 23.

26 E. Barkan, 'Introduction: Historians and Historical Reconciliation' (2009) 114(4) *The American Historical Review* 899.

27 L. Stan, 'Truth Commissions in Post-Communism: The Overlooked Solution?' (2009) 2 *Open Political Science Journal* 1.

28 O. Bakiner, 'Between Politics and History: The Baltic Truth Commissions in Global Perspective', in C.M. Horne and L. Stan (eds.), *Transitional Justice and the Former Soviet Union: Reviewing the Past, Looking Toward the Future*, Cambridge University Press, Cambridge, 2018, at 155.

29 T.U. Baik, 'Fairness in Transitional Justice Initiatives: The Case of South Korea' (2013) 19 *Buffalo Human Rights Law Review*, 169, at 170.

30 These included the Skweyiya Commission, Stuart Commission, the Douglas Commission and the Motseunyane Commission. Numerous other reports were written, including by organisations investigating their own violations. See further S. Ellis, 'Mbokodo: Security in ANC Camps, 1961–1990' (1994) 93(371) *African Affairs* 279.

Truth commissions are therefore defined in a myriad of ways. However, it is agreed that they examine past human rights abuses. Despite this, the term truth commission has also been used, for example, to describe three processes to investigate the global economic crisis that began in 2008 and its effects in Iceland, Ireland and Greece. These three institutions were the Icelandic Special Investigation Committee created in 2008, the Irish Parliamentary Banking Inquiry created in 2014 and the Greek Committee on Public Debt created in 2015.[31] These processes are agreed by almost everyone in the field not to fall within the definition of what qualifies as a truth commission. This is not to argue about their merits, but simply to state that they do not fall within what is accepted to be a truth commission from a definitional point of view.

A variety of definitions of what constitutes a truth commission exist. The United Nations in 2004 characterised a truth commission as 'official, temporary, non-judicial fact-finding bodies that investigate a pattern of abuses of human rights or humanitarian law committed over a number of years'.[32] A more encompassing definition is provided by Hayner, who has argued that a truth commission: (1) is focused on the past, rather than ongoing events; (2) investigates a pattern of events that took place over a period of time; (3) engages directly and broadly with the affected populations, gathering information on their experiences; (4) is a temporary body, with the aim of concluding with a final report; and (5) is officially authorised or empowered by the State under review.[33] Her earlier definition (1994) was criticised by Mark Freeman, because it included in the definition non-state commissions of inquiry. Freeman argued that formal truth commissions are only established or authorised by states.[34] Thus, Freeman argues that a truth commission is an ad hoc, autonomous and victim-centred commission of inquiry set up in and authorised by a state for the primary purposes of: (1) investigating and reporting on the principal causes and consequences of broad and relatively recent patterns of severe violence or repression that occurred in the state during determinate periods of abusive rule or conflict; and (2) making recommendations for their redress and future prevention. This definition contains the terms 'autonomous' and 'victim-centred', which many other definitions do not.

---

31 I. Kovras, S. McDaid and R. Hjalmarsson, 'Truth Commissions after Economic Crises: Political Learning or Blame Game?' (2017) 66 *Political Studies* 173.

32 UN Security Council, *The Rule of Law and Transitional Justice in Conflict and Post-Conflict Societies*, UN Doc. S/2004/616 (23 August 2004).

33 P.B. Hayner, *Unspeakable Truths: Confronting State Terror and Atrocity*, 2nd edn, Routledge, New York, 2011.

34 M. Freeman, *Truth Commissions and Procedural Fairness*, Cambridge University Press, Cambridge, 2006, at 18–19.

A more problematic definition is that of Dancy, Kim and Wiebelhaus-Brahm,[35] which contains the phrase that the institution investigates 'a pattern of abuses to personal integrity rights that occurred over a period of time, some of which were perpetrated by state actors'. However, it can be questioned why a truth commission should be limited to personal integrity rights only, what 'a period of time' means, and why the violations need to have been committed by the state. On the specific issue of a pattern of violations, some truth commissions would be excluded, such as that set up in Grenada: while that truth commission was established to deal with the period from 1976 to 1991, in reality it only focused on a few events.

Thus, there is no single, universally accepted definition of what a truth commission is. Because there is no agreement amongst academics on exactly the elements that constitute it, there is no composite list of which truth-seeking commissions qualify as truth commissions.[36] As Eric Brahm notes:

> There is a growing body of comparative research that seeks to produce empirical evidence and, thereby, contribute to policy debates on the relative merits of truth commissions. However, these efforts have been plagued by a lack of attention to case selection. The lack of consensus on what constitutes the universe of truth commission cases has contributed to a pattern of inconclusive, inconsistent findings.[37]

One of the most specific prerequisites for a truth commission is the acceptance by many that only official state institutions, or those sanctioned or authorised by the state, are truth commissions. This has been a problem, as past definitions of truth commissions were narrowly prescriptive and did not deal with all the necessary conceptual components of what a truth commission is. Yet non-formal processes ought not necessarily be excluded simply because they are not state-created or state-sanctioned. Broadening out the definition to include unofficial processes, and thus to allow more processes to fall within the definition, will ensure that more processes will be given formal recognition. This is crucial where official truth commission institutions are not permitted or cannot be established. At least if we are talking about the assembly of a large dataset of commissions, a strong argument could be made that the definition should err on the side of inclusion, and researchers should use their discretion to determine what the appropriate case selection process would be for their research question.

However, a revised definition of a truth commission is also necessary to ensure that it better captures all the aspects of what truth commissions are

35 Dancy, Kim and Wiebelhaus-Brahm, *supra* note 11.

36 See one list at Dancy, Kim and Wiebelhaus-Brahm, *supra* note 11.

37 E. Brahm, 'What is a Truth Commission and Why Does it Matter?' (2009) 3(2) *Peace and Conflict Review* 1.

functionally and their roles, including how they are established and what they do. A broader definition opens up the possibility of instigating more transitional justice processes in a variety of places where massive human rights abuses have occurred. In order to ensure that a truth commission is beneficial for a society in transition, and gives the society the best opportunity to deal with the past, the process must in all optimal ways promote a non-return to conflict. Truth commissions must be established in ways that promote success. They should also deal not only with the past, but should also deal at times – because the past and present are so interlinked – with both. The definition should also encompass what they do, such as issuing a final report with recommendations. In addition, incorporating the word 'usually' or 'ordinarily' into the definition mean that truth commissions should have some degree of flexibility in the way in which they are defined, and thus not meeting all aspects of how others define truth commissions should not exclude a particular truth commission.

The present author has therefore recently suggested that a truth commission is:

> (1) a temporary investigative institution that (2) focuses on understanding past violence and human rights abuse and its causes, which can focus also on on-going events if necessary; (3) usually investigates patterns of violence that took place over a (usually relatively recent) period of time and the reasons for why they occurred; (4) ordinarily issues a final report with recommendations; (5) is officially authorized, empowered or sanctioned by the State, but may be established by an intergovernmental organisation or United Nations where the state is unwilling or unable to do so.[38]

This definition may be more useful for a variety of reasons, including the fact that it promotes a non-return to conflict and violence by stipulating that a truth commission also focuses on issues like the causes of the problems that gave rise to the conflict and violence in the past. This is usually implicit in what truth commissions do, but is not usually contained in the definitions. However, while this is a useful way to classify truth commissions, it does not contain all those aspects necessary to ensure their effectiveness. Thus, issues that ought to be included are independence, resources, hearings and a range of other matters. For that reason, the present author has argued for another non-prescriptive, future-orientated definition that guides future processes on how to establish and set up such institutions.[39]

---

[38] J. Sarkin, 'Redesigning the Definition a Truth Commission, But Also Designing a Forward-Looking Non-Prescriptive Definition to Make Them Potentially More Successful' (2018) 19(3) *Human Rights Review* 349.

[39] Ibid.

## 1.3. THE ROLES OF TRUTH COMMISSIONS

As far as the purposes of truth commissions are concerned, there seems to be an emerging consensus that they are set up for transitional justice reasons to impact the states where they are created. They are seen to do a variety of things, including investigating past events, giving a voice to victims, perpetrators and relatives, establishing an official record of the causes of the conflict, and providing recommendations for institutional reforms. They also report on the truth of these matters, provide official recognition of the truth, and dispel misconceptions that could instigate future hindrance, while trying to ensure acceptance of a new 'shared' truth about the past.[40] While there are seen to be a number of main goals,[41] Borer has argued that truth commissions have about 25 different roles.[42] This will be returned to.

The role of truth recovery is seen to be the most critical role that truth commissions play, hence their names. This role is considered important because establishing truth is often a key concern of transitional or post-conflict states.[43] In 2006, Freeman noted that a truth commission's remarkable ability to shed light on contested historical events and to disseminate information is the most powerful attraction and reason for the bourgeoning popularity of the mechanism.[44] However, the pursuit of truth is undertaken for a variety of other reasons, including reducing deniability about past crimes. These processes allow victims to receive public acknowledgement of their suffering. By attaining official recognition of what has occurred to them, victims may be able to have their legal status issues addressed. For example, if there has been a disappearance, it should be possible to obtain a presumption of death certificate that would allow the person's financial affairs to be dealt with.

Truth, in its wide or in its narrow form, also benefits from such processes. Truth discovery at a macro (or wide) level allows the society at large to learn about the bigger picture – what was done, by whom was it done, to whom was it done, and why it occurred. Thus, a historical narrative is drawn up that allows for a fuller version of the history to be reclaimed and settled, and for

40 P. Domingo, *Dealing with Legacies of Violence: Transitional Justice and Governance Transitions*, Overseas Development Institute, 2012, at 4.

41 M. Popkin, *Peace Without Justice: Obstacles to Building the Rule of Law in El Salvador*, Pennsylvania State Press, Philadelphia, 2000, at 80.

42 T.A. Borer, 'Truth Telling as a Peace-Building Activity: A Theoretical Overview', in T.A. Borer (ed.), *Telling the Truths: Truth Telling and Peace Building in Post-Conflict Societies*, University of Notre Dame Press, Notre Dame IN, 2006, at 17.

43 C. Lawther, 'Transitional Justice and Truth Commissions', in C. Lawther, L. Moffett and D. Jacobs (eds.), *Research Handbook on Transitional Justice*, Routledge, London, 2017, at 348.

44 Freeman, *supra* note 34, at xiv.

society to move on. At the same time, smaller, individual accounts of traumas (or narrow versions of the truth) are collected that end up painting a macro version of what occurred. In this way, the idea that it was rogue elements embarking on unsanctioned activities becomes very hard to justify. A public report, drafted by a credible, legitimate and diverse truth-seeking process can be a long-term benefit to that society and help to prevent a repeat of the violence and to rebuild the state.[45] However, if the process is tainted by perceptions of bias, lack of representation, or an understanding that the process was not thorough or was insufficient in some way, the process itself might not be enough. Thus, there might be a demand in the future for the issues to be dealt with again. The understanding may be, in at least some quarters, that the pain of the past has not been addressed properly. As a result, violence and conflict may occur. While many believe that time heals, the passing of time does not mean that people forget. It does not allow the issues to be erased. In many parts of the world, there are those who seek answers for events that happened decades and/or even centuries ago.

## 1.4. THE FORM AND SCOPE OF TRUTH COMMISSIONS

The multiplicity of truth commissions has necessarily seen an expansion in their form and scope. While they possess similarities in what they do, they vary significantly in almost all their organisational aspects. Truth commissions have been established by a large number of methods around the world. Some have been created by the United Nations (El Salvador and Guatemala), international non-governmental organisations (Rwanda) or domestic NGOs (Brazil). Governmental commissions have been established by executive order (Chile) and legislation (South Africa). Some have only one or two commissioners; some have had more, such as the South African TRC, which had 17 commissioners. While most truth commissions usually have a mandate to operate for two or three years, some exist for much longer. Others have existed for shorter periods. Some have wide-ranging powers, such as the power to search, seize and subpoena, while others have to rely on voluntary participation. One institution (the South African TRC) had the power to grant amnesty, while a number of others have had the power to recommend amnesty. Some have issued extensive recommendations to promote a variety of matters, including guarantees of non-repetition, while others have issued very few proposals. Some truth commissions have had their recommendations

45 J. Paulson and M.J. Bellino, 'Truth Commissions, Education, and Positive Peace: An Analysis of Truth Commission Final Reports (1980–2015)' (2017) 53(3) *Comparative Education* 351.

complied with, while others have seen few of their recommendations followed by the state. Some commissions garner very little public attention. Part of the reason for this is because of how the institution is constituted, which can lead to the problems. It must be noted that '[s]ome commissions – in order to safeguard witnesses, if not the commissioners themselves – have been forced to conduct their hearings and deliberations in private.'[46] Nevertheless, many truth commissions involve as wide a swath of the population as possible (Sierra Leone, Timor-Leste and South Africa), while others operate in secret and at the margins of society (Guatemala) because of the way they are set up or the way they are run. However, public involvement and public awareness is dependent on the design and establishment of the process being credible and politically legitimate.

Some of these commissions, especially the South African TRC, have been extensively retrospectively examined and assessed. Many others have received very little media or academic coverage. The fact that so little notice is given to such mechanisms in locations such as the DRC, Burundi, Mauritius, Togo and Nigeria, besides others, means that the comparative aspects of these processes have not been sufficiently absorbed into the studies of truth commissions. This means that the lessons and value that these institutions can provide have not been taken up. Analytically, the study of these tools, both academically and for states considering designing such processes into their own contexts, is reduced if the full assortment of historical outcomes is poorly documented. It is understandable to some extent why this occurs, because of problems such as the difficulties of accessing these places, often an absence of local scholarship, language and other barriers, besides other limiting concerns. The fact is that the lack of scholarship on these processes means that the comparative benefits of these processes are lost. The more that is known about how other models have worked, the richer the knowledge and understanding of these processes and the lessons that can be gleaned for future processes.

## 2. THE IMPACT AND LEGACY OF TRUTH COMMISSIONS

Through the various chapters of this book, issues concerning the impact and legacy of truth commissions are examined. The two critical issues therefore are: what have been the impact and legacies of truth commissions thus far, and how should their efficacy be measured? These are important issues, because if

---

46 D.A. Crocker, 'Truth Commissions, Transitional Justice, and Civil Society', in R.I. Rotberg and D.A. Crocker (eds.), *Truth v. Justice: The Morality of Truth Commissions*, Princeton University Press, Princeton NJ, 2000.

answers could be found, it would help to ensure that truth commissions are understood better and that the arguments made in favour or against them are based on a scientific approach. If that was the case, then the two opposing schools (those who broadly support them and those that generally oppose them) of thought on these institutions would have solid evidence to base their arguments in favour or against these bodies, rather than by using vague assertions and anecdotes.

As far as truth commissions are concerned, impact has been defined as 'the causal effect of a truth commission process on individuals' and institutions' decisions, interests, beliefs and values' and how truth commissions affect a 'set of political, institutional, societal and judicial transformations'.[47] In broad terms, legacy denotes what those that came before have left behind. It is usually seen to be the lasting effect or outcome of a process. It has often been used by the Olympics or other sporting tournaments to indicate what lasting effect a specific sporting event has had for the community where that activity occurred.[48] The United Nations Office of the High Commissioner for Human Rights (OHCHR) has noted (directly concerning hybrid courts, but nevertheless highly relevant for truth commissions) that legacy concerning an institution is its 'lasting impact' and 'should be used to devise strategies that maximize the impact of a mechanism in its design and operations'.[49]

In the context of truth commissions, impact is what is usually felt immediately or over a short period of time. Legacy, on the other hand, is about how the effects of a past institution continue to be felt over a longer period of time, but it is also about how its role is viewed rather than what its impact was. In some ways, legacy is about enduring impact that may be different from its impact while it did its work. Legacy is about the issues that define the role of the institution, which will not always be what its impact was. Legacy is about understanding what about the institution endures and survives beyond the life of the body. Legacy thus refers to the longer-lasting direct and indirect consequences of past commissions, as felt or realised usually by the people affected by it. Legacy, in this context, is often linked to the role of the institution in dealing with violence, democratisation, reconciliation, developing a human rights culture and a range of other matters. It is about looking back to see influence and effect. Usually, legacy is something beneficial or positive to the receiver of the legacy. Although legacy can also be negative or something that has a deleterious effect, it is often used to imply positive achievements, particularly

---

47 O. Bakiner, 'Truth Commission Impact: An Assessment of How Commissions Influence Politics and Society' (2013) 8(1) *International Journal of Transitional Justice*, 6, at 13.

48 H. Preuss, 'The Conceptualisation and Measurement of Mega Sport Event Legacies' (2007) 12(3–4) *Journal of Sport & Tourism* 207.

49 OHCHR, *supra* note 13.

when it is associated with a person or institution. The legacy of an institution can be planned or unintentional. Some institutions plan legacy projects, while others attempt to define their own legacy. However, it is unusual for an institution's own attempts to define its legacy to be successful. This is because there are many issues that affect how an institution is perceived. Often issues over which the institution has no control affect its legacy. Moreover, its legacy can be purposefully undermined for political or other reasons.

There are two levels upon which the legacy of truth commissions ought to be considered. The first is their impact globally on transitional justice mechanisms and processes, and how the roles of these institutions are seen around the world. In this context, their legacy is the effect of such institutions globally and how they have become the go-to mechanisms in almost every place where there has been conflict and where a process is sought to deal with the consequences of such violence. In this sense, the roles of prior truth commissions are examined to see what model ought to be followed in the place where such a process is planned. The second issue that should be considered when the legacy of truth commissions is assessed is what kind of effect specific truth commissions have had on the countries in which they operated. These two legacy matters of truth commissions need to be considered, as truth commissions have both global and national dimensions. On a global level, legacy is how the global policy-making, donor and civil society communities interpret their records and achievements in deciding whether to continue supporting or employing truth commissions as institutions to tackle past human rights violations. It is about whether the vestiges of past truth commissions are viewed positively or negatively, and whether they are likely to continue to be used. On the domestic level, the issue surrounding the legacy of truth commissions is about deciding what exactly these institutions have left behind in the places where they have done their work.

It is important to note that impact and legacy are not the same – whereas impact can be measured more quantifiably, as it looks at specific markers (although it is not always measured on that basis), legacy is more about how an institution is viewed or perceived. Thus, legacy is largely a *perception* of what a truth commission has achieved and leaves behind it after it finishes its work. Legacy is more about attitude and perception rather than something based on an entirely objective assessment. Legacy is usually more simplistically assessed. While both impact and legacy ought to be measured more objectively, the methodologies in use to evaluate them can often fall short in this regard. Impact is usually about how the situation has been affected over a shorter period of time, whilst legacy, with respect to truth commissions and other institutions, refers to the way that the body has left its mark in the form of lasting change from a perception point of view. In other words, legacy is often viewed as how people believe the institution left its mark over a longer period of time. There is clearly overlap, but it is important that impact and legacy should not be used synonymously or interchangeably. Thus, while a truth commission's impact may have been enormous and critical, its legacy may not always be such, as there may be an issue or two that define the way it is seen (its legacy). Impact may be positive initially or in the short term, but can change over time. A truth commission's legacy may also change over time because how it is viewed may change for a variety of reasons. Finally, the legacy that exists can, on occasion, be different for diverse audiences because they see things at times in different ways. Thus, depending on the audience, the perception of what was or was not achieved might be very different. Thus, the South African TRC has a very positive legacy internationally, but not so much in the country. The legacy of the South African process is even less positively viewed domestically today than what it was at the end of the process or shortly thereafter. The legacy of the truth commission is also more critically viewed amongst Black South Africans, who are less positively disposed towards the supposed achievements of the TRC.

## 3. HOW ARE TRUTH COMMISSIONS JUDGED?

It is important to note that on a global level, as a result of their work in the many countries where they have operated, truth commissions have become very popular mechanisms for use in post-conflict societies around the world. However, they are not universally admired, as there seems to be more of an antipathy towards such institutions in the Global North. This is undoubtedly due to a Western proclivity for retributive justice. As far as impact is concerned, the problem is often that researchers assess impact through the lens of what would be expected within the countries of the Global North, and not accounting for the history, capabilities and social context of the state in which the truth commission takes place. Expectations need to be reflective of the places where the institutions work, and not of the biases of outside researchers who helicopter in for a short period of time, or in fact never visit the sites of the truth commissions. Studies made after brief stays in the regions affected do not always understand what is possible, in practice, in the places where such institutions are established, given the constrictions of the circumstances such as in Burundi, the DRC or Nigeria.

At times, there is a negative disposition towards truth commissions that comes from misconceptions of their roles and ability to achieve certain objectives. For some, the aversion towards these institutions stems from a view of truth commissions as substitutes for societies making harder choices, a 'second-best' rationalisation not using retributive justice as the means of dealing with its past. While this is true for some places, truth commissions are often mutually supportive processes to accountability procedures, rather than antagonistic to them.[50]

Regardless, the work done to review truth commissions often comes from those who take a critical stance towards them.[51] The negative views that these researchers hold concerning truth commissions seem, at times, to cloud their judgement concerning truth commissions' role and impact. These analyses criticise the institutions, but rarely sufficiently understand the complexity of those places and the wider context of their constrictions and obstacles. However, it is not possible to dismiss the merits of truth commissions without first positing realistic alternatives, or secondly posing the counterfactual question of what might happen if no truth commission is established. Thus, solutions and alternatives that are practicable and achievable ought to be suggested. To decide whether there are viable alternatives to truth commissions, or whether inaction is preferable, the role of truth commissions also needs to be measured against countries where no truth commission was established, to see if it is possible to make conclusions based on positive or negative correlations.

One place we can look to as an example of the absence of a truth commission in a situation that may have benefited is Namibia. Michelle Parlevliet argues that in Namibia, where no mechanisms were used to address the gross human rights abuses committed prior to independence (1994):

> [a] clear case can be made that the lack of accountability has had lasting repercussions for Namibian democracy, the relationship between state and citizens, and the conduct of the state security forces. As such, it supports the claim that a violent past, if not dealt with, will impact negatively on a society following a transition.[52]

Therefore, we can surmise that only comparing and examining countries where truth commissions were used gives a somewhat skewed understanding of their role. While it is difficult to draw exact conclusions, some useful observations can be made as to whether they have more or less positive legacies. It stands to reason that similar types of countries with similar types of problems and contexts need to be compared to see if better, more contextualised-researched results can be arrived at.

---

50 See further on this issue, H. Kim and K. Sikkink, 'Explaining the Deterrence Effect of Human Rights Prosecutions for Transitional Countries' (2010) 54(4) *International Studies Quarterly* 939.

51 J. Rowen, *Searching for Truth in the Transitional Justice Movement*, Cambridge University Press, Cambridge, 2017.

52 M. Parlevliet, 'Truth Commissions in Africa: The Non-Case of Namibia and the Emerging Case of Sierra Leone' (2000) 2 *International Law Forum* 99, at 100.

In many ways, it is clear to many governments, the wider international community, civil society in a variety of places and victims that truth commissions are seen as the best device available in the places where they are established. However, they are at the mercy of many variables and extraneous factors that impact their work. For this reason, the real question is not whether they are useful or not, but rather how to make them more effective. Another related question is how to improve them so that they can have more positive impacts on the societies in which they operate. If these questions could be dealt with, it would impact on how to improve upon their legacy, discovering what works and what does not, magnifying best practice methods so that future truth commissions may learn lessons and proceed with greater efficiency. From these lessons, decisions can be made regarding how to tailor the distinct mechanism that is a truth commission to the variety of contexts in which they can be deployed. This is especially important for future truth commission creators, as well as those who work in such institutions.

On the other hand, this is not to argue that truth commissions are not susceptible to valid criticisms on a range of organisational and activity-related matters. Like all types of institutions that do a variety of different types of work in an array of different places, truth commissions have their problems. Of course, there are no perfect institutions of any type, anywhere in the world. Institutions are created and managed by human beings, and are therefore at the mercy of individual decision-making and the problems that occur due to logistics and human error. In addition, a range of issues outside the body's control affects them. Most institutions suffer from funding limitations, for example. They are deeply affected by perceptions of them, over which they have limited control. They can try and affect those views by what they do, what they say, whom they hear, what they omit, whether they do outreach effectively and a range of other matters. The perceptions and reality are not always in agreement, as interested parties challenge, complicate or obfuscate the truth-creation process. All institutions (truth commissions and others) can be improved in what they do and the way they do it. Truth commissions, however, have a more complex task than most other types of institutions. As their role is specifically geared towards influencing public attitudes towards past events and how the future could be better, issues of public perception and legitimacy affect them significantly.

Truth commissions are criticised for what they do, even though this type of reproach is not always fair. The criticisms of truth commissions have been made sometimes due to a limited view of the roles they play. At times, such criticism is based on a very expansive view of what their role ought to be, rather than its realistic aims. This clouds a more objective analysis of what truth commissions are really capable of achieving. The ongoing dispute over what exactly commissions should achieve in their work makes the individual context seen in each country all the more vital, but also has the effect of blurring an assessment of what has been achieved.[53]

They are often criticised for not finding enough truth, not holding enough hearings, not being sufficiently transparent, not doing enough to reach the public or victims, not achieving sufficient reconciliation, or not doing enough to promote issues of human rights and democracy. For these reasons, some researchers inquire as to whether these mechanisms play the positive roles that others posit. However, it should be noted that truth commissions are deeply affected by weak mandates and limited resources. Moreover, some of the models adopted are out of place with local conditions, are unsuited to the specific context and do little to empower local communities and capacities.[54] On occasion, international voices and institutions have ignored local understandings of justice,[55] and have been ignorant about the existence and usages of such concepts on the ground.[56] Often, negative assessments are unfounded, as the critique is based on idealistic expectations of what they should do, rather than on an understanding of what they are legally entitled to do, and what they can pragmatically achieve in the context within which they are established. As these institutions generally operate in places where rapid political change is taking place, they are often limited in what they can achieve because they are subject to the political forces that operate there. Besides mandate limitations, truth commissions are also limited in the scope of what they can do, because they function for two or three years, mostly have limited budgets, and their work is difficult and time-consuming. This does not stop them being extensively criticised for not doing more to achieve a variety of objectives, mandated or not.[57]

These issues severely affect what truth commissions can achieve and ought to be taken into account more often in questions about success and impact.[58] With this in mind, how can they be expected to do the tremendous amounts of work necessary to achieve their mandates? How much truth collection is sufficient in that context? What is realistically possible and achievable in

---

53 Mendeloff, *supra* note 9.

54 See P. Lundy and M. McGovern, 'Whose Justice? Rethinking Transitional Justice From the Bottom Up' (2008) 35(2) *Journal of Law and Society* 265.

55 See L. Waldorf, 'Mass Justice For Mass Atrocity: Rethinking Local Justice as Transitional Justice' (2006) 79(1) *Temple Law Review* 1.

56 See E. Stanley, 'Transitional Justice: From the Local to the International', in P. Hayden (ed.), *The Ashgate Research Companion to Ethics and International Relations*, Ashgate, London, 2009.

57 J. Langer, 'Are Truth Commissions Just Hot-Air Balloons? A Reality Check on the Impact of Truth Commission Recommendations' (2017) 29(1) *Desafíos* 177.

58 E. Brahm, 'Uncovering the Truth: Examining Truth Commission Success and Impact' (2007) 8(1) *International Studies Perspectives* 16, at 17.

short periods of time with resource constraints? Furthermore, we should ask how exactly truth should be measured in order to determine whether the truth recovery component of a truth commission's work has been successful. Broadly, the impact of truth commissions concerning truth is about their role in recovering and narrating an overview assessment of the past, although it is also about the truth of specific cases. This refers to the truth individual victims seek, and this is where the abilities of truth commissions are somewhat limited by their capacities. As previously mentioned, their ability to fulfil their mandate is limited by the factors working against their achieving the most comprehensive results possible.[59] What is achievable by one well-resourced and sufficiently mandated truth commission is usually unobtainable by others. Logically, this suggests that we should be cautious in using the achievements of one commission as a benchmark for others, unless they are in similar positions.

Too little attention has been paid to the issue of funding across truth commissions. Limited resources impact what they can and cannot do. Obviously expenditure is dependent on the differing costs for each country. The types of expenses ought to be considered more holistically. Thus, for example, when issues are raised about the number of hearings, or where they were held, part of such an examination needs to consider the costs involved. Critically, more resources would be needed to do so and thus limited resources at times affect impact. Greater success, or wider impact, would occur if more funding were to be available.

It is also necessary to examine more closely the costs associated with truth commissions. While truth commission processes are undoubtedly expensive, they are notably cheaper to run than tribunals.[60] There are also arguments that consider truth commissions to play more effective roles.[61] However, the cost factor needs thorough research, as this would help determine what types of expenses are vital to the truth commission's ability to make an impact.

There are myriad variables that affect how truth commissions are perceived. Most of those are not connected to whether they have performed usefully. The issue of truth commissions' efficacy is directly connected to attitudes

59 C. Lawther, 'Peace Without the Past? Truth, Transition and the Northern Ireland Case', in C. Corradetti, N. Eisikovits and J.V. Rotondi (eds.), *Theorizing Transitional Justice*, Ashgate, London, 2014.

60 E. Wiebelhaus-Brahm, *Truth Commission and Transitional Societies. The Impact on Human Rights and Democracy*, Routledge, New York, 2010, at 15.

61 M. Minow, 'Making History or Making Peace: When Prosecutions Should Give Way to Truth Commissions and Peace Negotiations', in R. Buchanan and P. Zumbasen (eds.), *Law in Transition. Human Rights, Development and Transitional Justice*, Hart Publishing, Oxford, 2014, at 211. See also R. Nagy, 'Transitional Justice as Global Project: Critical Reflexions', in R. Buchanan and P. Zumbasen (eds.), *Law in Transition. Human Rights, Development and Transitional Justice*, Hart Publishing, Oxford, 2014.

towards them. Whilst there are undoubtedly truth commissions that have played a limited role, many have at least some positive effect on their affected nations. However, it must be remembered that they operate in very political spaces. The fact that they are 'often buffeted by powerful national political actors,'[62] impacts their effectiveness. It also impacts how their effectiveness is perceived. Because their work has deeply political effects, they are challenged and critiqued often for political reasons, rather than for issues specifically related to their exercise of their mandates. The government, or non-governmental groups, may have an intrinsic dislike for the truth commission process and what that process is trying to achieve, and so may foster an unduly complex and obstacle-laden environment in which they operate. Sometimes, a truth commission is heavily criticised for simply political reasons, rather than measured criticism of their efficacy. One event, or one statement by a politician who is against the process as a whole or attempting to achieve a political advantage, can undermine the institution. Such examples have been seen in Kenya and Nigeria. A public statement by a politician or negative public perceptions of a truth commission may overshadow whatever positive activities the institution carries out. Yet more damaging to such an institution is when governments ignore their reports and their recommendations.

## 4. CRITERIA FOR TRUTH COMMISSION IMPACT ANALYSIS

The various conclusions about the impact of truth commissions have arrived at conflicting results. Olsen et al., analysing the effects of a number of truth commissions, found that they are more effective at ensuring that human rights are more widely respected when they are practised in combination with trials and amnesties. They argue that truth commissions in isolation do not have a positive impact on the country they take place in, and can in fact be damaging.[63] The authors contend that the purpose of truth commissions and reconciliatory mechanisms is to prevent the atrocities from ever occurring again, with this goal better achieved when real justice is brought to the initial perpetrators.

In evaluating the impact and legacy of truth commissions, a key difficulty is that the parameters and scope of truth commissions vary widely. As a result,

62 K. Richards and R.A. Wilson, 'Truth and Reconciliation Commissions: Anthropological Perspectives', in H. Callan (ed.), *International Encyclopedia of Anthropology*, Wiley-Blackwell, Hoboken, 2017, at 10.

63 T.D. Olsen, L.A. Payne and A.G. Reiter, *Transitional Justice in Balance: Comparing Processes, Weighing Efficacy*, United States Institute of Peace Press, Washington D.C., 2010, at 457.

there are few standardised objectives to review how they work and what they do around the world. This is especially true since there is no commonly agreed definition as to what they are and which past truth commissions are considered to fall within the definition of a truth commission, or not.

One of the biggest problems is that there is also no clear position on the roles and objectives that truth commissions play. There are conflicting positions. As noted earlier, Borer argues that there are about 25 or 26 roles that truth commissions play including: accountability, acknowledgement, amnesty, apology, coexistence, confession, dignity, forgiveness, healing, human rights culture, justice, mercy, national unity, *nunca más* or never again, peace, punishment, reconciliation, reconstruction, remorse, reparations, repentance, responsibility, restoration, retribution, and rule of law.[64] She does not mention items such as historical investigations, research, archives promotion, memory, non-repetition, good governance, searching for, recovering and identifying the human remains of victims, and promoting democratisation. However, some of these issues might overlap with other items on her list (eg. *nunca más* and non-repetition). In fact, there are many more roles that truth commissions play besides the limited roles usually outlined. However, this wider, more comprehensive set of roles for truth commissions is not considered or examined when the effect or impact of truth commissions come to be investigated.

Because truth commissions have so many goals to achieve, only a few of these objectives are used to determine impact and legacy, resulting in much inconsistency in conclusions on how the impact of these institutions are measured and compared.[65] There are very few studies[66] that have used many criteria to arrive at overall conclusions concerning truth commissions' impact and legacy. Additionally, most of those studies that have come to overall conclusions have not examined *all* truth commissions, and their legacy and impact. They have relied on the generality of findings to arrive at their results. Generally, the findings on these issues are simply repeated. They are also relied on too frequently as a means to support a particular understanding or agenda. The research studies used have not come to one set of results.

Generally, the perception of truth commissions' main role is truth-gathering. However, that is a limited view of truth commissions' goals and targets; it even represents a very limited understanding of what such institutions do as far

---

64 Borer, *supra* note 42, at 17.

65 M.B.J. Hirsch, M. Mackenzie and M. Sesay, 'Measuring the Impacts of Truth and Reconciliation Commissions: Placing the Global "Success" of TRCs in Local Perspective' (2012) 47(3) *Cooperation and Conflict* 386.

66 See the main two research articles relied on: O.N.T. Thoms, J. Ron and R. Paris, 'State-Level Effects of Transitional Justice: What Do We Know?' (2010) 4(3) *International Journal of Transitional Justice* 329; and Olsen, Payne and Reiter, *supra* note 63.

as truth is concerned. Their roles as far as truth is concerned are numerous. Truth commissions, besides holding hearings and interviewing victims, also conduct historical research. In addition, they can create a climate for others to examine and re-examine the past.[67] They can create a favourable environment to conduct such research. Crucially, truth commissions leave behind archives that can be consulted in the future, and assist often in the process of developing a focus on collecting historical documentation.[68] Moreover, truth commissions also assist with processes of opening up archives, especially where they have belonged to secretive states or to the security services, despite the reluctance of many states to allow truth commissions access to such materials. Taking these attributes into account, the impact of truth commissions within the societies in which they operate should not be underestimated.

Truth commissions also play crucial roles in bringing to the public a consciousness of the events that have taken place during conflict periods, and in the piecing together of past narratives.[69] This can have clear benefits for the present and future of the affected societies.[70] Achieving these aims is crucial in order to try and limit denialism or revisionism.[71] Truth commissions have not always been successful in this regard. They may not succeed in overcoming arguments as to what occurred as put forward by the perpetrators of the crimes, and so these may become the accepted narrative, as occurred with the truth commission in the Former Yugoslavia. However, whether that particular institution qualifies as a truth commission can be questioned.

Another vital aspect of considering the impact and legacy of truth commissions is that they may be successful in bringing some level of truth to those who have been harmed, but it may not be enough. For that reason, criticism still persists. For example, in the South African truth commission context, despite the large amounts of information brought forward, many crimes and their consequences were not revealed. Questions remain as to whether or not the truth, or sufficient truth, was obtained. Other questions that are asked are: how should the role of truth commissions in amnesty processes be considered? Should that role be assessed by how many come forward or by how much cooperation is achieved

67 O. Bakiner, 'One Truth Among Others? Truth Commissions' Struggle for Truth and Memory' (2015) 8(3) *Memory Studies* 345.

68 B. Jones and I. Oliveira, 'Truth Commission Archives as "New Democratic Spaces"' (2016) 8(1) *Journal of Human Rights Practice* 6.

69 M. Andrews, 'Grand National Narratives and the Project of Truth Commissions: A Comparative Analysis' (2003) 25(1) *Media, Culture & Society* 45.

70 G. Grandin, 'The Instruction of Great Catastrophe: Truth Commissions, National History, and State Formation in Argentina, Chile, and Guatemala' (2005) 110(1) *The American Historical Review* 46.

71 M. Imbleau, 'Initial Truth Establishment by Transitional Bodies and the Fight Against Denial', in W.A. Schabas and S. Darcy (eds.), *Truth Commissions and Courts: The Tension between Criminal Justice and the Search for Truth*, Kluwer, Dordrecht, 2004.

with perpetrators? Does it depend on public attitudes towards the process? Does it matter that the state was not going to prosecute and that there was an understanding that perpetrators were going to avoid accountability but for the processes at the truth commission? These doubts aside, the fact that at least some truth has been attained means some justice has been dispensed, and that without such a mechanism, it is likely that not even this would have been achieved. This should be kept in mind when evaluating potential alternatives, and whether such options are viable.

Clearly, truth commissions influence the societies in which they work in many different ways. These can be direct and indirect; Bakiner notes that they have 'direct political impact, indirect political impact through civil society mobilization, vetting and judicial accountability'.[72] Thus, for example, truth commissions are often seen to have a cathartic effect for a society as a whole.[73] This is because truth commissions document and acknowledge 'a legacy of conflict and human rights violations as a step toward healing wounds'.[74] Nevertheless, that effect may not be felt by all, depending on the context and the place. However, a truth commission does usually have at least some impact on the society concerned. Catharsis is a key legacy issue, in that the ways in which it is achieved and finding what works best need to be better understood. Truth commission hearings and the role they play ought to be part of considerations about impact. Hearings have a multitude of benefits, including the building of past narratives, as well as memory.[75] Truth commissions also write or rewrite history and affect memory in a range of ways. Too often, however, the role of memory[76] is undervalued. It is not usually measured or considered when appraisals are made.[77] Nor are the benefits that truth commission testimony has for victims – the benefits of their acknowledgement, both for them and the society as a whole.

While these issues are generally measured to some extent, the effect of the truth commissions themselves on the achievement of reconciliation is not usually isolated. Truth commission impact on reconciliation should more often be considered as a form of impact. This is important, as truth commissions are

---

72 Bakiner, *supra* note 47, at 7.

73 J. Zalaquett, 'Balancing Ethical Imperatives and Political Constraints: The Dilemma of New Democracies Confronting Past Human Rights Violations' (1992) 43(6) *Hastings Law Journal* 1425.

74 A. Chapman and P. Ball, 'The Truth of Truth Commissions: Comparative Lessons from Haiti, South Africa, and Guatemala' (2001) 23(1) *Human Rights Quarterly* 1, at 2.

75 C.E. Cole, 'Commemorating Mass Violence: Truth Commission Hearings as a Genre of Public Memory' (2018) 83(3) *Southern Communication Journal* 149.

76 A. Assmann, 'History, Memory, and the Genre of Testimony' (2006) 27(2) *Poetics Today* 261.

77 A.V. Tovares, 'Going Off-Script and Reframing the Frame: The Dialogic Intertwining of the Centripetal and Centrifugal Voices in the Truth and Reconciliation Commission Hearings' (2016) 27(5) *Discourse & Society* 554.

likely to create longer-lasting peace if there is a reconciliatory attitude amongst the people of the previously conflicted area.[78] Changing the attitudes, societal goals and violent dispositions of the population is key to ensuring that harmony can be restored. Even if the existence of truth commissions is controversial in many places, or the role they play contentious, the fact that they are part of the landscape in places where violence and conflict have existed can act as a pressure reliever, if nothing else. A variable to be considered in truth commission analysis, but often missed, is that truth commissions provide space for a state to consider what ought to be done on a range of matters. They create an opportunity to focus on a spectrum of crucial issues, including what the state ought to look like, what steps need to be taken to protect the state and its people and the nature of potential reparations, as well as how to achieve nation-building, social cohesion and reconciliation. They try to find political and social solutions to ensure that the trauma does not reoccur.[79]

Truth commissions open the space up for that society in general to focus on the past, and deal with it as a national agenda item. It has been stated that:

> What truth commissions do well is to create a more open public dialog about the past abuses, providing the language of human rights to discuss events that might otherwise be unspeakable in the public sphere. Truth commissions contribute to the aims of liberal democracy in these ways by creating, to some degree, greater transparency in government and allowing a larger range of voices to participate in public and political discourse.[80]

Truth commissions exemplify the values of democracy, human rights, the rule of law, accountability, countering impunity and transparency, to name just a few. They also build an understanding of and respect for these matters and in particular human rights. Moreover, they assist in transforming 'social norms',[81] thereby enhancing notions of accountability, transparency and a range of allied issues. As we know, truth commissions' recommendations are not always followed or complied with exactly. However, the democratic space for dialogue and discussion on those matters, as well as others, opens as a result of the process. This change in the political and social atmosphere caused by a truth commission can have powerful effects on how the state acts in consequence. These are difficult matters to quantify, but can be taken

---

78 D. Bar-Tal and G.H. Bennink, *From Conflict Resolution to Reconciliation*, Oxford University Press, Oxford, 2004, at 23.

79 L.M. Johnson, 'Transitional Truth and Historical Justice: Philosophical Foundations and Implications of the Truth and Reconciliation Commission' (2006) 38(2) *International Studies in Philosophy* 69.

80 Richards and Wilson, *supra* note 62, at 5.

81 Bakiner, *supra* note 47, at 7.

into account by including surveys to measure changes in attitudes before, during and after the existence of such an institution. This is another reason why a broader examination of the role of truth commissions is necessary, one that examines their impact and legacy years after they have completed their work.

Truth commissions' recommendations are important as far as guarantees of non-repetition are concerned. The question therefore is: have their roles and their recommendations (where implemented) contributed to the society not resuming conflict and returning to violence? Changes in violence levels are vital as a yardstick by which a truth commissions' impact is measured, since dealing with the past in post-conflict societies is critically about past violence. As such, steps need to be taken by the truth commission to understand and deal with the causes of the violence. While, at a global level, little empirical proof exists that the results of the work of truth commissions engender peace, many of the localities where truth commissions have frequently occurred have not returned to the same degree of violence as occurred previous to the truth commissions' work and findings. The Latin American states where truth commissions operated certainly show a consistent and lasting move away from previous violence. The same is true in many other places, including South Africa and Nigeria, although various types of violence that are potentially unrelated do exist in those places. In many other states, there is a reversion back to higher levels of violence, if not outright conflict, some years after there was a peace agreement or transition that had ended or brought down those levels. In fact, some countries have reverted many times back to violence, including Ethiopia (12 times), Myanmar/Burma (13) and India (20).[82] Generally speaking, during the years that truth commissions operate in their countries, political violence generally remains low. It often stabilises or decreases, as occurred in South Africa, as just one example. However, more work is needed to determine what the correlation is between truth commissions and the post-completion resumption of violence, taking into account previous levels of violence. Obviously, each country's context is different, but some comparative analysis may be helpful.

While there is a focus by researchers on scrutinising truth commission recommendations, how they are taken up and whether they change state policy, what also needs to be evaluated is what role of the truth commission process plays in how the state and its institutions are reformed. That role does not only come from truth commission recommendations, but is part of a process that a truth commission engenders. Also needed is an evaluation of changes in the way the state and its institutions conduct themselves in

82 UCDP/PRIO Armed Conflict Dataset, 2009.

light of truth commission processes that promote reform, including greater accountability and openness. The issue of recommendations will be returned to when considering the methodology employed in measuring impact and legacy.

Besides those roles, truth commissions also educate the society that they are in. They develop an awareness of important matters and create a culture where these issues become part of the very foundations of the state. Issues of education and nation-building need to be given far more weight, amongst other considerations, when the roles that truth commissions play are examined. Truth commissions also have intrinsic key roles in building a human rights culture besides the role they play in nation-building, social cohesion, tolerance, social exclusion and a range of similar issues. Truth commissions are capable of affecting the tone of the national dialogue and often promote a greater openness and a spirit of greater inclusion. Truth commissions can help to better identify what people in a post-conflict society value, and allow the government to use this knowledge to focus on those issues. In Peru, for instance, a focus of the truth commission was on asking people how they foresaw a lasting peace, to which the overwhelming answer was an increase in development and quality of life, allowing the government to prioritise effectively and to ensure a peaceful transition.[83] This is just one important instance of how truth commissions can have a positive, meaningful political effect on their countries.[84]

An issue requiring further consideration is the question of timing when establishing a truth commission. When should a truth commission be established: immediately after the conflict or transition has occurred, some years later, or many years later? Timing and sequencing are an essential aspect of how successful these institutions can be. Comparative approaches could be useful in examining places where sequencing and timing have played a role.

## 5. METHODOLOGIES TO DETERMINE IMPACT AND LEGACY

Measuring the effect and impact of truth commissions in the country where the truth commission has done its work has until now been somewhat haphazard. As can be seen from the criteria section above, there are myriad

83 L.J. Laplante, 'Transitional Justice and Peace Building: Diagnosing and Addressing the Socioeconomic Roots of Violence through a Human Rights Framework' (2008) 2(3) *International Journal of Transitional Justice*, 331, 351.

84 Amnesty International, 'Truth, Justice and Reparation: Establishing an Effective Truth Commission', 2007, https://www.amnesty.org/en/documents/POL30/009/2007/en/.

yardsticks that could be used as indicators to measure impact. However, the choice of variables used in some studies is also problematic.[85] Very few studies compare truth commission outcomes using a sufficient number of variables, perhaps because there is a lack of data in general. In fact, one of the biggest problems is likely to be the lack of accurate, complete and consistent data across a range of countries on a wide range of issues, so vital to making proper evaluations concerning impact and effect.

While many of the aforementioned yardsticks are difficult to measure, it is not impossible. Many more criteria should be taken into consideration when examining truth commission impact. The effects of truth commissions, on societies more broadly, need to be better understood to determine what their effects are and how they can have even more positive roles. However, while more realistic indicators are needed to evaluate impact and legacy, the question remains as to whether it is really possible objectively to determine impact and legacy using such a complex set of variables. With so many objectives for impact assessment, can all of these targets be assessed? Can 'pragmatic indicators' actually be established for all of these ambitions? Are some impossible to measure because questions of causality and equifinality make it impossible to isolate the role of the truth commission in the events that occurred? How *does* one isolate the specific role of the truth commission alone in such chaotic contexts where they take place? Is it possible to identify whether there was a single causal link or several, and if the latter what the relative weights of each were? To add to the confusion, there are effects caused by specific actions of truth commissions, but also the consequences of the transitional justice process generally, which are specifically planned. At the moment, too little empirical evidence exists to solve such issues.

Taking all these questions into account, it is important to make determinations about how much of a truth commission's success can be ascribed to the truth commission itself, and how much to the role of other actors. While it is difficult to ascribe responsibility exactly, processes need to be more objective in these matters. The answers may be contextual to different truth commissions, and will be partly dependent on the mandate of the truth commission.

At the same time, impact must be measured to some degree by what is realistic and possible, rather than by looking to see, for example, if victims' expectations have been achieved.[86] While meeting expectations is important from one vantage point, a more realistic set of markers is necessary to determine what is really possible in the context of the conditions in which a truth commission

---

85 Hirsch, Mackenzie and Sesay, *supra* note 65.

86 On victim expectations see H. Guthrey, 'Expectations and Promises in the Quest for Truth: Examining Victims' Perceptions of Truth Commission Participation in Solomon Islands and Timor-Leste' (2016) 22(4) *Peace and Conflict: Journal of Peace Psychology* 306.

has carried out its work. As discussed above, the criteria by which the process is judged require more complexity, and the processes to measure said criteria need to be reassessed.

In this context, a variety of methodological problems have affected the processes to examine and assess the roles and impact of truth commissions. There have been numerous complications concerning how impact is measured.[87] While there is much reflective work on truth commissions, it is only more recently that the impacts of these institutions have begun to be more fully reviewed and analysed.[88]

While most studies review one commission only,[89] others review a number, but use variables that are not very extensive. Moreover, choosing which countries to evaluate to determine the impact of truth commissions has been a problem. More factors ought to be evaluated and more countries included in such studies.[90] Choosing, for example, three countries only, and furthermore those countries that had many problems, in order to make generalisations is problematic. Such limited samples can (and often do) lead to skewed results.[91] This is especially so when the choice of states is not made scientifically.[92] Additionally, little is done to examine truth commission processes some years after they have completed their work, yet this is vital to understanding their long-term impact and legacy.[93] Data gathered over time can and should be used to measure changes over the course of the truth commission, so as to gauge how their work had an effect. Results are often seen to be static; however, in reality, results change frequently, and measuring those changes can help to determine the variables that are affecting the changes themselves, such as levels of violence.

A further problem is that many researchers rely on only a few criteria to determine what impact means and what ought to be used to determine it. For example, whether a truth commission issues a report, whether it does so in a certain time and whether the state endorses such a report are all criteria that have been used to determine impact. Bakiner states, for example, 'I define

---

87 Hirsch, Mackenzie and Sesay, *supra* note 65.

88 B. Stewart and E. Wiebelhaus-Brahm, 'The Quantitative Turn in Transitional Justice Research: What Have We Learned About Impact?' (2017) 1(5) *Transitional Justice Review* 97.

89 See for example D.P. Espinosa, T. Rovira, R.M. Velázquez, E. Cueto, S. Seminario, C. Sandoval, I. Reátegui, I. Jave, 'Between Remembering and Forgetting the years of political violence: psychosocial impact of the Truth and Reconciliation Commission in Peru', *Political Psychology*, 2017, 38(5), 849–66.

90 See further O.N.T. Thoms, J. Ron and R. Paris, *The Effects of Transitional Justice Mechanisms.' A Summary of Empiric Research Findings and Implications for Analysts and Practitioners*, Centre for International Policy Studies, Ottawa: University of Ottawa (2008).

91 See further Brahm, *supra* note 58.

92 Stewart and Wiebelhaus-Brahm, *supra* note 88, at 101.

93 Hirsch, Mackenzie and Sesay, *supra* note 65.

truth commission impact as the effect of truth commissions on government policy and judicial processes, independent of the simultaneous effects of post-conflict institution building and other transitional justice and conflict resolution measures'.[94] He also mentions that impact must be measured by determining the ways in which truth commissions affect 'human rights policy and judicial accountability'.[95] On the other hand, some have argued that simply completing their mandated tasks and publishing their reports represent fair ways to determine their impact.[96] However, whether a truth commission completes its mandate or issues a report does not reflect its impact. It does not measure whether those tasks were done adequately or effectively. It also does not measure whether or not the reports themselves had positive consequences, but rather how the report was viewed and used.

Impact is best measured using a range of methodological tools, and a scale to measure the extent of its effect. Such tools would also make it possible to measure truth commission results on specific issues, making it possible to hone in accurately on which of the various truth commissions have achieve the best ones. If the same processes were used consistently across all truth commissions, much more could be learnt about truth commission impact. Measurements would need to be taken over time rather than at a single point. More empirical and relevant indicators are needed, as well as more research on issues in the truth commissions' respective countries, so that valid and useful impact assessments can be made. Filling these gaps in evaluation methodology in itself raises a number of problematic questions such as: who would do it? Why has it not been done before? Why is this type of deep and comparative study not really attempted or realised in many other fields? Whilst it is true that creating more complex and thorough evaluation methods will be difficult, without doing just that, asserting outcomes is much more subjective than it is scientific.

The methodological approaches applied to determine impact and effectiveness include statistical modelling, a variety of types of surveys, and experimental, ethnographic and mixed-method approaches.[97] Occasionally, interviews have been used, but they are not the best way to measure impact on their own. Using interviews also supposes similarity in the understanding of the concepts that interviewees are being questioned about, and they gauge perception of these matters rather than offering objective outcomes. Truth commission studies have also used multiple choice questions and focus groups

---

94 Bakiner, *supra* note 47.
95 Ibid.
96 Brahm, *supra* note 58.
97 Bakiner, *supra* note 47, at 7.

to arrive at results. These quicker types of research techniques have been used because there have been many problems and obstacles for researchers wanting to conduct research in some places where truth commissions have worked.[98] Some of the questions pertaining to impact look for simple 'yes' or 'no' answers rather than a spectrum of positions that ought to be carefully measured and evaluated. Thus, some impact assessments use blunt evaluations rather than nuanced assessments that measure scale. This does not allow all the issues to be discussed or to emerge, or for the full complexity of these issues to be seen.

Some of these techniques give rise to problems. They are not always usefully employed to investigate these issues. Furthermore, while different studies have used a host of different variables to determine impact, they do not always have a systematic methodology to correctly measure those variables. A much more rigorous, scientific and holistic process needs to be undertaken using many more determinates.

Problematically, impact assessments are done at a single point in time rather than before, during and after truth commissions have done their work. Retrospective analyses of specific truth commissions are often done after the work of the truth commission has been completed. No baseline is taken or measured. It is not often that the legacy of that truth commission is examined in the context of what has happened in the years after the truth commission has finished its work, except for in some instances, such as in Timor-Leste.[99] While an impact assessment is conducted usually for a single truth commission,[100] sometimes this is done for a number of truth commissions.[101] However, this does not occur very often. The focus in the literature is generally on the more widely publicised and well-known truth commissions.[102] Despite scores of other less well-known processes having taken place, especially since the 1990s, complete information is not available for many of these truth commissions.

As much of the lasting effects of truth commissions are on the psychology of the post-conflict nation, more needs to be done to understand how societal attitudes can be measured and reflected. Another problem is that the process to determine impact is at times based on subjective perspectives rather than usually on objective criteria. It is true that to some extent, impact, as far as truth commissions are concerned, is determined by how the community views

98 K. Höglund and M. Öberg, *Understanding Peace Research: Methods and Challenges*, Routledge, New York, 2010, at 149.

99 A. Rothschild, 'Victims versus Veterans: Agency, Resistance and Legacies of Timor-Leste's Truth Commission' (2017) 11(3) *International Journal of Transitional Justice* 443.

100 See for example G. Millar, 'Local Evaluations of Justice Through Truth Telling in Sierra Leone: Postwar Needs and Transitional Justice' (2011) 12(4) *Human Rights Review* 515.

101 Rowen, *supra* note 51.

102 J. Sarkin and T. Davi, 'The Togolese Truth, Justice and Reconciliation Commission: Lessons for Transitional Justice Processes Elsewhere' (2017) 24 *Peace and Conflict Studies* 1, at 2.

what the role of the truth commission should have been, and also to what extent the criticisms that have been directed at the institution have resonated in the community and now sully its citizens' evaluation of its impact. Attitudes to the transitional justice process that may have been blatantly or overtly manipulated (but at times may have occurred indirectly because of the cut and thrust of the political environment) can sway how the institution is viewed. Prejudices can cause a truth commission and its work to also be negatively viewed. The subjectivity of such analyses of truth commissions is an issue, and more objective criteria ought to be sought to determine what role the truth commission has played and the impact it achieved, by evaluating all the role that a truth commission played, with comparative studies, taking into account wider variables and realistic expectations.

One major issue with truth commission impact assessment is the data that is used to do the evaluation. Much of the retrospective analysis has been conducted on the basis of literature reviews and using databases, rather than by doing fieldwork. However, more needs to be done in countries where truth commissions have been held, in order to determine the part they have played in finding truth and creating reconciliation, amongst other expected aims. Too often the circumstances of these countries are not dealt with sufficiently when reviewing the truth commission. As Hayner has stated, various 'assumptions have been restated over and over again in untested assertions by otherwise astute and careful writers, thinkers, and political leaders'.[103] It has also been argued that the task of determining the 'roles, values, or effects of truth commissions are dauntingly complex'.[104] This is more problematic when it is noted that often *new* data is not sought to determine impact: much of the data used to make such assessments is existing data.[105] These data collections are not specifically geared to the task at hand. Where they are focused on transitional justice, they are oriented to a variety of processes within transitional justice rather than specifically truth commissions. They are not usually specifically oriented towards truth commissions and the issues they work on. They are also seen to produce 'patchy and contradictory' results.[106] Sometimes datasets on truth commissions examine limited issues, such as one dataset that measured their

---

103 P.B. Hayner, *Unspeakable Truths: Confronting State Terror and Atrocity*, Routledge, New York, 2001, at 7.

104 M. Urban Walker, 'Troubles with Truth Commissions: Putting the Moral Aims of Truth Commissions to the Fore', in S.E. Bird, M. Fraser and O. Anelli (eds.), *Performance of Memory as Transitional Justice*, Intersentia, Cambridge, 2015.

105 See an example of a dataset, C.E. Loyle and H.M. Binningsbø, 'Justice During Armed Conflict from 1949 through 2011: A New Dataset' (2017) 62(2) *Journal of Conflict Resolution* 442.

106 L. Mallinder and C. O'Rourke, 'Databases of Transitional Justice Mechanisms and Contexts: Comparing Research Purposes and Design' (2016) 10(3) *International Journal of Transitional Justice* 492.

impact on human rights and democracy.[107] This often means that the data relied on is more general in nature, rather than specific for the purpose needed. More recently, there have been projects reviewing issues such as how truth commission reports have been taken up, and how their recommendations have been implemented.[108] However, these have been, until recently, unfortunately rare. Much more data needs to be collected. The same limited databases cannot be used to arrive at simplistic and less-than-adequate conclusions. Rather than using generalised information to determine impact, more specific impact-focused data ought to be used. Much more empirical information is needed to make findings concerning impact and effect. A wide range of dependent variables in each country affects what each truth commission sets out to achieve, making evaluations of the effectiveness of these commissions difficult. Therefore, as is noted above, much more information collected before the evaluations are made is needed, specifically concerning the topics that truth commissions focus on.

To give an important example, data is needed to shed light on the extent to which reconciliation has progressed during the life of the truth commission, but also in the years that follow. Impact is not a static matter for aspects of the work of a truth commission. For some matters, such as reconciliation, the impact of a truth commission on that society can and usually *does* change over time. For truth recovery, what is found during the life of a truth commission remains static and cannot change unless new information is found, which would not be ascribed to the truth commission regardless.

When it comes to truth commission recommendations, the proposals themselves can be measured in terms of how much sense they make and how realistic they are in terms of implementation. However, whether and/or how they are taken up by the state is not in the power of the truth commission. And while it is common to measure a truth commission's impact by examining how its recommendations are complied with, sometimes the state is not ready or able to take up those recommendations. For some, that is reason to argue that a truth commission has been a failure because the expectations of victims, concerning the adoption of recommendations, have not been met.[109] This can, amongst other factors, have to do with reparations and for what and to whom they are paid.[110] Too often the impact of truth commissions on development matters is not seen to have flowed from reparations debates and dialogue.

107 E. Wiebelhaus-Brahm, *Truth Commissions and Transitional Societies: The Impact on Human Rights and Democracy*, Routledge, New York, 2010.

108 Paulson and Bellino, *supra* note 45.

109 Langer, *supra* note 57, at 182.

110 L.J. Laplante, 'On the Indivisibility of Rights: Truth Commissions, Reparations, and the Right to Development' (2007) 10 *Yale Human Rights and Development Law Journal* 141.

Another problem with some of the data used is that it has at times been ordered in particular ways so as to be able to better understand what the information that has been collected means. That process of ordering the data is done via what is termed data coding. This refers to codes being allocated to the data in order to organise and group it, and thus to be able to evaluate it and arrive at conclusions looking at the data collectively. However, for coding to occur, the meaning of the data needs to be found using refining techniques. There are many questions relating to how this is done and whether the process is reliable, particularly when done by single researchers.[111] Questions exist about the techniques,[112] and the extent to which investigators' presuppositions affect the coding and thus affect the outcomes of the research.[113] The allocation of codes can be done in ways that allow only some of the many possibilities of what the information could mean to be refined into specific codes for computation. The coding process does not always allow for a more nuanced understandings and for follow-ups to obtain more in-depth analysis of a specific matter.

## 6. CONCLUSION

In many ways, the world has become far more focused on dealing with past atrocities. Transitional justice processes have become more and more commonplace. Within that context, truth commissions have become common ways to deal with a contested past and massive human rights abuse. With the growing prominence of truth commissions, it is vital to evaluate their effectiveness, so as to better understand the impact that they have and to improve on their efficacy in the future. This is especially true when taking into account that there will very likely continue to be a prevalence of truth commissions around the world. It is therefore vital for those societies and for victims that the conveners of these commissions know what works and what does not, so as to effectively deal with the past. If the lessons were fully known and understood, post-conflict countries would move forward in ways that are more likely to achieve harmony and sustainable peace.

To determine what works and what does not, all truth commission processes need to be fully evaluated. It is not sufficiently understood that truth

---

111 M. Syed and S.C. Nelson, 'Guidelines for Establishing Reliability When Coding Narrative Data' (2015) 3(6) *Emerging Adulthood* 375.

112 E. Blair, 'A Reflexive Exploration of Two Qualitative Data Coding Techniques' (2015) 6(1) *Journal of Methods and Measurement in the Social Sciences* 14.

113 J. Campbell, C. Quincy, J. Osserman and O. Pedersen, 'Coding In-Depth Semistructured Interviews: Problems of Unitization and Intercoder Reliability and Agreement' (2013) 42(3) *Sociological Methods & Research* 294.

commissions play a multitude of roles and that they use a variety of tools to mend broken societies and produce sustainable peace. Many issues must be considered in determining what a truth commission has done and whether it has fulfilled its mandates effectively and left a positive legacy. A variety of these issues should be used to determine a truth commission's impact. A more realistic and pragmatic set of indicators should be used to measure what truth commissions can do, rather than only to quantify what they have done in isolation.

A recurring problem is that truth commission results have been evaluated in a number of ways, using varied methodologies.[114] There has been a lack of a consistent approach in the evaluation of truth commissions; in some studies, the ways in which such evaluations are conducted are less than comprehensive. At times, too few impact and result areas are examined, and when they are, they are examined in ways that are often superficial. As a result, there has been no consistent approach to examining the impact of truth commissions.[115]

To determine what truth commissions do, and how they do it, a more consistent set of criteria needs to be used. The data that is used also has to be much more holistic and must examine many more issues, in more depth. More needs to be done to understand what effects truth commissions have, using indicators in order to assess what limits their roles and how this can be remediated in future processes.

The incredible difficulties of implementing a successful truth commission need to be given far more weight in assessing a truth commission's role. Fundamentally, whether truth commissions are successful or not is not something that they have much control over. Issues such as the politics of the country, their resources, the cooperation they receive from other institutions and individuals, and the mandates given to them, over which they have no control, are major determinants of their ultimate success. These conditions have important effects, causing resource deficiencies, both human and material, which considerably impact their outcome. It must be kept in mind that despite the difficulties they suffer from, they endure as transitional tools. Their problems have not dampened people's desire to have the truth be told and for the other aspects of what truth commissions do to be carried out. The overall conclusion must be that they are the best option for achieving a multitude of objectives in post-conflict regions.

Even though they play critical roles in helping to broaden the understanding of the general public about the atrocities committed, truth commissions' impact on truth recovery is not always used as the major indicator of success.

---

114 E. Skaar and C.G. Malca, 'Conclusions', in E. Skaar, C.G. Malca and T. Eide (eds.), *After Violence*, Routledge, New York, 2015.

115 E. Skaar and E. Wiebelhaus-Brahm, 'The Drivers of Transitional Justice: An Analytical Framework for Assessing the Role of Actors' (2013) 31(2) *Nordic Journal of Human Rights* 127.

Some may point to the fact that a large amount of truth remains hidden in societies where there have been massive violations, either because the perpetrators of atrocities do not come forward or are not truthful in their testimony. However, it is beyond doubt that truth commissions have a positive impact on bringing evidence to light. This is particularly true as far as truth as narrative and memory are concerned. The ability of truth commissions to provide catharsis for post-conflict societies and their victims must not be underplayed, particularly as victims are invited to come forward and publically share their stories, which gives them a platform to be heard and find peace in their acknowledgement.[116]

However, as noted earlier in this chapter, there are dozens of roles that truth commissions play in dealing with the past. One of those is making recommendations to address the causes of violations and to ensure they are not repeated. Using the lens of recommendations made by truth commissions to the state is one useful way that impact ought to be measured. The change brought on by truth commissions may not adequately meet the demand of some critics, who argue that change needs to be measured in whether truth commission recommendations are effected by the state. Often this is determined in very narrow ways, including whether the state acknowledges the role of the truth commission. Often, if the state does not conduct the reforms specifically recommended to it by a truth commission, the truth commission is blamed. Even if reform does occur, but not exactly as recommended by the truth commission, that process is not given any credit. This is, however, a very limited view of how change is seen to have been effected by truth commissions. Truth commission recommendations, for example, may play a variety of roles in societal change, even if not specifically adopted in the exact manner recommended. The fact that a state instigates some change in a particular policy can at times be connected to the role of a truth commission, even if it was not specifically expressed by the truth commission, or not specifically articulated in the way that it was adopted by the state.

In conclusion, truth commissions will be enduring institutions in the landscape of post-conflict and transitional societies. This is their major legacy. Because of the ways they are mandated to achieve their goals, their limited resources and the political environment that they operate in, the question is not whether they are successful or sufficiently impact the environment in those places. The real issue is how to improve them to make them more successful and more impactful, and to ensure that their legacy is a more peaceful and harmonious society. For that to be achieved, there is much that needs to be

116 Bakiner, *supra* note 47.

done to give them greater independence, more resources and protection against sustained and ongoing political pressure, and to support them before and during their lifecycle, as well as protecting and strengthening their legacy. While the state has the primary role in achieving this, so do many other players.

# IS ANYONE LISTENING?

## A Review of the Research on Attitudes Towards Truth Commissions

Filipa RAIMUNDO and Joana REBELO MORAIS*



## 1. INTRODUCTION

Less than 30 years after the first studies on truth commissions appeared, the list of goals these transitional justice mechanisms are expected to achieve has grown substantially.[1] Among these goals, the emergence of an acceptable 'truth' about the previous regime or conflict appears to be consensual. 'Truth' is therefore expected to constitute an important legacy of truth commissions.[2] However, are

* The authors would like to thank participants at the conference at NOVA Law School in February 2018 in Lisbon and the anonymous reviewers for comments on earlier versions of this chapter. This publication received support from FCT through the project PTDC/CPO-CPO/30730/2017.

1 See the introduction to this book by Sarkin on the various types of objectives that truth commissions have.

2 The notion of 'truth' entered the transitional justice lexicon at a very early stage, when the first investigation commissions were established as a means to overcome the obstacles facing accountability efforts, particularly in Latin America and South Africa (see I. KOVRAS, *Truth Recovery and Transitional Justice. Deferring human rights issues*, Routledge, Abingdon, 2014). Because the word became associated with a particular type of mechanism, the two are often used together. Yet there is ample variation in how scholars think about this issue,

they seen generally as the ideal mechanism for truth-telling? What is the link between the emergence of a consensual version of 'the truth' and the approval of the work of a truth commission? Does exposure to and participation in truth commissions affect the emotional and psychological wellbeing of individuals? These and other questions bring another essential legacy of truth commissions to the forefront: their impact on citizens.

As this chapter reflects, there are a number of challenges associated with collecting and analysing survey data on transitional justice.[3] Yet the existing

and also in how they refer to it. As an illustration, within the contributions analysed for this chapter, we found six different terms used to refer to the issue of 'truth', including: truth-sharing (R. David, 'What we know about transitional justice: survey and experimental evidence' (2017) 38(1) *Advances in Political Psychology* 151); truth-finding (J. Gibson, 'The Contributions of Truth to Reconciliation: Lessons From South Africa' (2006) 50(3) *Journal of Conflict Resolution* 409); E. Kiza, C. Rathgeber and H. Rohne, *Victims of war: an empirical study on war-vicitimization and victims' attitudes towards addressing atrocities*, Hamburger Institut für Sozialforschung, Hamburg, 2006); truth-achievement (M. Cárdenas, D. Páez, B. Rimé and M. Arnoso, 'How Transitional Justice Processes and Official Apologies Influence Reconciliation: the case of the Chilean "Truth and Reconciliation" and "Political Imprisonment and Torture" Commissions' (2015) 25(6) *Journal of Community and Applied Social Psychology* 515); truth-revelation (P. Aguilar, L. Balcells and H. Cebolla-Boado, 'Determinants of Attitudes Toward Transitional Justice: An Empirical Analysis of the Spanish Case' (2011) 44(10) *Comparative Political Studies* 1397); truth-telling (Kiza, Rathgeber and Rohne, *supra* this note; M. Bratton, 'Violence, partisanship and transitional justice in Zimbabwe' (2011) 49(3) *Journal of Modern African Studies* 353; R. David and S. Choi, 'Victims on Transitional Justice: Lessons from the Reparation of Human Rights Abuses in the Czech Republic' (2005) 27(2) *Human Rights Quarterly* 392; B. Rimé,, P. Kanyangara, V. Yzerbyt and D. Paez, 'The impact of Gacaca tribunals in Rwanda: psychosocial effects of participation in a truth and reconciliation process after a genocide' (2011) 41(6) *European Journal of Social Psychology* 695; K. Brounéus, 'The trauma of truth telling effects of witnessing in the Rwandan Gacaca courts on psychological health' (2010) 54(3) *Journal of Conflict Resolution* 408); and truth-seeking (Kiza, Rathgeber and Rohne, *supra* this note; P. Vinck, P. Pham, S. Baldo and R. Shigekane, *Living with Fear. A population-based survey on attitudes about peace, justice and social reconstruction in Eastern Democratic Republic of Congo*, Human Rights Center, University of California, Berkeley, 2008; P. Vinck, P. Pham and T. Kreutzer, *Talking Peace. A population-based survey on attitudes about security, dispute resolution and post-conflict reconstruction in Liberia*, Human Rights Center, University of California, Berkeley, 2011; P. Pham, P. Vinck, E. Stover, A. Moss, M. Wierda and R. Bailey, *When the War Ends. A Population-Based Survey on Attitudes about Peace, Justice and Social Reconstruction in Northern Uganda*, Human Rights Center, University of California, Berkeley, 2007; C. Samii, 'Who wants to forgive and forget? Transitional justice preferences in postwar Burundi' (2013) 50(2) *Journal of Peace Research* 219; S. Parmentier and E. Weitekamp, 'Punishing perpetrators or seeking truth for victims: Serbian opinions on dealing with war crimes' (2013) 13 *International Criminal Law Review* 43; E. Nussio, A. Rettberg and J.E. Ugarriza, 'Victims, nonvictims and their opinions on transitional justice: findings from the Colombian case' (2015) 9(2) *International Journal of Transitional Justice* 336). In most of these contributions, when more than one term is used, no clear and distinctive definition is provided, and the same expression is used with different meanings by different authors. In this chapter, we will adopt the term 'truth-telling'.

3 See H. van der Merwe, 'Delivering justice during transition: research challenges', in H. van der Merwe, V. Baxter and A. Chapman (eds.), *Assessing the Impact of Transitional Justice: Challenges for Empirical Research*, United States Institute of Peace Press,

literature shows that these types of data are uniquely useful for improving our knowledge and reaching a better understanding of the performance of transitional justice mechanisms – mainly because they are an excellent tool with which to grasp the micro-level legacies of transitional justice and truth commissions in particular.

The chapter uses a bibliographic search to produce a review of the literature using attitudinal data on truth commissions and/or on the issue of 'truth', noting their main findings and discussing their theoretical and methodological features. To do this, the chapter is divided into three sections. The first offers an overview of those contributions, highlighting their main features and methodological choices. The second looks at three different sub-groups: preferences, assessment, and effects. The third presents some general conclusions and recommendations for future research and practice in the field of transitional justice in general and truth commissions in particular.

## 2. 36 STUDIES ON ATTITUDES TOWARDS 'TRUTH' AND TRUTH COMMISSIONS

A sizeable share of the impact assessment studies in the field of transitional justice focuses on the institutional effects of mechanisms as trials, truth commissions and vetting measures. These studies tend to highlight the macro-level legacies, such as the emergence of a human rights culture,[4] the elimination of authoritarian enclaves, institutional transformation,[5] greater social and political inclusion, a better quality of democracy, or the implementation of other transitional justice mechanisms.[6] The underlying idea has often been that transitional justice mechanisms are crucial tools that must be adopted while crafting and strengthening the new rules of the game, and that even after successful democratic consolidation, efforts should be made to avoid impunity and oblivion. These studies have focused on a wide range of countries in Latin America and Africa, but their excessively normative component vis-à-vis their empirical support is often criticised. Consequently, in recent years some

Washington D.C., 2009, at 115–142; M. Ben-Josef Hirsch, M. Mackenzie and M. Sesay, 'Measuring the impacts of truth and reconciliation commissions: placing the global "success" of TRCs in local perspective' (2012) 47(3) *Cooperation and Conflict* 386.

4 See for instance E. Wiebelhaus-Brahm, *Truth Commissions and Transitional Societies. The Impact on Human Rights and Democracy*, Routledge, London and New York, 2010.

5 See for instance H. Yusuf, *Calling the judiciary to account for the past: transitional justice and judicial accountability in Nigeria* (2008) 30(2) *Law and Policy* 194.

6 See for instance: A. Ferrara, *Assessing the Long-Term Impact of Truth Commissions. The Chilean Truth and Reconciliation Commission in Historical Perspective*, Routledge, London and New York, 2015.

studies have emerged that suggest the macro-level effects of transitional justice mechanisms are difficult to prove and can, on many occasions, be more negative than positive.[7]

We know less about the legacy of these mechanisms at the individual level, be it among citizens directly and indirectly affected by repression (also known as the 'end-users'),[8] or the population in general. The first few studies focused almost exclusively on the subject of reconciliation and, more recently, on the issue of trust in institutions.[9] Sub-Saharan Africa was often the primary focus of the former, while the latter has called attention to the many cases in Eastern Europe in which different transitional justice mechanisms, such as vetting measures, have been adopted. However, in the past 15 years, we have witnessed a considerable increase in the number of public opinion studies in this field. The prevailing view among the authors of these contributions is that many of the challenges facing societies in transition – either from war to democracy or from dictatorship to democracy – need to be overcome at the individual level. This is because they are concerned with how people relate to each other after years of violence and repression, how open they are to accepting a particular version of the past, and how willing they are to forgive the wrongdoers or political opponents. Given the growing interest in this type of data, it is time to identify the main characteristics and highlights from these studies.

Table 1 summarises the main characteristics of 36 survey-based studies on truth commissions and the issue of 'truth' in transitional justice.[10] Our main question when searching for publications on this topic was: 'how have scholars measured individual attitudes, perceptions and emotions regarding truth commissions and truth revelation, and what can we learn from their contributions?' The goal has not been to develop a comparative study of attitudes and perceptions in this field or to focus too much on the findings in those studies; as we shall see, the majority of them measure different things in different ways. Instead, the aim was to call attention to the main differences in the methodology

---

7 See for instance: D. Mendeloff, 'Truth-seeking, truth-telling and postconflict peacebuilding: curb the enthusiasm?' (2004) 6(3) *International Studies Review* 355; L. Vinjamuri and J. Snyder, 'Advocacy and scholarship in the study of war crime tribunals and transitional justice' (2004) 7(1) *Annual Review of Political Science* 345.

8 A. Macdonald, 'Local understandings and experiences of transitional justice: a review of the evidence', Justice and Security Research Programme, London School of Economics and Political Science (LSE), London, 2013, https://assets.publishing.service.gov.uk/media/57a08a49ed915d622c00066b/JSRP6.Macdonald.pdf.

9 See for instance C. Horne, *Building Trust and Democracy. Transitional Justice in Post-Communist Countries*, Oxford University Press, Oxford, 2017.

10 Although we refer to a few comparative pieces throughout the chapter, we decided not to include them in the table because they either provide aggregate data about several cases or they include countries that fall slightly outside our definition of what is a post-authoritarian or a post-conflict regime. See for instance Kiza, Rathgeber and Rohne, *supra* note 2; M. Cárdenas et al., 'Determinants of approval of the work of truth commissions in the southern cone: a comparative study' (2016) 31(3) *Revista de Psícologia Social* 423.

used to collect survey data, including the sample, the method and the survey instruments, and to note relevant trends and issues. As such, the main points described in the following sections are an attempt to identify major trends. The discussion about how authors have arrived at the results is as important as the findings in themselves.

All the studies were selected using a snowball-sampling technique, and the criteria for selection was the inclusion of questions about truth commissions or truth revelation.[11] When analysing these publications, some of the questions we had in mind included: 'did the questionnaire include questions about truth commissions or truth revelation?', 'what sort of sample does it use?', 'what is its main goal?' and 'what are its main findings?' The final list of selected publications covers 20 countries, with the cases of Rwanda and South Africa slightly overrepresented, as they account for almost a quarter. Given the criteria used in the selection of publications, many important contributions that do use attitudinal data to analyse the impact of transitional justice at the micro level have been excluded, because they do not cover attitudes towards truth commissions or the issue of 'the truth'.[12]

The first column in Table 1 indicates the country and the authors of the publication (full references in the appendix). The second column classifies the cases as either post-authoritarian or post-conflict and shows either the period in which human rights violations were committed or the period covered in the publication. The third column offers a classification, dividing the publications into three types: those focused on preferences (if the questions about truth-telling/truth commissions are used to measure individual preferences); those focused on assessment (if the questions about truth-telling/truth commissions are used to measure how citizens evaluate the mechanisms implemented in their country); and those focused on effects (if the questions about truth-telling/truth commissions are used to measure how citizens feel after participating in these processes or after finding out about their existence). The fourth column describes the main topic and dependent variable (DV), where applicable (some publications, particularly reports, are purely descriptive and therefore have no DVs). The fifth column indicates the type of sample, distinguishing

11 This review was not based on an established method because of a lack of resources. However, the authors have been as rigorous as possible in building the database.

12 See for instance J. Hall et al., 'Exposure to violence and attitudes towards transitional justice' (2018) 39(2) *Political Psychology* 345; R. David, 'The past or the politics of the present? Dealing with the Japanese occupation of South Korea' (2016) 22(1) *Contemporary Politics* 57; J. Barceló, 'The emotional underpinnings of attitudes towards transitional justice' (2017) 66(2) *Political Studies* 480; J. Gibson, J. Sonis and S. Hean, 'Cambodians' support for the rule of law on the eve of the Khmer Rouge trials' (2010) 4 *International Journal of Transitional Justice* 377; M. Biro, 'Attitudes toward justice and social reconstruction in Bosnia and Herzegovina and Croatia', in E. Stover and H. Weinstein (eds.), *My Neighbor, My Enemy. Justice and Community in the Aftermath of Mass Atrocity*, Cambridge University Press, Cambridge, 2004.

between cross-sectional and longitudinal, and national or regional studies. The sixth column explains the data collection method and the size of the sample used in the survey design. The last column indicates the data source and the period during which the data were collected. We must make one caveat: most of these studies do not focus specifically on the impact of truth-telling/truth commissions; instead, many of them focus on transitional justice in broad terms and only address those issues in part. As such, the column 'topic and DVs' only refers to those sections that deal specifically with our topic of interest.

**Table 1. Studies on attitudes towards 'truth' and 'truth commissions'**

| Country | Background | Type | Topic and DVs | Sample and method | Data source and year |
|---|---|---|---|---|---|
| **Argentina** Arnoso et al. (2014) | PA (1976–1983) | Preferences & Assessment | Attitudes and impact of TJ mechanisms | Cross-sectional, national; non-representative of victims and non-victims ($n$=265) | The authors [date not specified] |
| **Argentina** Zubieta et al. (2015) | PA (1976–1983) | Assessment & Effects | Perceived efficacy; the social impact of participation in a TRC | Cross-sectional, national; non-representative of victims and non-victims ($n$=518) | The authors [date not specified] |
| **Burundi** Samii (2013) | PC (1972 & 1993) | Preferences | Support for 'forgiving and forgetting' (DV) | Cross-sectional, regional; stratified sample of civilian population in 17 provinces (excludes demobilised combatants and active members of the security forces) ($n$=N/A) | The author and colleagues in partnership w/ Iteka – Ligue Burundaise des Droits de l'Homme (2007) |
| **Cambodia**[a)] Pham et al. (2009) | PA (1975–1979) | Preferences | Truth-seeking (several survey instruments) | Cross-sectional, national; representative of the population; random selection of 125 communes out of 1,621; sampling frame – Census 2008; cluster random sampling ($n$=1,000) | The authors in partnership w/ the Center for Advanced Study (2008) |
| **Cambodia**[a)] Pham et al. (2011) | PA (1975–1979) | Preferences | Truth-seeking (several survey instruments) | Cross-sectional, national; 30% of the sample overlapping with the 2008 sample; 70% cluster random sampling ($n$=1,000) | Initiative for Vulnerable Populations (2010) |

*(continued)*

Table 1 *continued*

| Country | Background | Type | Topic and DVs | Sample and method | Data source and year |
|---|---|---|---|---|---|
| **Central African Republic** Vinck and Pham (2010) | PC (1960–2003) | Preferences | Attitudes about justice mechanisms | Cross-sectional, regional; adult residents; random selection method in five administrative regions; sampling frame – Census 2003; random-route (*n*=1,879) | Initiative for Vulnerable Populations (2009) |
| **Chile** Manzi and González (2007) | PA (1973–1990) | Effects | Forgiveness and reparation | Cross-sectional, regional; non-representative sample, university students in Santiago (*n*=615) | The authors (2004) |
| **Chile** Cárdenas et al. (2015) | PA (1973–1989) | Assessment & Effects | Attitudes towards the TRC; perceptions of the country's socio-emotional climate | Cross-sectional, regional; stratified sample in Santiago, Valparaíso, Concepción, Antofagasta; random route (*n*=1278) | [Not specified] |
| **Chile** Martínez et al. (2015) | PA (1973–1990) | Assessment | Belief in victims' willingness to forgive those responsible for violence during the military dictatorship | Cross-sectional, regional; adult citizens in urban areas; convenience sample (Santiago, Valparaíso, Concepción); self-administered questionnaire (*n*=1,276) | The authors (2010–2011) |
| **Colombia** Rettberg (2008) | PC (1949–2015) | Preferences | Attitudes towards TJ mechanisms, including truth-seeking (survey instrument) | Cross-sectional, regional; convenience sample; sample frame – members of victims organisations and participants in events organised by Fiscalía General de la Nación (*n*=1,014) | The author (2008) |
| **Colombia** Nussio et al. (2015) | PC (1949–2015) | Preferences | Differences in attitudes towards TJ between victims and non-victims (DV) | Cross-sectional, regional; 42 municipalities (*n*=1,843) | Justice and Peace Survey, International Organization for Migration (2012) |

*(continued)*

Table 1 *continued*

| Country | Background | Type | Topic and DVs | Sample and method | Data source and year |
|---|---|---|---|---|---|
| **Czech Republic** David and Choi (2005) | PA (1948–1991) | Effects | Victims' feeling of rehabilitation (DV) | Cross-sectional, national; non-representative, former political prisoners; self-administered questionnaire (*n*=826) | The authors (1999–2000) |
| **Eastern DRC** Vinck et al. (2008) | PC (1996–2006) | Preferences | Attitudes towards TJ mechanisms, including truth-seeking (survey instrument) | Cross-sectional, regional; representative of the adults living in the selected area; multi-stage sampling strategy in Ituri district in Oriental province and North and South Kivu (*n*=2,620) | The Berkeley-Tulane Initiative on Vulnerable Populations (2007) |
| **Ecuador** Reyes et al. (2015) | PC (1984–1988) | Assessment & Effects | Perceived efficacy; the social impact of participation in a TRC | Cross-sectional, national; non-representative sample of victims and non-victims (*n*=387) | The authors (2013) |
| **Liberia** Vinck et al. (2011) | PC (1989–2003) | Assessment | Truth and the role of the TRC (set of survey instruments) | Cross-sectional, regional; representative of the population at the county level; random multi-stage cluster sampling in 260 Enumeration Areas (*n*=4,501) | Initiative for Vulnerable Populations (2010) |
| **Northern Uganda** Pham et al. (2005) | PC (1985–2005) | Preferences | Attitudes about TJ mechanisms (including truth commissions) | Cross-sectional, national; representative of the population in the respective districts; random-sampling; four northern districts (Gulu, Kitgum, Lira, Soroti) (*n*=2,585) | Human Rights Center, University of California-Berkeley; International Center for Transitional Justice (2005) |
| **Northern Uganda** Pham et al. (2007) | PC (1985–2005) | Preferences | Peace and Truth (several survey instruments) | Cross-sectional, regional; representative of the population in the respective districts; random multi-stage cluster sampling in eight districts (*n*=2,875) | The authors in partnership w/ the BBC World Service Trust (2007) |

*(continued)*

Table 1 *continued*

| Country | Background | Type | Topic and DVs | Sample and method | Data source and year |
|---|---|---|---|---|---|
| **Northern Uganda** Pham et al. (2010) | PC (1985–2005) | Preferences | Attitudes about TJ mechanisms (including truth commissions) | Cross-sectional, regional; representative of the population in the respective districts; random multi-stage cluster sampling in four districts (*n*=2,498) | Initiative for Vulnerable Populations (2010) |
| **Paraguay** Arnoso et al. (2014) | PA (1954–1989) | Effects | Perceived efficacy; the social impact of participation in a TRC | Cross-sectional, regional (*n*=400) | The authors [date not specified] |
| **Paraguay** Arnoso et al. (2015) | PA (1954–1989) | Assessment & Effects | Emotional impact of participation in a TRC | Cross-sectional, regional; convenience sample; self-administered questionnaire (*n*=1,992) | The authors (2012) |
| **Peru** Espinosa et al. (2015) | PC 1980–2000 | Assessment & Effects | Perceived efficacy; the social impact of participation in a TRC | Cross-sectional, regional; non-representative, university students in Lima (*n*=99) | The authors (2013) |
| **Peru** Espinosa et al. (2017) | PC 1980–2000 | Assessment | Support for remembrance and forgetting | Cross-sectional, regional; multi-stage random cluster sampling in three cities (*n*=1,200) | Institute of Public Opinion of PUCP (2011/12) |
| **Rwanda** Longman et al. (2004) | PC 1994 | Assessment | Attitudes towards the major TJ initiatives | Cross-sectional, regional; multi-stage cluster sampling in four communes (*n*=2,091) | The authors in partnership w/ local university students (2002) |
| **Rwanda** Rettig (2008) | PC 1994 | Assessment | Contribution of Gacaca to truth and reconciliation | Longitudinal; representative of Sovu's adult unincarcerated population; random sample, Sovu residents eligible to attend Gacaca (*n*=505) | The author (November 2006 and May 2007) |

*(continued)*

Table 1 *continued*

| **Country** | **Background** | **Type** | **Topic and DVs** | **Sample and method** | **Data source and year** |
|---|---|---|---|---|---|
| **Rwanda** Brounéus (2010) | PC 1994 | Effects | Impact of Gacaca on psychological health | Cross-sectional, regional; multi-stage, stratified cluster random sample in 4 provinces (*n*=1,200) | The authors in partnership w/ the International Rescue Committee (2006) |
| **Rwanda** Rimé et al. (2011) | PC 1994 | Effects | Reconciliation, wellbeing and Emotional climate of victims after Gacaca (DV) | Cross-sectional, regional; non-representative; four provinces (*n*=755) | The author in partnership w/ the *National University of Rwanda* (2006) |
| **Serbia** Parmentier and Weitekamp (2013) | PC (1991–1999) | Preferences | Support for seeking truth, establishing accountability, providing reparation and promoting reconciliation (DVs) | Cross-sectional, national; non-representative; quota-sampling method using geographical distribution, age and gender, self-administered questionnaire (*n*=922) | The authors in partnership w/ the Association Joint Action for Truth and Reconciliation (2007) |
| **Sierra Leone** Sawyer and Kelsall (2007) | PC (1991–2002) | Assessment | Knowledge and evaluation of the trials and the TRC | Cross-sectional, national (*n*=300) | The authors in partnership w/ a local counterpart (2005) |
| **South Africa** Gibson and Gouws (1999) | PA (1948–1994) | Effects | Blame attribution following apartheid (DV) | Panel, national; individuals answering both surveys (*n*=1,285) | The authors (1996–1997) |
| **South Africa** Gibson (2004) | PA (1948–1994) | Effects | Interracial Reconciliation Index after TRC (DV) | Cross-sectional, national (*n*=3,727) | The author in partnership w/ Decision Surveys International (2000–2001) |
| **South Africa** Gibson (2005) | PA (1948–1994) | Assessment | Perceived efficacy of the TRC | Cross-sectional, national; representative of the national population; random selection (*n*=3,727) | The author (2000–2001) |

*(continued)*

Table 1 *continued*

| Country | Background | Type | Topic and DVs | Sample and method | Data source and year |
|---|---|---|---|---|---|
| **South Africa** Kaminer et al. (2001) | PA (1948–1994) | Effects | Psychiatric health and forgiveness attitudes of survivors (DV) | Cross-sectional; regional; survivors from African communities, non-random sample (*n*=134) | The authors [date not specified] |
| **South Africa** Backer (2010) | PA (1948–1994) | Effects | The effect of the TRC on victims | Longitudinal, regional; victims of HR violations in Cape Town; randomised (*n*=153) | The author in partnership w/ local organisations (2002–2003 and 2008) |
| **Spain** Aguilar et al. (2011) | PA (1936–1975) | Preferences | Support for truth commission, trials and removal of symbols (DVs) | Cross-sectional, national; random sample (*n*=2,936) | Centro de Investigaciones Sociológicas (2008) |
| **Uruguay** Arnoso and Costa (2015) | PA (1973–1985) | Assessment & Effects | Perceived efficacy; the social impact of participation in a TRC | Cross-sectional, national; self-administered questionnaire (*n*=721) | [Not specified] |
| **Zimbabwe** Bratton (2011) | PC (1960–2000) | Preferences | Determinants of support for retributive justice (DV) | Cross-sectional, national; multi-stage stratified sample (*n*=1,200) | Mass Public Opinion Institute (2009) |

Source: Compiled by the authors. For full references see Appendix 1.

Notes: PA: post-authoritarian; PC: post-conflict (the classification refers exclusively to the type of situation that led to the implementation or demand for transitional justice mechanisms); a) Cambodia is considered a post-authoritarian society, even though it has not completed its transition to democracy.

The first aspect to highlight in Table 1 is the number of studies focusing on post-authoritarian societies compared to those focusing on post-conflict situations. While the former tend to concentrate mainly on the legacies of the European, Latin American and African authoritarian regimes that collapsed or were overthrown during the last quarter of the 20th century, the latter focus on more recent experiences, particularly in Africa, where some countries have yet to democratise. The number of studies focusing on each is similar, as illustrated by Figure 1, which suggests scholars have been as interested in collecting survey data in countries where truth-revelation mechanisms can still play a role as they have been in assessing how individuals evaluate the performance of mechanisms that have already been implemented and how participation in truth commissions affects their wellbeing.

**Figure 1. Distribution of single case studies on public attitudes towards 'truth' and truth commissions, by country**

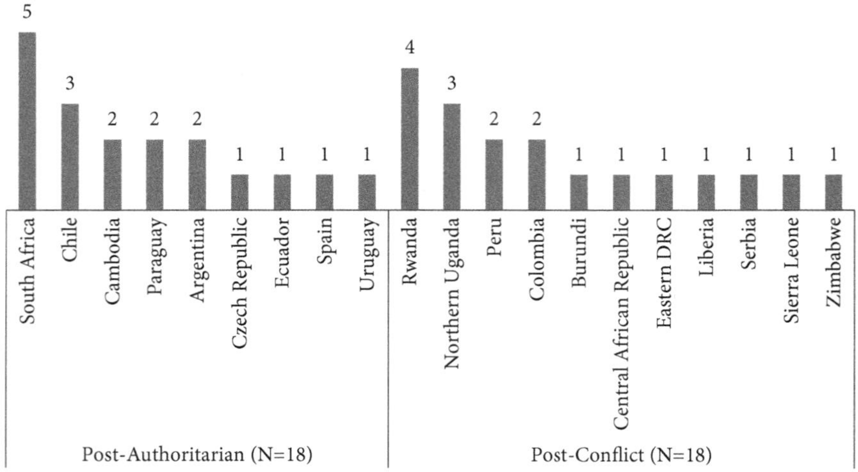


Source: Compiled by the authors from Table 1.

This distinction between post-authoritarian and post-conflict cases matters because, while the former represent transitional justice processes that take place during a transition to democracy, post-conflict cases represent processes that take place in societies going through a transition from war to peace, whether or not leading to a democratic regime. One important implication of this is that in post-conflict societies transitional justice is often implemented in the midst of power-sharing arrangements and disarmament, demobilisation and reintegration (DDR) processes, which may be incompatible with accountability goals, an issue that has been framed in the literature as the 'peace versus justice' dilemma. Another important aspect to take into account is that in post-authoritarian societies, state institutions can be reformed and restructured, while in post-conflict societies, state structures tend to be in ruins and need to be rebuilt, which often means these societies experience difficulties implementing these mechanisms without support from international actors. Finally, while in post-authoritarian societies the distinction between perpetrators and victims in most cases is reasonably straightforward, the opposite is true in post-conflict scenarios, and particularly when there are no clear winners.

Most of the studies analysed used samples larger than 1,000 individuals, which the authors constructed with help from local partners. As far as we are aware, only three of these studies use either panel data or longitudinal data; all other studies use cross-sectional data. The samples and sampling methods are, however, very diverse. Many are regional studies conducted in urban and rural areas; very few are representative samples of the national population, and a small number use university students to build their samples.

The issue of who sponsors or conducts these studies should not be overlooked. As Ben-Josef Hirsch et al. note, 'when promoters of the TRC process conduct surveys, focus groups and interviews, it may be difficult to determine if their enthusiasm in advertising the benefits of the process during the pre-focus group information sessions has an impact on participants' responses during focus groups.'[13] This also holds true for the survey results.

One other aspect that ought to be taken into account is whether – and if so, which – transitional justice mechanisms have been implemented before the data collection process, which is believed to alter how individuals interpret these mechanisms. For instance, perceptions of specific mechanisms are likely to be influenced by perceptions of aspects of procedural fairness regarding mechanisms applied in one's country.[14] Only in experimental studies, which are often used to access the individual effects of transitional justice mechanisms, is the context unimportant (at least in theory), due to the characteristics of the method. In the publications included in this review, not all authors provide this type of information.

Knowing whether the data was collected before or after the mechanisms were implemented matters because the vast majority of these studies use cross-sectional data, which means that they are only able to draw a picture of a given moment. In some cases, authors do mention that they are measuring attitudes towards potential future mechanisms, but that information is often lost in the methods sections and very rarely taken into account when interpreting the results. Table 2 offers a quick overview of the mechanisms implemented in the countries covered by the studies, ranking them by the number of mechanisms, from highest to lowest. The table shows that there is great interest in studying countries in which few mechanisms have been implemented. Yet scholars do not reflect enough on the impact of the transitional justice context for this type of data collection process. In a comparative study on war victimisation, the authors first asked respondents whether they knew what a truth commission was and only then asked them to express their views on the usefulness of such a mechanism. This allowed the researchers to analyse whether prior knowledge of a truth commission affects individual perceptions. In one of the studies on Rwanda, the authors explain, 'the survey was conducted after Gacaca judges were elected but before trials had begun, so people's opinions are not based on having watched Gacaca in operation'.[15]

---

13 Ben-Josef Hirsch, Mackenzie and Sesay, *supra* note 3, at 394.

14 See Kiza, Rathgeber and Rohne, *supra* note 2, at 63; C. Lillie and R. Janoff-Bulman, 'Macro versus Micro Justice and Perceived Fairness of Truth and Reconciliation Commissions' (2007) 13(2) *Peace and Conflict: Journal of Peace Psychology* 221.

15 T. Longman, P. Pham and H. Weinstein, 'Connecting justice to human experience: attitudes toward accountability and reconciliation in Rwanda', in Stover and Weinstein (eds.), *supra* note 12.

**Table 2. Transitional justice mechanisms already adopted at the time of the data collection process**

| Country | Survey year | Amnesty | Trials | TRC |
|---|---|---|---|---|
| Argentina: Arnoso et al. (2014) | N/A | x[a)] | x | x |
| Argentina: Zubieta et al. (2015) | N/A | x[a)] | x | x |
| Chile: Manzi and González (2007) | 2004 | x | x | x |
| Chile: Martínez et al. (2015) | 2010–2011 | x | x | x |
| Chile: Cárdenas et al. (2015) | N/A | x | x | x |
| Eastern DRC: Vinck et al. (2008) | 2007 | x | x | x |
| Peru: Espinosa et al. (2015) | 2015 | x | x | x |
| Peru: Espinosa et al. (2017) | 2011–2012 | x | x | x |
| Sierra Leone: Sawyer and Kelsall (2007) | 2005 | x | x | x |
| Uruguay: Arnoso and Costa (2015) | N/A | x | x | x |
| Northern Uganda: Pham et al. (2005) | 2005 | x | b) | x[c)] |
| Northern Uganda: Pham et al. (2007) | 2007 | x | b) | x[c)] |
| Northern Uganda: Pham et al. (2010) | 2010 | x | b) | x[c)] |
| Serbia: Parmentier and Weitekamp (2013) | 2007 | - | x | x |
| Cambodia: Pham et al. (2009) | 2008 | - | x | - |
| Cambodia: Pham et al. (2011) | 2010 | - | x | - |
| Central African Republic: Vinck and Pham (2010) | 2009 | - | d) | - |
| Czech Republic: David and Choi (2005) | 1999 | - | x | - |
| Rwanda: Longman et al. (2004) | 2002 | - | x[e)] | - |
| Rwanda: Rettig (2008) | 2006–2007 | - | x | - |
| Rwanda: Brounéus (2010) | 2006 | - | x | - |
| Rwanda: Rimé et al. (2011) | 2006 | - | x | - |
| South Africa: Gibson and Gouws (1999) | 1996–1997 | f) | - | x |
| South Africa: Gibson (2004) | 2000–2001 | f) | - | x |
| South Africa: Gibson (2005) | 2001 | f) | - | x |
| South Africa: Backer (2010) | 2008 | x | - | x |
| Ecuador: Reyes et al. (2015) | 2013 | - | - | x |
| Liberia: Vinck et al. (2011) | 2010 | - | - | x |
| Paraguay: Arnoso et al. (2014) | N/A | - | - | x |
| Paraguay: Arnoso et al. (2015) | 2012 | - | - | x |
| Spain: Aguilar et al. (2011) | 2008 | x | - | - |
| Colombia: Rettberg (2008) | 2008 | g) | - | - |
| Colombia: Nussio et al. (2015) | 2012 | g) | - | - |
| Burundi: Samii (2013) | 2007 | - | - | - |
| Zimbabwe: Bratton (2011) | 2009 | - | - | - |

Source: Compiled by the authors.

Note: a) The self-amnesty was annulled; b) No trial took place, but the ICC opened investigations in 2004; c) Some authors identify up to two truth commissions in Uganda, but this is not consensual in the literature; d) The trial had not started but the ICC had already confirmed charges against Bemba in 2009; e) Gacaca judges had already been elected but the trial had not begun; f) The TRC only concluded its work in 2002; g) An amnesty law was passed in 2016.

A common feature of almost all of these studies is the issue of potential differences between those who have been exposed to violence and repression and those who were not. Most studies find differences in the attitudes of victims and non-victims, except the study on Colombia, in which these differences have not been confirmed. In the Colombian study, the authors divided the sample into victims and non-victims based on the definition of victim used in a national reparation law.[16] This was accomplished by asking respondents to indicate from a list whether they had been victims or first-degree relatives of victims of the armed conflict. The same procedure was used in the study of Spanish attitudes towards transitional justice, but in this case – apart from distinguishing between direct and indirect victims – the questionnaire also asked if individuals or their relatives had experienced a range of situations during the Civil War (1936–1939) and the authoritarian regime (1939–1974), including death in combat, death in bombardment, homicide, death penalty, disappearance, imprisonment, flight from Spain, forced into hiding, expelled from work, arrested or fined. A different strategy was used in the case of the two studies using only victims in South Africa (Cape Town) and the Czech Republic. In both cases, the authors resorted to victims' associations that shared their contact lists. Consequently, the latter two works do not use representative samples of the population, while the former do.

In most other studies, however, authors use perception-based indicators of victimisation with two or three categories. In the surveys conducted in Latin America, the authors distinguished between indirect victims ('Are there any victims of ... among your family members or close friends?'), direct victims ('Do you consider yourself a victim of ...?'), and non-victims or persons unaffected by political violence. In Ecuador, a scale was used to distinguish between direct and indirect victims and non-victims. In Serbia, the authors distinguished between direct (physical injuries on the respondent) and indirect victimisation (having lost family members) and also included questions about potential physical, material and psychological suffering. They argue, 'in a violent conflict like the Yugoslav one it is virtually impossible to make such clear-cut distinctions between those who are only perpetrators and those who are only victims since individuals can and sometimes do assume different roles, even "reverse" roles, in different phases of a conflict'.[17] A slightly different wording is used in the studies on Rwanda, which refer to those who were hunted, beaten, raped or tortured as 'survivors', as opposed to those who did not share those experiences, including Hutus living in the country at the time of the genocide.

What is also likely to influence the findings produced by these studies is the share of victims in the population. Figure 2 shows the distribution of

16 Law 1448 of 2001: *Por la cual se dictan medidas de atención, asistencia y reparación integral a las víctimas del conflicto armado interno y se dictan otras disposiciones.*

17 Parmentier and Weitekamp, *supra* note 2.

victims and non-victims in the samples used in the 36 studies included in this review. While there is a majority of non-victims in the studies conducted in Argentina (70 per cent), Ecuador (61 per cent), Peru (50 per cent) and Colombia (85 per cent), the opposite is the case for the case studies on Chile (43 per cent), Cambodia (7 per cent), the Eastern DRC (19 per cent) and Liberia (22 per cent).

**Figure 2. Distribution of victims (direct and indirect) and non-victims among respondents in nine surveys, in percentages**

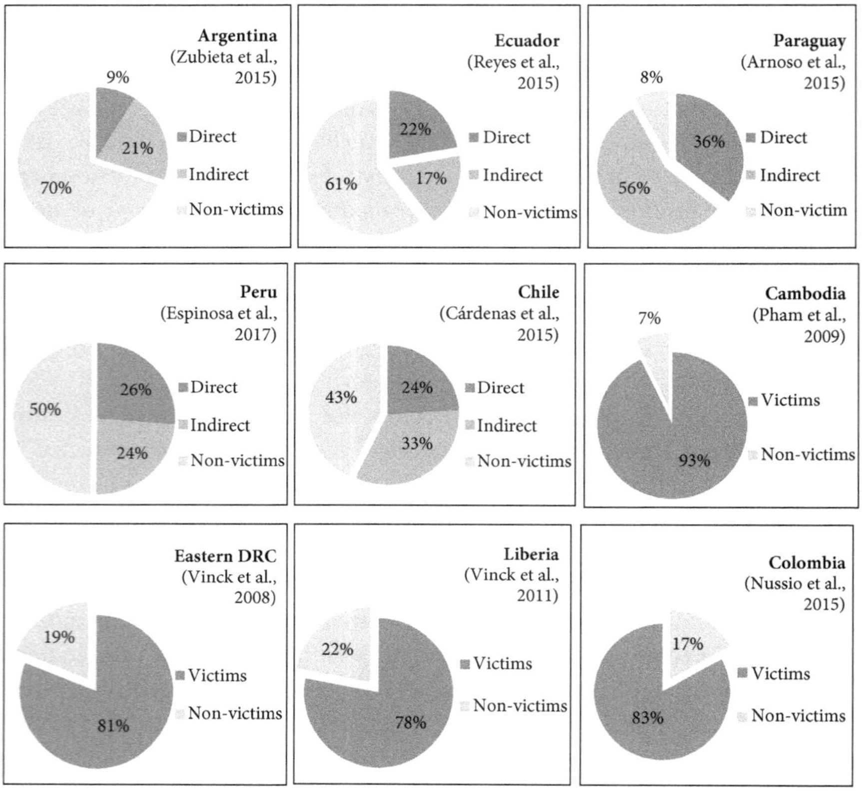


Source: Compiled by the authors. For full references see Appendix 1.

Below we explore the methodological, contextual and epistemological aspects of these studies, examining their findings and grouping the contributions into three categories.

## 3. THE LEGACY OF TRUTH COMMISSIONS AT THE INDIVIDUAL LEVEL

The works summarised in Table 1 have been divided into three different groups: those dedicated to the issue of preferences, with the aim of characterising popular perceptions of transitional justice mechanisms as well as their determinants; those devoted to the issue of assessment, with the aim of finding out how individuals evaluate the transitional justice mechanisms implemented in their own country; and those dedicated to the issue of emotional and psychological effects, with the aim of identifying how citizens feel after having participated in transitional justice processes or after knowing about their existence.[18] What they have in common is the use of public opinion data to examine the legacy of truth revelation and truth commissions at the individual level. Given that their goals are different, the type of question they ask and their findings raise different issues, which call for a separate analysis of the contributions in each group.

## 3.1. INDIVIDUAL PREFERENCES: TRUTH REVELATION 'YES', TRUTH COMMISSION 'PERHAPS'

Studies focused on individual preferences often adopt a holistic approach to transitional justice with the aim of identifying whether individuals prefer retribution over forgiveness or truth-seeking over forgetting. Consequently, questions about the issue of 'truth' or the idea of a 'truth commission' are not at the core of these survey questionnaires and should be seen as dimensions or categories of competing (or at least distinctive) transitional justice processes.

Two types of questions stand out as being more frequently used in these studies: multiple choice questions (in which respondents can choose between two or more answer options) and rating scale questions (typically using Likert-type scales).

In the former case, individuals are asked to pick two or more options from a list. In the surveys carried out by the Initiative for Vulnerable Populations in the Central African Republic or northern Uganda, the number of options available was in some occasions as high as 10. In response to the question 'what should happen to those responsible for the violence?', 'have them tell the truth' was one of 10 possible answers.

Multiple-choice questions with forced-choice have also been used on many occasions. In Samii's study in Burundi, respondents were asked to choose between two statements: 'to achieve peace and reconciliation, it is necessary to know the truth about what happened before the war', or 'in order to achieve peace and reconciliation, it is good to forget about the past'.[19] In Parmentier and Weitekamp's study in Serbia, individuals were asked to choose between four possible answers to the question 'do you think it is important for people

---

18 The distinction between the three is not always obvious and in some cases the questionnaire included more than one type of questions and the publication covers more than one approach.

19 Samii, *supra* note 2.

to tell about their experiences about the war?'[20] There were three variations on the positive answer: 'yes, but only the victims/the perpetrator/both victims and perpetrators should be given a chance to tell stories'.

In the case of Colombia, respondents were asked to position themselves on a scale: 'do you agree that ... It is better for victims to know the truth about what happened, who did it and why, than to leave it in the past'.[21] In Zimbabwe, respondents were asked to state what statement was closest to their view: 'revealing the truth about what happened in the past is necessary' or 'it is best to forget what happened in the past'.[22] This was one of six pairs of questions in which respondents were asked to choose between competing views of dealing with the past. Both in Liberia and in Eastern DRC, respondents were asked: 'is it important to know the truth about what happened?'[23] Their responses were limited to 'yes' or 'no', and in both cases, respondents were very clear about expressing their support for truth revelation.

In practical terms, this holistic approach often results in the construction of indices of support combining multiple dependent variables (e.g. Spain or Colombia) or in the analysis of the various components of transitional justice individually to find out what determines support for punishment or forgiveness, and retribution or truth (e.g. Burundi). These are also the type of studies that have been of most interest to political scientists.

Regarding the context in which these questions were asked, the most common pattern seems to be that surveys are carried out when at least one transitional justice mechanism has been implemented. In many cases, there is a public debate or a stated intention to adopt other mechanisms at the time the study is being carried out. In the case of Spain, where an amnesty law approved in 1977 has stopped retribution until the present day, the authors are interested in knowing whether an 'investigation commission (independent from the government) should be created to clarify human rights violations that took place under Francoism'.[24] The authors of the study on Serbia, where an international court was established to deal with crimes committed during the war, explicitly express their aim to focus on the 'possibilities (or opportunities) and the potential of a restorative approach'.[25]

The different experiences in each country are likely to affect how individuals feel about transitional justice mechanisms, and this needs to be taken into account in any attempt to compare individual attitudes. As the authors of one of the studies on Cambodia note, '[t]he results suggest how adult Cambodians define

---

20 Parmentier and Weitekamp, *supra* note 2, at 56.
21 Nussio, Rettberg and Ugarriza, *supra* note 2.
22 Bratton, *supra* note 2, at 363.
23 Vinck, Pham, Baldo and Shigekane, *Living with Fear, supra* note 2.
24 Aguilar, Balcells and Cebolla-boado, *supra* note 2.
25 Parmentier and Weitekamp, *supra* note 2, at 46.

justice has changed over times and may have been influenced by proceedings at the ECCC'.[26]

From an epistemological perspective, publications focusing on preferences show that the theoretical relationship between goals and transitional justice mechanisms may not necessarily be found in practice. In other words, the meaning respondents attribute to words such as 'justice' or 'truth' varies considerably and does not always reflect the way in which academics and practitioners think about transitional justice. The study on Eastern DRC, for instance, revealed that around 51 per cent of respondents believe 'justice' means 'establishing the truth'.[27] Similarly, in northern Uganda, 42 per cent of respondents believe the best way to establish 'the truth' is by investigating the principal perpetrators, the Lord Resistance Army (LRA). In Cambodia, 43 per cent of respondents defined justice as the means to reach the truth. In addition, cultural and historical issues must also be taken into account. For example:

> in an ethnographic study, Alayza and Crisóstomo (2007) reports that an important group of concerned organisations understand reconciliation as forgetting and forgiveness because in Andean cultural representations reconciliation refers to forgiveness or *pampachanakuy* in Quechua, which means burying something in the pampas, evoking the idea of letting the past go.[28]

The findings of these studies confirm that individuals distinguish clearly between finding the truth and setting up a truth commission. Figure 3 shows the data available in the studies under analysis on the percentage of respondents who agreed that establishing the truth was important or necessary and the percentage of respondents who stated that a truth commission would be the most appropriate mechanism to accomplish it. In most countries, respondents agree with the idea that truth revelation matters – albeit for different reasons, such as 'to achieve peace and reconciliation' (Burundi); 'to move forward' (Zimbabwe); 'to prevent future violence' (Liberia and northern Uganda); and 'to make individuals feel better' (Serbia). With the exception of Burundi, support for truth revelation is always above 50 per cent among citizens and respondents in these studies. Yet they do not consider truth commissions to necessarily be the best way to reveal the truth or to achieve peace. In Liberia, for example, only 5 per cent believe truth commissions to be the ideal way to ensure truth revelation. In Cambodia,

---

26 P. Pham, P. Vinck, M. Balthazard and S. Hean, *After the first trial. A population-based survey on knowledge and perception of justice and the extraordinary chambers in the courts of Cambodia*, Human Rights Center, University of California, Berkeley, 2011, at 29.

27 Vinck, Pham, Baldo and Shigekane, *Living with Fear, supra* note 2.

28 A. Espinosa, D.P. Rovira, T. Velázquez, R.M. Cueto, E. Seminario, S. Sandoval, F. Reátegui and I. Jave, 'Between remembering and forgetting the years of political violence: psychosocial impact of the Truth and Reconciliation Commission in Peru' (2017) 38(5) *Political Psychology* 849.

the contrast is even more evident: while 86 per cent of respondents agree it is necessary to find the truth, a large majority (45 per cent) said they did not know what would be the best mechanism to accomplish it, with only 8 per cent showing support for the establishment of a truth commission. In Eastern DRC, the overwhelming majority of respondents (88 per cent) expressed support for truth revelation, yet a significant percentage (56 per cent) said the judicial system was better equipped to deal with the truth than a truth commission. While citizens in Eastern DRC have a clear preference for the revelation of the truth, this does not mean they oppose accountability measures. In fact, in 2007, more people believed that in order to achieve peace it was more important to arrest those responsible for crimes (28 per cent) than it is to establish the truth (20 per cent). On the other hand, most of the population (51 per cent) thought obtaining justice meant establishing the truth. This picture changed in 2010, as the percentage of respondents in favour of amnesty (45 per cent) was clearly higher than those in favour of a truth commission (32 per cent) as a way to achieve peace.

**Figure 3. Support for 'truth' and 'truth commissions'**

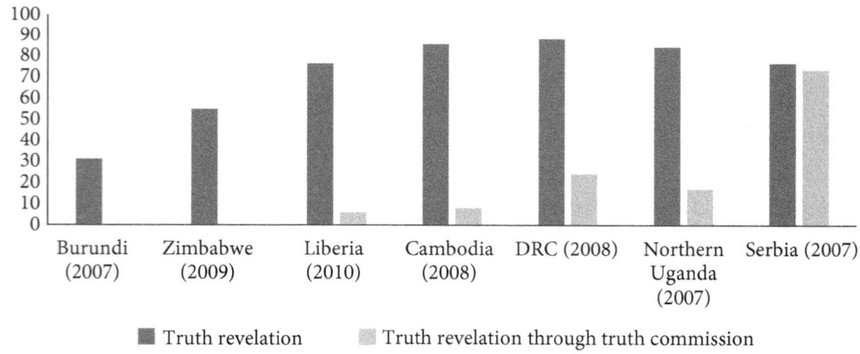


Source: Compiled by the authors. For full references see Appendix 1.

Note: Figures are not directly comparable as the types of question used were different in each study.

The same authors of the study in Eastern DRC and Cambodia conducted the studies in northern Uganda and found that an overwhelming majority (95 per cent) of respondents were 'in favour of a written historical record of what had happened during the war' and, more importantly, only a slightly lower percentage (89 per cent) said they would be willing to contribute to that written record by talking openly about their personal experiences. However, even in this case, the proportion of respondents expressing a preference for the establishment of a truth commission was reasonably low (29 per cent). In-depth interviews provided researchers with an explanation for this low level of support: unlike in the DRC, where a previous state-sponsored commission earned a bad reputation, in northern Uganda, local truth-telling experiences appear to have a had a positive impact on support for truth revelation, even if this did not translate into support for truth commissions themselves.

It is more challenging to compare Serbia with other cases, and in particular the figures concerning support for truth revelation through the establishment of a truth commission. Here, respondents were asked to express their preferences on a scale ranging from 'strongly disagree' to 'strongly agree'. Truth commissions were just one option among many that included courts and other public forums.

In identifying the determinants of support for transitional justice mechanisms, researchers have reached similar results, albeit in highly diverse contexts. For example, the findings from Burundi (post-conflict) and Spain (post-authoritarian) both highlight the role of political factors in shaping attitudes towards transitional justice. In the former case, the results do not support the idea that 'those who oppose punishment or truth-seeking ... do so out of fear about how punishment and truth-seeking may undermine peace or individual safety'; rather, the author finds 'partisan motivations, and particularly ethnic-partisan motivations' play a more important role,[29] even though there was a general rejection of retributive measures among the population. In the latter case, 'those who are more likely to support these measures are people who are closer to the left, younger and non-religious, but also people whose families sided with the Republicans during the Civil War and/or were victimised during the dictatorship'.[30] This suggests political-partisan factors can be equally important in both contexts.

Briefly, these studies reveal public attitudes are influenced by three major factors: preference for retributive justice (i.e. prosecution); earlier experiences with similar commissions with a bad reputation; and lack of knowledge about transitional justice mechanisms. To what extent citizens' knowledge may partly explain their preferences is something to be explored in the next section.

## 3.2. POOR KNOWLEDGE, MODERATE APPROVAL

Unlike preferences, which tend to be more normative, individual assessment is, to some extent, a policy-based evaluation. We can compare this to David Easton's distinction between specific and diffuse support for democracy.[31] In Easton's view, evaluating the performance of political institutions is different from assessing the political regime itself. Therefore, citizens can assess the performance of institutions negatively and still express support for democracy as the best form of government. The same holds true for transitional justice: asking citizens to evaluate the performance of specific mechanisms is different

29 Samii, *supra* note 2, at 213.

30 Aguilar, Balcells and Cebolla-Boado, *supra* note 2, at 1420.

31 D. Easton, *A Systems Analysis of Political Life*, John Wiley, New York, 1965.

from asking them to express their views on transitional justice in abstract terms. Hence, the questions used to grasp individual assessment do not provide a measurement of how much citizens support different transitional justice approaches per se – i.e. punishment, forgiveness, remembrance – in the way the studies focused on preferences do; instead, they focus on how individuals assess the way the mechanisms implemented in their country performed. As such, low satisfaction with a truth commission does not mean citizens do not favour truth-revelation mechanisms. In turn, their assessment may be associated with levels of politicisation, partiality, poor performance, low resources and manipulation, among other things.

Again, unlike what we have seen in the studies on transitional justice preferences, in which there is ample variation in how scholars formulate the questions and in how they measure individual preferences, some similarities can be found among individual assessment studies. This is because there is a greater propensity to apply the type of survey instruments used in earlier publications – the studies by James Gibson on the South African truth commission are among those that have been replicated more often. This facilitates comparisons:

> our results provide evidence that confirms the findings of previous studies (Gibson 2004); that is, when a TRC is perceived as fulfilling important functions related to the knowledge of the truth, and when their report contributes to further activities in seeking justice by the civil society, then a TRC is positively valued.[32]

One of the aspects frequently mentioned in the literature is that few individuals report knowing about transitional justice mechanisms, particularly truth commissions. This is true both when respondents are asked whether they know what a truth commission is and when asked whether they have heard about the truth commission implemented in their country. In addition, we do not always know what individuals have in mind when answering questions about the potential benefits of a future truth commission. Such is the case, for instance, in the study on Colombia, where the same 80 per cent who admitted never having heard about a truth commission said they were convinced it would be a good solution to their own problem.[33] In order to solve this, some authors choose to provide a description of the mechanism they want to obtain information on, and only then collect participants' views. In the case of Peru, for instance, researchers offered participants a summary of the activities of the two truth commissions before posing the question. In South Africa, the questions used in the survey included brief information about the truth commission: 'The TRC granted amnesties to some of those who came forward

[32] Cárdenas et al., *supra* note 10, at 439.

[33] A. Rettberg, *Reparación en Colombia ¿Qué quieren las víctimas?*, Deutsche Gesellschaft für Technische Zusammenarbeit, Bogotá, 2008, at 83.

and admitted committing atrocities. Do you approve of amnesty being given to those who admitted committing atrocities?'[34]

What these studies find is that the level of knowledge is not related to the level of approval of truth commissions. Figure 4 shows some preliminary (and so far unpublished) data collected in seven Latin American countries. Each column represents the country in which the data was collected – meaning citizens were asked whether they knew and how much they approved of the work of the truth commission(s) established in their country. The case of Uruguay – with the highest level of knowledge and lowest level of approval – and the case of Paraguay – with the lowest level of knowledge and among the highest levels of approval – illustrate how the two aspects are not related.

In addition, there seems to be a minimal relationship between the timing of the publication of reports and the level of knowledge expressed by citizens. The most recent commission among those represented in the graph is Brazil's, where the report was published at the end of 2014, and yet the level of knowledge among Brazilian respondents is considerably lower than among respondents from Argentina, which is generally thought to have created the first truth commission (1983) and Uruguay, which had two truth commissions – one in 1985, and the other in 2000. It seems that the best-known commissions are those whose reports were disseminated more widely.

**Figure 4. Knowledge and approval of the work of the truth commission in post-authoritarian democracies**

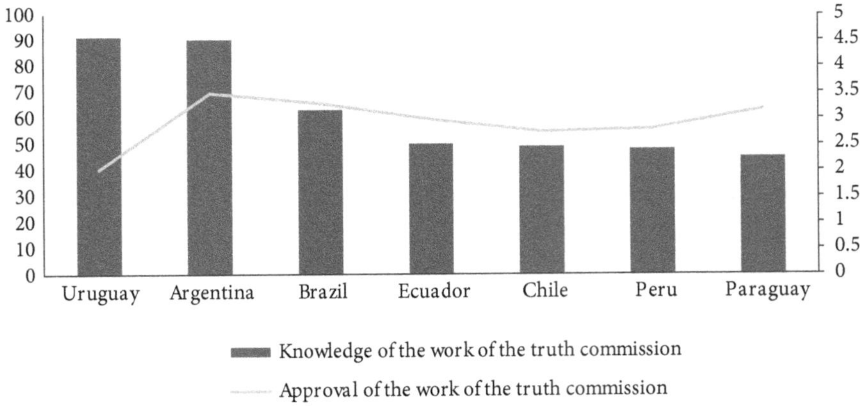


Source: Compiled by the authors based on D. Páez, A. Espinosa and A. Mathias, 'Evaluation of TRC, political orientation, attitudes towards past, perception of emotional climate and social trust: a meta-analytical integration of surveys in Argentina, Brazil, Chile, Ecuador, Paraguay, Peru, and Uruguay', paper presented at the 'Attitudes Towards Transitional Justice: A Global Overview' conference, Institute of Social Sciences, University of Lisbon, 1 February 2018.

---

34 D. Backer, 'Watching a bargain unravel? A panel study of victims' attitudes about transitional justice in Cape Town, South Africa' (2010) 4 *International Journal of Transitional Justice* 443, at 450.

The debate over whether local experiences and traditional methods are better or not at disclosing the truth is another one raised in these studies. The case of the Gacaca courts in Rwanda is an example of transitional justice administered through a traditional form of dispute resolution. After surveying a region in which this mechanism was present, Rettig finds the majority of participants and non-participants believed lies were being systematically told at Gacaca courts. Although this is no different from other courtroom situations, the fact that Gacaca judges received no training may have hindered the process.

Some of these studies show that citizens often have preconceived ideas about what these mechanisms can do, meaning they either have high hopes about what can be achieved or they have a negative image due to an earlier experience. It is important, therefore, to know whether it was a matter of false expectations, negative experiences, misinformation or some other issue related to how the researcher operationalised the concepts and the methods used. In some cases, their evaluation is also related to the individual level effects of participating in these mechanisms, an issue that will be explored next.

## 3.3. NEGATIVE EMOTIONS

One important difference between studies focusing on individual effects and the previous ones is that they usually analyse the individual impact of transitional justice mechanisms as independent variables: that is, the impact of taking part in or being exposed to a truth commission or other truth-telling mechanism is used as a potential explanatory factor for an individual's psychological and emotional climate. This is different from the studies on preferences and evaluation analysed so far, in which scholars are interested in characterising and explaining individual attitudes. Hence, in the study of effects, authors are often concerned with explaining feelings of rehabilitation, reconciliation or healing among individuals. For that reason, this type of research is always conducted in countries in which at least one transitional justice mechanism has been adopted, as is shown in Table 2.

Second, while questions about effects are also addressed to individuals with no personal experience of transitional justice mechanisms, authors often distinguish between those who did and did not participate in transitional justice mechanisms, and the former group may include victims and perpetrators. This contrasts with the previous studies, which look for differences between victims and non-victims. This difference is concerned with both the researcher's goals (to understand whether direct exposure has a positive or negative effect on the individual) and with the method being used. Most of these studies use experimental methods in which the stimulus consists of having taken part in a truth commission hearing or some other form of truth-telling. The studies on the individual effects of the South African truth commission are pioneering, but other countries and regions, such as Rwanda and Latin America, have attracted attention more recently.

The works on the effects of truth commissions and other truth-telling mechanisms seem to converge around the idea that, more often than not, participation in these mechanisms leads to negative emotions and experiences. One of the studies on Rwanda finds that those who served as witnesses on Gacaca courts experience more significant levels of post-traumatic stress disorder (PTSD) and depression than those who did not. An unpublished study on seven Latin American countries shows that truth and reconciliation commissions often elicit more negative than positive emotions, including sadness, anger or shame.[35] The study on the Czech Republic shows that truth-telling exercises may lead to lower feelings of rehabilitation if the story told does not receive sufficient coverage.[36]

The conclusions from these studies are in line with what authors have found when analysing the effects of participation in other transitional justice mechanisms, such as trials.[37] Exploring in more detail how these mechanisms have been implemented and the type of criticism and controversy they have generated seems to be of key importance. As one early study on the South African truth commission describes in the conclusions:

> to date, the TRC has made few friends in South Africa. Many victims are still aggrieved, popular expectations of retributive justice are unmet, many see the commission's work as a witch hunt, and the TRC has on several occasions done enormous damage to its own legitimacy.[38]

---

35 D. Páez, A. Espinosa and A. Mathias, 'Evaluation of TRC, political orientation, attitudes towards past, perception of emotional climate and social trust: a meta-analytical integration of surveys in Argentina, Brazil, Chile, Ecuador, Paraguay, Peru, and Uruguay', paper presented at the conference 'Attitudes Towards Transitional Justice: A Global Overview', Institute of Social Sciences, University of Lisbon, 1 February 2018.

36 R. David and S. Choi, *supra* note 2.

37 See for instance C. Martín-Beristain, D. Páez, B. Rimé and P. Kanyangara, 'Psychosocial effects of participation in rituals of transitional justice: a collective level analysis and review of the literature of the effects of TRCs and trials on human rights violations in Latin America' (2010) 25(1) *Revista de Psicología Social* 47; T. Longman, 'The domestic impact of the International Criminal Tribunal for Rwanda', in S.R. Ratner and J.L. Bischoff (eds.), *International War Crimes Trials: Making a Difference?*, University of Texas Law School, Austin TX, 2004.

38 A. Gibson and A. Gouws, 'Truth and reconciliation in South Africa: attribution of blame and the struggle over apartheid' (1999) 93(3) *The American Political Science Review* 501, at 515.

## 4. CONCLUSIONS AND RECOMMENDATIONS FOR FUTURE RESEARCH AND ACTION

In this chapter, we sought to highlight the potential of collecting survey data and the challenges faced by researchers looking to collect these types of data. In order to do that, we offered a review of 36 research articles, book chapters and reports on 'truth' and truth commissions in 20 post-authoritarian and post-conflict societies. The aim of conducting such a review was to identify the main issues raised in these works and to highlight their main findings on the potential legacies of transitional justice at the micro level.

In the first part of the chapter, we discussed some of the issues we believe deserve further attention from academics, particularly in order to enhance the comparative potential of these studies. First, whether the study is being conducted in a post-authoritarian or post-conflict society can have an important effect because there are a number of contextual aspects associated with the political culture, institutional infrastructure and overall social environment that may potentially affect individuals' attitudes. Second, distinguishing between victims and non-victims, or participants and non-participants, in the transitional justice process is an important aspect related to personal experiences that may or may not affect perceptions. Finally, the transitional justice context in which the surveys are implemented should also not be ignored, namely clearly identifying what mechanisms have been implemented and when.

In the second part, we argue that some broad trends do emerge among existing studies, although the variety of data collection tools and methods is one of the aspects that stands out – thus revealing the challenges of conducting comparative work in this field. We then divided all contributions into three issues: preferences, evaluation and effects. First, we have shown there is usually a consensus around the idea of finding 'the truth', but that this is not necessarily a sign of support for the implementation of truth commissions. The number of ways in which these questions have been asked leads us to recommend being cautious in interpreting these results. In fact, by adopting a somewhat holistic approach, many of these studies are more interested in exploring support for retribution or forgiveness, rather than capturing support for truth commissions. Second, we have shown that knowledge and approval of truth commissions often do not go hand-in-hand. In these studies, there have been more attempts to replicate existing questions than in the previous ones, but they are somewhat limited in what they can tell us about the performance of the transitional justice mechanisms that are being evaluated. Third, we have shown that exposure to truth-telling mechanisms, particularly truth commissions, seems to have an adverse effect on the wellbeing of individuals, contributing to the somewhat negative image these mechanisms have gained in the past few years.

Regarding future research, we make four main recommendations. First, studies should begin with a discussion of the concepts used and an explanation of how transitional justice is understood and reflected in the questionnaire. Second, there seems to be a great need for either a standardisation of terms or a better clarification of what different expressions such as 'truth-seeking' and 'truth-telling' mean. Third, there is an urgent need to begin to develop comparable survey instruments. This does not imply that scholars should stop doing research that addresses the specificities of each case, but there are many questions that can be adopted in a similar way in many countries. Fourth, the combination of different data collection methods appears to be particularly useful, especially the use of focus groups and in-depth interviews both before and after the implementation of survey questionnaires.

## APPENDIX: LIST OF CASE STUDIES BY COUNTRY

*Argentina*

M. Arnoso, M. Cárdenas, M. Muratori, E. Zubieta, D. Páez and J. Bombeli, 'Argentina: diferencias intergeneracionales ante las medidas de justicia transicional' (2014) 25(2) *Revista Latinoamericana de Derechos Humanos* 151.

E.M. Zubieta, J.I. Bombelli and M. Muratori, 'Argentina: el impacto de la implementación de medidas de Justicia Transicional Post Dictadura' (2015) 15(32) *Psicologia Política* 101.

*Burundi*

C. Samii, 'Who wants to forgive and forget? Transitional justice preferences in postwar Burundi' (2013) 50(2) *Journal of Peace Research* 219.

*Cambodia*

P. Pham, P. Vinck, M. Balthazard and S. Hean, *After the first trial. A population-based survey on knowledge and perception of justice and the extraordinary chambers in the courts of Cambodia*, Human Rights Center, University of California, Berkeley, 2009.

P. Pham, P. Vinck, M. Balthazard, S. Hean and E. Stover, *So we will never forget. A population-based survey on attitudes about social reconstruction and extraordinary chambers in the courts of Cambodia*, Human Rights Center, University of California, Berkeley, 2011.

*Central African Republic*

P. Vinck and P. Pham, *Building peace, seeking justice. A population-based survey on attitudes about accountability and social reconstruction in the Central African Republic*, Human Rights Center, University of California, Berkeley, 2010.

*Chile*

J. Manzi and R. González, 'Forgiveness and reparation in Chile: the role of cognitive and emotional intergroup antecedents' (2007) 13(1) *Peace and Conflict: Journal of Peace Psychology* 71.

M. Cárdenas, D. Páez, B. Rimé and M. Arnoso, 'How Transitional Justice Processes and Official Apologies Influence Reconciliation: the case of the Chilean "Truth and

Reconciliation" and "Political Imprisonment and Torture" Commissions' (2015) 25(6) *Journal of Community and Applied Social Psychology* 515.

M. Martínez, M. Cárdenas and D. Páez, 'Justicia transicional y predictores del perdón político en Chile' (2015) 26(1) *Revista Latinoamericana de Derechos Humanos* 78.

*Colombia*

A. Rettberg, *Reparación en Colombia ¿Qué quieren las víctimas?*, Deutsche Gesellschaft für Technische Zusammenarbeit, Bogotá, 2008.

E. Nussio, A. Rettberg and J.E. Ugarriza. 'Victims, nonvictims and their opinions on transitional justice: findings from the Colombian case' (2015) 9(2) *International Journal of Transitional Justice* 336.

*Czech Republic*

R. David and S. Choi, 'Victims on Transitional Justice: Lessons from the Reparation of Human Rights Abuses in the Czech Republic' (2005) 27(2) *Human Rights Quarterly* 392.

*Eastern DRC*

P. Vinck, P. Pham, S. Baldo and R. Shigekane, *Living with Fear. A population-based survey on attitudes about peace, justice and social reconstruction in Eastern Democratic Republic of Congo*, Human Rights Center, University of California, Berkeley, 2008.

*Ecuador*

C. Reyes, G. Grondona and M. Rodriguez, 'Evaluación del Impacto de la Comisión de la Verdade n Ecuador: aportes psicosociales en la actual discusión sobre la reparación a las víctimas' (2015) 15(32) *Psicologia Política* 119.

*Liberia*

P. Vinck, P. Pham and T. Kreutzer, *Talking Peace. A population-based survey on attitudes about security, dispute resolution, and post-conflict reconstruction in Liberia*, Human Rights Center, University of California, Berkeley, 2011.

*Northern Uganda*

P. Pham, P. Vinck, M. Wierda, E. Stover and A. Giovanni, *Forgotten Voices. A Population-Based Survey on Attitudes about Peace and Justice in Northern Uganda*, International Center for Transitional Justice and Human Rights Center, University of California, Berkeley, 2005.

P. Pham, P. Vinck, E. Stover, A. Moss, M. Wierda and R. Bailey, *When the War Ends. A Population-Based Survey on Attitudes about Peace, Justice, and Social Reconstruction in Northern Uganda*, Human Rights Center, University of California, Berkeley, 2007.

P. Pham, P. Vinck, E. Stover, A. Moss, M. Wierda and R. Bailey, *Transitioning to Peace. A Population-Based Survey on Attitudes about and Social Reconstruction and Justice in Northern Uganda*, Human Rights Center, University of California, Berkeley, 2010.

*Paraguay*

M. Arnoso, M Cárdenas, D. Páez and C. Martín, 'Paraguay: de las violaciones a los derechos humanos a la justicia transicional' (2014) 5(1) *Salud & Sociedad* 98.

M. Arnoso, M. Bobowik and C. Beristain, 'La Comisión de Verdade y Justicia en Paraguay: la experience emocional en los rituales de conmemoración y la eficácia percebida de la comisión' (2015) 15(32) *Psicologia Política* 137.

*Peru*

A. Espinosa, D.P. Rovira, T. Velázquez, R.M. Cueto, E. Seminario, S. Sandoval, F. Reátegui and I. Jave, 'Between remembering and forgetting the years of political violence: psychosocial impact of the Truth and Reconciliation Commission in Peru' (2017) 38(5) *Political Psychology* 849.

A. Espinosa, M. Schmitz and R.M. Cueto, 'Impacto Psicosocial de la Comisión de la Verdad y Reconciliación (CVR) en una Muestra de Estudiantes Universitarios de Lima-Perú' (2015) 15(32) *Psicologia Política* 157.

*Rwanda*

K. Brounéus, 'The trauma of truth telling effects of witnessing in the Rwandan Gacaca courts on psychological health' (2010) 54(3) *Journal of Conflict Resolution* 408.

T. Longman, P. Pham and H. Weinstein, 'Connecting justice to human experience: attitudes toward accountability and reconciliation in Rwanda', in E. Stover and H. Weinstein (eds.), *My Neighbor, My Enemy. Justice and Community in the Aftermath of Mass Atrocity*, Cambridge University Press, Cambridge, 2004.

M. Rettig, 'Gacaca: Truth, Justice and Reconciliation in Postconflict Rwanda?' (2008) 51(3) *African Studies Review* 25.

B. Rimé, P. Kanyangara, V. Yzerbyt and D. Paez, 'The impact of Gacaca tribunals in Rwanda: psychosocial effects of participation in a truth and reconciliation process after a genocide' (2011) 41(6) *European Journal of Social Psychology* 695.

*Serbia*

S. Parmentier and E. Weitekamp, 'Punishing perpetrators or seeking truth for victims: Serbian opinions on dealing with war crimes' (2013) 13 *International Criminal Law Review* 43.

*Sierra Leone*

E. Sawyer and T. Kelsall, 'Truth vs. justice? Popular views on the Truth and Reconciliation Commission and the Special Court for Sierra Leone' (2007) 7(1) *The Online Journal of Peace and Conflict Resolution* 36.

*South Africa*

D. Backer, 'Watching a bargain unravel? A panel study of victims' attitudes about transitional justice in Cape Town, South Africa' (2010) 4 *International Journal of Transitional Justice* 443.

J. Gibson, 'Does Truth Lead to Reconciliation? Testing the Causal Assumptions of the South African Truth and Reconciliation Process' (2004) 48(2) *American Journal of Political Science* 201.

J. Gibson, 'The truth about truth and reconciliation in South Africa' (2005) 26(4) *International Political Science Review* 341.

J. Gibson and A. Gouws, 'Truth and reconciliation in South Africa: attribution of blame and the struggle over apartheid' (1999) 93(3) *The American Political Science Review* 501.

D. Kaminer, D.M. Stein, R. Mbanga, N. Zungu-Dirwayi, 'The Truth and Reconciliation Commission in South Africa: relation to psychiatric status and forgiveness among survivors of human rights abuses' (2001) 178 *British Journal of Psychiatry* 373.

*Spain*

P. Aguilar, L. Balcells and H. Cebolla-Boado, 'Determinants of Attitudes Toward Transitional Justice: An Empirical Analysis of the Spanish Case' (2011) 44(10) *Comparative Political Studies* 1397.

*Uruguay*

M. Arnoso and S. Costa, 'Actitudes Hacia el Pasado de Violencia Colectiva y Actividades de Justicia Transicional en Uruguay' (2015) 15(32) *Psicologia Política* 185.

*Zimbabwe*

M. Bratton, 'Violence, partisanship and transitional justice in Zimbabwe' (2011) 49(3) *Journal of Modern African Studies* 353.

# ASSESSING THE LONG-TERM IMPACT AND LEGACY OF TRUTH COMMISSIONS

Anita FERRARA



## 1. INTRODUCTION

Truth commissions are temporary bodies that aim to disclose the truth about past human rights violations. Drawing on Hayner's widely used definition, truth commissions are created to investigate patterns of human rights abuses over a period of time, to engage directly and broadly with the affected population and to issue a final report recommending reparations programmes and institutional reforms to ensure such abuses do not reoccur.[1]

These bodies have been used in more than 30 countries since the fall of the military regime in Argentina in 1983. From an historical perspective, the first generation of truth commissions included those established in the Southern Cone of Latin America. Despite the limitations of the initial commissions, these represented the baseline and were a source of inspiration for later truth commissions. Since then, 'truth commissions have become a staple of post-conflict or post-authoritarian transitions across numerous and diverse contexts'.[2]

---

1 P.B. HAYNER, *Unspeakable Truths: Transitional Justice and the Challenge of Truth Commissions*, 2nd edn, Routledge, New York, 2011, 11.

2 N. VALJI, 'Trials and Truth Commissions: Seeking Accountability in the Aftermath of Violence', The Centre for the Study of Violence and Reconciliation, 2004, www.csvr.org.za/images/f_e_s.pdf.

Truth commissions have changed considerably since their early establishment and they are no longer regarded as 'quick-fix' solutions to overcome complex transitions or as a substitute for criminal justice. These bodies have developed significantly over the past three decades, expanding their mandates and objectives and becomingly increasingly innovative in their processes, thus forming very sophisticated and complex enterprises. Therefore, a large amount of literature has been written on the supposed benefits of truth commissions claiming that they provide victims with an opportunity to tell their story, promote accountability and the rule of law, produce an authoritative account of state crimes, recommend institutional reforms, and promote reconciliation. Since truth commissions in the last two decades have become increasingly popular mechanisms for dealing with the past, the trend in recent research has been towards evaluating the impact and merit of these bodies. One of the most active debates in the research on transitional justice is focused on the problem of how to assess the impact and effectiveness of truth commissions and other transitional justice mechanisms. While there has been some attempt made to identify common guidelines in order to evaluate the effectiveness and efficacy of such bodies, the results of the first empirical studies, both qualitative and quantitative, have so far produced mixed and sometimes contradictory results. Several studies have identified a series of conceptual, methodological and epistemological problems related to the assessment exercise and most recent research attempts to explore ways to overcome these challenges.[3]

Other scholars have identified the need to conduct long-term impact assessments of truth commissions, claiming that a long-term perspective can tell us more about the deeper social, political or institutional changes that such mechanisms seek to achieve.[4] Yet studies that examine the effects of truth commissions years after their work has concluded are rare. The few empirical studies that do exist that assess the long-term impact of truth commissions suggest that the consequences and effects of truth commissions are long-lasting and evolve over time.[5] The cases of Argentina and Chile demonstrate

3 H. van der Merwe, V. Baxter and A.R. Chapman (eds.), *Assessing the Impact of Transitional Justice: Challenges for Empirical Research*, United States Institute for Peace Press, Washington D.C., 2009; O.N.T. Thoms, J. Ron and R. Paris, 'State-Level Effects of Transitional Justice: What Do We Know?' (2010) 4(3) *International Journal of Transitional Justice* 1; M. Ben-Josef Hirsch, M. Mackenzie and M. Sesay, 'Measuring the Impacts of Truth and Reconciliation Commissions: Placing the Global "Success" of TRCs in Local Perspective' (2012) 47(3) *Cooperation and Conflict* 386; O. Bakiner, 'Truth Commission Impact: An Assessment of How Commissions Influence Politics and Society' (2013) 8(1) *International Journal of Transitional Justice* 6.

4 Thoms, Ron and Paris, *supra* note 3, at 8; E. Brahm, 'Uncovering the Truth: Examining Truth Commission Success and Impact' (2007) 8(1) *International Studies Perspectives* 6, 17–19.

5 A. Ferrara, *Assessing the Long-term Impact of Truth Commissions: The Chilean Truth and Reconciliation Commission in Historical Perspective*, Routledge, London, 2015;

that advancements in public acknowledgement and apologies, prosecutions, institutional reforms, reparations and other areas came years after the truth commissions had ended their work. For this reason, a longer-term evaluation of truth commissions is necessary since some of the objectives that truth commissions initially set out to achieve can take many years, if not decades, to materialise.

This chapter aims to provide a possible framework and set of criteria against which to make a long-term impact assessment of truth commissions (see further Sarkin's introductory chapter on the criteria and methods to determine truth commission impact). It defines long-term impact as the ability of truth commissions to 'act as a catalyst for a series of social, political and institutional transformations, which can occur in post-truth commission phases'. Just as the process of dealing with the past is nonlinear, being characterised by advancements and setbacks, so too is the impact of a transitional institution like a truth commission, which is embedded in that process. Three main assumptions are thus put forward to evaluate the long-term impact of a truth commission (see Sarkin's introductory chapter on these and other issues). Firstly, the long-term impact of a truth commission can depend on a multitude of factors, including the evolution of the political context, institutional reforms, external factors, leadership change, sequencing and combination with other transitional justice mechanisms and timing.[6] Moreover, it requires sustained commitment by multiple actors and forces in both society and institutions. Therefore, follow-up mechanisms, state action and engagement of civil society are required in order for the work of a truth commission to be upheld. Secondly, since many variables determine the impact of a truth commission, the researcher should follow up any unexpected findings that could not have been anticipated at the outset. Although this aspect further complicates the search for causality, this chapter argues that having fixed expectations and goals might limit our understanding of the potential of truth commissions. Thirdly, in order to grasp how or to what extent the effects of a truth commission might change, evaluations need to be conducted at multiple points in time after the conclusion of the truth commission's work, rather than at single point. The post-commission process can be divided into a number of different phases. A short-term impact analysis can be conducted in the period immediately following the establishment of the truth commission; a medium-term analysis could be conducted 10 years after the truth commission has concluded its work. For the purpose of this study,

---

E. Wiebelhaus-Brahm, *Truth Commissions and Transitional Societies: The Impact on Human Rights and Democracy*, Routledge, London, 2010.

6 L.E. Fletcher, M. Harvey and J.R. Weinstein, 'Context, Timing and the Dynamics of Transitional Justice: A Historical Perspective' (2009) 31 *Human Rights Quarterly* 163; E. Skaar and C.G. Malca, 'Conclusions', in E. Skaar, C.G. Malca and T. Eide (eds.), *After Violence*, Routledge, New York, 2015.

a timeframe of 20–30 years after the conclusion of the truth commission is considered the minimum amount of time necessary to conduct an evaluation of its longer-term impact. In order to see the outcomes of truth commissions and to have a clearer understanding of the underlying historical processes at work, one must perhaps be prepared to wait. Whilst several decades appears to be a lengthy timeframe in transitional justice terms, it is certainly not long if truth commissions are regarded as part of the broader, complex historical process.

## 2. A FRAMEWORK FOR EVALUATING LONG-TERM IMPACT

This section examines what stage the current assessment literature has reached and identifies the major challenges of undertaking this type of research. It then suggests a possible framework and set of criteria to conduct a long-term impact assessment of truth commissions.

The first quantitative studies, using large-N regression analysis, have measured the impact of truth commissions mainly on democratisation and human rights practices. Yet, as Hayner noted, the goals of democracy and respect for human rights are not the only goals that are attainable, nor are they the expressed aims of truth commissions.[7] Very few studies have assessed truth commissions against other goals, such as raising public awareness of past atrocities, promoting acknowledgement and apology, aiding institutional reforms and reconstruction, reintegrating victims into society, promoting memory, and building shared narratives.[8]

The decision of researchers to measure the impact of truth commissions on democracy and human rights is based on the fact that more data is now available from different countries. Using a mixed-method approach, Wiebelhaus-Brahm's statistical findings show that truth commissions have a negative effect on human rights practices and a negligible impact on democracy.[9] However, the findings of Wiebelhaus-Brahm's qualitative analysis of four separate case studies (Chile, South Africa, El Salvador and Uganda) suggest that truth commissions have a positive impact on both human rights practices and democracy. Another study by Olsen et al. concludes that the impact of transitional justice measures on democracy and human rights practices depends on the combination of transitional justice mechanisms that are implemented. According to Olsen et al., truth commissions make a positive contribution when combined with trials

7 Hayner, *supra* note 1, at 25.
8 See Sarkin's introductory chapter on issues concerning the wider goals of truth commissions.
9 Wiebelhaus-Brahm, *supra* note 5.

and amnesty, whereas truth commissions alone tend to exacerbate the problems in a transitional country. Their study suggests that the use of multiple mechanisms is the most effective way to generate positive change.[10] Contrary to Wiebelhaus-Brahm and Olsen et al., Kim and Sikkink's study finds that both truth commissions and human rights prosecutions have a positive impact on democracy and human rights. They argue that human rights trials and truth commissions help to spread an accountability norm, which increases respect for the rule of law.[11] The results from these first quantitative studies suggest that contradictory conclusions are reached even by studies looking at the same outcomes, such as democracy and human rights, and using the same methodology, for example large-N regression analysis. However, Brandon and Wiebelhaus-Brahm further explain the factors that led to such divergent findings, including definitional and measurement issues, different sampling strategies, and construction of diverse statistical models.[12] Finally, all the above quantitative studies rely on Polity IV or Freedom House as the main datasets to measure democracy and on CIRI (Cingranelli-Richards Human Rights Data Project) as the main dataset to measure improvements in human rights. These datasets include several indicators on which truth commissions are unlikely to have an impact, such as public participation, electoral rules, freedom of the press and freedom of religion.[13] While recognising the importance of these quantitative studies, this chapter argues that it is nevertheless the case that the value of empirical quantitative study is limited due to the lack of necessary data and the difficulty of measuring these effects statistically. Transitional justice is a recognised 'hard-to-measure area of social change'.[14] Therefore, the chapter contends that qualitative analysis of specific case studies is still required in order to assess both the limitations and the possibilities of truth commissions. Moreover, the case study offers a better understanding than a quantitative analysis of the complex social and political dynamics, as well as of the interplay between numerous factors that could affect the contributions of these bodies. However, in order to avoid the limitations that would result from analysing one single case, a multiple case study design is required. The multiple case study includes both within-case analysis of single cases and comparisons of several different cases.[15]

10 T.D. Olsen, L.A. Payne and A.G. Reiter, *Transitional Justice in Balance: Comparing Processes, Weighing Efficacy*, United States Institute of Peace Press, Washington D.C., 2010.

11 H. Kim and K. Sikkink, 'Explaining the Deterrence Effect of Human Rights Prosecutions for Transitional Countries' (2010) 54(4) *International Studies Quarterly* 939.

12 S. Brandon and E. Wiebelhaus-Brahm, 'The Quantitative Turn in Transitional Justice Research: What Have We Learned About Impact?' (2017) 1(5) *Transitional Justice Review* 97.

13 Brahm, *supra* note 4, at 25–26.

14 C. Duggan, 'Editorial Note', Special Issue: 'Transitional Justice on Trial: Evaluating Its Impact' (2010) 4(3) *International Journal of Transitional Justice* 315.

15 A. Bennett, 'Case Study Methods: Design, Use, and Comparative Advantages', 2012, https://pdfs.semanticscholar.org/7d11/098671a75e7b289fd65adab2eb236c5cf580.pdf.

Furthermore, both qualitative and quantitative studies to date have failed to conduct longer-term impact assessment of these temporary bodies. Even for the most well-known cases, the existing literature on assessment tends to analyse short-term transitional justice outcomes, focusing on the degree to which a commission completed its objectives within a designated period of time.[16] Wiebelhaus-Brahm also distinguishes the 'success' of a truth commission from its long-term impact.[17] A book written by the present author represents one of the first efforts to empirically analyse the long-term impact of one of the oldest truth commissions: the Chilean case.[18] She argues that it is extremely important to understand the long-term impact of truth commissions, in order to determine whether or under what conditions these bodies contribute to the transition and/or to other social and political changes within a country. Her study examines the extent to which and how the Chilean truth commission contributed to the development of the transitional justice measures that ensued, and how the relationship with those subsequent developments was established over time. Moreover, she analyses the ability of the truth commission to effect deeper social and political changes over time. She concludes that the Chilean truth commission had unexpected consequences, which are more visible today than they were in the short-term. A long-term impact assessment helps to clarify why certain truth commissions with limited mandates and power have had longer-lasting effect than other truth commissions that were created with far-reaching mandates and better access to resources. Drawing on the conclusions of her previous investigation based on the Chilean case, the author proposes in this chapter a framework, which can be applied to other truth commissions to assess their longer-term impact. The author argues that it is very problematic to measure truth commissions' effects against pre-established end goals, such as democracy, rule of law and reconciliation. Multiple dynamics and the interaction between many factors, including unexpected ones, determine the long-term impact of a truth commission. Therefore, the author argues in favour of the need to examine the post-truth commission process and trace the role of truth commissions as catalysts for the development of wider transitional justice processes. The chapter argues that the impact of a truth commission over the longer term should be measured according to two main criteria: its impact on other transitional justice mechanisms and its impact on wider society and public institutions.

In particular, truth commissions should be evaluated against their ability to:

1. support, strengthen and interact with other transitional justice mechanisms, including reparations, trials and memorialisation; and

---

16 Thoms, Ron and Paris, *supra* note 3, at 8.

17 Wiebelhaus-Brahm, *supra* note 4, at 17–19.

18 Ferrara, *supra* note 5.

2. promote a change in attitudes, beliefs and practices at the political, social and institutional level.

The major methodological problem in assessing transitional justice measures lies in the difficulty of establishing a causal relationship between the truth commission and a series of dependent variables that are of interest, such as democracy, human rights protection and the rule of law. Recent studies have found it difficult to treat truth commissions as independent variables, with the result that most of the benefits attributable to truth commissions are instead seen as the outcome of other factors.[19] Proving causal relationships between transitional justice mechanisms and certain outcomes is extremely difficult because transitions are non-linear processes and the changes sought through a transitional justice mechanism will be the result of manifold interactions between numerous factors that are difficult to predict, let alone control. This means that it is highly problematic, if not impossible, to establish causal relationships. Since multiple variables are involved in these complex socio-political processes, it is extremely difficult to assess the impact of a particular cause on future outcomes.[20] Truth commissions take place in the context of broader socio-political, economic and institutional reforms, where factors other than truth commissions may cause certain effects.

The argument presented in this chapter is that the long-term analysis can best be achieved through a qualitative methodology that involves process tracing. Process tracing is a research method for tracing causal mechanisms using detailed, 'within-case' empirical analysis of how a causal process plays out in an actual case. Moreover, by establishing explanations that document the intervening variables and processes through which truth commissions bring about certain outcomes, process tracing differs from and complements statistical inferences.[21] Since process tracing is a case-based approach, it needs to be combined with comparative methods in order for the researcher to be able to make generalisations about causal processes. Cross-case comparative evidence has to demonstrate that the population of other positive cases is relatively causally similar to the selected case, thereby enabling generalisations to be made.[22] Finally, the systematic comparison of individual cases could overcome the limitations of a single case study analysis, while at the same time maintaining the focus on context-specific dynamics that allow for the

19 Wiebelhaus-Brahm, *supra* note 4, at 28.

20 K. Sikkink and C.B. Walling, 'The Impact of Human Rights Trials in Latin America' (2007) 44(4) *Journal of Peace Research* 427, at 443.

21 Bennett, *supra* note 15.

22 B. Derek, 'Process-Tracing Methods in Social Science', *Oxford Research Encyclopedia of Politics*, Oxford University Press, Oxford, 2018.

identification and tracking of causal processes. Other qualitative methodologies, including public opinion surveys, discourse analysis, focus groups and in-depth interviews, remain the most suitable methodologies to measure changes in public attitudes and beliefs, political elites' discourses and institutional practices over time.

The following sections explore in more detail the interaction between truth commissions and other transitional justice mechanisms, including reparations, trials and memorialisation, in order to gauge the long-term effects of truth commissions. The last section analyses a set of criteria to measure the ability of truth commissions to change attitudes, beliefs and practices of political elites and the broader public over the longer term.

## 3. UNDERSTANDING THE IMPACT OF TRUTH COMMISSIONS ON OTHER TRANSITIONAL JUSTICE MECHANISMS

Many studies have argued that truth commissions should be considered as the beginning of a longer-term process that will provide the foundation for the subsequent establishment of further transitional justice initiatives to deal with past human rights violations. In fact, in many countries, truth commissions either preceded or were established concurrently and in combination with other transitional justice mechanisms, such as reparations, apologies, amnesties, criminal trials, memorialisation and institutional reforms. In such cases, scholars have suggested that it is unwise to assess the effects of a single transitional justice mechanism in isolation.[23] According to Dancy, Hunjoon and Wiebelhaus-Brahm, 'it is irresponsible to assume the independence of events in reference to transitional justice mechanisms'.[24] De Greiff argues that transitional justice mechanisms should exhibit 'external coherence' and be designed in such a way as to bear a close relationship with other transitional justice institutions.[25] While the most prevalent assumption in the literature seems to be that the more transitional justice mechanisms the better, it remains to be seen whether or under what conditions multiple transitional justice mechanisms can truly interact with and support each other in order to better respond to victims' demands. Brandon and Wiebelhaus-Brahm assert that quantitative studies

---

[23] G. Dancy, K. Hunjoon and E. Wiebelhaus-Brahm, 'The Turn to Truth: Trends in Truth Commission Experimentation' (2010) 9(1) *Journal of Human Rights* 45, at 59.

[24] Ibid.

[25] P. De Greiff, 'Justice and Reparations', in P. De Greiff (ed.), *The Handbook of Reparations*, Oxford University Press, Oxford, 2006.

have rarely investigated the effect of interaction between transitional justice mechanisms, which would allow the researcher to examine their cumulative effects.[26]

In 2007, a dataset was created by Sikkink and Walling to document the emergence and dramatic growth of the use of truth commissions and domestic, foreign and international human rights trials globally. Their data on truth commissions shows that almost two-thirds of the countries that had truth commissions also held trials to deal with past human rights abuses. Furthermore, every country in the Americas region that established a truth commission also held domestic trials.[27] Finally, according to this study, countries that established truth commissions were more likely to choose additional transitional justice measures.[28]

As many countries today have established multiple transitional justice mechanisms, there is a need to further explore how truth commissions have interacted and/or contributed to other transitional justice mechanisms. Given that many truth commissions have proved to be the first step towards other transitional justice initiatives, it is now possible to investigate whether truth commissions can be considered to have acted as a platform for some of the subsequent transitional justice policies and how this relationship or interaction occurred. Given the non-linearity of the transitional process and the impact of other factors on the transition, the relationships between the truth commissions and the transitional justice mechanisms that were implemented at different key moments during the transition and post-transition phases will need to be traced in depth by new studies. This type of analysis, although not necessarily proving causality, aims to find the direct and indirect contributions that the work of a truth commission can have on subsequent measures, even years after the conclusion of its work. This section highlights the links between truth commissions and other transitional justice measures, suggesting what type and degree of relationship can be established.

## 3.1. TRUTH COMMISSIONS' RELATIONSHIP WITH REPARATIONS

Many truth commissions in their final reports have recommended the establishment of reparations programmes. These have been implemented either immediately after the closure of the truth commissions or through a much longer process that has unfolded over many years, if not decades. Some truth

26 Brandon and Wiebelhaus-Brahm, *supra* note 12, at 123.

27 Sikkink and Walling, *supra* note 20, at 430.

28 Ibid, at 442.

commissions have recommended the payment of monetary reparations; others have formulated broader reparations programmes, including granting access to land, healthcare or education, or symbolic reparations and rehabilitation measures. Some truth commissions have prioritised individual reparations, while others have also implemented collective reparations.

We still know very little about the status or standards of the reparations policies implemented and the impact they have had on the lives of the victims and their relatives. Most importantly, the nature of the relationship between truth commissions and reparations is yet to be investigated. Does the truth revelation legitimise reparations? Should the implementation of reparations be made compulsory in the recommendations? What is the degree to which victims themselves should participate or their approval be sought in the design of reparations programmes? These and other questions require major investigation. In addition, there is a need for more comparative studies to be conducted on the qualitative and quantitative difference between reparations that follow the establishment of truth commissions and those that are established independently of a truth-seeking mechanism. Without at this stage elaborating on the finer details of this relationship, several reasons are suggested as to why truth-telling strengthens the subsequent reparations and how truth commissions and reparation policies are closely interconnected.

First, in the aftermath of large-scale or systematic violations or more generalised conflict, the number of victims in need of redress may be vast and the harm caused to victims and survivors may be devastating and irreparable. The design of reparations programmes requires a vast amount of documentation on the number of victims, the kind of violations suffered and their immediate consequences. Truth commissions can be invaluable in gathering and delivering this information.

Second, the reparations programmes represent an acknowledgement by the state of its responsibilities for the harm done to the victims, which, as the experience of many cases has shown, is regarded by victims and their families as one of the most important aspects of the reparations. It is therefore crucial to first recognise the victims and what happened to them and then make reparations. Without previous recognition of their status as victims and the harm they suffered, victims would have regarded those reparations as empty measures undertaken by public authorities to buy their silence.[29]

Third, the truth that is revealed, documented and publicly disclosed by truth commissions lays the foundation upon which a social and political consensus can be built to implement a programme of reparations by the state. According to

---

[29] L. Magarrel, 'The Nature and Objectives of Reparations', Reparative Justice Series, International Centre for Transitional Justice, New York, 2007.

a renowned Chilean human rights activist and academic, uncovering the truth has an advantage that lies in the fact that it obliges a society to acknowledge the evidence and the evidence itself provides the legitimacy required to deliver reparations to the victims. This is one of the main reasons why truth and reparations are strictly inseparable and why it is so important that the truth-seeking processes engage the broader public as much as possible, so that the extent of the violations committed, and the harm and suffering inflicted on victims, reaches the public consciousness.[30]

Fourth, material and symbolic reparations are necessary in order to facilitate the full reintegration of victims who have been marginalised by society. In fact, the delivery of socio-economic reparations provides concrete financial help, which improves people's daily lives and restores their dignity. A wife of one of the detained-disappeared in Chile affirmed that 'the pension granted by the Chilean TC was crucial and helped to recover some of the dignity we had lost in the previous years, when we had nothing'.[31] Although material reparations are essential, to be effective they need to be accompanied by symbolic measures. The public dimension of symbolic reparations embodies the wider society's recognition of the victims and what happened to them. Victims often seek recognition from both state and society, in order to feel that their stories and experiences have been fully embodied in the dominant discourse. Therefore, the public recognition of the harm done is fundamental to the reintegration of victims into public and civic life. For many victims in Chile, the fact that their relative's name appeared in the final truth commission report, and/or was inscribed on a memorial wall erected in memory of the detained-disappeared, provided them with a sense of healing and restoration.[32] It is also important to note the symbolic dimension surrounding the presidential discourse when presenting the findings of the truth commission report to the nation. His public apology was an important symbolic reparation received by the relatives of the victims.[33]

Finally, and strictly connected to the reintegration of victims into public life, there is a need for active participation in the debates regarding the design and scope of reparations. Truth commissions are established mainly as victim-oriented mechanisms and they should represent a more inclusive process for the victims. This means that a truth commission must pay attention to the needs and opinions of victims and actively involve them in discussions about reparations packages. Moreover, victims know what their priorities

30 E. Lira, personal interview, 25 March 2009.

31 Instituto de Investigación en Ciencias Sociales (ICSO), 'Reparaciones en Chile: Historias de Vida', Boletines y otras publicaciones, January 2012, http://www.icso.cl/wp-content/uploads/2012/01/Reparaciones-Historias-de-Vida-Obs-UDP-2011.pdf.

32 Personal interviews with victims' relatives in Chile.

33 Ibid.

and expectations are, and excluding them from the design of the reparations packages could jeopardise the entire process.[34] In Chile, the reparation policies were discussed beforehand with the association of the victims' relatives, which actively participated in the formulation of the final proposal. The relatives' association sent a detailed report to the Chilean president outlining the requests that had been made by victims.[35] Even though the final proposal was the result of a political agreement, many of the victims' suggestions were incorporated into it.

It is important to remember that the payment of reparations remains one of the most problematic aspects of a post-truth commission process. Although the revelation of the truth is a form of reparation to the victims, the reparative effect of a truth commission can be dramatically diminished by the lack of implementation of reparations and/or by the failure to include the demands of victims and survivors within the process of design and implementation.

## 3.2. THE RELATIONSHIP BETWEEN TRUTH COMMISSIONS AND TRIALS

The debate on the interaction between truth commissions and trials has entered a new forum, since these two justice mechanisms are no longer viewed as incompatible but rather as complementary and inextricably interconnected. Their complementarity has today been widely acknowledged by the UN, by transitional justice scholars and practitioners, and by civil society.[36] The theoretical focus of the earlier literature has shifted away from defining the supposed benefits of one mechanism over another towards a deeper discussion of the best conditions under which truth commissions could or ought to cooperate effectively with courts, whether at the national or international level. Some countries, such as Sierra Leone and East Timor, have established truth commissions in conjunction with national and international courts that operate according to new models of cooperation. However, while these cases

---

34 L. Magarrell, 'Outreach to and Engagement of Victims on Reparations, Lessons Learned from Truth and Reconciliation Processes', paper presented at Reparations for Victims of Genocide, Crimes against Humanity and War Crimes: Systems in Place and Systems in the Making, The Hague, 1–2 March 2007.

35 Agrupación de Familiares de Detenidos-Desaparecidos (AFDD), Respuesta de Agrupación de Familiares de Detenidos-Desaparecidos a la Comisión Nacional de Verdad y Reconciliación, Santiago, 1990.

36 N. Roht-Arriaza and J. Mariezcurrena (eds.), *Transitional Justice in the Twenty-First Century: Beyond Truth versus Justice*, Cambridge University Press, Cambridge, 2006; UN Security Council, Report of the Secretary General, *The Rule of Law and Transitional Justice in Conflict and Post-Conflict Societies*, UN Doc. S/2011/634.

have revealed that truth commissions and trials can happen concurrently, they also demonstrate that the lack of adequate coordination policies and the overlap between the functions of their mandates can produce serious flaws and endanger or jeopardise the entire process.[37]

Therefore, the latest studies are investigating and discussing in more detail how the sequencing and operations of these two kinds of transitional justice mechanism can become more fruitful so that one process does not hamper the effectiveness of the other. Bisset offers a more thorough analysis of the difficult and complicated relationship between truth commissions and trials through an investigation of their operational arrangements at the national and international level.[38] She identifies potential areas of conflicts in their operative mechanisms when a truth commission interacts with national trials, or with the International Criminal Court and/or with third states. Yet her study highlights a number of complications that can emerge as a result of this relationship, especially in cases where these two mechanisms have operated simultaneously. Moreover, the new trend towards complementarity between truth commissions and trials has been coupled with the establishment of truth commissions with broader mandates and greater truth-seeking investigative powers, rendering them, in some cases, quasi-judicial bodies.[39]

Later truth commissions were endowed with the power of subpoena and/or search and seizure, and of witness protection, as well as with the power to grant confidentiality. While this has made truth commissions increasingly more robust, in practice it has also led to a series of operational conflicts with the courts.[40] In her study, Bisset dedicates more attention to the problem of the interaction between these two mechanisms when truth commissions possess quasi-judicial powers. In contrast, earlier truth commissions, including the Chilean and Argentinian truth commissions, had very restricted mandates and did not possess any judicial power. Therefore, earlier truth commissions were established as completely distinct and autonomous processes from trials.

Paradoxically, this helped to facilitate the interaction between earlier truth commissions and the national and international courts, sometimes many years after the work of the truth commissions had concluded. In fact, despite their limited legal mandates and powers, earlier truth commissions managed to publish authoritative and highly valued accounts that provided a

---

37 E.M. Evenson, 'Truth and Justice in Sierra Leone: Coordination between Commission and Court' (2004) 104(3) *Columbia Law Review* 730.

38 A. Bisset, *Truth Commissions and Criminal Courts*, Cambridge University Press, Cambridge, 2012.

39 Ibid, at 31–33.

40 Ibid.

comprehensive picture of the human rights violations that had been committed, as well as documentation containing the testimonies of thousands of victims and witnesses. The sharing of this information and evidence is one of the main contributions of the earlier truth commissions to later national and international trials. Finally, as a result of developments in international law and an increase in international prosecutions for international crimes, courts in foreign countries urgently needed to collect a huge amount of information and evidence to build cases against perpetrators who had committed international crimes in other countries. For this reason, the findings of truth commissions have, over time, become useful evidence upon which foreign judges and prosecutors have drawn in order to prosecute the perpetrators of the worst human rights violations.[41] The Pinochet case in Spain is a prime example of this tendency. The Chilean truth commission report was extensively used by Spanish judges and lawyers to build the case against Pinochet in 1998.[42] In other emblematic cases against perpetrators of human rights violations, foreign judges and prosecutors have built cases on the basis of the evidence provided in the truth commission reports. Among the most famous cases are the *Guatemala Genocide case* against former Guatemalan president José Efraín Ríos Montt and seven other high-ranking military officers,[43] as well the case against ex-Chadian dictator Hissène Habré.[44]

The commission reports provide the contextual elements necessary to prove that the crimes committed were not isolated acts but followed a pattern of widespread and systematic policy directed against the civilian population. In fact, the conclusions of the truth commissions are based on the analysis and collection of thousands of statements from victims, witnesses and perpetrators, as well as on many official and unofficial documents. All this documentation is invaluable for the work of the prosecution.

Moreover, truth commissions offer details about the function, structure and nature of a repressive organisation, and provide prosecutors and judges with evidence to identify the chain of command, the hierarchical structure and the kind of military orders that were being issued from above, all of which are crucial elements in establishing the extent of the responsibility of

41 Ibid, at 152–157.

42 R.J. Wilson, 'Prosecuting Pinochet: International Crimes in Spanish Domestic Law' (1999) 21(4) *Human Rights Quarterly* 927, at 950–951.

43 N. Roht-Arriaza, 'Guatemala Genocide Case' (2006) 100(1) *American Journal of International Law* 207, at 207; N. Roht-Arriaza, 'Prosecuting Genocide in Guatemala: The Case before the Spanish Courts and the Limits to Extradition', Centre for Global Studies Working Paper No. 2, George Mason University, Fairfax VA, spring 2009.

44 R. Brody, 'Victims bring a Dictator to Justice. The Case of Hissène Habré, Bread for the World', June 2017, https://www.brot-fuer-die-welt.de/fileadmin/mediapool/2_Downloads/Fachinformationen/Analyse/Analysis70-The_Habre_Case.pdf.

the perpetrators. International jurisprudence generally analyses the key features of the structure of an organisation to determine the level of control that the accused had over an entire organisation, a specific division or over certain individuals. In addition, the consideration of the hierarchical structure is also relevant for determining the existence and extent of the defendant's knowledge about the offences, as well as the level and degree of their involvement in the planning, instigation, issuing of commands, committing or concealment of these offences.[45]

Finally, truth commissions are official bodies established using authorised procedures operating under certain specific legal norms that regulate their public functions. Therefore, although the findings of a truth commission do not provide legal evidence, they constitute the corroboration from a public body of a factual truth, as well as the qualified opinion of respected persons that have been called to comply with a public function.[46] For all these reasons the reports of truth commissions have acquired a probative value in many foreign countries.

As the cases of Argentina, Chile, Peru and Guatemala have shown, truth commissions and their archives are also increasingly used as evidence in many domestic trials against those responsible for the human rights abuses. Argentina was the first country where a successful relationship between the truth commission and the courts was established. The information collected by the *Nunca Más* report of the CONADEP Commission was largely used to condemn some of the most powerful leaders of the military junta,[47] while in Chile this process unfolded many years later. Among the most emblematic examples of this trend in domestic courts, we can mention the *Myrna Mack case* in Guatemala,[48] where the Court valued highly the report of the Guatemalan Commission for Historical Clarification, which was used as evidence of the historical context in which serious human rights violations occurred, as well as evidence of the military operations and tactics used to exterminate those

45 J. Méndez et al., *Amicus Curiae* presented at the Supreme Court of Justice during the Fujimori trial from the International Center for Transitional Justice (ICTJ), Expediente A.V. 19-2001 (Acumulado A.V. 45-2003), August 2008, Section no. 4 (Aportes de la experiencia comparada sobre la prueba de la responsabilidad penal del superior jerárquico), available in Spanish at https://www.ictj.org/sites/default/files/ICTJ-Peru-Fujimori-Amicus-2008-Spanish.pdf.

46 International Centre for Transitional Justice (ICTJ), 'Consideraciones Técnicas a partir del Derecho Internacional y el Derecho Comparado sobre el Valor Probatorio de Algunas Pruebas Documentales en Procesos Penales'.

47 E. Crenzel, 'Argentina's National Commission on the Disappearance of Persons: Contributions to Transitional Justice' (2008) 2(2) *International Journal of Transitional Justice* 173.

48 *Caso Myrna Mack*, Sentencia de primera instancia, Tribunal Tercero de Sentencia Penal, Narcoactividad y Delitos contra el Ambiente, C-5-99, Oficial 3ro. 3 October 2002.

considered as internal enemies, like the anthropologist Myrna Mack. This was the first time that senior military officials were brought to trial or convicted for human rights violations committed during the civil war. In another historic trial, this time against the former president of Peru Alberto Fujimori, the Supreme Court, in its final judgment, highlighted the probative value of the findings and conclusions contained in the final report of the Peruvian truth commission.[49]

There are several reasons why truth commission reports and archives can make a significant contribution to justice. First, the state archives documenting the repression and/or secret agencies' records have been and still are largely inaccessible because they have been destroyed, concealed and/or kept in secret intentionally by former perpetrators.[50] In this context, the value of the truth commissions' archives is enormous, considering that in many countries they represent the only documentary evidence available that reconstructs the history of the repressive periods and provides details on how the authoritarian state structures worked. Secondly, truth commissions usually receive documents and records from a variety of sources, including governmental records such as civil registries, judicial and medical documents, press releases, police and security forces' records, land records, NGOs' archives, investigative journalism reports, radio and television recordings, and international organisations' reports. From the analysis of all this heterogeneous material, it is possible to discover how the repressive state worked, the location and the organisations of the different torture centres, and information regarding the official agents (such as doctors, judges or journalists) involved in the cover-up of human rights violations.[51] Therefore, truth commissions analyse the structure, activities and functions of the repressive organisations that committed the crimes. This information constitutes crucial evidence for judges and prosecutors.[52] Thirdly, truth commissions are able to cross-check all the information they have collected and analysed, which allows them to corroborate its reliability and trustworthiness. Finally, one definite contribution that truth commission

49 Corte Suprema de Justicia de la República, Sala Penal Especial, Expediente A.V. 19-2001, 7 April 2009, Parte II.

50 R.A. I Fugueras, 'Rights, Memory, Truth and Justice: Archives for Human Rights', in Archivos, Memoria y Derecho a la Verdad: Memorias Seminario Internacional, conference proceedings, Bogotá, 26–28 November 2008.

51 C.L.G. Gutiérrez, 'Fuentes para el Estudio de la Represión en Iberoamérica: Entre Archivos y Centros Documentales', paper presented at Actas del XIV Encuentro de Latinoamericanistas Españoles, Congreso Internacional 1810–2010: 200 años de Iberoamérica, Santiago de Compostela, 15–18 September 2010.

52 T.H. Peterson, 'The Role of the Archives in the Strengthening of Democracy', in Archivos, Memoria y Derecho a la Verdad: Memorias Seminario Internacional, conference proceedings, Colombia, 26–28 November 2008.

archives have made towards prosecutions is that all the information gathered is centrally organised, which greatly assists in the investigatory process. In the past few years, regional human rights bodies such as the Inter-American Court of Human Rights have also relied on the findings of truth commission reports to support many of their judgments.[53]

Few studies have investigated this trend towards the judicialisation of truth commissions. While this trend was inevitable in the Latin American context, which is highly legalised, it was nevertheless an unanticipated outcome, since truth commissions in that region were initially created as non-judicial mechanisms. This fact certainly raises some questions regarding the desirability of such a practice, and it raises serious concerns about whether or not this trend towards the judicialisation of truth commissions could affect the original aims and objectives of truth commissions. Moreover, there are other important concerns about how this could adversely affect the *modus operandi* of truth commissions, such as the issue of due process or confidentiality, including the disclosure of witness or perpetrator statements. More research is needed to analyse which factors facilitate or constrain the interaction between these two mechanisms, whether at the national or international level. While UN agencies and international NGOs have strongly argued in favour of complementarity, further investigation is needed to discover how the division of labour can be effectively carried out between the two mechanisms and to identify the implications of other factors, such as the legal context, sequencing and timing.

## 3.3. TRUTH COMMISSIONS AND MEMORIALISATION

Since the establishment of the earlier truth commissions, research has started to investigate the contribution of truth commissions to the construction of collective and historical memory. The relationship between truth commissions and memorialisation is a complex one that merits deeper analysis and understanding.

Many truth commissions, including those in Chile, Guatemala, South Africa, Ghana and Sierra Leone, have recommended the establishment of symbolic reparations such as memorials, peace parks, museums and many other forms of commemoration to restore the dignity of those who suffered horrendous crimes. Memory initiatives represent an official, public acknowledgement and recognition of the private suffering of the victims. This is one of the main reasons

53 A. Ferrara, 'The Inter-American Court of Human Rights and Truth Commissions', in K. Fernandez, C. Pena and S. Smart (eds.), *Chile and the Inter-American System of Human Rights*, Institute of Latin American Studies, London, 2017.

why public memorialisation is linked to the state's reparation policies. Memorials are part of a broader programme of reparation policies, which aim to focus on victim needs, redress the damage inflicted upon the victims and contribute to the victims' healing process.[54] A survey of victims of violence revealed that, for those surveyed, memorialisation initiatives were the second-most important form of state reparation after financial compensation.[55]

Memorials, originally regarded as a soft cultural and artistic phenomenon, have become a primary terrain of contestation where a wide array of actors address the enormous and challenging complexities of a traumatic past. With the passing of time, civil society and victims' groups have increasingly emphasised the importance of memorials, cemeteries and museums as public spaces for civic engagement that provide forums for debate on the controversial issues of the past that can be used to educate the general public about what happened and why.[56] Consequently, memorial projects are acquiring growing importance as a potential educational tool to promote learning and critical thinking, and also to facilitate active participation rather than representing static places, detached from other transitional justice initiatives, that turn visitors into passive observers.[57] Memorialisation initiatives have the potential to help citizens enter into a dialogue about what happened in the past and to construct a more cohesive collective memory of the past.[58] Both truth commissions and memorials share the goal of integrating the victims' stories into the official narrative. In Argentina, Chile, South Africa and Morocco, significant efforts have been made to transform the places where human rights abuses occurred into official sites of remembrance.[59]

These are public spaces where society can try to come to terms with what happened there and learn some of the painful stories suffered by the victims of repression. In this way, memorial projects contribute towards opening up spaces where the voices of those once marginalised and excluded by society can be integrated into the nation's historical memory. Londres 38 (a former torture centre) in Chile, Robben Island Museum (a former prison for liberation activists, including Nelson Mandela) in South Africa, and the ESMA

---

54 S. Brett, L. Bickford, L. Ševcenko and M.R. Tobar, 'Memorialization and Democracy: State Policy and Civic Action', FLACSO, ICTJ and International Coalition of Historic Site Museums of Conscience, Santiago, 2008; see also A. Wilde, 'Avenues of Memory: Santiago's General Cemetery and Chile's Recent Political History' (2008) 5(3) *A Contracorriente* 134.

55 E. Kiza, C. Rathgeber and H.-C. Rohne, 'Victims of War: An Empirical Study on War-Victimization and Victims' Attitudes Toward Addressing Atrocities', Hamburg Institute for Social Research, Hamburg, June 2006.

56 M. Gómez-Barris, 'Witness Citizenship: The Place of Villa Grimaldi in Chilean Memory' (2012) 25(1) *Sociological Forum* 27.

57 Brett, Bickford, Ševcenko and Tobar, *supra* note 54, at 5–8.

58 Ibid.

59 B. Ivanisevic, 'Comparative Study on the Impact of Truth Commissions', ICTJ, May 2009, at 10.

(the naval base school used as the Clandestine Centre of Detention, Torture, and Extermination) in Argentina are all examples of this trend.

Moreover, to take place, memorialisation requires the documentary evidence that the truth commission records provide, and in this way memorialisation has a close dependency on truth commission records. Documentary evidence, when represented in physical, geographical spaces, stimulates public awareness of the atrocities committed in the past and strengthens the impact of truth commissions. Therefore, memorialisation and truth commissions are mutually reinforcing and extremely interdependent endeavours.[60] For this reason, the relationship between memorialisation and truth commissions is crucial and should not be underestimated.

The above sections have underlined the possible links and kind of interactions between truth commissions and other transitional justice mechanisms, highlighting the need to further explore the inherent complexities and dynamics of such processes. Understanding the complex relationships between truth-seeking, reparations measures, memory and criminal justice can greatly expand and enhance our knowledge about the impact of truth commissions over the longer term.

## 4. THE TRANSFORMATIVE LONG-TERM ROLE OF TRUTH COMMISSIONS

Van Der Merwe et al. argue that the toughest test of a specific transitional justice mechanism's efficacy is how effectively it builds institutions, policies and practices that will enable the nascent democracy to deal with existing social conflict and violence.[61]

According to this analysis, the second criteria against which truth commissions should be evaluated is their ability to change attitudes, beliefs and practices at the socio-political and institutional level. Three main indicators can be identified to measure this ability, namely the extent to which:

1. multiple actors, including the political elites, state actors and former perpetrators, have acknowledged and recognised past atrocities;
2. society has changed its attitudes and beliefs towards the victims on the one hand, and the perpetrators of human rights violation on the other; and
3. there has been a social repudiation of the institutional practices of the past.

---

60 J. Barsalou and V. Baxter, *The Urge to Remember: The Role of Memorials in Social Reconstruction and Transitional Justice*, United States Institute of Peace Press, Washington D.C., 2007, at 9–10.

61 H. van der Merwe, V. Baxter and A.R. Chapman, 'Introduction', in van der Merwe, Baxter and Chapman, *supra* note 3.

The above changes are fundamental ingredients of societal transformation, which can take years, if not decades, to occur. The truth commissions may trigger this long-term process of change by facilitating public and official recognition of the crimes committed in the past, engaging the wider society in a debate about the past, legitimising the victims' voices and sending a strong message of repudiation of past practices and ideologies.

Firstly, the aim of the official and public recognition of past human rights abuses is to give satisfaction to the victims, to de-legitimise those responsible for the crimes committed, and to encourage the perpetrators and their supporters to admit and publicly assume responsibility for their past actions. By genuinely recognising the violations as illegitimate and immoral, the institutional actors and the former perpetrators demonstrate their willingness to make compromises and show their respect for a set of norms and values upon which the future political order could be built. This process of recognition, although no substitute for justice, is fundamental to the rebuilding of the moral and normative edifice of an entire society. It is only this process that can restore the dignity of the victims, promote trust among citizens as well as in public institutions, and rebuild a moral order in the country. Therefore, truth commissions can trigger a positive cycle that, in the long term, may produce profound social and political change.

Although President Aylwin issued an apology immediately after the release of the Chilean truth commission report in 1991, in both Argentina and Chile it took years for the representatives of the military – the institution that had committed most of the crimes during the dictatorships – to recognise its institutional responsibilities and apologise. In Peru, the president publicly supported the truth commission's work and apologised on behalf of the state. However, the army has refused to apologise for crimes committed by military forces during the conflict, and the truth commissions' findings and recommendations have been strongly opposed by the Army. In El Salvador, there has been no official acceptance of responsibility for abuses committed by government forces during the armed conflict between 1980 and 1992. However, in some truth commission processes (for example in Sierra Leone), a huge number of perpetrators appeared before the truth commission hearings to admit their crimes. In Timor-Leste, thousands of perpetrators admitted their actions and carried out acts of reconciliation.[62] The official endorsement of the truth revealed by truth commissions may enable a discursive shift to take place, one which strongly challenges previous denials and/or justification of past crimes, thus creating a space where alternative versions of the previously accepted narrative can be legitimised. A truth commission process that is from

[62] Ivanisevic, *supra* note 59.

the beginning perceived as impartial and legitimate is likely to be more widely accepted by society in the long term. While acknowledgement and apologies have traditionally been regarded as important objectives of truth commissions, few studies have investigated, across different countries, the time taken or the extent to which the various sectors within society have recognised past crimes, thus contributing to a country's reconstruction after a violent past. In the view of the author, this should be one of the most important indicators to measure the impact and legacy of a truth commission over the longer term.

Secondly, it has been argued that, in order to have a transformative impact on society and its institutions, truth commissions have to be able to engage the wider society as far as possible. The official revelation of the truth to the public is crucial for generating society's awareness of the extent and magnitude of the crimes committed and for exposing the political and institutional failings that caused them. In order to fully develop its transformative potential, a truth-seeking process needs to be sustained by a civil society that is highly mobilised and has strong public engagement with the issues of the past. These are among the most crucial factors that have the capacity to generate social and political condemnation of the crimes committed and to de-legitimise the institutional actors that sustained such violent practices and ideologies. When the process of truth-seeking raises public awareness, the commitment to change past practices from various sectors of society, including the perpetrators and their accomplices, is more likely to happen. Public attitudes towards truth commissions and the degree to which their findings have a social impact should be periodically observed in order to understand how and under what circumstances attitudes might change. Systematic studies that examine public perceptions about policies to deal with the past or shifts in public opinions are, however, rare.

Thirdly, if a high level of social de-legitimisation of former perpetrators is achieved alongside a repudiation of past practices, it could indirectly influence institutional change. Institutional actors that are placed under public scrutiny, either for crimes committed in the past or for their past negligence, might embrace more democratic attitudes and values in order to regain social and political legitimacy and salvage their reputation. Although many other factors – including the altered political situation, institutional reforms, power relations and strategic calculations – contribute towards changing institutional attitudes and beliefs, this chapter argues that the public and official disclosure of the truth about the extent and magnitude of past human rights violations also plays an important role. Conversely, an absence of public debates on the issue of the past and a lack of acknowledgement on the part of former perpetrators impedes the process of collective condemnation. Thus, the moral and social pressures generated by a truth commission can, in the longer term, lead to a change in attitude and belief at the institutional level, making those institutions more responsive to the demands of victims and society in general.

In this way, truth-telling efforts and public engagement with the issue of past human rights violations can gradually transform the political, legal and social interactions that take place. Although the exposure of the truth can begin this long process of political and social transformation, it nevertheless requires long-term commitment and effort on the part of multiple state actors, institutions, civil society and the broader society.

Changes in attitudes, beliefs and practices can be measured by qualitative methodologies, including public opinion surveys, discourse and content analysis, focus groups and in-depth interviews. Although it should be borne in mind that not all countries produce much information in the period following the conclusion of a truth commission, this study argues that a considerable quantity of data is crucial in order understand the long-term impact of truth commissions. Moreover, in order to document a transition, data needs to be gathered over time and in a consistent manner. Finally, if one lesson can be drawn for future research, it is the critical importance of collecting baseline data. Therefore, for ongoing truth commissions and future truth commissions, the collection of data is extremely important, both during and immediately after the truth commission process. In this way, attitudinal and behavioural change in society and political elites will be measured using more reliable sources and databases.[63]

## 5. CONCLUSION

Despite the increasing popularity of truth commissions and their worldwide institutionalisation, there is still little understanding of their long-term effects and consequences. This chapter suggests a framework for evaluating truth commissions over the longer term in order to appreciate the social, political or institutional changes that such processes seek to achieve. As the chapter has shown, truth commissions have in many cases contributed to the development of later transitional justice mechanisms, including trials, reparations and memorialisation initiatives, thus enhancing and strengthening their legacy. While the chapter has indicated the possible links and kind of interactions between truth commissions and other transitional justice mechanisms, it suggests the need to further explore the inherent complexities and dynamics of such interaction processes.

In the previous section, the chapter argued that truth commissions should be evaluated by their ability to change attitudes, beliefs and practices at socio-political and institutional level. Truth commissions have the potential to set the

[63] See further on these issues Sarkin's introduction to this volume.

stage for a series of transformative processes to unfold, which over the longer term will be able to shift the public discourse on the past, de-legitimise past institutional practices, pave the way for the recognition of wrongdoings and support a more inclusive dialogue on the past. Future longitudinal studies could investigate more thoroughly how and under what circumstances these pathways of impact may develop over time. Experience has demonstrated that truth commissions are complex processes, whose contribution to accountability and transformation efforts in their societies depend on a variety of factors, including contexts, socio-political developments, sequencing with other transitional justice mechanisms and timing.

Today we can start to measure the long-term success of a truth commission by looking at its trajectory. The creation of follow-up mechanisms, the amount and type of reparations paid in the ensuing years, the status of implementation of the recommendations for institutional reforms, the level of social recognition of truth, the preservation of the truth commission archives and the creation of memorialisation initiatives are all crucial indicators of the long-term impact of truth commissions.

This chapter concludes that truth commissions should be seen as one part of a broader political project. Truth commissions are not enough in themselves, but they can constitute the beginning of a slow and protracted process of historical change. They can help a society to rebuild its moral and ethical values, which in turn may create the basis for a more just political order. The truth revealed by a truth commission can be used as evidence in future trials, catalyse the social repudiation of human rights atrocities, sensitise the population to the human rights abuses and finally prompt democratic reform. For this reason, in the years that follow a truth commission, it is fundamental to follow up its work to avoid major setbacks; for if a truth commission is seen as only a temporary measure for addressing the past, and if it is not part of a broader project of democratisation, it will only provide short-term benefits and its achievements will therefore be less far-reaching. It is also essential that the process of democratisation continues, as a new generation of leaders succeeds the old and the fear of past conflicts fades away. For all of this to happen, the passage of time is a crucial factor. The process of reckoning with a burdensome past concerns society as a whole and has to be continuously addressed in the social and public sphere. Thus, in order to see the dynamic process of truth commissions, we may have to wait much longer than transitional justice discourse currently allows. It may be that the work of a truth commission and its legacy will be of significance to future generations.

# THE GLOBAL TEXTUAL LEGACIES OF TRUTH COMMISSIONS

## Narratives on Sexual Violence in the Reports of Sierra Leone, Liberia, Kenya and Beyond

Susanne BUCKLEY-ZISTEL*



## 1. INTRODUCTION

In October 2017, UNESCO added a further item to its Memory of the World register: the 454 dossiers and 103 recordings of the Frankfurt Auschwitz trial (1963–1965) covering 183 days of court hearings. They detail the trials of 22 people accused of murder or complicity in murder at the death camp Auschwitz-Birkenau at the hands of National Socialists during the Second World War. UNESCO's Memory of the World initiative aims to secure documents of historical significance for future generations. In awarding the status to the Auschwitz trial, UNESCO has stated that the documentation of

* The research for this chapter has been conducted in the context of the research project 'Redressing Sexual Violence in Truth Commissions. The Labelling of Women as Victims and its Social Repercussions' funded by the Deutsche Forschungsgemeinschaft (DFG), to which I am very grateful. I am also grateful to Anne Menzel, Anna Emil and Jürgen Bast for their comments on an earlier draft of this chapter.

transitional justice processes is an important cultural heritage deserving global attention and preservation. Written and oral recordings hence form part of the legacy of mechanisms that deal with past violent conflicts and repressive regimes. In doing so, UNESCO has accorded significance to a particular object: text.

In line with UNESCO's appreciation of texts of transitional justice institutions, this chapter thus focuses on texts produced by truth commissions as part of their legacy. As presented elsewhere in this volume, the global legacy of truth commissions is often considered in terms of reparations and reforms or less tangible societal aspects such as the effect on the relationship between the conflicting parties. By contrast, the present chapter operates on the basis of text. It is concerned with the global textual legacy of truth commission reports that depict the findings of the commissions based on individual statements, corroborated facts and background research. In truth commission hearings, individuals narrate what they have experienced and witnessed so that recounting these ordeals produces a cacophony of voices on violence. The truth commission reports, however, do not simply repeat these voices, rather they interpret them. There is thus a very strong normative element to the reports: they assess, organise and evaluate the fragmented accounts on often extreme violence by individuals, turning them into narratives with clear storylines, and in so doing provide meaning to a sequence of events that seem beyond comprehension.

In other words, truth commissions offer narratives about past atrocities that are fixed in writing, printed on paper and made available as reports for future reference. Importantly, these reports can be considered as inter-texts because they are shaped by the meaning inherent in previous texts and themselves help to shape future texts, transgressing time and space and leading to a global understanding of truths about violence in the context of war and repression. Inter-textuality suggests that texts are related to each other, add layers of depth to knowledge and influence the recipients' prior understanding.[1] The textual legacy of truth commission reports therefore lies in the meaning they produce and how this will inform thinking – and textual writing – in the future about other instances of violence.

In the following analysis, I focus on the texts produced by truth commissions, not on the actual work of commissions. I look at the kind of meaning produced in national truth commission reports and how this shapes our global understanding of the atrocities committed in the context of violent conflict and repression.

---

1 M. Shapiro, 'Textualising Global Politics', in J. Der Derian and M. Shapiro (eds.), *International/Intertextual Relations: Postmodern Readings of World Politics*, Lexington Books, Lexington, 1989.

In order to narrow the scope of the analysis, I focus on one particular form of violence: sexual violence.[2] On a general note, even though all truth commissions today incorporate a focus on sexual violence, this has not always been the case.[3] Earlier commissions, such as those in Argentina, El Salvador and Chile, did not take sexual or gender-based aspects into consideration but assumed a gender-blind approach to truth.[4] After being made aware of the lack of redress of sexual abuses, the truth commissions of South Africa and Guatemala, which initially had gender-blind mandates, have subsequently paid particular attention to these forms of violence, and more recent commissions, such as those in Peru, East Timor, Haiti, Ghana, Sierra Leone, Liberia and Kenya, have explicitly included sexual and gender-based aspects in their mandates from the outset.[5]

This chapter starts with a brief introduction of the truth commission reports on which the analysis is based – Sierra Leone, Liberia and Kenya – before analysing systematically how they narrate sexual violence. A key finding is that the reports shy away from simple explanations for sexual violence but offer a broad spectrum of motives as to why male combatants assault women.[6] This depiction is highly normative and closely linked with a strong feminist agenda, according to which sexual violence should not only be prevented in and of itself but societal gender relations should more broadly be changed. This particular feminist stance – I argue by way of conclusion – is a central component of the global textual legacy of the truth commission reports.

---

2 This adds an important aspect to the academic debate because almost all of the literature on redressing sexual violence in truth commissions focuses on victims, both male and female, which can be explained by the general attention truth commissions pay to victims (in contrast to more perpetrator-centred legal institutions), as well as by a more general rise in victim research. What is largely absent from the analysis, though, is a focus on perpetrators, so that this chapter also contributes to the emerging field of perpetrator studies. See for instance T. Williams and S. Buckley-Zistel, *Perpetrators and Perpetration of Mass Violence. Action, Motivations and Dynamics*, Routledge, Abingdon, 2018.

3 See S. Buckley-Zistel, 'Truth Commissions, Human Rights and Gender: Normative Changes in Transitional Moments', in T. Debiel, T. Held and U. Schneckener (eds.), *Peacebuilding in Crisis. Rethinking Paradigms and Practices of Transnational Cooperation*, Routledge, Abingdon, 2016.

4 K. Theidon, 'Gender in Transition: Common Sense, Women, and War' (2007) 6(4) *Journal of Human Rights* 435; F. Ni Aolain and C. Turner, 'Gender, Truth and Transition' (2007) 16 *UCLA Women's Law Journal* 229.

5 V. Nesiah, 'Truth Commissions and Gender: Principles, Policies, and Procedures', ICTJ, New York, 2006.

6 The focus of this chapter is mainly on heterosexual violence. Importantly, though, the truth commission reports specifically address male-to-male sexual violence. Since this is described as a phenomenon but not explained, I have decided to omit the important topic of violence against men in this chapter.

## 2. DEPICTING SEXUAL VIOLENCE IN TRUTH COMMISSIONS

There is a small body of academic literature that discusses the prevalence and causes of sexual violence as depicted in transitional justice mechanisms, offering a textual analysis as advanced in the chapter. In a study on Peru and Guatemala, Michele Leiby draws on the reports of the respective truth commissions in order to assess the prevalence and dynamics of sexual violence, as well as to establish patterns of such violence.[7] On the basis of court transcripts, Tusty ten Bensel examines the nature of sexual violence during the war in Sierra Leone, focusing on how sexual violence evolved over time.[8] She treats the statements made in court as representations of reality, rather than as statements that were produced within, and thus shaped by, the court setting. In contrast, Inger Skjelsbæk assesses court transcripts in order to reveal which narratives about the perpetration of sexual violence are constructed by the court.[9] She illustrates how courts – i.e. institutions mandated to redress sexual violence – try to make sense of the deeds and thus takes the statements made in front of the court as narratives – rather than factual truths – to highlight how perpetration is explained on a continuum from normal to abnormal behaviour. This chapter is inspired by Skjelsbæk's approach and analyses the way in which truth commission reports narrate the perpetration of sexual violence. The analysis draws on narrative theory as well as on a conceptual framework for categorising narratives, outlined below. To narrate a particular occurrence in one way or another does not suggest that this narrative is an accurate picture of a factual event, but rather an interpretation of this particular event. As illustrated below, this often leads to rather stereotypical notions of masculinity and femininity.

## 3. THE TRUTH COMMISSIONS OF SIERRA LEONE, LIBERIA AND KENYA

The narrative of a truth commission is inter alia shaped by the nature and scope of the violence, the commission's mandate, and the conditions under

7 M.L. Leiby, 'Wartime Sexual Violence in Guatemala and Peru' (2009) 53(2) *International Studies Quarterly* 445, at 445.

8 T.T. Bensel, 'Framing in the Making: The Evolution of Sex Offender Motivation in Sierra Leone' (2014) 24(1) *International Criminal Justice Review* 59.

9 I. Skjelsbæk, 'Perpetrators of Sexual Violence in Armed Conflict', in T. Williams and S. Buckley-Zistel (eds.), *Perpetrators and Perpetration of Mass Violence. Action, Motivations and Dynamics*, Routledge, Abingdon, 2018; I. Skjelsbæk, 'The Military Perpetrator: A Narrative Analysis of Sentencing Judgments on Sexual Violence Offenders at the International Criminal Tribunal for the Former Yugoslavia (ICTY)' (2015) 3(1) *Journal of Social and Political Psychology* 46.

which the commission was established.[10] Even though the focus of this chapter is on text, these aspects provide the conditions under which the texts were produced. The following offers what can only be a very sketchy overview of the commissions analysed in this chapter. Since the focus here is to advance the notion of textual legacies, this chapter works on the level of the report that has been released, so that the wider particular idiosyncrasies of the commissions, such as their politicisation and internal struggles, are not relevant.

The Sierra Leone Truth and Reconciliation Commission (SLTRC, November 2002–October 2004) was established following 10 years of civil war, which was ended by the Lomé Peace Agreement of 1999. The war was characterised by extreme violence on all sides. In stipulating its mandate, the Truth and Reconciliation Commission Act of 2000 identified its objectives as being:

> to investigate and report on the causes, nature and extent of the violations and abuses … to the fullest degree possible, including their antecedents, the context in which the violations and abuses occurred, the question of whether those violations and abuses were the result of deliberate planning, policy or authorisation by any government, group or individual, and the role of both internal and external factors in the conflict.[11]

Moreover, in contrast to previous truth commissions that omitted sexual violence from their mandates, the bill stipulates paying 'special attention to the subject of sexual abuses'.[12] Importantly, even though the mandate does not make explicit reference to women and girls, the Commission's final report clarified that this demographic had been the overwhelming victims of such abuse, and thus required special attention.[13] To achieve these objectives, the SLTRC conducted public hearings throughout Sierra Leone for victims and perpetrators and collected about 8,000 statements, 13 per cent of which came from perpetrators – unprecedented for a truth commission.[14] The final report was presented in 2004 and consists of approximately 1,800 pages – 3,600 pages including all the appendices, in three volumes, with Volume III being divided into III a and III b. It includes a chapter entitled 'Women in Armed Conflict' (Vol III b, Chapter 3), in which gender crimes against women are addressed.

---

10 S. Buckley-Zistel, 'Narrative Truths: On the Construction of the Past in Truth Commissions', in S. Buckley-Zistel, C. Braun, T. Koloma Beck and F. Mieth (eds.), *Transitional Justice Theories*, Routledge, Abingdon, 2014.

11 Sierra Leone Truth and Reconciliation Commission Act 2000, www.sierra-leone.org/Laws/2000-4.pdf.

12 Ibid.

13 SLTRC, *Witness to Truth. Final Report of the TRC*, Freetown, 2004, at IIIb 85.

14 P.B. Hayner, 'The Sierra Leone Truth and Reconciliation Commission. Reviewing the First Year', ICTJ, New York, 2004.

This chapter also focuses on possible reasons for these crimes, by assessing the cultural and traditional history of Sierra Leone and the role of women in society in general. Parts of the report draw on academic literature, in particular on the book *Women, War and Peace* by Elisabeth Rehn and Ellen Johnson Sirleaf, and as a result read like literature reviews.[15]

The Liberian Truth and Reconciliation Commission (LTRC, 2006–2009) was established following 14 years of civil war characterised by an extremely high rate of violence. The Comprehensive Peace Agreement was signed in 2003 by the three warring factions and 18 political parties. The Agreement stipulates promoting respect for human rights (Art. XII) and mandated the creation of a Truth and Reconciliation Commission. After an initial political struggle, the Truth and Reconciliation Act was established in June 2005, mandating the Commission to investigate the country's history between 1979 and the end of the war in 2003:

> Investigating gross human rights violations and violations of international humanitarian law as well as abuses that occurred, including massacres, sexual violations, murder, extra-judicial killings and economic crimes, such as the exploitation of natural or public resources to perpetuate armed conflicts, during the period January 1979 to October 14, 2003; determining whether these were isolated incidents or part of a systematic pattern; establishing the antecedents, circumstances factors and context of such violations and abuses; and determining those responsible for the commission of the violations and abuses and their motives as well as their impact on victims.[16]

Importantly, there is an explicit reference to sexual crimes, as well as to the contextualisation of all crimes in the cultural and historical structures of the society. The final report is based on over 22,000 statements from people in Liberia and the diaspora, as well as over 500 public testimonies made by victims, perpetrators and witness. These 500 pages include chapters on the mandate, methodology, the background of the conflict, victims, findings and recommendations. The final report is supplemented by 13 appendices, the first of which is entitled 'Women and the Armed Conflict' and focuses on the gender dimension and gender-specific experiences of the conflict.

Finally, Kenya established a Truth, Justice and Reconciliation Commission (TJRC, 2009–2013) in the wake of the post-election violence of 2007–2008, during which people were killed and evicted from their homes; the violence had a strong ethnic component. In late 2008, Kenya's Parliament passed a

---

15 E. Rehn and E.J. Sirleaf, *Women, War and Peace: The Independent Experts Assessment on the Impact of Armed Conflict on Women and Women's Role in Peace-Building*, UNIFEM, New York, 2002.

16 https://web.archive.org/web/20170502235720/http://trcofliberia.org:80/about/trc-mandate.

bill establishing the TJRC and mandated it with 'establishing an accurate, complete and historical record of human rights and economic crimes ... between 12 December 1963 and 28 February 2008', with particular reference to 'rape, sexual slavery, enforced prostitution, forced pregnancy, forced sterilization, or any other form of sexual violence of comparable gravity' (Article 2(g)).[17] The mandate focuses not only on crimes committed after the 2007 elections but dates back to the country's independence. This is based on the assumption that the social fissures that gave rise to the violence existed well before the elections. The final report was published in 2013 and consists of 2,665 pages in four volumes, with Volume II being divided into II A, B and C. In Volume II A, Chapter 6 deals specifically with sexual violence and covers the whole period under investigation; in Volume II C, Chapter 1 addresses the role of women in Kenyan society.

In summary, sexual violence has been a focal point in the mandates, investigations and reports of all three commissions. What is important to emphasise is not only that the commissions were mandated to investigate sexual violence, but that they also assessed the historical development of societal gender relations and the scope of patriarchy in order to situate war-related sexual violence in the *longue durée* of the country. Many of the reports contain lengthy sections on gender asymmetries, most evident in the most recent commission in Kenya, which experienced the shortest period of acute violence. Moreover, the reports (and investigations) of all three commissions assess sexual violence not only against women but also against men, which is a very important development.[18]

However, due to the diverse contexts, the reports also differ in a number of ways. The scope and form of the violence in Sierra Leone and Liberia were extreme, lasted for many years and involved different non-state combatant groups. In Kenya, the post-election violence was fierce but only lasted several months, and state-armed groups such as the police played an instrumental role.[19] In addition, due to the time span covered by the commission, the Kenyan report also investigated a number of other instances of (sexual) violence, often in relation to evictions, as well as to violent struggles. Regarding the scope of

17 United States Institute of Peace, 'The Truth, Justice and Reconciliation Commission Bill, 2008', 2008, https://www.usip.org/sites/default/files/file/resources/collections/commissions/Kenya-Charter.pdf.

18 Due to its scope, the present chapter only focuses on sexual violence against women, though. It also does not take into account the ambivalent role of women who might also perpetrate violence. See for instance D.K. Cohen, 'Female Combatants and the Perpetration of Violence: Wartime Rape in the Sierra Leone Civil War' (2013) 65(3) *World Politics* 383.

19 S.F. Materu, *The Post-Election Violence in Kenya: Domestic and International Legal Responses*, Springer, Berlin, 2014, at 52.

the documents, it is important to note that the reports for Sierra Leone and Kenya are much longer and thus much more comprehensive and detailed than the Liberian report, which is also why they have been used more strongly for the analysis below. The publication of the reports of Liberia and Kenya were both subject to political turmoil (irrespective of sexual violence) and a division amongst the commissioners, such that their results might be more of a compromise between different viewpoints of the commissioners.[20]

## 4. NARRATING THE TRUTH

In order to understand how the reports shape our understanding of the atrocities committed, it is paramount to pay close attention to their respective narratives. In general, truth commissions are spaces in which a particular truth about an event is constructed.[21] The established regime of truth determines how the violent past is interpreted, what counts as a crime in need of investigation, who can be classified as a victim or a perpetrator, and what underlying patterns of causality are invoked. Narrative theory is therefore useful for examining the reproduction of the truth about an event, such as the perpetration of sexual violence, when it is presented in a spoken, written or visual form, such as the report of a truth commission.

According to narrative theory, the world is not presented in the form of 'well-made stories, with central subjects, proper beginnings, middles and ends, and a coherence that permits us to see "the end" in every beginning',[22] but our desire for coherence, integrity and closure forces us to structure events into meaningful actions. We therefore produce 'a clear sequential order that connects events in a meaningful way for a definite audience'.[23] This seems particularly relevant in the face of (sexual) violence, which appears to be beyond comprehension. Here, storytelling might allow us 'to feel that we actively participate in a world that for a moment seemed to discount, demean, and disempower us'.[24] For Hayden White, '[t]he production of meaning … can be regarded as a

20 K. Lanegran, 'The Kenyan Truth, Justice and Reconciliation Commission: The Importance of Commissioners and Their Appointment Process' (2015) 1(3) *Transitional Justice Review* 41; C. De Ycaza, 'A Search for Truth: A Critical Analysis of the Liberian Truth and Reconciliation Commission' (2013) 14(3) *Human Rights Review* 189.

21 For a more detailed discussion see S. Buckley-Zistel, *supra* note 10.

22 H. White, *The Content of the Form: Narrative Theory and Historical Representation*, John Hopkins University Press, Baltimore, 1987, at 24.

23 L.P. Hinchman and S.K. Hinchman, 'Introduction', in L.P. Hinchman and S.K. Hinchman (eds.), *Memory, Identity, Community*, State of New York Press, Albany, 1997, at xx.

24 M. Jackson, *The Politics of Storytelling: Violence, Transgression, and Intersubjectivity*, Museum Tusculanum Press, Copenhagen, 2002, at 16.

performance, because any given set of real events can be emplotted in a number of ways'.[25] There is no simple truth to be uncovered, but truth is the outcome of this process of narration. The narratives uttered in a truth commission construct the truth about a violent past, and this has significant implications for uncovering truth in truth commissions because it suggests that the meaning of an event – such as the perpetration of sexual violence – cannot simply be unveiled but must be created anew by use of a narrative.

Narratives often bear some form of family resemblance in following particular logics, assumptions and tropes, which structure a text. Tropes are commonly recurring motifs or discursive styles that are historically contingent. They are phrases, ideas or images that are frequently used in a particular narrative, such as in the report of a truth commission, as well as globally across reports. Tropes thus allow for the comparison of the narratives of truth commissions, as illustrated below.

The strength of a narrative approach is that it embeds stories historically and relationally in the context from which they emerge, suggesting that it is only within this spatio-temporal framework that they can be understood and interpreted. Thus, the telling of the narrative and the understanding of elements included in the process of selecting and organising events – such as the statements made in front of the commission, its mandate, etc. – is profoundly affected by the prevailing environment in which the narration takes place.

## 5. ANALYSING NARRATIVES ON WARTIME SEXUAL VIOLENCE

To reiterate, the objective of this chapter is to assess how truth commission reports shape our understanding of sexual violence through their narratives and how this contributes to their global textual legacy. In order to achieve this objective, I draw on Paul Kirby's categorisation of explanations for sexual violence.[26] Kirby offers three narratives (which he calls modes) – instrumentality, unreason and mythology – that shed light on the implicit structure of the understanding of wartime sexual violence. These narratives serve to assess how the perpetration of sexual violence is explained in the reports of the truth commissions in this chapter. Instrumentality refers to rational behaviour, i.e. the calculation of costs and benefits in order to advance personal interests. This is often material and might be based on greed. Unreason refers to affect,

25 White, *supra* note 22, at 44.

26 P. Kirby, 'How Is Rape a Weapon of War? Feminist International Relations, Modes of Critical Explanation and the Study of Wartime Sexual Violence' (2013) 19(4) *European Journal of International Relations* 797.

i.e. non-rational behaviour, and may be linked to emotions (including anger, desire, trauma, etc.) or the unconscious. Mythology is based on identity and the collective habits and beliefs, as well as cultural norms, and might include militarised discourses, customary practices and so on. Kirby's categorisation is useful for the purpose of this chapter, but it is important to note that others have offered alternative classifications for the organisation and discussion of wartime violence.[27] In the following, I analyse the reports of the truth commissions in Sierra Leone, Liberia and Kenya along the lines of Kirby's three narratives and in doing so explore these categories further.

Regarding methodology, the reports were analysed with the aid of a software programme (MAXQDA) for qualitative research with data based on text.[28] The analysis was based on codes emerging from the reading of the documents, as well as from preconceived categories derived from the current state of the art in the literature on sexual violence during violent conflict, i.e. on inductive as well as deductive modes. This software allows for comparing and contrasting each of the truth commission reports using the same analytical categories. In this study, however, the objective was not to systematically compare the three reports, but to deepen knowledge by assessing a broader sample of truth commission reports and to provide a wider spectrum of insights regarding global textual legacies. Critically, it has to be admitted that looking for particular categories in a text at the same time obstructs the view from others, i.e. it leads to a selective engagement with the source and a 'rubbing out' of alternative explanations.[29] It is thus necessary to keep this restriction in mind. Moreover, a significant ethical consideration when using software to analyse texts is that it reduces the very real and painful experiences of people to mere textual blocks, categories and codes, which has a dehumanising effect. It is thus important not to lose sight of the individuals behind the words.

The following discusses a small selection of report excerpts that were considered to be representative of the wider narratives, and mainly draws on Sierra Leone since it has the longest sections on sexual violence. These excerpts are organised around tropes that are explained with reference to academic scholarship on the perpetuation of sexual violence. There is a

27 M.E. Baaz and M. Stern, *Sexual Violence as a Weapon of War?: Perceptions, Prescriptions, Problems in the Congo and Beyond*, Zed Books, London, 2013; L.J. Shepherd, '"Victims, Perpetrators and Actors" Revisited: Exploring the Potential for a Feminist Reconceptualisation of (International) Security and (Gender) Violence' (2007) 9(2) *The British Journal of Politics & International Relations* 239; I. Skjelsbæk, 'Sexual Violence and War: Mapping out a Complex Relationship' (2001) 7(2) *European Journal of International Relations* 211; J.N. Clark, 'Making Sense of Wartime Rape: A Multi-Causal and Multi-Level Analysis' (2014) 13(5) *Ethnopolitics* 461.

28 I am deeply indebted to my research assistant Anna Emil who carried out the MAXQDA coding.

29 For a discussion see M.E. Baaz and M. Stern, 'Curious Erasures: The Sexual in Wartime Sexual Violence' (2018) *International Feminist Journal of Politics* 1, at 4.

strong similarity between the arguments in the literature and in the reports, an aspect that requires closer attention to global text production per se but would exceed the scope of this chapter.

An important qualification regarding the source of the reports is needed before proceeding. Authors of truth commission reports are first and foremost persons employed by the commission and it is their view that shapes the content of the report, rather than the statements made by victims and witnesses. In other words, the authors filter information and interpret it according to their own horizon and agenda. The statements analysed below thus need to be considered as statements of the employees of the commission, not as a reflection of the statements before the commission.

## 5.1. INSTRUMENTALITY

Instrumentality, for Kirby, covers incentives, interests, dispossession and accumulation – it is a rational action in the context of war and violence.[30] In the truth commission reports of Sierra Leone, Liberia and Kenya, the instrumentality narrative is invoked by a number of different tropes. To begin with, reference is made to the strategic use of sexual violence to intimidate a community and to spread terror. This is often related to the application of the term 'rape as a weapon of war' and highlights the strategic use of sexual violence for military gains. In this sense, rape is an instrument of a larger campaign of violence, based on a broader consensus.[31] The strategic use of intimidation rests on the assumption that it changes behaviour, instils fear and undermines confidence by degrading and intimidating the victims,[32] as apparent in the quotations from Kenya and Sierra Leone:

> The Commission ... finds that state security-led interventions in situations of conflict were the single most important cause of sexual violations including gang rape and sexual torture. Security agents used sexual violence as a weapon to terrorise, suppress, intimidate and humiliate communities ...[33]

> The Commission finds that all the factions pursued a deliberate strategy of perpetrating torture on women and girls perceived to be associated with the 'enemy', by inflicting or threatening to inflict sexual violence, other acts of violence and cruel and inhuman acts upon them or on persons close to them.[34]

---

30 Kirby, *supra* note 26, at 806.

31 D.E. Buss, 'Rethinking "Rape as a Weapon of War"' (2009) 17(2) *Feminist Legal Studies* 145, at 150.

32 D.A. Lewis, 'Unrecognized Victims: Sexual Violence against Men in Conflict Settings under International Law' (2009) 27(1) *Wisconsin International Law Journal* 1, at 3.

33 TJRC, *Report of the Truth, Justice and Reconciliation Commission*, Nairobi, 2013, at 46.

34 SLTRC, *supra* note 13, at II 104.

This trope is closely linked to one that can be labelled the destruction of the social fabric of a community. Here, too, deliberation, intentionality and strategy are central components of the motivation behind perpetrating sexual violence. The destruction of social and cultural cohesion within a group is said to reduce the group's external value; it is humiliated and degraded in the process.[35] This is particularly visible in incidences where husbands, brothers and sons are forced to witness the rape of female members of their family, thereby insulting them in their socially prescribed role as the protectors of 'their' women. Moreover, it creates and recreates relations of superiority and inferiority between the parties to the conflict. In the reports this is illustrated as follows:

> On occasion, civilians were forced to witness the rape of a family member, a mother, sister or daughter. This was aimed at stigmatising family members thereby weakening the bonds of the family, since it is the most basic component of society.[36]
>
> The Commission finds that the RUF and the AFRC deliberately embarked on systematic strategies to abduct and rape women and girls between the ages of ten and 14 years. The Commission finds that the systematic raping of women was intended to humiliate, defile and violate women, their families and communities. The practice of systematic rape sowed terror among the local population and debased societal norms and customs.[37]

From a more individualistic perspective, the trope of opportunism, denoting self-interest and striving for (material) gain,[38] is referred to as a motivation to perpetrate sexual violence. For Cohen, particularly in wars that are lengthy or very violent, sexual violence offers an incentive to combatants.[39] Rape is thus explained as one aspect of looting, it is a '"war booty" in terms of rewarding the victorious soldiers (male) with the rape of the women',[40] as apparent in the following quotations:

> As tensions flared, many Kamajor members learned to use the war for private gain. Although they were under oaths, taboos and a disciplined code of conduct that

---

35 R. Seifert, 'The Second Front. The Logic of Sexual Violence in War' (1996) 19(1–2) *Women's Studies International Forum* 35, at 39.

36 SLTRC, *supra* note 13, at IIIa 486.

37 Ibid. at II 102.

38 T. Williams, 'The Complexity of Evil: A Multi-Faceted Approach to Genocide Perpetration' (2014) 3(1) *Zeitschrift für Konfliktforschung* 71, at 84; A. Fahlberg and M. Pepper, 'Masculinity and Sexual Violence: Assessing the State of the Field) (2016) 10(8) *Sociology Compass* 673, at 676.

39 D.K. Cohen, 'Explaining Rape during Civil War: Cross-National Evidence (1980–2009)' (2013) 107(3) *American Political Science Review* 461.

40 M.E. Baaz and M. Stern, 'Why Do Soldiers Rape? Masculinity, Violence, and Sexuality in the Armed Forces in the Congo (DRC)' (2009) 53 2 *International Studies Quarterly* 495, at 498.

> forbade them from engaging in certain acts, they nonetheless looted, raped, killed innocent civilians and conscripted children into their ranks.[41]
>
> More youths joined the war when they saw how 'profitable' the experience had proved for others. Instead of enduring long periods of unemployment, they looted money and goods. Rather than possessing no stake in society, no property and no hope for the future, they became 'commandos' who could acquire guns, sex, food and drugs at their will.[42]

One aspect related to opportunism is to obtain a bush wife or to take advantage if her partner was not present:

> In a large number of cases, women were handed over to combatants and became their 'bush wives' for the purpose of satisfying not only their sexual needs but also to perform a host of different duties including domestic chores.[43]
>
> In addition to the 'bush wife' phenomenon, where women were assigned to a combatant for the purposes of both sex and to perform domestic duties, another category of violation carried out on women was to keep them isolated for the purpose of being available to satisfy the sexual needs of several combatants. Whenever combatants had the urge, there was a ready-made harem of women to rape.[44]

A further instrumental use of sexual violence, according to the reports, was to strengthen group cohesion. Importantly, it is not peer group pressure that leads to violence, but the desire to create a peer group. According to Clark, '[w]hen group members jointly engage in crimes … including rape, this can enhance intra-group ties'.[45] Similarly, Cohen argues that combatant groups with relatively low levels of social bonding might be particularly prone to strengthening bonds through gang rape.[46] The trope is apparent in the following words:

> Child soldiers were often forced by their captors to commit heinous atrocities in order to demonstrate loyalty to them and their cause. Atrocities often included carrying out the killings, amputations and rape of loved ones, community members, relatives and peers. Atrocities against family and community made it extremely difficult for child soldiers to escape and return home.[47]

---

41 SLTRC, *supra* note 13, at IIIb 354.
42 Ibid, at IIIb 352.
43 Ibid, at IIIb 159.
44 Ibid, at IIIb 161.
45 Clark, *supra* note 27, at 470.
46 Cohen, *supra* note 39, at 464.
47 SLTRC, *supra* note 13, at IIIb 263.

## 5.2. UNREASON

The next narrative suggests that perpetrators of sexual violence do not act as rational agents but that they are beyond reason.[48] A number of sections in the reports sustain the argument that unreason serves as an explanatory narrative; in other words, it is based on the notion that violent conflict is a state of exception which defies normality. Rape, it is argued, becomes an outlet for men of the moment of war, since war precipitates madness.[49] In this sense, according to one trope, violence is described as an abnormality in its scope and form; it is cruel and inhuman.

> The Commission finds that all of the armed groups were responsible for the enforced sterilisation, torture and mutilation of women and girls. In particular, the Commission finds the RUF – through its practice of disembowelling pregnant women – responsible for the violations of 'enforced sterilisation', torture and mutilation of women and young girls for no reason other than to torture and inflict cruel and inhuman treatment on them.[50]

Unreasonable behaviour is further explained by the abuse of drugs, which could account for the irrationality of combatants.[51]

> The use and abuse of drugs was widespread among the various armed factions. Many perpetrators lost all sense of reason and had no regard for human life, women's included. In a drug-affected state, combatants committed atrocities without feeling and with total impunity. While drug use cannot excuse the conduct of perpetrators or the atrocities they committed, it is a factor to consider, particularly in the case of child and youth perpetrators, as drugs have been proven to alter minds and affect reason.[52]

Another trope that runs strongly through the reports is that a war-related breakdown of social norms unleashes unconstrained violence. As Baaz and Stern discuss, it is argued that 'war suspends the social constraints that hinder men from being sexual animals that they "naturally" are/can be'.[53] Norms, which under normal circumstances restrain people from responding to their

---

48 Kirby, *supra* note 26, at 809.

49 M.E. Baaz and M. Stern, 'Making Sense of Violence: Voices of Soldiers in the Congo (DRC)' (2008) 46(1) *The Journal of Modern African Studies* 57, at 79.

50 SLTRC, *supra* note 13, at IIIb 156.

51 B. Ingelaere and N. Wilén, 'The Civilised Self and the Barbaric Other: Ex-Rebels Making Sense of Sexual Violence in the DR Congo' (2017) 35(2) *Journal of Contemporary African Studies* 221.

52 SLTRC, *supra* note 13, at IIIb 170.

53 Baaz and Stern, *supra* note 27, at 18.

sex drives at will, no longer exist and basic instincts come to the fore. This turns all men into potential rapists if and when they are let loose,[54] an idea highlighted in the following quotations:

> Studies have shown that cases of sexual violence escalate in the contexts of conflict, a factor attributed to a breakdown of the social order – perpetrators taking advantage of the disorder to commit sexual violence with impunity – and the use of sexual violence as an instrument of terror.[55]

> From a wider societal perspective, the Commission has identified a total breakdown of all morality and norms, along with levels of cruelty that are quite frightening in terms of their long-term effects.[56]

Research, in particular from a neuropsychological point of view, further argues that violence is perpetrated as a result of exposure to traumatic incidences.[57] When committing violent acts, combatants 'receive rewarding incentives through the release of hormones that prevent post traumatic stress disorder symptoms'.[58] Trauma as a trope resonates in the following words:

> The perpetrator consciously or unconsciously transfers all the humiliations and pains he has gone through to the innocent victim. These acts are climaxed by celebrations with group members. They rejoice at this moment because they feel that they are now above the common world, above its limits and laws and all codes of race and prohibitions that constitute it. They dance, drink, take drugs, gang rape and this final stage is celebrated by the whole group in extreme ways after this initiation. SJ [who provided the testimony] explains this ceremony, which has to be understood as an effect of the traumatic aspect of the rite.[59]

Emasculation is another trope used to explain sexual violence. This masculinity-in-threat connotes feelings of inadequacy in men, which is said to contribute to the perpetration of sexual violence. Feelings of shame and masculine insecurity are compensated for via various tactics including sexual aggression and violence.

---

54 S. Turner, 'Victims of Chaos and Subaltern Sexualities? Some Reflections on Common Assumptions about Displacement and the Prevalence of Sexual and Gender-Based Violence', in S. Buckley-Zistel and U. Krause (eds.), *Gender, Violence, Refugees*, Berghan, Oxford, 2017.

55 TJRC, *supra* note 33, at II 721.

56 SLTRC, *supra* note 13, at 169.

57 T. Elbert, R. Weierstall and M. Schauer, 'Fascination Violence: On Mind and Brain of Man Hunters' (2010) 260(2) *European Archives of Psychiatry and Clinical Neuroscience* 100.

58 U. Krause, 'Escaping Violence and Being Safe? Post-conflict Refugee Camps and the Continuum of Violence', in S. Buckley-Zistel and U. Krause (eds.), *Gender, Violence, Refugees*, Berghan, Oxford, 2017, at 189.

59 SLTRC, *supra* note 13, at IIIa 560.

'In these contexts,' it has been suggested, 'sexual violence is one mechanism for reaffirming one's sense of power, security, and identity'.[60] This argument strongly resonates in the following quotation:

> The changed gender roles and identities that the war brought about have left many men feeling powerless. Many of those forced to watch helplessly as their mothers, wives, sisters and daughters were raped and sexually abused admit to shame and inability to live up to the hegemonic model of masculinity. The easiest way for them to regain their power has been through exerting control over women through sexual and physical violence.[61]

Spirituality and ritual violence is another identifiable trope that connects to the narrative of unreason. Here, too, rational thinking is replaced by irrationality, with a higher power guiding the actions.

> There is particular concern at the large number of reported cases of raped children. Attacks are perpetrated not only out of sexual desire, but also due to belief in rape as a ritual capable of increasing power and virility.[62]

> The Commission recorded testimony that pregnant women were killed by the Kamajors in order to extract parts of their bodies for use in initiation ceremonies. Furthermore some Kamajors carried 'charms' or 'fetishes' with them which were constituted of human remains, including the mutilated genitalia of women.[63]

## 5.3. MYTHOLOGY

The mythology narrative situates the perpetration of sexual violence within socio-cultural boundaries, and provides a symbolic framework for action, as well as collective beliefs, religions and ideologies rooted mainly in collective identities. For Kirby, mythology suggests that 'wartime sexual violence is a continuation of political power in a more dispersed and collective sense, designating some as legitimate and others as illegitimate depending on their circulation within the rules and norms of the group.'[64]

One identifiable trope in the reports that relates to mythology is the differentiation between in-group and out-group. This refers to belonging to a combatant group and the identification that comes with the group's culture, such as its militarisation. 'In the war-zone men are not only set to be men,

60 Fahlberg and Pepper, *supra* note 38.
61 LTRC, *Report of the Truth and Reconciliation Commission*, Monrovia, 2004, at III 52.
62 Ibid.
63 SLTRC, *supra* note 13, at IIIa 496.
64 Kirby, *supra* note 26, at 811.

but to be militaristic men,' Skjelsbæk argues, so that '[a]n understanding of militaristic culture is key in attempting to understand the gender dimension of the war-zone.'[65] This male camaraderie and shared identity, so the argument goes, makes it easier for men to perpetrate sexual violence.

> Another symbol of identification for new converts is the dreadlocks. In times of their action, they are usually badly dressed with military trousers and T-shirts, worn out boots or slippers. They do not care about what they wear as long as they are filled with the notion of being in control of the situation. Everyone is under their command. In this position they can get what they want forcefully. Converts display sadistic behaviour to non-members. This explains the nature of atrocities committed against civilians, which range from amputation, mutilation, arson and rape.[66]

Ethnic or national belonging is another potential trope for the perpetration of sexual violence. Clark argues that this produces a permissive environment, for it imbues sexual violence with a strong symbolic meaning.[67] Women become the target of violence due to being the bearers of symbols such as 'the mother of the nation'; targeting them becomes synonymous with targeting the other ethnic group. In the words of the commissions:

> In recent conflicts, because of their sex and the fact that they are often viewed as symbolic bearers of cultural and ethnic identity, women have increasingly become the specific target of violence, especially sexual violence.[68]
>
> Indeed, data received by the Commission through interviews, statements and oral submissions revealed clear patterns of consistent and widespread sexual violence targeting women and men during the electioneering period as well as during ethnically and politically-instigated conflict that have over time characterised Kenya's elections. Of the total 1 104 statements received by the Commission in regard to sexual violence, nearly a quarter (255) was committed in the context of political/ ethnic clashes.[69]

The reports also pick up the argument that women are subjected to sexual violence due to the prevailing gender asymmetries in society. It has been argued that some men display their masculine identity through the use of violence, which is intrinsically connected to the assertion of social status and the value of the self; in other words, violence literally 'makes men'.[70]

65 Skjelsbæk, *supra* note 27, at 216.
66 SLTRC, *supra* note 13, at IIIa 560.
67 Clark, *supra* note 27, at 467; Skjelsbæk, *supra* note 28, at 216.
68 TJRC, *supra* note 33, at IIc 86.
69 Ibid, at IIa 735.
70 N. Cahn, F. Ni Aolain and D.F. Haynes, 'Gender, Masculinities, and Transition in Conflicted Societies' (2009) 44(1) *New England Law Review* 101, at 105.

Patriarchy thus serves as an explanatory trope for the 'socially constructed relationship between rape and power'.[71] This resonates in the reports:

> This report determines that through the investigations of the TRC, many of the causes and origins of violence against women during wartime are rooted in the socio-cultural, traditional and political history of Liberia. It is also firmly linked to the low socio-political status of women, with the added perception of male superiority. This rendered women and girls extremely vulnerable to exploitation and violence during both war and peace.[72]

> Consequently, it was easy for armed combatants to treat women with disdain and appropriate a sense of ownership of women's bodies for themselves, as they probably were wont to do, albeit to a lesser extent, in peacetime. The patriarchal hegemony that had existed in Sierra Leone continued and worsened during the conflict, evolving in the most macabre manner. The cultural concept that a woman was 'owned' by a man played itself out in many of the violations that women suffered during the conflict.[73]

The above discussion shows that the truth commission reports combine various narratives about the perpetration of sexual violence, a subject increasingly being emphasised in the literature.[74] Moreover, the reports do not simply state the empirical facts from the testimonies, but have proved to be an often very strong normative analysis of causes and patterns, offering an interpretation rather than a mere documentation. In analysing the narratives on sexual violence in the reports, it becomes apparent that they bear strong similarities to the current state of the art of academic literature on sexual violence. In other words, the reports often apply scholarly arguments to evaluated empirical data.

## 6. CONCLUSION

The objective of this chapter was to analyse the global textual legacy of the truth commission reports by focusing on one particular aspect: wartime sexual violence. The legacy manifests itself in how the reports shape our understanding of these atrocities, i.e. how they influence what we know and how we think about such atrocities, and how this shapes future thinking and writing about truth-seeking processes in other cases of dealing with past violence.

---

71 Clark, *supra* note 27, at 464.

72 LTRC, *supra* note 61, at III 81.

73 SLTRC, *supra* note 13, at IIIb 170.

74 See Leiby, *supra* note 7; Kirby, *supra* note 26; Skjelsbæk, *supra* note 27.

Through committing the stories to words in reports, something is left behind: the materiality of a document, but also, more importantly, the intangible effect of how the perpetration of sexual violence is explained in the particular context, as well as in subsequent truth commissions reports. As inter-texts, the reports will shape future texts globally.

From the vantage point of this chapter, the global textual legacy of a truth commission report is how it ascribes meaning to gender relations. Analysing the narratives of truth commissions allows for insights into the construction of these relations in the text. If one follows Butler, then there is an intricate relationship between performance, for example writing, and materiality, such as the constructed gender identities and relations.[75] These identities and relations are produced by social, cultural and historical conditions, which determine how gender is understood, a process that is constantly affirmed and challenged by iteration and re-iteration of societal norms. In this sense, the way we speak (or write) about men and women informs how gender identities and gender relations are constituted. The global legacy of the truth commission report thus lies in the narration of gender relations and how this influences future commissions in their particular way of depicting sexual violence.

In the present reports, this is done with a strong feminist agenda. The texts are highly normative, advancing social change and a reduction of societal gendered power asymmetries, a trend that is more generally discernible in truth commissions which – over time – first added women, then gender and lastly feminism to their agendas.[76] Importantly, feminism does not simply account for sexual violence, it 'politicizes sexual violence as an act related to social power; because it takes as an analytical baseline the embeddedness of gender practices within a historically located hierarchical system of differentiation which privileges those defined as masculine at the expense of those defined as feminine; and because it connects analysis with politics and ethics at a fundamental level'.[77] The reports, therefore, make very clear statements about prevailing gender relations in their respective societies and thus strongly advocate for transforming them.[78]

The chapter has looked at the global legacy of truth commissions from a different angle. By focusing on their textual legacies, it has highlighted the

75 J. Butler, *Bodies that Matter: On the Discursive Limits of 'Sex'*, Taylor & Francis, Florence, 2011.

76 Buckley-Zistel, *supra* note 3. See also C. Bell and C. O'Rourke, 'Does Feminism Need a Theory of Transitional Justice? An Introductory Essay' (2007) 1(1) *International Journal of Transitional Justice* 23.

77 Kirby, *supra* note 26, at 799.

78 For a critique of mainstream feminist agendas in transitional justice see C. O'Rourke, 'Feminist Scholarship in Transitional Justice: A De-Politicising Impulse?' (2014) 51 *Women's Studies International Forum* 118.

significance of the texts themselves (rather than recommendations emerging out of the text) and argued that it is also important to look at this intangible heritage. The truths produced by commissions, the interpretation offered in the reports and the narratives recounted in the writing shape future thinking and understanding of violence and how it is portrayed. It is unlikely that any of the truth commission reports used for this study will qualify for the UNESCO Memory of the World register – they are not sufficiently extraordinary – but they will still leave an imprint on the reports to come.

# THE IMPLEMENTATION RECORD OF TRUTH COMMISSIONS' RECOMMENDATIONS IN LATIN AMERICA

Elin SKAAR*



## 1. INTRODUCTION

One of the most theoretically neglected and empirically under-researched, yet potentially one of the most important, legacies of truth commissions are their recommendations. As discussed elsewhere in this volume, truth commissions have become a significant means of confronting human rights abuses committed by the military, state agents, paramilitaries or opposition forces during repressive regimes or periods of armed conflict. The prime function of a truth commission is to investigate and document human rights violations, and to make its findings public through a report. Another central function of truth commissions is to make recommendations to the government with two main aims: to address violations of the past and to prevent such violations from reoccurring in the future.

* I would like to thank Jeremy Sarkin and two anonymous reviewers for helpful comments on an earlier draft.

There are between 50 and 70 truth commissions in existence worldwide – depending on the criteria one uses to define the universe of truth commissions.[1] The South African Truth and Reconciliation Commission is arguably the world's best known, and the one that has received the most scholarly attention. However, the model of a truth commission was developed and perfected in Latin America. As of 2018, this region has had 13 official (that is, state-endorsed) truth commissions in 11 different countries that have completed their work since the early 1980s. Adding the two official commissions that never published a report and various non-official truth commissions, there have been a total of more than 20 truth commission efforts in Latin America. Widely known commissions include Argentina's National Commission on the Disappeared (CONADEP), Chile's National Commission on Truth and Reconciliation (Rettig Commission), and Peru's Truth and Reconciliation Commission. Lesser known truth commissions include those of Ecuador, Haiti, Panama and Paraguay. A latecomer on the truth commission scene in Latin America is Brazil – which published its final report almost three decades after the country's transition from military dictatorship to democracy in 1985, in response to a presidential initiative.[2] Truth commissions have recently also been established in Colombia and Bolivia, suggesting that this form of documenting human rights violations is far from passé in the region.[3]

In addition to documenting the violations committed by the prior regime(s), these truth commissions have made a series of recommendations to their governments, which, if implemented, may potentially have a significant impact on the reconstruction of democracy and peaceful social order. Yet we know very little – in fact, next to nothing – about the implementation record of truth commissions' recommendations, since hardly any scholars have ventured into this field yet. This chapter tries to amend some of this scholarly gap by examining the implementation record of recommendations made by Latin American official truth commissions – 13 in total. Although this chapter focuses specifically on Latin American truth commissions, the findings

---

1 Contrast for example P.B. Hayner, *Unspeakable Truths: Transitional Justice and the Challenge of Truth Commissions*, 2nd edn, Routledge, London and New York, 2011, and T.D. Olsen, L.A. Payne and A.G. Reiter, *Transitional Justice in Balance: Comparing Processes, Weighing Efficacy*, United States Institute of Peace Press, Washington D.C., 2010.

2 F. Ghelfi, S. Hourcade, L.P. Zaldua and M. Perelman, 'Brazil's National Truth Commission: Recommendations for a pending democratic agenda', in E. Skaar, J. García-Godos and E. Wiebelhaus-Brahm (eds.), *From Word to Practice: The Fate of Truth Commission Recommendations in Latin America*, Vol. II (forthcoming).

3 A truth commission was included in the government–FARC peace accord in Colombia in 2017 and was formally inaugurated by President Juan Manuel Santos in April 2017. See press release at https://colombiareports.com/colombia-creates-historic-truth-commission/ (accessed 19.02.2018). The Bolivian truth commission was formally established August 2017. See press release at http://santiagotimes.cl/2017/08/21/bolivia-launches-truth-commission-to-investigate-military-dictatorships-crimes/ (accessed 19.02.2018).

should be relevant – both theoretically and empirically – for the study of the implementation record of truth commission recommendations in other parts of the world.

The chapter consists of six sections. Following this short introduction, the next section provides an overview of the literature dealing specifically with truth commission recommendations. The third section focuses on Latin American truth commission reports, while section 4 gives an overview of their recommendations. Section 5 analyses the implementation record of Latin American truth commissions in general, but also offers some concrete examples from specific commissions. Concluding remarks are made in section 6.

## 2. WHAT DO WE KNOW ABOUT TRUTH COMMISSION RECOMMENDATIONS AND THEIR IMPLEMENTATION RECORD?

One of the ideas put forward in this chapter is that well-implemented recommendations will likely enhance a truth commission's impact and relevance in the society in which it operates. Scholars of transitional justice have in recent years become increasingly concerned with the impact of truth commissions and other transitional justice mechanisms. As documented in detail elsewhere in this volume, attempts at gauging impact produce very different and sometimes even contradictory results.[4] This section zooms in on the scholarly literature that focuses specifically on the impact of truth commission recommendations.

First, some reflections on the functions and relevance of truth commissions. Truth commissions serve different functions, through which they (at least theoretically) might contribute to various goals. The *transformative* potential of truth commissions arguably lies specifically in the body of recommendations put forward in their final reports. Although truth commissions are usually not aimed at transforming societies' economic structures, their transformative potential lies in their contribution to changing social norms and practices. The list of truth commission recommendations is often extensive and usually includes proposals to reform legal, security, political and social institutions. Truth commissions also frequently recommend reparations and various other measures to further address past violations.

Under certain conditions, these recommendations can be transformative if they change individual or societal behaviour in a positive direction, or if they lead to structural changes that affect individual and societal behaviour.

4 See, for example the literature overviews provided in the chapters written by Anita Ferrara and by Filipa Raimundo and Joana Rebelo Morais in this volume.

To give an example, truth commission recommendations could lead to law reform or institutional reform that would increase access to justice more widely, beyond the individuals or groups targeted directly by the recommendation. Police reforms in response to a truth commission recommendation could strengthen a key institution to uphold the rule of law. Police reforms would also benefit the population writ large and could have future spin-off effects such as more respect for human rights in general. Law revision initiated to benefit marginalised groups in a conflict could have larger societal benefits. Truth commission recommendations could also further rights-based political processes. If constitutions are revised to broaden standing before the constitutional court and access to redress is increased as a result, this could benefit a wide range of rights (health, housing, education, environment, etc.). This in turn may, in the long run, enhance structural change and reduce inequality.

The extent of possible recommendations raises questions about expectations and the possibility of implementation. In general, there are many obstacles to implementing truth commission recommendations. Governments may have other priorities. Powerful stakeholders who are threatened by the recommendations may create roadblocks. Anecdotal evidence shows that the implementation record of truth commission recommendations is generally weak.[5] However, there is hardly any empirical research to support this claim as the relationship between the nature of recommendations and the prospects for their implementation has largely been neglected in scholarly literature. Most qualitative studies of truth commissions stop their analysis when the truth commission has handed over its report and hence make little or no reference to the recommendations.

Nevertheless, there is a small but steadily growing literature that is concerned with what happens after a truth commission has launched its report. In Latin America, there are a handful of studies that have tried to assess the importance of truth commission recommendations. As early as the mid-1990s, Marc Ensalaco, in his analysis of the then recently established truth commissions in Chile and El Salvador, wrote:

> The most important contributions of these most recent TCs [truth commissions] … derived from their advisory function. The commissions' recommendations concerning the adaptation of the political constitutions and legal statutes to reflect international human rights standards, and institutional reforms of the judiciaries and militaries, consisted of the legal and institutional prerequisites of societies that are truly protective and promotive human rights.[6]

---

5 Hayner, *supra* note 1, at 6.

6 M. Ensalaco, 'Truth commissions for Chile and El Salvador: A report and assessment' (1994) 16(4) *Human Rights Quarterly* 656, at 666.

However, given the short time span between the issuing of the reports and the publication of Ensalaco's article, we could interpret this positive evaluation more as an expression of what the author had hoped that the commissions would contribute to in the future based on what was written in the final reports, rather than on an actual analysis of the implementation record.

Mike Kaye provides a more thorough assessment of the implementation record of the recommendations made by two investigative commissions in Central America – the Salvadoran Commission on the Truth and the Honduran Commission on Disappearances.[7] Kaye provides an evaluation of these commissions' contributions to justice, reconciliation and democratisation. Although Kaye's analysis was carried out shortly after these two commissions released their final reports, he provides some indication of their implementation status. For instance, he points out that some military officials were removed from positions of authority in El Salvador due to their involvement in human rights violations.[8] However, most recommendations had failed to be implemented at the time of writing. Interestingly, Kaye notes that '[w]hile the truth commission and the Valladares Report were very similar in terms of their reconciliation measures and their support for criminal prosecutions, the level of implementation was far higher in Honduras than in El Salvador'.[9]

Shifting focus to Peru, Lisa J. Laplante and Kimberly Theidon analyse the implementation record of the Peruvian truth commission recommendations, particularly with respect to recommendations made regarding reparations to victims, exemplified by the government's 'Plan of Reparations 2005–2006' approved by executive decree in 2005. They find that, at least initially, the government was unwilling to allocate the resources necessary to implement the reparation plan.[10]

Eric Wiebelhaus-Brahm, in his analysis of Chile's Rettig Commission and the Salvadoran Commission on the Truth, finds that recommendations were more likely to be implemented when party politics are more competitive and when civil society is more robust.[11] In an earlier article, Brahm argues that if we want to understand the contribution of truth commissions to democratisation processes, 'recommendations related to political institutions are of particular relevance because, unlike reparations, they impact all

7 M. Kaye, 'The role of truth commissions in the search for justice, reconciliation and democratisation: The Salvadorean and Honduran cases' (1997) 29(3) *Journal of Latin American Studies* 693.

8 Ibid, at 704.

9 Ibid, at 707.

10 L.J. Laplante and K.S. Theidon, 'Truth with Consequences: Justice and Reparations in Post-Truth Commission Peru' (2007) 29(1) *Human Rights Quarterly* 228.

11 E. Wiebelhaus-Brahm, *Truth Commissions and Transitional Societies: The Impact on Human Rights and Democracy*, Routledge, New York, 2010.

of society. Truth commissions typically make reform recommendations to prevent the repetition of past crimes and, thereby, identify ways to help former opponents live side by side peacefully'.[12]

Although these earlier studies advance our understanding of the relevance and impact of truth commissions by broadening their focus to include the reports' findings, they did not look at recommendation implementation systematically. Moreover, since the assessments were carried out shortly after the commissions had completed their report, there was little time to implement anything, and so the findings may not be significant. With the passage of time, scholars of transitional justice have the benefit of operating within a larger time frame for analysing and assessing implementation. Anita Ferrara, in her detailed analysis of the Chile Rettig Commission and what happened after it had completed its work at the end of the 1990s, makes a strong argument for why it is important to employ a long-term perspective when one tries to understand the larger contributions of truth commissions.[13] She shows how the Rettig Commission was the precursor to reparation programmes, more truth-finding initiatives, memorialisation projects, and criminal prosecution for human rights violations.

To date, the most comprehensive and systematic exploration of the impact of truth commission recommendation implementation is the work of Onur Bakiner. Distinguishing between direct and indirect impact, Bakiner assesses existing theoretical explanations in light of empirical evidence drawn from fifteen truth commissions from around the world, several of which are Latin American.[14] He argues that direct political impact may take place through the implementation of recommendations and indirect political impact through civil society mobilisation. He further argues that truth commissions may also have positive judicial impact by contributing to human rights accountability and negative judicial impact by promoting impunity. Finally, he concludes that truth commissions do promote political and judicial change, albeit modestly, especially when human rights and victims' groups pressure governments for policy implementation.[15] An important point regarding causality – i.e. 'proof' that there is a causal link between x and y – is that:

> truth commissions' recommendations are incorporated into policy in some countries because politicians take the initiative to implement them, whereas in other cases

---

12 E. Brahm, 'Uncovering the Truth: Examining Truth Commission Success and Impact' (2007) 8(1) *International Studies Perspectives* 16, at 24.

13 A. Ferrara, *Assessing the Long-Term Impact of Truth Commissions: The Chilean Truth and Reconciliation Commission in Historical Perspective*, Routledge, London, 2015.

14 O. Bakiner, 'Truth Commission Impact: An Assessment of How Commissions Influence Politics and Society' (2014) 8(1) *International Journal of Transitional Justice* 6.

15 Ibid.

> implementation takes place despite the reluctance, or even hostility, of the political leadership, as a result of continuous civil society mobilization.[16]

In his book *Truth Commissions: Memory, Power, and Legitimacy*, which includes an analysis of some of the most well-known and one of the lesser known Latin American truth commissions, Bakiner argues that often the impact of truth commissions is felt long after the commission itself has ceased to exist.[17] In line with Ferrara's 2015 findings in the Chilean case, Bakiner argues that the positive judicial impact of truth commissions (i.e. human rights accountability)

> tends to appear several years after the end of the process, in great part as a result of broader changes in politicians' and judges' attitudes on human rights trials; and *negative judicial impact* (i.e., impunity) favors only a small subsection of perpetrators, while the overall climate of impunity is likely caused by factors other than truth commissions' amnesty procedures.[18]

Bakiner concludes that '[t]he processes that generate the largest effects are direct political impact and delayed political impact through civil society mobilization'.[19] These conclusions suggest that recommendations can play a catalytic role and outline causal mechanisms through which recommendations may cement commissions' legacies. As implementation is often the product of lengthy struggles, it is necessary to collect data over long periods of time in order to accurately assess truth commission impact, and the implementation record in particular.

## 3. LATIN AMERICAN TRUTH COMMISSION REPORTS

This chapter focuses on the implementation record of recommendations made in the final reports of Latin American truth commissions. These undertakings were in response to the widespread human rights abuses that took place in the region either during times of military dictatorship in the 1970s and 1980s, or during internal armed conflict from the 1950s up to the present. This geographical focus is relevant for several reasons. As mentioned above, Latin America saw the origins of the first official truth commissions in the early 1980s and contains

---

16 Ibid, at 14.

17 A third of 16 truth commissions discussed in Onur Bakiner's book are Latin American: Argentina, El Salvador, Guatemala, Haiti and Peru. O. Bakiner, *Truth Commissions: Memory, Power, and Legitimacy*, University of Pennsylvania Press, Philadelphia, 2016.

18 Ibid, at 113.

19 Ibid, at 112.

a sizeable number of truth commissions. Since many of the commissions were established in the 1980s and 1990s, there is an ample timeframe for observing the implementation of recommendations. Furthermore, the region was the 'pilot' for the post-Cold War UN's active involvement in establishing truth commissions in connection with its involvement in peace processes (El Salvador in 1991–1992 and Guatemala in 1996–1997), which allows us to compare and contrast these commissions with the commissions that were purely domestic initiatives. In addition, Latin America is the continent that has seen the highest number of alleged human rights violators prosecuted in national courts. This allows us to explore potential connections between the documentation made by truth commission reports and subsequent prosecution for the crimes that have been documented.[20] Finally, Latin America has also been a forerunner in establishing reparation programmes for victims/survivors and their families. Particularly in recent years, there has been an increased focus on bottom-up, victim-centred and/or victim-driven reconciliation processes. Since many truth commissions make recommendations encouraging reparations for victims and their families, it may be interesting to examine whether there are any direct connections between the recommendations made by truth commissions and government-sponsored reparation programmes. This is a hitherto empirically unexplored causal connection, with the notable exception of Ferrara's detailed analysis of the connections between the first Chilean truth commission, the Rettig Commission, and subsequent governmental and non-governmental efforts in transitional justice, such as reparations.[21]

The subsequent section examines only the truth commissions that fit with Priscilla Hayner's classic 2011 definition:

> A truth commission (1) is focused on the past, rather than ongoing, events; (2) investigates a pattern of events that took place over a period of time; (3) engages directly and broadly with the affected population, gathering information on their experience; (4) is a temporary body, *with the aim of concluding with a final report*; and (5) is *officially authorised or empowered by the state* under review.[22]

Table 1 provides an overview of all the formal, that is, state-sponsored, truth commissions established in the Latin American region that have completed

20 E. Skaar, C. Collins and J. García-Godos, 'Conclusions: the uneven road towards accountability in Latin America', in E. Skaar, J. García-Godos and C. Collins (eds.), *Transitional Justice in Latin America: The Uneven Road from Impunity towards Accountability*, Routledge, London, 2016, at 275–298.

21 Ferrara, *supra* note 13.

22 Hayner, *supra* note 1, at 11–12.

their work and subsequently submitted a final report to the government.[23] Although we expect governments to feel responsible for the implementation of recommendations made by only state-sponsored (i.e. formal) truth commissions, it is worth noting that there are at least three important investigations that have been carried out by non-governmental organisations (NGOs): the Archbishop of São Paulo and the World Council of Churches' *Brasil: Nunca Mais* project; Servicio Paz y Justicia's *Uruguay: Nunca Más*; and the Human Rights Office of the Archbishop of Guatemala's *Recuperación de la Memoria Histórica* project. These non-formal truth commissions also issued reports that were taken seriously by at least some sectors of society.

The truth commissions in Table 1 are listed in chronological order according to the year they issued their final reports.

**Table 1. Latin American truth commissions**

| Country | Name of Commission (English translation) | Commission established by | Year of final report |
|---|---|---|---|
| **Argentina** | National Commission on the Disappeared (CONADEP) | President (1983–84) | 1984 |
| **Uruguay** | Investigative Commission on the Situation of Disappeared People and its Causes | Parliament (1985) | 1985 |
| **Chile** | National Commission for Truth and Reconciliation (Rettig Commission) | President (1990–91) | 1991 |
| **El Salvador** | Commission on the Truth for El Salvador | UN (1992–93) | 1993 |
| **Haiti** | National Truth and Justice Commission (CNVJ) | President (1994–96) | 1996 |
| **Guatemala** | Commission for Historical Clarification (Memoria del Silencio) | UN (1997–99) | 1999 |
| **Panama** | Panama Truth Commission | President (2001–02) | 2002 |

*(continued)*

23 We exclude from this list the formal truth commissions that did not complete their reports (Bolivia's National Commission for the Investigation of Forced Disappearances (1982–1984) and Ecuador's Truth and Justice Commission (1996–1997)). The truth commission in Honduras is also not included here. The preliminary report on disappearances in Honduras, entitled 'The Facts Speak for Themselves' (referred to in the quote that follows as the Valladares Report) was released on 29 December 1993 by the National Commissioner for the Protection of Human Rights, Leo Valladares Lanza. As stated by Kaye, 'As the investigations into the disappeared were undertaken on Valladares' initiative and the CNDH was not created with the specific mandate of reviewing past human rights violations in Honduras, the commissioner's work *does not conform to the traditional truth commission model*. Despite this, the Valladares Report clearly falls within the framework established above for defining what constitutes a truth commission' (emphasis added): Kaye, *supra* note 7, at 700.

Table 1 *continued*

| Country | Name of Commission (English translation) | Commission established by | Year of final report |
|---|---|---|---|
| **Uruguay** | Commission for Peace | President (2000–02) | 2003 |
| **Peru** | Truth and Reconciliation Commission (CVR) | President (2001–03) | 2003 |
| **Chile** | National Commission on Political Imprisonment and Torture (Valech I) | President (2003–05) | 2004, 2005[24] |
| **Paraguay** | Truth and Justice Commission | President (2004–08) | 2008 |
| **Ecuador** | Truth Commission to Impede Impunity | President (2008–10) | 2010 |
| **Brazil** | National Truth Commission (CNV) | President (2012–14) | 2014 |

Sources: Compiled by the author from P.B. Hayner, *Unspeakable Truths: Transitional Justice and the Challenge of Truth Commissions,* 2nd edn, Routledge, London and New York, 2011; monthly bulletins from ICTJ (see http://ictj.org/); and reports published by United States Institute of Peace's Truth Commission Digital Collection (see http://www.usip.org/publications/truth-commission-digital-collection).

The final reports issued by the 13 official, state-sponsored truth commissions spread across 11 Latin American countries differ immensely in scope and detail. The length of their reports varies from around 50 pages for the parliamentary commission in Uruguay to eight large volumes of thousands of pages in the case of the Peruvian truth commission. Availability varies too: some reports can be bought in almost any book store (such as the CONADEP report in Argentina), while others are available only electronically (Peru), or hardly available at all in any format (Panama and Uruguay). The reports were written at different points in historical or 'world' time in response to a variety of different national conflicts, and situated in very different national, sub-regional and international political and legal contexts. Ten of the commissions operated in post-authoritarian contexts, whereas two carried out their work after the end of internal armed conflict (El Salvador and Guatemala) or a mix of the two (Peru). A little more than half of the commissions were set up immediately or soon after the transition to democracy and/or peace. The remaining half (those of Panama, Paraguay and

[24] The report published on 29 November 2004 detailed the results of a six-month investigation. A revised version was released on 1 June 2005. The commission was reopened in February 2010 for 18 months, adding more cases. For more details on the Valech report, see C. Collins, 'Truth-Justice-Reparations Interaction Effects in Transitional Justice Practice: The Case of the "Valech Commission" in Chile' (2017) 49(1) *Journal of Latin American Studies* 55.

Ecuador, plus the second truth commissions in Chile and Uruguay, and that of Brazil) were established a decade or more after the transition to democratic rule. In this sample, only two commissions, both set up as part of UN-sponsored peace processes in El Salvador and Guatemala, invited commissioners from abroad to provide an aura of neutrality in the midst of very tense political settings. The rest consisted of national commission members. Only Haiti's truth commission had a mix of nationals living in Haiti and Haitians from the diaspora. In spite of all these obvious differences, these 13 commissions do not differ all that much in terms of what types of recommendations they made upon completion of their work.[25]

## 4. A THOUSAND RECOMMENDATIONS[26]

The 13 state-sponsored truth commissions have, in their final reports, jointly made roughly one thousand recommendations to their respective governments. These may be divided into eight major categories:

(i) *institutional reform* (such as reform of the courts, the police, the military);
(ii) *legal or administrative reform* (i.e. recommendations to the effect that new laws be created or existing laws be revised);
(iii) *constitutional reform* (i.e. recommendations that call for the constitution to be amended);
(iv) *criminal justice* (i.e. recommendations that call for the prosecution of individuals for past crimes);
(v) *reparations* for victims;
(vi) *non-repetition measures* (i.e. the aim of the truth commission recommendation is to reduce in the future the types of human rights violations that occurred in the past);
(vii) *follow-up measures* (i.e. recommendations urging the government to create a body to monitor/coordinate the implementation of truth commission recommendations and/or further address past human rights violations); and
(viii) *other measures* (i.e. the truth commission recommendation provides some means of addressing past human rights abuses not covered by the other categories).

---

25 E. Skaar, E. Wiebelhaus-Brahm and J. García-Godos, *Beyond Words. Implementing Latin American Truth Commission Recommendations, Vol. I* (forthcoming).

26 This section draws on a draft of Chapter 3, 'Mapping the Universe of Truth Commission Recommendations in Latin America. A Descriptive Analysis', in Skaar, Wiebelhaus-Brahm and García-Godos, *supra* note 25.

Six of the truth commissions have made recommendations in all of these thematic fields (see Table 2).

Note that the categories are not mutually exclusive. For example, non-repetition measures may include legal, institutional and constitutional reform, while non-repetition measures are also considered one component of reparations. Since not all legal or institutional reform measures, nor all reparations, aim at non-repetition, we include non-repetition measures as a separate category of truth commission recommendations.[27] According to Naomi Roht-Arriaza, 'guarantees of non-repetition' is 'the most amorphous' of all tasks included in the international transitional justice soft law framework, which essentially has to do with states' obligations to combat impunity and grant reparations to victims. The basic idea is to prevent a recurrence of the serious human rights violations or international crimes committed in the past. In practice, according to Roht-Arriaza, 'it generally means vetting or restructuring of security forces, and measures to increase the independence and effectiveness of the formal judiciary'. Yet she advocates expanding the realm of 'guarantees of non-repetition' 'to encompass a more transformative non-repetition of the conditions likely to lead to renewed conflict' – including through truth commission recommendations. We follow Roht-Arriaza's broad approach here to include all transitional justice measures that have non-repetition of human rights violations as an explicit or implicit aim – depending on the context in which the violations have taken place.[28]

**Table 2. Thematic focus and number of Latin American truth commission recommendations**

| TC | Total number of TC recommendations | Thematic areas covered by TC recommendations | Thematic areas not covered by TC report's recommendations |
|---|---|---|---|
| Argentina TC (CONADEP) 1984 | 9 | 6 | *Constitutional reform, other* |
| Uruguay TC 1985 | 2 | 1 | *Institutional reform, legal reform, constitutional reform, criminal justice reparations, non-repetition measures, follow-up measures* |

*(continued)*

[27] This is in line with the UN approach, which with the appointment of the UN Special Rapporteur in 2011 has counted 'guarantees of non-recurrence' as a separate element of transitional justice, along with truth, justice and reparations.

[28] For a full discussion of the origins and developments of the term 'guarantee of non-repetition', see N. Roht-Arriaza, 'Measures of Non-Repetition in Transitional Justice: The Missing Link?', UC Hastings Research Paper No. 160, 2016, at 1–42.

Table 2 *continued*

| TC | Total number of TC recommendations | Thematic areas covered by TC recommendations | Thematic areas not covered by TC report's recommendations |
|---|---|---|---|
| Chile TC (Rettig Commission) 1991 | 110 | 6 | *Follow-up measures, other* |
| El Salvador TC 1993 | 43 | 7 | *Criminal justice* |
| Haiti TC (CNVJ) 1996 | 166 | 8 | |
| Guatemala TC 1999 | 87 | 6 | *Constitutional reform, other* |
| Panama TC 2002 | 11 | 7 | *Constitutional reform* |
| Uruguay TC (Peace Commission) 2003 | 10 | 6 | *Constitutional reform, criminal justice* |
| Peru TC (CVR) 2003 | 82 | 8 | |
| Chile TC (Valech I) 2004 | 42 | 7 | *Criminal justice* |
| Paraguay TC 2008 | 202 | 8 | |
| Ecuador TC 2010 | 156 | 8 | |
| Brazil TC (CNV) 2014 | 43 | 7 | *Other* |
| **Total number of TC recommendations** | **1,059** | | |

Source: Compiled by the author from original truth commission reports.

Note: For background material and more detailed analysis, see E. Skaar, E. Wiebelhaus-Brahm, and J. García-Godos, *Beyond Words. Implementing Latin American Truth Commission Recommendations, Vol. I* (forthcoming).

As Table 2 shows, the number of recommendations ranges from two for Uruguay's first truth commission to 202 for Paraguay's truth commission. However, regardless of whether a truth commission has made only few or many recommendations, all truth commissions – with the exception of the two Uruguayan truth commissions – have made recommendations in six or more of the thematic areas listed above. Ongoing research shows some interesting findings with respect to the distribution of recommendations across these thematic areas. By far the three largest categories of truth commission recommendations are non-repetition, institutional reform and legal reform. If we add constitutional reform to this list, around 75 per cent of all recommendations are what we may call systemic: that is, recommendations aimed at reforming state institutions, laws or constitutions – thereby contributing to non-repetition of human rights violations. Reparations make up around 14 per cent of the total number of recommendations, whereas follow-up measures, calls for criminal prosecutions and constitutional reform constitute less than five per cent each of the total share of truth commission recommendations. Finally, the 'other' category lumps together the truth commission recommendations that do not fit any of the other seven categories, adding up to around two per cent of the total share of truth commission recommendations. The next section presents some preliminary findings of the implementation record of these different types of recommendation.

## 5. IMPLEMENTATION ACROSS LATIN AMERICA

Skaar, Wiebelhaus-Brahm and García-Godos, in their analysis of the implementation record of the entire universe of around 1,000 recommendations across 13 truth commission reports, have made some interesting – albeit tentative – findings. To assess the level of implementation, they draw on a combination of primary and secondary sources, such as government documents, newspaper articles and interviews with former truth commission members, academics, government officials and representatives from the NGO sectors. It is necessary to stress that the data is uneven across the 13 truth commission cases.[29] Missing information could mean two things: either that the recommendation in question has not been implemented – in which case the overall implementation rate will be *lower* than their findings suggest – or that the recommendation in question has in fact been implemented, but has gone under the radar of the data-collecting teams – which would mean that the implementation rate is actually *higher* than their data suggests. If the latter is true, it possibly means that the reform or other type of recommendation has not substantially changed behaviour or beliefs, and thus is not more visible. Another caveat is that implementation is an ongoing activity, so assessing implementation is a moving target. Certain recommendations could therefore have been implemented after the data collection for the project ended in mid-2017 – in which case, implementation rates would be higher than the data suggests.

---

[29] Data is particularly thin in the case of Paraguay, which also had the highest number of recommendations of all the truth commission reports. See F. Reátegui and T. Gómez, 'Paraguay's Truth and Justice Commission: Recommending justice without political change', in Skaar, García-Godos and Wiebelhaus-Brahm (eds.), *supra* note 2.

Keeping these caveats in mind, the preliminary findings from this comparative project show that the average implementation rate for the different types of recommendation runs between 20 and 40 per cent. The preliminary findings of Skaar, Wiebelhaus-Brahm and García-Godos further suggest that among the most commonly implemented types of recommendation across the 13 truth commission are the following: the establishment of a follow-up body or a human rights institution, either as an independent body or within the judiciary; symbolic and material reparations to victims and their families; memorialisation; search for the disappeared; and human rights education.[30] Common to all these measures is that they are things that civil society is likely to pay the most attention to. This may lend some support to the claim that missing data might undercount implementation rates.

By contrast, the least commonly implemented types of recommendation seem to be system-oriented recommendations, particularly ones dealing with institutional reform, legal reform and constitutional reform. There are big variations in the implementation rates of different kinds of non-repetition measures, which frequently overlap with other types of recommendation.

One of the most commonly implemented types of recommendation is the establishment of a follow-up body to oversee the general implementation of recommendations. All of the truth commission reports – with the exception of the report issued by Uruguay's 1985 truth commission – recommended that such a body be set up, either as a human rights institution located within the Ministry of Justice or as an independent body like the National Institute of Human Rights in Chile recommended by the Valech Commission or the Follow-up Secretariat recommended by the Comisión para la Paz in Uruguay.[31] Although governments have generally been both willing and able to set up these follow-up bodies, they vary a lot with respect to how successful or effective they have been in terms of overseeing the implementation of all the other recommendations made by the truth commission (in some cases more than one hundred).[32]

Offering material or symbolic reparations to victims also seems to be a general government priority after the end of political conflict and atrocities in many countries. This is quite likely because governments in most countries have been under considerable pressure from victim organisations, as well as from

30 Skaar, Wiebelhaus-Brahm and García-Godos, *supra* note 25.

31 S. Hourcade, F. Ghelfi, L.P. Zaldua and M. Perelman, 'Chile's Rettig and Valech Commissions: When recommendations become state policy', and F. Ghelfi, S. Hourcade, L.P. Zaldua and M. Perelman, 'Uruguay's Commission for Peace: An unfulfilled experience?', both in Skaar, García-Godos and Wiebelhaus-Brahm (eds.), *supra* note 2.

32 Skaar, Wiebelhaus-Brahm and García-Godos, *supra* note 25.

civil society in general, to address the needs of the victims. Offering material reparations is only possible where there are sufficient resources and where there is a minimum of political agreement on who should qualify as victims eligible to receive reparations. Countries like Argentina, Chile, Brazil, Peru and Guatemala have prioritised material reparations to victims, in the areas of health, housing, education and pensions. Some countries, such as Chile and Peru, have established extensive national reparation programmes. Peru and Guatemala have opted for collective reparations in addition to individual reparations. Half-hearted attempts have been made in Haiti to secure material reparations for victims.[33] In Panama, symbolic and material reparations have been partially implemented.[34] No reparations have been paid by the government in El Salvador in the 25 years that has lapsed since the Commission on the Truth for El Salvador made recommendations for reparations in its report.[35]

With respect to symbolic reparations, public apologies have been made by the presidents of Chile, Argentina, Uruguay and Ecuador, but not in El Salvador and Guatemala. Interestingly, though, the military in Guatemala has apologised for its involvement in extensive human rights violations – whereas the Brazilian armed forces have not. Another type of symbolic reparation that some (i.e. Guatemala and Chile), though not all (i.e. Panama), governments seem quite happy to comply with is to establish a national day of commemoration of victims of human rights abuses.[36]

In general, though, many of the countries analysed here have seen a trend towards memorialisation projects, especially over the last decade or so, and particularly in the Southern Cone plus Peru and Guatemala.[37] Memorials are often considered to have elements of both reparation and non-repetition. That is, they are established primarily to commemorate the victims, but through spreading information and knowledge of atrocities, they are also meant to prevent such violations from happening again. Typical commemoration activities include the naming of parks and streets after victims, while the establishment of collective memory cites (like specific graveyards) has been particularly

33 L.-M.M. Selvik, 'Haiti's Truth and Justice Commission: Forgotten recommendations, living demands', in Skaar, García-Godos and Wiebelhaus-Brahm (eds.), *supra* note 2.

34 A. Rudling, 'Panama's Truth Commission: Recommendations – out of sight, out of mind?', in Skaar, García-Godos and Wiebelhaus-Brahm (eds.), *supra* note 2.

35 E. Martínez-Barahona, S. Rubio-Padilla, H. Centeno-Martín and M. Gutiérrez-Salazar, 'El Salvador's Truth Commission: Recommending peace in exchange for justice', in Skaar, García-Godos and Wiebelhaus-Brahm (eds.), *supra* note 2.

36 Skaar, Wiebelhaus-Brahm and García-Godos, *supra* note 25.

37 For central works on the Southern Cone, see C. Collins, K. Hite and A. Joignant, *The politics of memory in Chile: From Pinochet to Bachelet*, Lynne Rienner Publishers, Boulder CO, 2013; K. Hite, *Politics and the Art of Commemoration*, Routledge, London and New York, 2013; F. Lessa and V. Druliolle (eds.), *The Memory of State Terrorism in the Southern Cone: Argentina, Chile, and Uruguay*, Palgrave Macmillan, New York, 2011.

important in multicultural societies where indigenous people have suffered disproportionately from human rights violations (Guatemala and Peru). Specific memory sites – such as the Museo de la Memoria (Memory Museum) in Santiago, Chile, or the Lugar de la Memoria, la Tolerancia y la Inclusion Social (Site of Memory, Tolerance and Social Inclusion) in Lima, Peru – have been established by the governments on the direct recommendation of truth commissions.[38] In other countries, where both state-initiated and victim-initiated memorials have flourished, the causal connections between the establishment of the actual memorial and a concrete recommendation in the truth commission report may be less clear. Finally, there are some countries, like Haiti, where no initiatives have been implemented to create memorials. By contrast, non-repetition measures have been taken seriously by the Haitian government: two thirds of the recommended measures (10 out of 15) have been fully implemented.

Several truth commission reports have recommended investigations into the detained-disappeared – as part of complying with the right to truth.[39] Investigations and opening of individual and mass graves to identify victims and return the bodies to the families have taken place in Chile, Argentina, Uruguay and Peru, but not in Guatemala. The search for children who have disappeared has had high priority in Argentina and Uruguay. By contrast, the Guatemalan government has failed to comply with the specific recommendation made by its truth commission report to investigate the disappearance of children, in spite of the fact that the country has the highest number of disappearances and killings (estimated at around 200,000 people). Of all the cases examined here, many of the victims were indigenous, and many were women and children.[40]

Another type of recommendation with a relatively high implementation rate has been human rights education, frequently considered to be part of non-repetition measures.[41] In addition to many truth commission reports

---

38 S. Hourcade, F. Ghelfi, L.P. Zaldua and M. Perelman, 'Chile's Rettig and Valech Commissions: When recommendations become state policy', and F. Reátegui and D. Uchuypoma, 'Peru's Truth and Reconciliation Commission: Recommending a piecemeal approach to transitional justice', both in Skaar, García-Godos and Wiebelhaus-Brahm (eds.), *supra* note 2.

39 Skaar, Wiebelhaus-Brahm and García-Godos, *supra* note 25.

40 H.C. Martín, 'Guatemala's Commission of Historical Clarification: The memory of silence or the silence of memory?', in Skaar, García-Godos and Wiebelhaus-Brahm (eds.), *supra* note 2.

41 Skaar, Wiebelhaus-Brahm and García-Godos, *supra* note 25. Note that the authors take a narrow view on education. In an explorative analysis of the various connections between truth commissions and education in 20 truth commissions worldwide (including nine of the truth commissions analysed in this chapter), Julia Paulson and Michelle J. Bellino in a recent article argue that truth commissions tend to recommend forward-looking reforms in the

recommending the publication and dissemination of the reports themselves, they also frequently recommend educating the public, or specific sectors, in the subject of human rights. In response to these recommendations, many governments have put in place human rights education for various groups, such as judges, the police, primary school children, university graduates, teachers, the general public, etc. Even countries like El Salvador, which has been very reluctant to implement any kind of systemic reforms of its institutions, has introduced human rights education as part of the curriculum for its armed forces.[42]

However, the picture of implementation is not all rosy. Less commonly implemented recommendations typically include those belonging to the large category of system-oriented or systemic recommendations, which make up almost three quarters of the total number of recommendations across all truth commission reports. There are, however, some positive developments: for instance, recommendations to ratify international human rights conventions and treaties, and to incorporate international human rights law into national legislation, seem to be given high priority by many governments. Legal reforms of this nature have been successfully implemented in countries like Argentina, Chile, Uruguay, Peru, El Salvador and Guatemala, and have been partially implemented in Haiti, but are hard to assess in the case of Panama. However, the question is whether this was done as a direct follow-up to the recommendations of the truth commissions, or whether we should interpret these legal changes as part of a larger picture of judicial reform taking place across Latin America in the 1990s and early 2000s.[43] Alternatively, and even more basically, it could be seen as the efforts of fragile new governments to curry favour with the international community.

While pushing through a new law normally requires simple majority in congress, constitutional amendments require a two-thirds majority and therefore more political consensus. Nevertheless, a small number of constitutional reforms have been successfully implemented, for instance in Guatemala and Haiti, in response to truth commission recommendations. Recommendations that target reforming the judiciary (especially supreme courts) or the military

area of education: J. Paulson and M.J. Bellino, 'Truth commissions, education, and positive peace: an analysis of truth commission final reports (1980–2015)' (2017) 53(3) *Comparative Education* 351.

42 Martínez-Barahona, Rubio-Padilla, Centeno-Martín and Gutiérrez-Salazar, *supra* note 35.

43 F. Agüero and J. Stark (eds.), *Fault Lines of Democracy in Post-Transitional Latin America*, North-South Center Press of the University of Miami, Miami, 1998; E.J. Buscaglia, M. Dakolias and W. Ratliff, *Judicial Reform in Latin America: A Framework for National Development*, Stanford University Press, Stanford, 1995; P. Domingo and R. Sieder, 'Rule of Law in Latin America: The International Promotion of Judicial Reform' (2001) 45(1) *Latin American Politics and Society* 153.

seem to be implemented less often. However, there are significant variations in recommendation implementation from country to country.

Implementation of truth commission recommendations is likely to be influenced by a number of factors, including: public awareness of the truth commission report and its recommendations; the legitimacy of the commission; the relative power of pro- and anti-commission sentiment; political will to implement the recommendations; sufficient resources; other reform trends in the Latin American region; and international factors.[44] The balance of forces between the 'drivers of justice' and 'the spoilers of justice' has rightly been stressed in the literature on transitional justice mechanisms in general, and is highly relevant as a contextual explanation for implementation – or the lack thereof.[45] A key issue is *who* will be affected by the recommendations and what power they have to promote or obstruct implementation. To illustrate this point, the Supreme Court in El Salvador, which was heavily criticised in the truth commission report for having done little to hinder or combat the rampant human rights violations taking place during the 12 years of civil war, was totally opposed to implementing any of the various reforms targeted at the judiciary in general and the Supreme Court in particular.[46]

Finally, the international community may play a role in pushing for implementation. We see this most clearly in the case of Haiti. A country in economic and institutional shambles, struck by one catastrophe after the other (massive earthquake, cholera epidemic), Haiti has been almost completely reliant on the UN and international donors in implementing the recommendations made by the truth commission.[47] In the case of Panama, it seems clear that wherever there has been implementation, however partial, the Inter-American Court of Human Rights and the Inter-American Commission on Human Rights have functioned as supporting actors.[48] However, it is important to highlight that the presence of international actors is no guarantee of implementation, as it is ultimately up to the national government to prioritise (and normally fund) the implementation of various reforms and activities. For instance, the UN was involved in the peace processes and the establishment of truth commissions in both El Salvador and Guatemala. Yet the implementation record of truth commission recommendations is much poorer in El Salvador than in Guatemala – principally due to the active reluctance of the government(s)

44 Skaar, Wiebelhaus-Brahm and García-Godos, *supra* note 25.

45 E. Skaar and E. Wiebelhaus-Brahm, 'Drivers of Justice after Violent Conflict: An Introduction' (2013) 31(2) *Nordic Journal of Human Rights* 119.

46 Martínez-Barahona, Rubio-Padilla, Centeno-Martín and Gutiérrez-Salazar, *supra* note 35.

47 Selvik, *supra* note 33.

48 Rudling, *supra* note 34.

in the former to comply with the truth commission report, especially where the spoilers were affected by the recommendations.

Where the national government accepts and endorses the truth commission report, is sympathetic to the recommendations made in the report, and has sufficient resources to carry out the recommendations, the implementation rate is higher. The Southern Cone countries – which have had relatively strong institutions and strong economies compared to those of the Andes, Central America or the Caribbean – generally tend to have done a better job overall of implementing the recommendations made by their truth commissions.[49]

## 6. CONCLUSION

Some of the main advantages of truth commissions identified by Jeremy Sarkin and Tetevi Davi include: their potential, through information-gathering, to illuminate the full range of abuses committed during a violent conflict or by an oppressive regime; their investigations being established in a state-sanctioned way, thus lending the findings legitimacy; the reports constituting common and authoritative narrative; and the ability of truth commissions to identify reparations for victims.[50] Following up on the last point, this chapter has provided an argument for why it is timely to shift focus from the operations of a truth commission to what happens in the wake of the submission of its final report if we wish to gain a deeper understanding of the potential contributions and long-term impact and legacies of truth commissions.

One of the most important insights from the research presented in this chapter is that a very important legacy of truth commissions is their recommendations, for the following reasons. First, truth commission recommendations may lead to the creation of something new and permanent beyond the operation of the truth commission, such as institutions set up to ensure human rights protection or museums to commemorate victims and their families. Second, truth commissions may give the impetus to, or provide support for, processes of institutional or legal reform. Third, recommendations may serve as catalysts for kick-starting larger societal processes of healing and reconciliation – especially recommendations that deal with memory or human rights education. The recommendations are hence part of the afterlife of truth commissions and, *if implemented*, may gain importance way beyond the operations of the truth commission and the publishing of its final report.

---

49 Skaar, Wiebelhaus-Brahm and García-Godos, *supra* note 25.

50 J. Sarkin and T. Davi, 'Examining the Criticism Levelled Against Transitional Justice: Towards an Understanding of the State of the Field' (2017) 11(1) *Human Rights & International Legal Discourse* 7, at 21–22.

There are hence strong reasons to argue that through the implementation of their different kinds of recommendations, truth commissions can contribute to positively changing social norms and practices, and hence mitigate the repetition of human rights abuses.

Another central finding of this chapter is that we need to apply a long-term perspective when analysing or assessing the long-term impact – or legacies – of truth commissions. In a way, this is the opposite argument that is used in relation to the actual operation of truth commissions, where 'experience has shown that *some* limits on the work of TCs are necessary, and even desirable, in order to prevent overly broad and grossly protracted enquires'.[51] Based on detailed empirical analysis, this chapter has demonstrated that it may take decades, even generations, for implementation of truth commission recommendations to take place. Returning briefly to Argentina's CONADEP, the first Latin American truth commission to publish a full report back in 1985: all of its eight recommendations have been implemented, albeit by different governments and over a long period of time. In fact, criminal prosecutions of political crimes committed during the military dictatorship in the 1970s are still ongoing in Argentine courtrooms today.[52] As the Argentina case further clearly illustrates, when assessing implementation one also needs to take into account that this is a non-linear, fluid process; there may be advances and setbacks over time. This should give hope to the truth commissions with poor implementation records, such as that of El Salvador.

Evidence from the 13 truth commissions analysed in this chapter shows that, at least in the Latin American region, the implementation record of truth commissions is far from poor or non-existent. Although uneven across different types of recommendations and across different countries, there has been a general tendency for both national governments and international actors to try to deal with the recommendations made by truth commissions. Impact has not been the explicit focus of this chapter, yet we can safely say that the implementation of a recommendation is a necessary first step for that particular recommendation to have any impact at all.

In conclusion, one of the global legacies of truth commissions may very well be what happens *after* they have completed their work – if their recommendations are successfully implemented. The legacy of truth commission recommendations is obviously most important at the national level. However, it

51 Ibid, at 20.

52 F. Lessa, 'Operation Condor on trial: Justice for transnational human rights crimes in South America' (2015) 9(3) *International Journal of Transitional Justice* 494–506. See also an up-to-date version: F. Lessa, 'Operation Condor on trial: Justice for transnational human rights crimes in South America' (2018), https://www.cambridge.org/core/journals/journal-of-latin-american-studies/article/operation-condor-on-trial-justice-for-transnational-human-rights-crimes-in-south-america/C2A765BAB0E45A1260053E1E8DC0AE82.

can certainly be argued that the expectations voiced through truth commission final reports and recommendations are part of what inspire the establishment of new truth commissions – both in Latin America and in other parts of the world.

## APPENDIX: LATIN AMERICAN TRUTH COMMISSION REPORTS

*Argentina, 1984*
Comisión Nacional Sobre la Desaparición de Personas (CONADEP)
Report: *Informe de la Comisión Nacional Sobre la Desaparición de Personas*

*Uruguay, 1985*
Comisión Investigadora Parlamentaria Sobre la Situación de Personas Desaparecidas y Hechos que la Motivaron
Report: *Informe Final de la Comisión Investigadora Parlamentaria Sobre Situación de Personas Desaparecidas y Hechos que la Motivaron*

*Chile, 1991*
Comisión Nacional de Verdad y Reconciliación (Rettig Commission)
Report: *Informe de la Comisión Nacional de Verdad y Reconciliación* (Informe Rettig), Vols. 1–3

*El Salvador, 1993*
Comisión de la Verdad Para El Salvador (CVES)
Report: *De la locura a la esperanca. La guerra de 12 años en El Salvador*

*Haiti, 1996*
Commission Nationale de Vérité et de Justice (CNVJ)
Report: *Si m pa rele: 29 September 1991 – 14 Octobre 1994*

*Guatemala, 1999*
Comisión Para el Esclarecimiento Histórico (CEH)
Report: *Guatemala: Memoria del Silencio*

*Panama, 2002*
Comisión de la Verdad de Panamá
Report: *Informe Final de la Comisión de la Verdad. 'La verdad os hará libres'*

*Peru, 2003*
Comisión de la Verdad y Reconciliación
Report: *Informe Final de la Comisión de la Verdad y Reconciliación* (abbreviated version: *Hatun Willakuy*)

*Uruguay, 2003*
Comisión Para la Paz (COMIPAZ/ComiPaz)
Report: *Informe Final de la Comisión para la Paz*

*Chile, 2004*
Comisión Nacional Sobre Prisión Politica y Tortura (Valech Commission)
Report: *Informe de la Comisión Nacional sobre Prisión Politica y Tortura* (Informe Valech)

*Paraguay, 2008*
Comisión Verdad y Justicia (CVJ)
Report: *Informe Final. Anive haguâ oiko*

*Ecuador, 2010*
Comisión de la Verdad Para Impedir la Impunidad
Report: *Informe de la Comisión de la Verdad Ecuador 2010: Sin verdad no hay justicia*

*Brazil, 2014*
Comissão Nacional da Verdade (CNV)
Report: *Relatório da Comissão Nacional da Verdade, Vols. I–III*

# IN THE AFTERMATH OF TRUTH

## Implementing Truth Commissions' Recommendations on Reparations – Following Through for Victims

Luke Moffett*



## 1. INTRODUCTION

Transitional justice emerged after the Second World War as a set of discrete measures, such as trials, truth commissions or reparations, to address the atrocities of a past regime and to transition societies away from the recurrence of atrocities.[1] Since the 1990s there has been an increasing emphasis on the need for multifaceted, comprehensive transitional justice measures to effectively deal with impunity and the consequences of mass violence.[2] It is no longer considered effective to pigeonhole discrete transitional justice mechanisms. Instead there is increasing discussion of a comprehensive package of measures that complement each other. Each of the areas of transitional justice – truth,

* Thanks to Adriana Rudling for the research assistance and helpful comments from Brianne McGonigle-Leyh, Eric Wiebelhaus-Brahm, Jeremy Sarkin and the anonymous reviewers. This chapter draws from research collected from the UK Arts and Humanities Research Council funded project 'Reparations, Responsibility and Victimhood in Transitional Societies' (AH/P006965/1), https://reparations.qub.ac.uk/.

1 R. Teitel, 'Transitional Justice Genealogy' (2003) 16(1) *Harvard Human Rights Journal* 69.

2 D. Orentlicher, *Independent study on best practices, including recommendations, to assist states in strengthening their domestic capacity to combat all aspects of impunity*, E/CN.4/2004/88 (27 February 2004), at para. 10.

justice, reparations, amnesties, guarantees of non-recurrence and, to a certain extent, demobilisation, disarmament and reintegration (DDR) – have their own particular focus, benefits and limitations. Although such measures can be complementary, there can also be overlap and tension between them, such as when trying to carry out prosecutions while at the same time seeking to secure truth, which requires careful crafting of social, political, economic and legal factors to avoid derailing the transition itself.

Given that the focus of this chapter is on truth commissions and reparations, it will mainly address the connection between these two measures.[3] Truth commissions and reparations, to a certain extent, have a symbiotic relationship through which they can complement and reinforce one another's goals in acknowledging the atrocities of the past, building social inclusion and trying to vindicate victims' suffering.[4] The first part of this chapter explores the bond between these two mechanisms, drawing upon different examples of how recommendations for reparations are constructed by truth commissions and their justification. The second part of this chapter analyses the implementation of reparation recommendations, finding that in most cases states fail to follow through, or only do so where they are forced by civil society through legal and political pressure. The third part of this chapter briefly discusses transitional societies where reparations are made without a truth commission and their impact on the transition, before reaching a conclusion. As such, it is more likely than not that truth commissions can facilitate the implementation of reparations. That said, transitional societies are complex and fragile, and cannot be easily socially engineered; the past is often still contested and fought through political and legal forums. Truth commissions can at least assuage these contests by shaking society awake to the atrocities of the past and morally motivating them to alleviate the consequences of those victims left to bear the burden of the past.

## 2. THE BOND BETWEEN REPARATIONS AND TRUTH COMMISSIONS

Reparations are intended to acknowledge and alleviate the suffering of victims. Truth commissions are established to recognise 'victims as rights holders, foster … civic trust, and contribute … to strengthening the rule of law.'[5]

---

3 That said, there is emerging practice of reparations being connected to trials for international crimes, as well as with amnesties (such as with the Kenyan TJRC Act, Article 41), but this latter connection is often associated with impunity and reparations being perceived as 'blood money'; see C. Moon, '"Who'll Pay Reparations on My Soul?" Compensation, Social Control and Social Suffering' (2012) 21(2) *Social & Legal Studies* 187.

4 Orentlicher, *supra* note 2, para. 59.

5 P. De Greiff, *Report of the Special Rapporteur on the promotion of truth, justice, reparation and guarantees of non-recurrence*, UN Doc. A/HRC/24/42 (28 August 2013), at para. 24.

There is some conceptual overlap between the two, with truth recovery seen as an important part of the measures of satisfaction in publicising victims' experience, vindicating the wrongfulness of their suffering and identifying the institutions and actors responsible.[6] There may be challenges in the implementation of reparations where truth commissions are broadly construed to include a range of historic victims. Truth commissions can catalyse societies' attention to victims' suffering and ongoing destitution, which in turn builds 'political and public support for the government to respond positively.'[7] At the other end of the spectrum, reparations cannot deliver the wider social and public conversation and confrontation with the past that a truth commission can catalyse. As Verdeja finds, reparations 'can only assist, not generate or sustain, a critical reappraisal of the past'.[8] Accordingly, reparations and truth commissions can complement each other. A truth commission can be crucial for, 'even if implicitly, acknowledging some form of collective responsibility towards the victims.'[9] Furthermore, reparations can be a substantive way to cement the work of a commission in alleviating the consequences of suffering for those most directly affected: the victims.

Truth commissions often make recommendations for reparations, which have now become a 'staple' of such commissions.[10] Freeman and Wiebelhaus-Brahm both in part define truth commissions by their ability to make recommendations on redress for victims.[11] Some peace agreements and legislation establishing truth commissions can specifically provide for reparations to be part of the commission's mandate. Others can be more ambiguous, such as the Sierra Leone Truth and Reconciliation Commission Act, which provides that its object is 'to address impunity, to respond to the needs of the victims, to promote healing and reconciliation and to prevent a repetition of the violations and abuses suffered.'[12] The Democratic Republic of Congo truth commission had the power to arrange settlements for compensation and restitution, or traditional forms of reconciliation between victimised communities and perpetrators, but

---

6 M. Lawry-White, 'The Reparative Effect of Truth Seeking in Transitional Justice' (2015) 64(1) *International and Comparative Law Quarterly* 141, at 145.

7 P.B. Hayner, *Unspeakable Truths: Transitional Justice and the Challenge of Truth Commissions*, Routledge, London and New York, 2010, at 163.

8 E. Verdeja, 'A Normative Theory of Reparations in Transitional Democracies' (2006) 37(3–4) *Metaphilosophy* 449, at 460.

9 R. Dudai, '"Rescues for Humanity": Rescuers, Mass Atrocities, and Transitional Justice' (2012) 34(1) *Human Rights Quarterly* 1, at 27.

10 De Greiff, *supra* note 5, at para. 43.

11 M. Freeman, *Truth Commissions and Procedural Fairness*, Cambridge University Press, Cambridge, 2006, at 18; and E. Wiebelhaus-Brahm, *Truth Commissions and Transitional Societies: The Impact on Human Rights and Democracy*, Routledge, London and New York, 2010, at 4. In contrast Hayner does not include recommendations for reparations as part of their definition: Hayner, *supra* note 7, at 12.

12 Article 6(1), Truth and Reconciliation Commission Act 2000.

it was never operationalised.[13] Divergences exist in the scope and complexity of reparations being proposed, from simply suggesting compensation or vague measures of reconciliation,[14] to a range of monetary and symbolic measures directed at different types of victims.

For instance, the Kenyan Truth, Justice and Reconciliation Commission (TJRC) categorised and prioritised victims, so as to concentrate resources on those most vulnerable.[15] The Commission organised victims of gross violations of human rights into the following categories: (1) violations of the right to life; (2) violations of the right to personal integrity, including sexual or gender-based violence; (3) forcible transfer of populations; (4) historical and contemporary land injustices; and (5) systematic marginalisation. The TJRC prioritised victims in categories 1 and 2 as those most vulnerable under the heading of Priority A.[16] The victims in this group would be eligible for monetary compensation via a 10-year annual pension, as well as medical and psychological vouchers for rehabilitation. Under the TJRC's reparation recommendations, all victims in the five categories are entitled to collective reparations, with other victims in Priority B only able to claim collective reparations. These collective reparations are to address the 'policies and practices that negatively impacted entire groups of people',[17] and include measures such as apologies, memorials and land restitution.[18] The purpose of these collective reparations is to recognise victims' experiences, acknowledge the state's responsibility, restore their dignity and ensure non-recurrence.[19] Despite being well thought out and innovative, none of these measures were ever implemented.

Reparations can also be justified to promote reconciliation, reflecting a dual political and transactional role: to recognise victims' suffering, to affirm their rights as citizens through social inclusion and to rebuild trust in state institutions, while at the same time aiming to minimise perceptions that combatants or perpetrators are benefiting from the peace more than victims.[20] The Peruvian Truth and Reconciliation Commission (CVR) justified reparation as 'a gesture and an action that recognizes and reaffirms the dignity and status of people.

13 Articles 41 and 42, loi n°/04/018 du 30 juillet 2004 portant organisation, attributions et fonctionnement de la Commission Verite et Reconciliation; and Hayner, *supra* note 7, at 253.

14 See Argentina – (CONADEP) *Nunca Mas: Informe de la Comisión Nacional sobre la Desaparición de Personas'* (Buenos Aires: EUDEBA, 1984).

15 The Truth, Justice, and Reconciliation Commission of Kenya, Report, Volume IV, (2013), at 97–122.

16 This included those in category 3 who had died as a result of displacement.

17 Kenyan TRJC Report, *supra* note 15, Volume IV, at 107.

18 Ibid, at 108.

19 Ibid, at 114.

20 Sierra Leone TRC Report, Chapter 7, at paras. 10–11; *Chega!* Timor Leste Commission for Reception, Truth and Reconciliation (CAVR), 2005, Part 11, at 36. See P. Hazan, 'Measuring the impact of punishment and forgiveness: a framework for evaluating transitional justice' (2006) 88(861) *International Review of the Red Cross* 19, at 44.

Reparations coming from the State is an expression of due respect to their status as citizens.'[21] Timor-Leste prioritised the issue of reparations for victims from the wider impact on Timorese societies as '[a]ll East Timorese people have been touched and victimised by the conflict in one way or another. … We are all victims but not all victims are equal. We must acknowledge this reality and lend a hand to those who are most vulnerable.'[22] It went on to distinguish reparations as:

> [a] form of justice is delivered which directly benefits the victim and will contribute to healing, national reconciliation and a further reduction in the possibility of violence. The most vulnerable victims of past atrocities will be afforded recognition and the means to enjoy their fundamental rights and fulfil their potential on an equal footing with other citizens of Timor-Leste.[23]

The Sierra Leone Truth and Reconciliation Commission (TRC) conceptualised reparations as forming part of a 'restorative system of justice' that also includes 'accountability, truth telling, [and] acknowledgement'.[24] Moreover, the implementation of reparations would be 'vital to the reconciliation process because it has the potential to assist those victims whose lives have been most devastated' and to help 'to facilitate relations between victims and perpetrators'.[25] The Kenyan TJRC Act defines reparation as 'means dignifying the victims by measures that will alleviate their suffering, compensate their social, moral and material losses, restitute their rights'.[26] The Argentinean CONADEP framed reparations along the lines of truth that '[t]he first indispensable reparation demanded by society after fundamental institutions had been restored was to ascertain the truth of what had happened, to "face up" to the immediate past and let the country judge.'[27] Its recommendations with regard to reparations were quite general, including that:

> appropriate laws be passed to provide the children and/or relatives of the disappeared with economic assistance, study grants, social security and employment and, at the same time, to authorize measures considered necessary to alleviate the many and varied family and social problems caused by the disappearances.[28]

---

21 Informe Final – Comisión de la Verdad y Reconciliación, (CVR) (2003), Volume 9, at 141.

22 Timor-Leste CAVR Report, *supra* note 20, at 35.

23 Ibid, at 36.

24 Sierra Leone TRC Report, *supra* note 20, Volume 3(B), Chapter 7, at para. 8.

25 Ibid, at para. 9.

26 Article 2(1), Truth, Justice and Reconciliation Commission Act No. 6 of 2008.

27 *Nunca Más (Never Again): A Report by Argentina's National Commission on Disappeared People*, Faber & Faber, London, 1986, at Part IV.

28 Ibid, at Part VI, Recommendation C; along with guarantees of non-repetition such as human rights training for the military, strengthen investigations of human rights violations and the adherence to such rights.

Reparations are not only recommended by official truth commissions, but also by 'unofficial'[29] truth recovery initiatives by civil society in the face of state impassivity. In Sierra Leone, before the war, chiefs played an important role in the community in mediating disputes through compensation between the aggrieved party and the wrongdoer, which became a source of grievance when it was used for extortion. As a result, the community truth initiative of *Fambul Tok* does not use compensation in its reconciliation committee meetings between victims and perpetrators.[30] In Zimbabwe, the *Breaking the Silence* report did not recommend compensation, but instead the recovery of the remains of those disappeared, and symbolic shrines to those disappeared to publicise in social memory of clandestine disappearances, to remedy the harm caused.[31] Importantly, the report noted that while there was a War Victims Compensation Act that would need to be amended, providing compensation to each individual victim would be impossible as too much time had lapsed, most of the evidence of abuses had been destroyed, and the sheer scale of violations would leave the state paying out hundreds of millions of dollars.[32]

In Guatemala, the *Recuperación de la Memoria Historia* (REMHI) report recommendations were aimed at a range of actors, including the guerrillas, the Church and the international community. It recommended reparations on the basis that 'the state has the obligation to adopt measures that help compensate some of these losses and that those groups who were affected by the violence can live with dignity.'[33] It recommended 'economic reparations or development projects, grants and study programmes, commemorations and monuments, and psychosocial projects for the victims and survivors.' These were similar to the official CEH commission recommendations.[34] Isaacs notes that the official and unofficial commission failed to make their recommendations 'stick', as acknowledging genocide was continually debated in formulating the reparations programme.[35] Other unofficial truth commissions – such as the Brazilian *Nunca*

29 De Greiff, *supra* note 5, at para. 21.

30 Fambul Tok International, *Community Healing in Sierra Leone, and the World – Our Second Year*, 2010, at 23.

31 Catholic Commission for Justice and Peace in Zimbabwe and Legal Resources Foundation, *Breaking the Silence: Building True Peace. A Report on the Disturbances in Matabeleland and the Midlands 1980 to 1988*, 1997, at 205 and 211–212. The report also recommended psychological rehabilitation for affected communities and human rights violators as well as community development.

32 Ibid, at 212.

33 Recovery of Historical Memory (REMHI), Oficina de Derechos Humanos del Arzobispado de Guatemala, (1998), Volume IV.

34 *Guatemala: Memory of Silence. Report of the Guatemalan Commission for Historical Clarification. Conclusions and Recommendations*, 1999, at 49–54.

35 A. Isaacs, 'Truth and the Challenge of Reconciliation in Guatemala', in J. Quinn (ed.), *Reconciliation(s): Transitional Justice in Postconflict Societies*, McGill-Queen's University Press, Montreal, 2009, at 140.

*Mais* report, SERPAJ and Ardoyne – are more concerned with documenting and mapping out human rights violations than making recommendations. Reparations require substantial financial commitment, which unofficial truth commissions would struggle to mobilise and administer. Even if unofficial truth commissions could somehow gather sufficient resources for reparations, they would be missing an important component of the official acknowledgement of the victims' harm, and might risk being seen as charity rather than vindication of victims' rights and social inclusion.[36] Nonetheless, Bickford suggests that unofficial truth commissions can stimulate debate and dialogue around the importance of reparations, as the REMHI did in Guatemala.[37] This is particularly apparent where communities and society have a close connection, trust and respect for non-state actors carrying out such investigations and producing such reports, in contrast to the state.

It is clear from these examples that recommendations and justifications for reparations by truth commissions are varied in their scope and detail. Across the globe there remain close natural connections between uncovering the truth and remedying individuals' harm. That said, each context has its own idiosyncrasies that must be taken into account. These can include cultural or religious dimensions to dealing with the past (such as *ubuntu* in the South African TRC), traditional or indigenous practices (as in Peru and Timor Leste), or existing reparations programmes (e.g. Sri Lanka). Given the numerous variables in a society, transitional justice is not an exact science to simply apply to each data set that will ensure consistency in results. However, there may be merit in the field of transitional justice outlining principles and standards of measures such as reparations, so as to give them increased legitimacy when they are domestically recommended by truth commissions. Human rights bodies have been important in this regard, in particular for reparations.[38] As such, the causality between truth commissions and reparations is not examined here in a quantitative way, but rather via more mid-range theorising, drawn from qualitative research.[39]

At best we can make broad suggestions that having a truth commission can at least open up public debate and awareness of victims' harm, thus giving impetus to establish reparations programmes to alleviate victims' suffering, or can provide a basis for national and international civil and criminal litigation for reparations. Official and unofficial truth commissions make similar assumptions that reparations are connected or at least part of a continuum of necessary

---

36 L. Bickford, 'Unofficial Truth Projects' (2007) 29(4) *Human Rights Quarterly* 994, at 996.

37 Ibid, at 1031.

38 See C. Sandoval, 'Two steps forward, one step back: Reflections on the jurisprudential turn of the Inter-American Court of Human Rights on domestic reparation programmes' (2017) 22 *International Journal of Human Rights* 1192.

39 R.K. Merton, 'On Sociological Theories of the Middle Range', in R.K. Merton (ed.), *Social Theory and Social Structure*, Free Press, New York, 1949, at 39–53.

measures society needs to address to move forward. Together these measures suggest both a corrective justice approach for individual victims, as well as broad societal transformation, in particular with the role of guarantees of non-repetition and truth itself as having reparative value to acknowledge the past and contribute to reconciliation. This reparative value of truth is key for unofficial truth commissions, but their informality may lose the effect of acknowledgement and reparation where it is not coming from an authoritative responsible actor.

Olsen et al. find that acknowledgement of violations through a public truth commission, and reparations for such crimes, can reinforce accountability.[40] However, this does not always follow. Truth commissions can make dealing with the past toxic, poisoning the discussion on reparations and paralysing momentum for its implementation. In Northern Ireland, the recommendation of a 'recognition payment' for all bereaved families by the Consultative Group on the Past (a public consultation group working around the establishment of a truth commission) gave rise to protests, which resulted in the whole scheme being eventually shelved by the government, due to the moral equivalence such a payment would have made between 'innocent victims' and killed combatants.[41]

This makes the design of and consultation on reparations and its process a vital part of shaping measures that can adequately and appropriately respond to victims' harm.[42] Victims have varying interests that change over time and conflict and compete with each other. Depending on their circumstances and the harm caused to them, some victims may prioritise truth recovery over reparations, or vice versa – or may seek both. Their expectations in engaging with a truth commission can vary from having a positive procedural experience or feeling satisfaction at the outcomes to being vilified or frustrated by the limited scope, procedure or recommendations.[43] This makes the process, design and participation of victims in truth commissions important in terms of how it can shape the scope of the subsequent or other transitional justice measures.[44]

In the 2004 Valech Commission in Chile, Collins points out that where the promise of reparations was unclear, victims came forward to testify anyway. Yet other victims were discouraged from testifying, given the 50-year embargo

40 T.D. Olsen, L.A. Payne, A.G. Reiter and E. Wiebelhaus-Brahm, 'When Truth Commissions Improve Human Rights' (2010) 4(3) *International Journal of Transitional Justice* 457, 475.

41 See L. Moffett, 'Reparations for "Guilty Victims": Navigating Complex Identities of Victim–Perpetrators in Reparation Mechanisms' (2016) 10(1) *International Journal of Transitional Justice* 146.

42 See C. Correa, J. Guillerot and L. Magarrell, 'Reparations and Victim Participation: A Look at the Truth Commission Experience', in C. Ferstman, M. Goetz and A. Stephens (eds.), *Reparations for Victims of Genocide, Crimes Against Humanity and War Crimes: Systems in Place and Systems in the Making*, Martinus Nijhoff, Leiden, 2009.

43 See Freeman, *supra* note 11.

44 Ibid.

on accessing the testimony and the fact that the exchange of reparations made some of them feel like they were being 'silenced or bought off'.[45] In contrast, in Peru many victims participated in the truth commission in the hope of obtaining reparations,[46] though some also sought truth and justice. There is to some extent an unspoken covenant that victims coming forward to testify to truth commissions will get more than a warm, healing feeling, which creates expectations of some form of substantive redress for their harm through reparations.[47] The failure to deliver reparations after a truth commission, whether part of its mandate or not, can only cause further distrust within a state and society that allowed individuals to be victimised.

From a victim's perspective, testifying before a truth commission means publicly opening themselves up to a traumatic event(s) of their past. They may do this as a good citizen, or perhaps for other reasons, such as to ensure that such atrocities do not reoccur. Yet there can be a 'cost' for victims in engaging with a truth commission, such as the risk of reopening psychological wounds, or suffering secondary victimisation if they are then attacked and diminished by the state or other actors in the engagement with truth commissions or claims for reparations. As Daly points out, this may have a social cost of 'domestic violence, reduced productivity, increased substance abuse'.[48] Moreover, victims' participation in a truth commission can be staged or manipulated for political ends, such as excluding victimised perpetrators, or can legitimise violence by state actors.[49] Nevertheless, truth commissions are to a certain extent dependent on victims coming forward. Without them, truth commissions are limited to their own investigations, archives and secondary sources. As part of the process, psychological support and counselling is needed to minimise the harm to victims and inform their expectations. Otherwise the processes and the failure to deliver reparations will cause them secondary victimisation. If there is an 'implicit bargain' that victims testify for truth commissions in exchange for more substantive redress through reparations, the failure to implement reparation recommendations in practice may be detrimental in the long run to future truth commissions, as victims appreciate the unlikelihood that such a process will provide them with redress.

---

45 C. Collins, 'Truth-Justice-Reparations Interaction Effects in Transitional Justice Practice: The Case of the "Valech Commission" in Chile' (2016) 49 *Journal of Latin American Studies* 55, at 71.

46 L.J. Laplante, 'From Theory to Practice: Implementing Reparations in Post-Truth Commission Peru', in B.R. Johnston and S. Slyomovics (eds.), *Waging War, Making Peace: Reparations and Human Rights*, Left Coast Press, Walnut Creek CA, 2009, at 81.

47 Lawry-White, *supra* note 6, at 170.

48 E. Daly, 'Truth Skepticism: An Inquiry into the Value of Truth in Times of Transition' (2008) 2(1) *International Journal of Transitional Justice* 23, at 41.

49 Correa, Guillerot and Magarrell, *supra* note 42, at 389.

There are also other drawbacks to closely connecting reparations with truth commissions. There is a danger that a truth commission will close the book on the past through a narrowly constructed mandate (temporal, territorial, violations),[50] not naming names,[51] or sealing information for decades.[52] These issues can have a detrimental effect on the scope of truth and acknowledgement, but also the extent of reparations. For instance, in South Africa the TRC recommended reparations only for those victims of the four categories of human rights violation (killing, torture, severe ill-treatment and abduction) and who were found to be victims by the commission.[53] However, less than 22,000 victims were recognised by the commission as being eligible, despite some South African victims' groups claiming the true number of victims to be over 100,000. As a result, the recommendations and the delayed implementation of a smaller amount of compensation by the South African government left many victims feeling 'betrayed'[54] and that the implementation of reparations was 'false reconciliation' or a way to buy their silence.[55]

Truth commissions' recommendations and a state's implementation of them can feel like an orchestrated, top-down way for the state to draw a line under the past and for society to move on, compelling victims to accept whatever little or limited reparations are proposed, rather than receive none at all.[56] Given the usually short temporal scope of a truth commission, it may just capture a snapshot of victims' current needs and harm, without encompassing something that can evolve over time, as they get older and their health and financial security deteriorates. These limitations can undermine these grander justifications of truth commissions, reparations and the goal of transitional justice of social inclusion, civic trust, dealing with the past to prevent its repetition, and reconciliation. However, on balance, from reviewing a number of truth

---

50 Such as the focus on civil and political rights, rather than economic, social and cultural rights. See L.J. Laplante, 'On the Indivisibility of Rights: Truth Commissions, Reparations and the Right to Development' (2007) 10(1) *Yale Human Right and Development Journal* 141; and M. Mamdani, 'Amnesty or Impunity? A Preliminary Critique of the Report of the Truth and Reconciliation Commission of South Africa (TRC)' (2002) 32(3–4) *Diacritics* 33, at 37.

51 Such as the Canadian TRC – see A. Woolford, 'The healing state? Residential schools and reparations in Canada', in J.M. Wemmers, *Reparation for Victims of Crimes against Humanity. The healing role of reparation*, Routledge, London, 2014, at 133.

52 On Chile, see Collins, *supra* note 45.

53 South African Truth and Reconciliation Commission Final Report, (1998) Volume 5, Chapter 5, at 176.

54 T. Madlingozi, 'On Transitional Justice Entrepreneurs and the Production of Victims' (2010) 2(2) *Journal of Human Rights Practice* 208, 215.

55 B. Hamber, 'The Dilemmas of Reparations: In Search of a Process-Driven Approach', in K. De Feyter, S. Parmentier, M. Bossuyt and P. Lemmens (eds.), *Out of the Ashes: Reparation for Victims of Gross and Systematic Human Rights Violations*, Intersentia, Antwerp, 2005, at 139.

56 Ibid, at 140; and Woolford, *supra* note 51, at 133.

commissions, reports by UN Special Rapporteurs and qualitative research in a number of contexts, it seems that the benefits of connecting truth commissions to reparations outweigh the risks, as can be seen in the discussion in section 4 of countries that have attempted reparations without a truth commission.

## 3. IMPLEMENTATION OF REPARATION RECOMMENDATIONS

In theory, reparations are designed to cement a truth commission's commitment to redressing and acknowledging the past by focusing on those who have been most affected by the violence. Yet in practice, the data on the implementation of reparation recommendations made by truth commissions is poor. Bakiner found in analysing 15 truth commissions that only two states had implemented reparation recommendations made by a truth commission.[57] This mirrors wider trends in transitional societies, where only 14 out of 84 have implemented reparations programmes.[58] This reflects that when it comes to implementation, the ball is in the government's court, with reparation recommendations being 'merely potentialities' and with implementation and institution reform beyond the powers and capacity of truth commissions.[59] However, it is possible to discern some trends of successful, partial and forced implementation of reparation recommendations.

'Successful' implementation of reparation can be defined as where subsequent bodies are established and deliver monetary and symbolic measures. This does not require a 'mirror image' approach, where recommendations have to be directly implemented word for word, but means that there is a margin of appreciation in implementing such measures to reflect the fact that the democratic process will modify the legislation of such provisions. What is important for a successful implementation is that it includes the majority of serious violations, munificence in the range of measures and mostly satisfies victims' expectation of remedy of their harm. Ideally this should be done in a timely manner to mitigate any further harm to victims. With this in mind, we can say that often more work is required by the government to work out the complex procedures in designing and implementing reparations from a truth commission's recommendations. Procedures such as drafting legislation, a victim registry and inter-institution cooperation can be planned from an early stage of the truth commission, factoring in their administration and funding,

57 See O. Bakiner, 'Truth Commission Impact: An Assessment of How Commissions Influence Politics and Society' (2014) 8(1) *International Journal of Transitional Justice* 6, at 18.

58 Olsen, Payne, Reiter and Wiebelhaus-Brahm, *supra* note 40, at 53.

59 De Greiff, *supra* note 5, at para. 38.

with recommendations and consultations with victims tailoring the appropriate measures and eligible beneficiaries.

The two successful examples identified by Bakiner (Chile and Sri Lanka) were planned as part and parcel of the measures of the transition. For instance, Ferrara points out that the successful payment of reparations in Chile to those who had been extra-judicially executed was down to reparations and the truth commission being viewed as the two 'main pillars' of the political transition.[60] Often, seeing reparations delivered comes down to the political will of the government to honour the recommendations of the truth commission. It may be that a truth commission's recommendation of reparations fails to engage with political, social or economic realities; as such, there is an art in making reparation recommendations 'policy friendly'.[61] In Sri Lanka, reparation recommendations were provided through existing reparation bodies, such as the Rehabilitation of Persons, Properties and Industries Authority (REPPIA).[62] However, this scheme offered a limited form of reparations and funding. Only more recently, after pressure from civil society and the international community, was an Office for Reparations set up in 2018 to more comprehensively redress the conflict. Both cases represent how reparation proposals have been developed over time to be more inclusive and comprehensive, due to changing political and social factors.

Some truth commissions can provide detailed recommendations on what reparations should look like, thereby helping to minimise the policy and legislative work required of the government in order to obtain successful implementation. The 2007 Ecuadorian truth commission in its recommendations provided a draft reparations bill, which was later enacted into law.[63] The intention of the commission was to help ensure that reparations were implemented, after examining other countries where reparation recommendations were often left unfulfilled.[64] The legislation itself mirrors the recommendations of the truth commission, such as its purpose and temporal scope. It is of course not an exact implementation; issues such as interpretation in good faith in the victim's benefit do not appear in the law that was passed, and the legislation dilutes certain provisions, such as scholarships, as recommended by the commission, which became training and advice on developing economic inclusion initiatives.[65] Nonetheless, a provision in the legislation speaks of the importance of truth and

60 A. Ferrara, *Assessing the Long-Term Impact of Truth Commissions: The Chilean Truth and Reconciliation Commission in Historical Perspective*, Routledge, London, 2014, at 65.

61 De Greiff, *supra* note 5, at para. 72.

62 Rehabilitation of Persons, Properties and Industries Authority, Legislative Act No. 29, 2 June 1987.

63 *Informe de la Comisión de la Verdad Ecuador*, 2010, Volume 5: Conclusiones y recomendaciones, at 395–413; Ley Reparación Victimas Judicialización Violaciones Derechos Humanos, 5 December 2013, Oficio No. SAN-2013-1642.

64 *Informe de la Comisión de la Verdad Ecuador, supra* note 63, Volume 5, at 361.

65 Article 6(5), Ley Reparación Victimas Judicialización Violaciones Derechos Humanos.

reparations being complementary and inseparable to prevent the repetition of such violations.[66]

Some truth commissions' recommendations cannot be implemented because they are too unrealistic or too vague, making it difficult to discern if the commission's requirements have been met. For instance, the South African TRC made over one hundred recommendations, mostly aimed at the government, but also including civil society such as the media, faith communities and businesses, some of which were unclear in how they would be implemented.[67] The scale of reparations required may take time to implement in practice, and having numerous reparation recommendation may necessitate a staggered approach, prioritising measures aimed at those most vulnerable. In Peru, despite the CVR recommending a range of reparations, collective measures for affected communities only began in 2006 and compensation in 2011; they were rushed through around the time of an election[68] and the required implementation across different ministries and agencies (education, health, social welfare) in the Peruvian context was 'uneven and slow'.[69]

There is a danger that truth commissions can be too prescriptive in their design of reparations recommendations, such as where they are too specific in terms of the regulations of the operation of a reparations programme, which is best settled by a reparations body itself. Where truth commissions provide for a specific amount of compensation, this might become worthless in the years it takes for the reparations to be implemented. This was the case in Ghana, where its high inflationary economy devalued the specific amounts set out for each type of violation by the National Reconciliation Commission, which trivialised victims' harm and created a hierarchy of victimhood.[70]

Truth commissions' recommendations have to be implemented through democratic processes such as parliaments. During such processes, a truth commission's findings can be dissected in terms of the scope of reparations or eligibility, such as drawing a line between victims and perpetrators or enabling one side to 'blame' the other.[71] The recommendations of truth commissions are best situated in tracing out the principles and shape of reparations, based on views from victims who have testified before it and other evidence, such as draft legislation and eligible victims; by contrast, a reparations programme should be based on wider research and victim engagement by itself, guided by expertise on

66 Ley Reparación Victimas Judicialización Violaciones Derechos Humanos, Preamble, para. 5.

67 South African TRC Report, *supra* note 53, Volume 5, Chapter 8, at 308.

68 C. Correa, *Reparations in Peru from Recommendations to Implementation*, International Center for Transitional Justice, 2013, at 15–16.

69 Ibid, at 21.

70 N. Valji, 'Ghana's National Reconciliation Commission: A Comparative Assessment', ICTJ, New York, 2006, at 23.

71 See C. Lawther, *Truth, Denial and Transition: Northern Ireland and the Contested Past*, Routledge, London, 2014.

reparations and responding to victims' harm. Yet legislating and implementing such measures through the democratic process can see such issues being manipulated or stifled, especially where the majority who supported or colluded in past violence continue to dominate the legislature and executive. This may fall short of the truth commissions' recommendations and victims' expectations for redress.

Truth commissions can carefully consider the financial and social implications of reparation recommendations and the challenges of implementation. The Peruvian CVR acknowledged that no matter what it proposed in terms of reparations, it was dependent on political will, resulting in it developing a detailed reparations policy in the hope that it would reflect the complex social and financial implications of its recommendations.[72] In the case of the Sierra Leone TRC, it recommended social services rather than individual compensation, not only because of victims' views expressed to the commission, but also so as to make such measures as 'feasible and practical as possible' given the resources available to the state.[73] Moreover, due to the widespread poverty caused as a result of the conflict, awarding individual cash payments in Sierra Leone could have potentially '[led] to additional division and strife as opposed to the sense of social solidarity that the reparations programme is meant to foster.'[74] Similarly, the Kenyan TJRC provided detailed recommendations for reparations with the intention that they would be 'practical and implementable'.[75] Hayner notes that truth commissions often aim to be 'realistic and policy-relevant' to ensure that their recommendations have the best chance of being implemented.[76] Despite this, the Sierra Leone and Kenyan commissions' recommendations have not yet been put into action. In Sierra Leone, interim reparations were made to some victims through funding from international donors, in contrast to the more substantial financial support given to ex-combatants under demobilisation and reintegration programmes.[77]

Truth commissions have also been conscious that victims' needs change over time, such as recommending pensions for those who are injured.[78] Those victims coming before a commission may emphasise the need for

72 See J. García-Godos, 'Victim Reparations in the Peruvian Truth Commission and the Challenge of Historical Interpretation' (2008) 2(1) *International Journal of Transitional Justice* 63, at 74.

73 Witness to Truth: Report of the Sierra Leone Truth and Reconciliation, Chapter IV, (2004), at para. 71.

74 Ibid.

75 Kenya Truth, Justice and Reconciliation Commission Report, Volume IV, at 98.

76 Hayner, *supra* note 7, at 163.

77 E. Conteh and M. Berghs, *'Mi At Don Poil': A Report on Reparations in Sierra Leone for Amputee and War-Wounded People, Amputee and War-Wounded Association*, Sierra Leone, Freetown, 2014, at 6.

78 Sierra Leone TRC Report, *supra* note 73, at paras. 71 and 168–171; South African TRC Report, *supra* note 53, Volume 5, at para. 41.

assistance over more substantive long-term reparations, such as access to health care, education and housing.[79] Waldorf suggests that victims were unsatisfied with the traditional reparations approach, which would return them to the *status quo ante*.[80] However, while victims coming before the Sierra Leone TRC did not prioritise compensation, in Ghana, nine out of 10 victims who appeared before the commission (some 2,000) did so to seek compensation.[81] Victims' interests should not all be reductively merged into what the majority wants or needs. Victims of extra-judicial executions can have differing needs from families of those disappeared, and those who have been seriously injured or tortured have distinct needs from victims of sexual violence or child soldiers. Reparations are intended to acknowledge and alleviate the suffering of those who suffer the most, with assistance aimed at helping the recovery of the generally affected population. With the passage of time, victims' needs may move on from immediate assistance with supporting themselves to more substantive reparations to seek acknowledgement and alleviation of their long-term suffering.

Timing can play an important part in the implementation or sequencing of transitional justice mechanisms, such as truth commission and reparations. Collins suggests a 'phased' approach to transitional justice. Instead of trying to do all transitional justice measures at once, she suggests that a more 'progressive realisation' can enable states to build momentum for transitional justice with measures that 'generate[] least internal resistance'.[82] Hayner suggests that in some countries, reparations have come in waves on the back of truth commissions or litigation at regional courts, such as in Chile and Argentina.[83] Firchow calls for greater research into the sequencing between reparations and reconciliation that can facilitate the community acceptance of the payment of reparations to victims and repair the social fabric of communities.[84] More broadly, timing is a key issue in transitional justice and its wider engagement with rule of law initiatives, development, democratisation[85] and reconciliation. However,

---

79 Of the 7,707 victims who testified before the Sierra Leone TRC, 49% sought home or shelter, 41% education, 27% health care and 18% cash – reflecting more than one measure by respondents, Chapter IV, at para. 30, figure 1. See also in Peru, L. Laplante, 'Transitional Justice and Peace Building: Diagnosing and Addressing the Socioeconomic Roots of Violence through a Human Rights Framework', (2008) 2(3) *International Journal of Transitional Justice* at 331, at 351–352.

80 L. Waldorf, 'Anticipating the Past: Transitional Justice and Socio-Economic Wrongs' (2012) 21(2) *Social & Legal Studies* 171, at 178.

81 Valji, *supra* note 70, at 22.

82 Collins, *supra* note 45, at 79.

83 Hayner, *supra* note 7, at 170–171.

84 P. Firchow, 'Do Reparations Repair Relationships? Setting the Stage for Reconciliation in Colombia' (2017) 11(2) *International Journal of Transitional Justice* 315, at 331.

85 See L.E. Fletcher, H.M. Weinstein and J. Rowen, Context, 'Timing and the Dynamics of Transitional Justice: A Historical Perspective' (2009) 31 *Human Rights Quarterly* 163, at 218–219.

kicking the issue of reparations down the road may mean that the momentum for delivery is lost when all the energy is placed on a truth commission. Hamber notes that the South African government failed to deliver symbolic reparations early on in the transition, at a time when it would have been more receptive to their delivery.[86] The difficulty with reparations is that it requires a mapping out of the universe of victims and creating at least a registry of those who have suffered and would be eligible, through legal and evidential requirements. Such programmes require time and resources to set up so that they deliver measures that are not merely symbolic, but are fair and efficient. Nevertheless, the sooner evidence and documentation of violations can be collected, the more quickly can victims' harm be alleviated, as well as ensuring that their harm does not develop into long-term vulnerability and marginalisation.

## 3.1. CHALLENGES TO IMPLEMENTATION

Reparations carry baggage, meaning that even the most carefully crafted recommendation from a truth commission can easily falter in the face of political contention or intransigence over such issues as who is seen as a deserving victim worthy of redress. In Peru, despite the CVR recommendation of an inclusive approach to reparations that encompassed victimised non-state actors, the issue became polemic as the government initially dragged its feet on implementation, prioritising redress for wounded government soldiers and screening measures aiming to exclude members of the Shining Path that increased the evidential burden of victims in claiming reparations.[87] Similarly, in South Africa, victims were tarred by the government as being economic opportunists in their claims for the TRC's reparation recommendations to be implemented.[88]

A lack of implementation is often due to a lack of political will on the part of the government, which after an authoritarian regime or post-conflict may still be struggling with the political, social and economic costs of the past. In some cases, the final reports of a truth commission are delayed (e.g. the 1986 Ugandan truth commission report was only released in 1994) or sealed (e.g. the 1974 Uganda Commission of Inquiry into Disappearances).[89] In Peru, while reparations

86 Hamber, *supra* note 55, at 147.

87 Laplante, *supra* note 46, at 87.

88 O. Makhalemele, 'Still not Talking: The South African Government's Exclusive Reparations Policy and the Impact of the R30,000 Financial Reparations on Survivors', in Ferstman, Goetz and Stephens, *supra* note 42, at 547.

89 This report has still not been officially published, but a leaked version is available online, where the commission recommends reparations including compensation for illegally detained prisoners, restitution of property of disappeared soldiers, and social services to widows and children of those disappeared: 1974 Commission of Inquiry into the Disappearances of People in Uganda since 25 January 1971, at 789–800, https://www.usip.org/index.php/publications/1974/06/truth-commission-uganda-74.

were eventually given, the years of delays around individual awards (over eight years) left victim feeling 'disillusioned and cynical' about the truth commission, 'nullifying [its] positive results', and about the government's commitment to redressing their suffering.[90] Political will can only take an implementation process so far. As acknowledged by the OHCHR, implementation is a major challenge, which also requires 'sufficient institutional capacity' and funds to undertake these measures.[91] As such, donors and international organisations can play an important role in the delivery of reparations, helping to fill in these gaps in resources, but also in terms of how they prioritise funding and development goals in shaping values in transitional societies. In such cases where the state has limited resources and is dependent on donors in the short term, the government can still play an important role in acknowledging its responsibility for violations and taking ownership over delivering redress to all victims of the violence.

In the face of elections or waning public support or interest in the transition, *force majeure* or unforeseen crises can deprioritise reparations, such as an economic slump (Argentina and Ghana) or natural disasters (Haiti and Nepal), can diminish the political impetus for seeing recommendations for reparations implemented. However, if there is a will, there is a way, and there are many avenues to fund reparations, whether through 'wealth taxes',[92] seizing the assets of perpetrators, donor contributions, issuing government bonds, or levies on natural resources.[93] That said, reparations programmes can often be long-term financial commitments that need to have a dedicated budget line in a government's expenditure to make them meaningful and effective, even if the amounts will taper off in time.[94]

Implementation can be delayed or derailed by the politics of reparations. Opposition parties or members of the former regime can use the political nature of reparations and any controversy associated with them, such as economic cost, corruption or benefiting victim-perpetrators, to weaken the political power of the government and its vision of transition. Successive governments or legislative bodies may try to 'ignore, evade and delay' if it does not suit their political ambitions or benefit their constituents.[95] For truth commissions that

---

90 L. Laplante and K. Theidon, 'Truth with Consequences: Justice and Reparations in Post-Truth Commission Peru' (2007) 29(1) *Human Rights Quarterly* 228, at 231 and 248; and similarly in South Africa – Hamber, *supra* note 55, at 144.

91 OHCHR, *Rule of Law Tools for Post-Conflict States: Truth Commissions*, HR/PUB/06/1 (2006), at 31.

92 South African TRC Report, *supra* note 53, Volume 5, Chapter 8, at 319.

93 1999 Peace Agreement between the Government of Sierra Leone and the RUF (Lomé Peace Agreement).

94 See P. De Greiff, *Report of the Special Rapporteur on the promotion of truth, justice, reparation and guarantees of non-recurrence*, UN Doc. A/69/518 (8 October 2014), at para. 56.

95 Waldorf, *supra* note 80, 177.

take years, it can mean that recommendations get caught in election cycles with victims and reparations used as 'political footballs'.[96] This can leave societies with 'partial implementation', in that some recommendations are delivered by the government, but not to the scale, intent or design of the truth commission, such as in South Africa where a fraction of the recommended amount of reparations was distributed to victims.[97]

## 3.2. PARTIAL IMPLEMENTATION

In practical terms, reparations programmes require substantial resources and administration to deliver successfully. This can mean that progressive recommendations by a truth commission on reparations may only be partially met by the government in the short and medium term after mass violence, due to other reconstruction needs. There is a role for international community and international or regional actors to help build capacity and assist in the delivery of reparations, such as the International Organization for Migration's support of the Sierra Leone reparations programme or the work of the International Committee of the Red Cross (ICRC) in recovery of the disappeared alongside national NGOs in Guatemala. Within a particular country, public, political and media attention to victims can fade, reducing the impetus to deliver reparations to them. For instance in Ghana, with the initial delay by the government in implementing reparations, where a budget was not established for reparations before the National Reconciliation Commission (NRC) report came out in 2005, despite being deferred from being published in 2004.[98] The Ghanaian NRC had recommended a comprehensive reparations programme that included apologies, a memorial, a monument, a national day of remembrance, restitution of property and compensation, as well as scholarships and health benefits for survivors and next of kin. Only in 2007 did the Ghanaian government pay out US$1.5 million in compensation to some 2,000 victims, ranging from $217 to $3,300 depending on their harm suffered, but it did not implement the more symbolic collective measures of an apology or monuments.[99] Victims were dissatisfied with the amount of compensation provided, but as Asare points out, public attention to dealing with the past had waned.[100] This reflects the challenges of trying to

---

96 P. Gallagher, 'A deflated political football: external perceptions of the campaign for a pension for those severely physically injured during the conflict in Northern Ireland', Master's thesis, 2017 – on file with the author.

97 The South African TRC recommended $2,700 for six years to 21,676 victims ($16,200 total), but instead the government provided a single payment of $4,900 to 17,408 victims.

98 Valji, *supra* note 70, at 25–27.

99 A. Ampofoa Asare, 'The Ghanaian National Reconciliation Commission: Reparation in a Global Age' (2008) 2(2) *The Global South* 31, at 35 and 49.

100 Ibid, at 49.

consult and engage victims in the design of reparation recommendations by a truth commission, particularly where there are multiple types of violations, different actors involved and a large geographical area. In such circumstances, conducting outreach and providing sufficient time to engage and build the capacity of victims' groups can be challenging.[101] This does not mean it should not be done, but that it needs to be considered in the design and delivery of reparation recommendations and implementation.

Implementation of reparations may also be limited by a lack of engagement shown by key actors, such as ex-combatants, in facilitating such measures. In the case of the Chile, reparations based on the commission's recommendations delivered monthly pensions to some 5,794 victims,[102] but failed to discover the whereabouts of many of those disappeared, as a result of the lack of cooperation from military personnel on the location of the victims' remains.[103] Other actors may also shape the transition, such as economic forces or donors, who may be more concerned with market stabilisation and economic development than spending already limited public finances on uncovering past crimes. Yet this is short-sighted, given that the failure to address past atrocities and causes of violence risks future conflict and marginalisation that will undermine any future development.

In the case of South Africa, the lack of financial backing for community measures meant that reparations were only partial. Although the TRC recommended more substantive individual compensation than the government provided, it also viewed apartheid as a crime against humanity and considered that it 'constructed' the system and 'destroyed' communities.[104] As such, there should also be a collective and community dimension to reparations. Community-focused rehabilitation sought to ensure reconciliation and transform the way in which services are provided to all South Africans, rather than being discriminatory, depending on the recipient's race.[105] Yet the South African President's Fund responsible for financing these community measures has not yet disbursed these funds.[106] In the face of the South African government's slow and ineffectual action, victims' groups, such as the Khulumani Support Group, have initiated litigation and political protests to demand reparations. In such cases where the state has not implemented such measures or done so only partially, civil society, in particular victims' groups, may try to force

---

101 Correa, Guillerot and Magarrell, *supra* note 42, at 393.

102 The Commission had originally identified 2,298 victims. E. Lira, 'Policy for human rights violations in Chile', in P. De Greiff, *The Handbook of Reparations*, Oxford University Press, Oxford, 2006, at 57–59.

103 Ferrara, *supra* note 60, at 62.

104 Mamdani, *supra* note 50, at 44.

105 South African TRC Report, *supra* note 53, Volume 5, Chapter 5, at para. 95.

106 F. Collins, 'R1.5-billion for apartheid victims but thousands still waiting for money', *The Times*, 28 August 2017.

implementation through social and political mobilisation or strategic litigation before domestic or international courts.

## 3.3. FORCED IMPLEMENTATION

In some cases, there can be decades between a truth commission's findings and victims receiving redress. Where reparations are delivered over such long periods, it is often only due to litigation or political mobilisation of victims, and in some cases political opportunism, as the state is approaching elections.[107] Forced implementation here thus refers to a lack of political will on the part of the state to implement a truth commission's recommendations, but it being compelled to do so because of domestic and/or international pressure.

There are a number of examples of reparations being delivered years after a truth commission recommends them. In the case of Chad, a truth commission was established in 1995 after Hissène Habré was deposed. It recommended reparations, but victims sought justice against Habré for nearly 30 years through the International Court of Justice and then the Extraordinary African Chambers. Only in 2017 were reparations ordered, similar to the truth commission's original recommendations against Mr Habré and the Chadian government, but there have still been delays in setting up the delivery of these reparations.[108] As the Habré case shows, it is also important to acknowledge the international dimensions of victims pursuing redress abroad where their government is unwilling or unable to provide it.[109] This is a long and arduous process that places a heavy burden on victims. There has been similar experiences in Chile, with the arrest of former president Augusto Pinochet in London reviving the issue of dealing with the past more comprehensively. This included revisiting the scope of victims and reparations: where the Rettig Commission had only examined those killed or disappeared, the Valech Commission in 2004 and 2010 covered those who had been imprisoned on political grounds and tortured by the regime.[110]

---

107 Such as reparations made in 2010 by the Ugandan government before the presidential election to the victims of the Mukura massacre in northern Uganda – 'Mukura Massacre of 1989: Justice and Reconciliation Project', Field Note XII, March 2011, at 17.

108 US$148 million or 82,290,000,000 CFA Francs: Appeals Chamber of the Extraordinary African Chambers, *The Prosecutor v. Hissein Habré*, dispositif, 27 April 2017, at 225–227. A similar ruling was made in the Chadian courts for joint liability of Mr Habré and the Chadian state – see N. Iskandar Diab, 'Challenges in the Implementation of the Reparation Award against Hissein Habré: Can the Spell of Unenforceable Awards across the Globe be Broken?' (2018) 16(1) *Journal of International Criminal Justice* 141.

109 See also the South African example and the ACTA claims against corporations; see J. Sarkin, 'Pursuing Private Actors for Reparations for Human Rights Abuses Committed in Africa in the Courts of the United States of America', in C. Villa-Vicencio and E. Doxtader (eds.), *Reparations in South Africa*, David Philip Publishers, Cape Town, 2004.

110 See Collins, *supra* note 45.

In Guatemala, despite reparations being outlined in the 1996 peace agreement and in the official and unofficial truth commissions, it was only because of continuing judgments against the state for mass violations of human rights and awards of reparations to dozens and even hundreds of victims in cases before the Inter-American Court of Human Rights that a domestic reparations programme was established to reduce the cost of paying reparations to all affected victims.[111] Yet despite creating a national reparations programme, the Guatemalan government has not yet implemented (at the time of writing in 2019) many of the collective and economic reparations to victims, such as the massacre cases of *Plan de Sanchez* and *Rio Negro* cases, which represented only a handful of the hundreds of sites where the genocide was committed.

Such a relationship between the national and international mechanisms on reparations has not always been top-down, but can be integrative. Generally, the Inter-American Court of Human Rights has tried to include victims that come before it within national reparations programmes, even where they have been excluded, such as Afro-Colombians in Colombia,[112] or has tried to increase the amount of compensation they would get in comparison to the national reparations programme.[113] There has been a symbiotic relationship in Latin America between national reparations programmes and the international Inter-American system, with them influencing each other on the scope of victims and appropriate measures.

It is easy to place blame for the lack of implementation at the door of a truth commission and its construction of recommendations. In Sierra Leone, the government laid the blame for the failure of reconciliation on the TRC for not developing a follow-up strategy, not securing sufficient financial support, and in raising expectations without any long-term planning.[114] However, this is not the mandate of truth commissions; it is the government that is responsible for delivering reparations. Even the legislation that designs the mandate of truth commissions can be vague as to the details of carrying out reparations, causing challenges in implementation. The Kenyan TJRC Act permits victims of gross violations of human rights to apply to the Commission for reparations; however, the Commission had no power to award or implement reparations, only to make recommendations on '(a) the basis and conditions upon which reparation may

---

111 N. Roht-Arriaza, 'Guatemala: Lessons for transitional justice', in C. Lawther, L. Moffett and D. Jacobs (eds.), *Research Handbook on Transitional Justice*, Edward Elgar, Cheltenham, 2017, at 449.

112 *Case of the Afro-descendant communities displaced from the Cacarica River Basin (Operation Genesis) v. Colombia*. Preliminary Objections, Merits, Reparations and Costs, Judgment of 20 November 2013, Series C No. 270, at para. 470.

113 See *Case of the Río Negro Massacres v Guatemala*, Preliminary Objection, Merits, Reparations and Costs, Judgment of 4 September 2012, Series C No. 250, at paras. 303–309.

114 R. Friedman, *Competing Memories: Truth and Reconciliation in Sierra Leone and Peru*, Cambridge University Press, Cambridge, 2017, at 113.

be granted; (b) the authority responsible for the reparation; and (c) measures that should be taken to grant urgent and interim reparation to victims.'[115] Reparations have not been dispersed to victims of the post-election violence in Kenya, despite the recommendations of the TJRC, government directives and victim litigation.[116]

Truth commissions rarely have implementation bodies, with the exception of the Rettig Commission in Chile, but even the delivery of reparations in Chile was through a separate administrative body, the CNRR (Corporación Nacional de Reparación y Reconcialiación). It can be undesirable for truth commissions to be burdened with the technical and administrative process of identifying and delivering reparations to victims, as it may affect their capacity to uncover truth.[117] However, it is worth remembering that without an implementation body and dependent on the political generosity of the government, victims often have to force implementation through political pressure or the courts, which even then do not guarantee delivery by themselves.

## 4. REPARATIONS WITHOUT A TRUTH COMMISSION

There is no road map for transitional justice: the different measures of truth, justice and reparations are lights meant to guide the way forward for society through a dark past. Many countries have chosen not to establish a truth commission, but instead have created a reparations programme. In addition, having a truth commission and a reparations programme may not satisfy victims' needs for redress, who can continue to pursue through the courts their own vision of remedy. In the case of Colombia, the 2005 Justice and Peace Law provided a transactional arrangement for demobilising paramilitaries, in which they contributed information and assets for truth recovery and reparations in exchange for more lenient sentences under the auspices of a criminal justice-dominated approach.[118] While this law focused on the responsibility of paramilitaries, neglecting the actions of state forces, this was in part remedied through the Victims' Restitution Law 2011. The subsequent peace process with FARC will see a further expansion of the reparations programme to victims of this group and others, as well as a truth commission and other measures.[119]

Transitional justice measures are meant to complement each other; one without the other can undermine the dual individual–societal dimensions

115 Article 42(3), TJRC Act 2008.

116 'Restorative Justice Fund not created 3 years after directive', *Capital News*, 19 March 2018.

117 Orentlicher, *supra* note 2, at para. 19(b).

118 Ley 975 de 2005, Ley de Justicia y Paz, Diario Oficial 45.980 (2005).

119 Final Agreement to end the armed conflict and build a stable and lasting peace, 24 November 2016.

embedded in each measure in dealing with the past. Reparations without truth-telling can hide away victims' harm from the public eye, with compensation being the manner in which the state tries to 'buy [their] silence or acquiescence'.[120] In cases of disappearances, victims' families may not be satisfied with compensation, but want to know the circumstances around the disappearance and fate of their loved one, in the hope of giving them a proper burial.[121] In Brazil, social movements in pursuing civil litigation in the absence of a truth commission eventually saw a reparations body established.[122] Brazil had a range of compensation schemes that were made up of a 'series of unrelated laws and decrees', but were not part of a comprehensive reparations programme.[123] The detachment and privatisation of harm caused victims to pressure the government into establishing a truth commission to publicise the harm caused, in particular around torture, but only years after the events. Comparably, the Canadian TRC on the historic abuse of First Nations people in residential schools followed on from a class action settlement, with its recommendations focusing on more symbolic measures and institutional reform to prevent repetition.[124] Together these examples may show that there is a continuum of transitional justice measures. Perhaps for each context it is not formulaic as simply finding the truth first, and then implementing reparations in consequence to the findings, but instead being comprehensive and finding the best temporal fit to advance an issue.[125]

In a way, victims' use of civil litigation to claim compensation has been secondary to their goal of seeking accountability and acknowledgement. To give two examples, in Brazil, victims of torture have made claims against the head of the Centre for Operations for Internal Defence, while in Northern Ireland victims of the Omagh bombing have sued leaders in the Real IRA who were never prosecuted.[126] The absence of a truth commission leaves the burden of

---

120 D. Orentlicher, *Report of the independent expert to update the Set of Principles to combat impunity*, E/CN.4/2005/102 (18 February 2005), at para. 59(d).

121 Ibid, at para. 63.

122 See C. Macdowell Santos, 'Transitional Justice from the Margins: Legal Mobilization and memory Politics in Brazil', in N. Schneider and M. Esparza (eds.), *Legacies of State Violence and Transitional Justice in Latin America: A Janus-Faced Paradigm?*, Lexington Books, Lanham MD, 2015.

123 I. Cano and P. Galvão Ferreira, 'The reparations program in Brazil', in De Greiff, *supra* note 102, at 102.

124 *Canada's Residential Schools: Reconciliation. Final Report of the Truth and Reconciliation Commission of Canada*, Volume 6, (2015), at 223–241.

125 Daly, *supra* note 48, at 39–40.

126 Macdowell Santos, *supra* note 122, at 61; and L. Moffett, 'Beyond Attribution: Responsibility of Armed Non-State Actors for Reparations in Northern Ireland, Colombia and Uganda', in N. Gal-Or, C. Ryngaert and M. Noortmann (eds.), *Responsibilities of the Non-State Actor in Armed Conflict and the Market Place: Theoretical Considerations and Empirical Findings*, Brill, Leiden, 2015.

uncovering the truth about the past on the shoulders of victims, who can try to pursue truth and reparations through civil litigation in courts or mobilise on the streets. Not all victims want reparations and truth. In Northern Ireland, injured victims have been advocating for a pension as a form of reparations, rather than truth. As one victim case worker noted, those injured were more concerned with 'improving their quality of life' than truth or justice.[127] However, for some victims, acknowledgement and truth are more important, in that reparations are seen an insult to the memory of their loved one. As such, victims do not speak with one voice and their needs and interests change over time, transitional justice mechanisms have to be flexible as far as possible to provide a certain level of choice for victims in whether or not they want to engage in them.

Reparations alongside or after a truth commission can promote better transparency and inclusion than awards made before one. After the peace agreement in the Solomon Islands, compensation was distributed to those who lost economic opportunities and property, but lacked guidelines and transparency, resulting in corruption, and failed to highlight the truth about the wider pattern of violations. The subsequent TRC recommended comprehensive reparations for a broader range of more serious violations, but has so far not received funding.[128] Similarly, the Moroccan Arbitration Panel, while offering compensation to thousands of victims, was considered to have failed to uncover the truth and provide reparations to all victims who had suffered under the regime.[129] As a result, the Equality and Reconciliation Commission (IER) was established to provide more comprehensive reparations and truth. Even with such measures, corruption can still be a substantial issue for any reparations programme, with or without a truth commission. The benefit of a truth commission beforehand is that it can awaken society to the importance of delivering reparations to victims, and show that the truth is not just empty words, but instead has real consequences for victims.[130]

## 5. CONCLUSION

Truth commissions and reparations are often invoked on the basis of healing the wounds of the past and bringing about reconciliation. Informing expectations of these measures and ensuring their delivery is an important,

---

127 Interview with victim group coordinator, IR06, Belfast, Northern Ireland, March 2017.

128 See N. Dicker, 'Development Aid for Reparations in the Solomon Islands', in R. Jeffery (ed.), *Transitional Justice in Practice: Conflict, Justice, and Reconciliation in the Solomon Islands*, Palgrave Macmillan, New York, 2017.

129 Hayner, *supra* note 7, at 172.

130 Laplante and Theidon, *supra* note 90.

if not vital, part of the transition. The best we can expect between the two is that one opens the door for the other, facilitating society to accept that truth and reparations are necessary to heal the wounds of the past. While this is not to burden reparations with the expectations of reconciliation, it can help to ease the differences amongst victims, who are left to bear the burden of the past, and the rest of society. At best, reparations can possibly address and acknowledge victims' suffering, which in turn can open up space for them to engage with reconciliation. For victims, reconciliation is an individual's choice, something that has to be voluntary and not the result of external pressure. The design and implementation of reconciliation is something best left to other social, moral, cultural or communal forces to broker, rather than via a legalised top-down process by lawyers and, by extension, reparations. Apologies are an important part of reparations and truth recovery, with responsible actors acknowledging their wrongdoing; however, apologies need to be carefully crafted in consultation with victims, so that it is meaningful to them and not merely a way for those responsible for causing harm to justify their violence.[131]

The global legacy of truth commissions is that they have helped to solidify the need for individual and community redress at the domestic level, beyond uncovering the facts of the past. There remains a broad spectrum of practice and implementation around recommendations for reparations by truth commissions. That said, there is a consistent view that a range of reparative measures, beyond compensation, need to be implemented by states to deliver remedies that are politically and symbolically imbued with promoting values of a transitioned society. In terms of achievements, there a range of practice and experience to draw from the dozens of previous and existing truth commissions that can be used to inform the establishment of new commissions. Truth commissions have helped to prioritise those who have borne the brunt of the violence and the hidden victims left out of the official state discourses on the past, and have helped to encourage victim participation and cement the need for reparations. Yet there remain common challenges around implementation, such as in countries like Guatemala, where ongoing violations continue to occur against indigenous and marginalised groups, and where the partial implementation of reparations and the completion of the truth commission's work have not by themselves achieved a transformative agenda.

Nevertheless, there remains a strong bond between truth commission and reparations. Truth commissions and reparations are two tools in the transitional justice toolkit, and while they can be complementary, they are designed to serve to some extent discrete functions. Recommendations for reparations by truth

131 See Queen's University Belfast's Human Rights Centre (HRC) and University of Ulste's Transitional Justice Institute (TJI) Submission on Reparations Issues pursuant to Article 75 of the Statute, 15 May 2015, ICC-01/04–01/07-3551, at para. 85.

commissions provide a supportive and normalising function, which ultimately recognises the need to move beyond truth to alleviate the ongoing consequences of mass atrocities for victims. It needs to be remembered that although there are ambitious goals for such transitional justice mechanisms, reparations and truth commissions can only make modest contributions to reconciliation, building civic trust and the rule of law.[132] In truth, the strength of truth commissions is their ability to 'narrow the range of permissible lies';[133] of reparations, the provision of measures that can ease victims' suffering so that they may regain some quality of life and dignity.

132 L. Magarrell, 'Reparations for massive or widespread human rights violations: Sorting out claims for reparations and social justice' (2003) 22(1) *Windsor Yearbook of Access to Justice* 85, at 94.

133 M. Ignatieff, *The Warrior's Honor: Ethnic War and the Modern Conscience*, Owl Books, New York, 1997, at 174.

# TRUTH COMMISSIONS AND SOCIAL JUSTICE

## 'Wishful Thinking or Not Very Thoughtful Wishing'?

Brianne McGonigle Leyh



## 1. INTRODUCTION

Though there are debates about the definition,[1] transitional justice is largely seen as 'the full range of processes and mechanisms associated with a society's attempts to come to terms with a legacy of large-scale past abuses, in order to ensure accountability, serve justice and achieve reconciliation'.[2] These measures include, amongst others, domestic and international(ised) trials, truth commissions, reparation programmes, vetting and lustration practices, documentation, memorialisation, legal reforms, and other efforts made to promote reconciliation. In general, the different processes aim to make a clear break from past abusive practices so that trust may be re-established between different groups in society and the state.[3] They are largely based on the notion

1 See C. Bell, 'Transitional Justice, Interdisciplinarity and the State of the "Field" or "Non-field"' (2009) 3 *International Journal of Transitional Justice* 5.

2 UN Security Council, Report of the Secretary-General, *The Rule of Law and Transitional Justice in Conflict and Post-Conflict Societies*, UN Doc. S/2004/616 (23 August 2004), para. 8.

3 J. Allen, 'Balancing Justice and Social Unity: Political Theory and the Idea of a Truth and Reconciliation Commission' (1999) 49 *The University of Toronto Law Journal* 315, at 319.

that backward-looking processes, namely those that acknowledge and address abuses suffered by victims, are necessary in order to help transition out of conflict or repression and into societies that respect democracy, human rights, and the rule of law.

Yet, despite the wide range of innovative responses that have been developed, it has become clear that the implementation of transitional justice processes is not a remedy for all of a society's problems. Nor should they be seen in this light. Rather, they are meant to help with the transition from authoritarian rule to democracy or from conflict to peace by addressing past abuses. Yet, as has often been the case, past abuses are addressed in an unsatisfactory manner, or not addressed at all. Trials cannot prosecute all crimes, vetting processes cannot cover all institutions or individuals, and reparations cannot redress all harms suffered. Some of the most pertinent criticism of transitional justice processes is that they tend to be rooted in westernised, liberal and legalistic approaches to justice.[4] They predominately focus on violations of civil and political rights (loss of life or violations of physical integrity), while largely ignoring violations of economic, social and cultural (ESC) rights, broader structures of inequality, poverty or corruption.[5] Issues such as social, cultural or religious discrimination or exclusion, the erosion of livelihoods through corrupt practices by a small elite, the denial of worker rights, and interference with access to food, water, education and healthcare are often left untouched by conventional transitional justice processes or only referred to as context, even when these problems are part of the specific abuses that took place.

A failure to confront these concerns is problematic because it generates and perpetrates mistrust and inequality between social groups, as well as within the institutions of the state, leading, in many cases, to a recurrence of violence.[6]

---

4 See K. McEvoy, 'Beyond Legalism: Towards a Thicker Understanding of Transitional Justice' (2007) 34 *Journal of Law and Society* 411.

5 See C. Chinkin, 'The Protection of Economic, Social and Cultural Rights Post-Conflict', paper series commissioned by the Office of the High Commissioner for Human Rights, 2009, http://www2.ohchr.org/english/issues/women/docs/Paper_Protection_ESCR.pdf; R. Mani, Editorial, 'Dilemmas of Expanding Transitional Justice, or Forging the Nexus between Transitional Justice and Development' (2008) 2 *International Journal of Transitional Justice* 253; D.N. Sharp, 'Addressing Economic Violence in Times of Transition: Toward a Positive-Peace Paradigm for Transitional Justice' (2012) 35 *Fordham International Law Journal* 779; E. Schmid and A. Nolan, '"Do No Harm"? Exploring the Scope of Economic and Social Rights in Transitional Justice' (2014) 8 *International Journal of Transitional Justice* 362. One notable exception has been the Mauritius Truth and Justice Commission, which operated from 2009–2011, which was mandated to investigate slavery and indentured labour during its colonial period.

6 See A.L. Boraine, 'Transitional Justice: A Holistic Interpretation' (2006) 60 *Journal of International Affairs* 17; B.A. Leebaw, 'The irreconcilable goals of transitional justice' (2008) 30 *Human Rights Quarterly* 95; M. Mahmood, 'Reconciliation without Justice' (1996) 46 *South African Review of Books* 3; R. Carranza, 'Plunder and Pain: Should Transitional Justice Engage with Corruption and Economic Crimes?' (2008) 2 *International Journal of Transitional Justice* 310, at 329.

Indeed, advocates of human security have long noted the associations between poverty and socio-economic/political inequalities with sources of conflict.[7] Accordingly, within the peacebuilding field, scholars have begun to call for transitional justice to ensure a transition to positive peace or 'just peace'.[8] There was increasing concern that transitional justice was failing to contribute to building or securing not just an absence of conflict but more equitable peace.[9] In response to the lack of real societal change in many post-conflict societies following the implementation of transitional justice processes, a number of commentators began to contend that transitional justice needs to be recalibrated into more holistic processes by moving away from its one-dimensional stance focusing almost exclusively on civil and political rights violations.[10] In 2008, Arbour, former UN High Commissioner for Human Rights, called for a categorical shift whereby transitional justice should aim to achieve 'social justice' as its ultimate objective. While she defined social justice as the 'minimum legal standards guaranteeing substantive equality (as reflected in international human rights instruments prohibiting discrimination and protecting economic, social and cultural rights) in the fulfilment of the idea of freedom from want',[11] others, for instance, have defined it in terms of redistribution and recognition.[12]

The term social justice has therefore become the conceptual umbrella term for loosely grouped-together concepts such as past violations of ESC rights, the socio-economic root causes of violence, marginalisation, structural violence, or socio-economic concerns of the future. The focus upon social justice has come at the same time as the push for a more 'transformative agenda' of transitional justice.[13] And, despite concerns expressed by a number of scholars about the

---

7 Human Security Report Project, 'Human Security Brief 2007', http://www.css.ethz.ch/en/services/digital-library/publications/publication.html/55856.

8 See Sharp, *supra* note 5.

9 See L.J. Laplante, 'Transitional Justice and Peace Building: Diagnosing and Addressing the Socioeconomic Roots of Violence through a Human Rights Framework' (2008) 2 *International Journal of Transitional Justice* 331.

10 See L. Arbour, 'Economic and Social Justice for Societies in Transition' (2007) 40 *New York University Journal of International Law and Policy* 1; W. Lambourne, 'Transitional Justice and Peacebuilding after Mass Violence' (2009) 3 *International Journal of Transitional Justice* 28; Sharp, *supra* note 5; Boraine, *supra* note 6; Chinkin, *supra* note 5.

11 Arbour, *supra* note 10, at 5, note 10.

12 N. Fraser, 'From Redistribution to Recognition? Dilemmas of Justice in a "Post-Socialist" Age', in K. Olson (ed.), *Adding Insult to Injury: Nancy Fraser Debates Her Critics*, Verso, London, 2008. There is no clear agreement on the definition of social justice. Sandoval defines it as 'all social changes aimed at providing people in a state with opportunities to live in a world free of poverty, marginalization, and discrimination and where they are able to exercise their rights and live with dignity'. C. Sandoval, 'Reflections on the Transformative Potential of Transitional Justice and the Nature of Social Change in Times of Transition', in R. Duthie and P. Seils (eds.), *Justice Mosaics: How Context Shapes Transitional Justice in Fractured Societies*, ICTJ, New York, 2017, at 169.

13 E. Daly, 'Transformative Justice: Charting a path to reconciliation' (2002) 12 *International Legal Perspectives* 73, at 74 and 80; M. Evans, 'Structural Violence, Socioeconomic Rights,

impracticability and dangers of expanding transitional justice,[14] the calls for social justice aims and greater transformative impact have made an important impression on UN and EU transitional justice policy,[15] with both organisations endorsing greater inclusion of social justice in transitional justice programming. As a result, not only are prevention of conflict, reconciliation and re-establishing the rule of law goals of transitional justice processes, but equally, if not more importantly, social justice and social transformation have also become goals.[16]

Of all the various transitional justice processes, scholars have noted that truth commissions are especially well suited to delivering on social justice goals.[17] In particular, their structures, processes and outcomes provide the necessary space and flexibility to address social justice concerns. But have truth commissions ever really been able to deliver on social justice promises? Or do they, like many other transitional justice processes, fall short of grand expectations? This chapter looks at the question of whether truth commissions have been able to live up to their transformative potential to bring about greater social justice and suggests that modesty is in order when looking at the legacy of truth commissions.

Over the past decade, an increasing number of studies has evaluated the impact of truth commissions on a range of issues from human rights, to democracy, to social reconciliation and beyond.[18] All of these studies, and their often conflicting findings, reflect the intrinsic difficulties of measuring truth commission impact. While a more comprehensive study is undoubtedly needed, this chapter is not aimed at carrying out a systematic and comparative review of case studies to assess impact. Rather, it is concerned with looking at modest and potential contributions of truth commissions to the *notion* of social

---

and Transformative Justice' (2016) 15 *Journal of Human Rights* 1, at 5; see also P. Gready and S. Robins, 'From Transitional to Transformative Justice: A New Agenda for Practice' (2014) 8 *The International Journal of Transitional Justice* 339.

14 See Mani, *supra* note 5; L. Waldorf, 'Anticipating the Past: Transitional Justice and Socio-Economic Wrongs' (2012) 21 *Social & Legal Studies* 171.

15 Guidance Note of the Secretary-General, *United Nations Approach to Transitional Justice*, March 2010, https://www.un.org/ruleoflaw/files/TJ_Guidance_Note_March_2010FINAL.pdf; Council of the European Union, *The EU's Framework on Support to Transitional Justice*, 2015, http://data.consilium.europa.eu/doc/document/ST-13576-2015-INIT/en/pdf.

16 See Arbour, *supra* note 10; Lambourne, *supra* note 10.

17 T. Pasipanodya, 'A Deeper Justice: Economic and Social Justice as Transitional Justice in Nepal' (2008) 2 *International Journal of Transitional Justice* 378, at 392–395. Reparations are also touted as one of the processes that lends itself to social justice concerns. See Sandoval, *supra* note 12, at 169–170.

18 See ICTJ, *Challenging the Conventional: Can Truth Commissions Strengthen Peace Processes?*, 2014; E. Wiebelhaus-Brahm, *Truth Commissions and Transitional Societies: The Impact on Human Rights and Democracy*, Routledge, London, 2010; T.D. Olsen, L.A. Payne and A.G. Reiter, *Transitional Justice in Balance: Comparing Processes, Weighing Efficacy*, United States Institute of Peace Press, Washington D.C., 2010; J.L. Gibson, 'The Contributions of Truth to Reconciliation: Lessons from South Africa' (2006) 59 *Journal of Conflict Resolution* 409; O. Bakiner, 'Truth Commission Impact: An Assessment of How Commissions Influence Politics and Society' (2014) 8 *International Journal of Transitional Justice* 6.

justice more generally. It highlights where truth commissions have, in limited circumstances, emphasised important social justice concerns, and where they should have emphasised these but have failed to do so. Section 2 looks at the structures of truth commissions, focusing on mandates and resources, and the procedure they may adopt, touching on inclusive processes. The section then focuses on the outcomes of various truth commissions, including their findings, recommendations and implementation. The many challenges to any significant contribution to the lives, and social justice concerns, of affected communities are noted throughout. Section 3 touches further on obstacles facing truth commissions when dealing with social justice, calling for both more modesty when looking at the legacy of truth commissions and more collaboration between other transitional justice and post-conflict responses. Section 4 concludes with final observations.

## 2. TRUTH COMMISSIONS AS A FAVOURED RESPONSE

Truth commissions have become a favoured response to serious human rights violations, particularly in contexts where the state or governing authority has not been forthcoming with the truth about wrongdoing.[19] To date, more than 40 truth commissions have been established around the world,[20] operating in a diverse range of geo-political environments. They have been endorsed by the UN, regional organisations and donor countries, as well as international and local civil society organisations.[21]

Generally, truth commissions are officially sanctioned, temporary, non-judicial investigative bodies designed to produce a final report describing the patterns of violence and abuse, its causes and its consequences.[22] They do this

19 L. Vella, 'Translating Transitional Justice: The Solomon Islands Truth and Reconciliation Commission', State, Society and Governance in Melanesia Discussion Paper 2014/2, at 3.

20 M. Aciru, 'Rethinking Post-Truth Commissions: Empowering Local Capacities to Shape the Post-Truth Commission Discourse' (2017) 11 *Human Rights and International Legal Discourse* 71, at 71; Vella, *supra* note 19, at 4; Bakiner, *supra* note 18, at 11.

21 R. Shaw and L. Waldorf, 'Introduction: Localizing Transitional Justice', in R. Shaw, L. Waldorf and P. Hazan (eds.), *Localizing Transitional Justice Interventions and Priorities after Mass Violence*, Stanford University Press, Stanford, 2010, at 3; C.L. Sriram, 'Justice as Peace? Liberal Peacebuilding and Strategies of Transitional Justice' (2007) 21 *Global Society* 579, at 583; UN Security Council, *supra* note 2; OHCHR, *Rule of Law Tools for Post-Conflict States: Truth Commissions*, HR/PUB/06/1 (2006).

22 OHCHR, *supra* note 21, at 1; Hayner asserts that a truth commission: (1) is focused on past, rather than ongoing, events; (2) investigates a pattern of events that took place over a period of time; (3) engages directly and broadly with the affected population, gathering information on their experiences; (4) is a temporary body, with the aim of concluding with a final report; and (5) is officially authorised or empowered by the state under review. P.B. Hayner, *Unspeakable Truths: Transitional Justice and the Challenge of Truth Commissions*, 2nd edn, Routledge, London, 2011, at 11–12.

by taking, collecting and analysing statements, holding public hearings, carrying out exhumations, and researching and investigating allegations of wrongdoing.[23] The benefits claimed to be the result of truth commissions are wide-ranging: disclosure of the truth, creation of an historical record, promotion of national healing, individual catharsis, and acknowledgement and redress for victims.[24]

Earlier commissions have often served as templates for later commissions, resulting in many common characteristics and reflecting globalised norms and values in their language and methods.[25] Yet, because they operate in specific cultural and political contexts, their operation, outcomes and impact vary considerably. While there is debate about whether truth-seeking processes promote reconciliation, repair harm or deter future abuses,[26] they do offer the structures, procedures and outcomes that, unlike other transitional justice processes, may enable greater attention to be paid to social justice concerns.

## 2.1. STRUCTURES

When looking at truth commission structures and how they can contribute (or have contributed) to social justice, it is important to look firstly at the articulated mandate of the truth commission. The mandate of a truth commission describes the commission's goals and objectives, designates the violations and time period under investigation, and specifies a timeframe for completion of the commission's work. Often, the mandate of a truth commission also specifies the acts that the commission may investigate. As noted by Bakiner, 'a truth commission is simultaneously enabled and constrained by its mandate'.[27] The situation prompting the creation of the truth commission, the resources available to it, the functioning of the government, and the political climate will all play a role in the drafting of the mandate and its goals and objectives.

The goals and objectives of a truth commissions vary greatly. Some general goals found in the governing structures of numerous truth commissions include: establishing an historical record (the truth about what happened); clarifying the main causes and effects of past violence and human rights abuses; making

23 OHCHR, *supra* note 21, at 1.

24 Allen, *supra* note 3, at 316; Bakiner, *supra* note 18, at 8–9.

25 G. Millar, 'Between Western Theory and Local Practice: Cultural Impediments to Truth-Telling in Sierra Leone' (2011) 29 *Conflict Resolution Quarterly* 177, at 180; Shaw and Waldorf, *supra* note 21, at 4.

26 See Allen, *supra* note 3, at 316; M. Freeman and P.B. Hayner, 'Truth-Telling', in D. Bloomfield, T. Barnes and L. Huyse (eds.), *Reconciliation After Violent Conflict: A Handbook*, International Institute for Democracy and Electoral Assistance, Stockholm, 2003; A.R. Chapman, 'Approaches to Studying Reconciliation', in H. van der Merwe, V. Baxter and A.R. Chapman (eds.), *Assessing the Impact of Transitional Justice: Challenges for Empirical Research*, United States Institute of Peace Press, Washington D.C., 2009.

27 Bakiner, *supra* note 18, at 14.

recommendations to prevent such events from recurring; and promoting national reconciliation, healing and unity. East Timor's Commission of Reception, Truth and Reconciliation (CAVR), for example, specified nine distinct objectives, among which were inquiries into human rights violations during the political conflict, identification of factors leading to violations, identification of practices to prevent a recurrence of violations, referral of violations to a prosecutor, and restoration of the dignity of victims.[28] In the Solomon Islands, the truth commission was mandated to, amongst other things, examine the nature, antecedents, root causes and extent of the violations or abuses that occurred and consider the impacts on health, education and legal and other sectors.[29] The truth commission of Liberia was given a broad mandate to address gross human rights violations, violations of international humanitarian law and economic crimes.[30] Likewise, the truth commission in Kenya was mandated to investigate the root causes of the 2007 post-election violence, including a broad array of violations committed by the state, such as massacres as well as economic crimes, beginning from Kenyan independence in 1963 until 2008.[31] In these examples, because human rights violations were not narrowly defined, the truth commission had the power and responsibility to investigate a broad set of human rights violations, extending beyond traditional violations of civil and political rights, such as extrajudicial killings and violations to bodily integrity. Moreover, they were empowered to examine root causes of the conflict, allowing them to move beyond the legal realm of human rights law and categorisation, to look at issues of marginalisation, poverty and/or corruption.

In contrast, there are other truth commissions that almost exclusively focused on violations such as torture, rape, prolonged arbitrary detention, disappearances, other forms of inhumane treatment, and killings. In El Salvador, for instance, the peace agreements establishing the truth commission only authorised it to investigate 'serious acts of violence', but did not specify particular crimes.[32] The final report notes that serious acts of violence were taken primarily

---

28 UN Transitional Administration in East Timor (UNTAET) Regulation 2001/10, 13 July 2001, section 3; Likewise, the terms of reference for the Indonesia–Timor-Leste Commission of Truth and Friendship (CTF) stated explicitly that their peoples strive 'to build a solid foundation for a future of peace; a future where human dignity and social justice are the guiding force of transformation'. See Republic of Indonesia and Democratic Republic of Timor-Leste, 'Terms of Reference for The Commission of Truth and Friendship', Jakarta, 9 March 2005.

29 Vella, *supra* note 19, at 8, citing TRC Act, section 5(1).

30 Liberia, Truth and Reconciliation Commission Final Report, Volume II: Consolidated Final Report, December 2009, at 2–3.

31 Kenya, Truth, Justice, and Reconciliation Commission, Act and Amendments (TJRC) – TJRC Act 2008, Article 5.

32 Peace Agreement signed at Chapultepec, Mexico, on 16 January 1992, Article 2. See also UN Security Council, Report of the UN Truth Commission on El Salvador, *From Madness to Hope: the 12-year war in El Salvador*, UN Doc. S/25500, 1993.

to mean violations to the right to life and physical integrity. Root causes or more systematic inequalities contributing to the harms suffered were not included. The terms of reference for the truth commission in Ghana included a more specific list: 'killing, abduction, disappearance, detention, torture, ill-treatment, and seizure of properties'.[33] Yet this list also limited the commission's investigatory powers to violations of civil and political rights and restricted its ability to fully investigate all crimes or violations experienced in, or underpinning, the conflict that were of a broader concern to victim communities. These limitations can, in turn, result in the creation of duplicative commissions, as was the case in Chile, and very often in commissions that are unable (or less able) to deliver on social justice demands simply because the mandate does not allow them to look at a broader set of violations or root causes of conflict.

Having the proper mandate is therefore key in order for truth commissions to be able to explore social justice issues and the broader contours of the conflict. However, a drawback to having a broader mandate is that truth commission staff are, due to resource or other constraints, unable to investigate all violations and therefore must prioritise. Very often, when this happens, traditional violations get prioritised over ESC rights violations, structural inequalities or corruption. This prioritisation takes place at all truth commissions and it is a reality that must be addressed. It reflects not only the importance of priority-setting but also the importance of resources for a truth commission's overall structure and how it operates.

The availability of financial resources will affect the pace and scope of investigations conducted by truth commissions. If resources are minimal, which they often are in post-conflict settings, then the scope of the investigation will be limited, thereby often minimising the legitimacy and relevancy of the commission when it comes to social justice concerns. Yet, even when there are serious financial limitations, it is vitally important that truth commission staff listen and reflect on the needs and concerns of the communities they are working for. In East Timor, the CAVR truth commission was operating on a limited budget but its staff still prioritised the taking of statements related to social justice concerns. The availability of strong human resources does indeed affect the scope of the investigation, since 'the commissioners and staff exercise considerable agency in terms of how they interpret the mandate, how they identify and carry out their tasks, what they choose to include in the final report and how they interact with victims, presumed perpetrators, politicians, bureaucrats, armed actors and civil society organizations'.[34] It is crucial that commissioners and other staff have knowledge of a broad range of human rights, including their interrelatedness,

[33] Ghana, National Reconciliation Commission Act 2002, Article 4.

[34] Bakiner, *supra* note 18, at 14.

and socio-economic policy. Without this knowledge, the process of taking and analysing statements and following up with investigations may inadvertently take a narrow, traditional path that may not reflect the full needs and concerns of the victim communities.

## 2.2. PROCESSES

The demands for an emphasis on social justice and on social justice transformations, which took place in, for instance, Colombia, Peru, Nepal, Liberia and East Timor, require a process whereby affected individuals can air grievances that touch on social justice concerns and efficient procedures that can review, process and analyse their statements, pronounce upon them in substantive findings, and lay out recommendations in a final report. Unlike other transitional justice processes such as trials or administrative vetting procedures, truth commissions can generally provide such processes. The processes and procedures adopted, including the participation of victims and victim communities, will all factor into whether socio-economic harms and socio-economic concerns come into play. If successful, victims can emphasise their socio-economic complaints, detailing their harms suffered and what they may want to see happen in the future. Truth commissions can be well placed to hear about and document these individual accounts, as well as provide a sequence of collective narratives to paint a clearer picture of the societal injustices, such as land inequalities or wider patterns of discrimination, experienced by a community.[35]

Because truth commissions are victim-focused, they allow for greater victim participation than most processes. In its most basic form, participation means the 'act of sharing or taking part'.[36] Yet the term 'participation' can include any number of things, ranging from non-dispositive forms of participation to more dispositive ones.[37] Participation can be seen as allowing for 'expression', where the victim may provide information and express emotion.[38] Often, the sheer number of victim statements taken sheds light on the inclusive participatory processes adopted. In contrast with the Commission of Truth and Friendship between Indonesia and East Timor, which interviewed 85 people and took statements from 62 witnesses,[39] the findings of the South African truth commission were

---

35 Evans, *supra* note 13, at 4.

36 I. Edwards, 'An Ambiguous Participant: The Crime Victim and Criminal Justice Decision-Making' (2004) 44 *British Journal of Criminology* 967, at 973.

37 Ibid, at 973.

38 Ibid.

39 R. Strating, 'The Indonesia-Timor-Leste Commission of Truth and Friendship: Enhancing Bilateral Relations at the Expense of Justice' (2014) 36 *Contemporary Southeast Asia* 232, at 245.

based on more than 20,300 statements taken from victims and survivors.[40] Such an undertaking reflects the expressive value a truth commission process can take on and signals to the wider society that victim voices are important. In some situations, however, even this type of participation could be viewed as 'empty ritual' in that if nothing relevant is done with the statements it could largely go towards maintaining the status quo and serving the interests of elite decision-makers.

There are also other non-dispositive forms of participation, such as consultation. Consultation could include larger surveys or meetings with experts to share specific information or advice. Again, some may view this as a token form of participation, since no obligations are tied to a consultation process and victim voices may be reduced to statistical jargon.[41] Other non-dispositive forms of participation include receiving 'information' or participation in the form of 'placation'.[42] Placation has a higher level of influence than receiving information or consultation, but those in power are not required to consider the participant's views. Often it means that a few hand-picked victims deemed 'worthy' are chosen to participate, but ultimately they have no real decision-making power. Finally, there are empowerment forms of participation, including 'partnership', 'delegated power' and 'citizen control'.[43] In these forms of participation, the participant has some decision-making control, though it may still be limited.

Tellingly, truth commissions rarely move into the more empowerment types of participation, usually remaining more non-dispositive. Participation in the statement-taking phase or investigatory phase alone is not enough to move past the phase of non-dispositive participation. There must be meaningful inclusion in the early phases, to give voice to victim needs and concerns and provide some sort of decision-making, such as determining the best methods for reaching communities, taking statements or understanding the statements in a given situation. In the Solomon Islands, Vella notes that the truth commission procedures were not in accordance with the context in which it was operating.[44] Going to villages and asking victims to simply come forward and tell their stories was in contrast with the local customs and practices for conflict resolution, which emphasise building of relationships of trust.[45] Moreover, framing the final analysis around human rights law, rather than storytelling and narratives, risked alienating the very populations the truth commission aimed to serve.[46]

---

40 South Africa, Truth and Reconciliation Commission Report, Volume 5, 1998, at 570; W. Verwoerd, 'Individual and/or Social Justice after Apartheid? The South African Truth and Reconciliation Commission' (1999) 11 *European Journal of Development Research* 115, at 117.

41 See S.R. Arnstein, 'A Latter of Citizen Participation' (1969) 35 *AIP Journal* 216.

42 Ibid, at 217.

43 Ibid.

44 Vella, *supra* note 19, at 12.

45 Ibid.

46 Ibid.

In terms of social justice and transformative discourses, there have been strong calls for localising peacebuilding and truth-seeking in particular.[47] These calls stress the importance of efforts to reach as many voices as possible. This may mean including not only respected local leaders but also less visible individuals in societies. It means making the proceedings accessible, public and transparent, using oral traditions, and relying on local knowledge and resources.[48] However, caution should always be exercised when viewing the 'local' as a homogenous category, and especially one that is in opposition to national/external/international actions.[49]

Nevertheless, even the broad non-dispositive participation provides 'a means by which issues that concern affected communities (rather than outside elites) may be raised'.[50] Empowerment may, in fact, come later from the individual or group capacity to make calculated choices and to then 'transform those choices into desired actions and outcomes'.[51] Numerous truth commission reports highlight the value of having strong victim participation in the shaping of their conclusions and understandings of not only what occurred but also of how the violations or abuse affected victims and communities.[52] And some authors see participation in truth processes as the key to moving towards greater political participation more generally.[53] Though empirical evidence on this point is lacking, Bakiner shows how civil society mobilisation around a truth commission can become an important contributor to policy reform when political will may be lacking.[54] Participation may, indeed, be the key to bringing social justice concerns to the attention of political elites.

## 2.3. OUTCOMES

Following their investigation and statement-taking procedures, truth commissions generally produce a final report. The size and substance of reports

47 R.M. Ginty, 'Gilding the Lily? International Support for Indigenous and Traditional Peacebuilding', in O.P. Richmond (ed.), *Palgrave Advances in Peacebuilding: Critical Developments and Approaches*, Palgrave Macmillan, London, 2010, at 349.

48 Ibid, at 349–350.

49 J. Wallis, 'Building a Liberal-Local Hybrid Peace and State in Bougainville' (2012) 25 *The Pacific Review* 613, at 631.

50 Evans, *supra* note 13, at 8; J. Gaventa and G. Barrett, 'So What Difference Does it Make? Mapping the Outcomes of Citizen Engagement', Institute of Development Studies Working Paper 347, University of Sussex, 2010, at 36.

51 R. Alsop, M. Frost Bertelsen and J. Holland, 'Empowerment in Practice: From Analysis to Implementation', World Bank, 2006, at 1.

52 See South Africa, Truth and Reconciliation Commission Report, Volume 1, 1998, at para. 80.

53 E. Brahm, 'Uncovering the Truth: Examining Truth Commission Success and Impact' (2007) 8 *International Studies Perspectives* 16, citing studies that link truth commissions to democratisation.

54 Bakiner, *supra* note 18, at 23.

varies greatly;[55] nevertheless, through their findings and recommendations (as well as through direct reparation awards, if in their mandates), truth commissions have the ability to bring attention to social justice concerns, including the interrelatedness of all types of violation, structural violence and needs of the future.[56] When looking at findings, Robinson notes that one of the primary contributions of truth commissions is the emphasis on social justice issues and how these relate to human rights realisation.[57]

The case with the first Liberian truth commission report is interesting in this respect.[58] On the one hand, in its findings the Liberian truth commission was able to attribute the root causes of the conflict to poverty, corruption, limited education opportunities, socio-economic inequalities, and land tenure and distribution, amongst other issues.[59] Moreover, in its recommendations, it stressed the need for individual and collective reparations and for institutional reforms to alleviate poverty and reduce illiteracy.[60] But is it enough to simply emphasise relevant social justice issues? Schmid contends that better analysis of ESC rights was needed. The first report failed to include any ESC rights violations on the list of gross violations of human rights,[61] and it made a clear prioritisation of civil and political rights and missed an important opportunity to explore legal obligations related to ESC rights. When there has been a poorly executed analysis of the causes and consequences of the violence or repression, there is a danger that the various concepts related to social justice become confounded and muddled, leading to imprecise or vague recommendations that are unlikely to be investigated further.

Truth commissions generally make context-specific recommendations because context matters,[62] and the type of social justice needed in each situation differs. For instance, in some situations it may be necessary to empower indigenous communities. In others, it may be about poverty reduction or a gender-specific approach. However, of the various types of recommendation,

---

55 For example, the truth commission in Uruguay produced a 20-page report, whereas the Peruvian report came in at 4,000 pages, available only electronically.

56 E. Skaar highlights the disparity between the attention given to recommendations in final reports, with some reports including only a handful of recommendations, such as Uruguay and Argentina, while others include hundreds (Paraguay 2008); see E. Skaar 'The Implementation Record of Truth Commissions' Recommendations In Latin America', in this volume.

57 A. Robinson, 'Truth Commissions and Anti-Corruption: Towards a Complementary Framework?' (2015) 9 *International Journal of Transitional Justice* 33, at 41.

58 See E. Schmid, 'Liberia's Truth Commission Report: Economic, Social, and Cultural Rights in Transitional Justice' (2009) 24 *Praxis: The Fletcher Journal of Human Security* 5.

59 Liberia, Truth and Reconciliation Commission Final Report, Volume I: Findings and Determinations, 2008, at 73–74.

60 Ibid, at 11–12.

61 Schmid, *supra* note 58, at 12.

62 Vella, *supra* note 19, at 1; Sandoval, *supra* note 12, at 167–168.

four general types emerge: (i) public endorsement of the commission's work by government leadership; (ii) government publication of the commission's final report; (iii) implementation of a reparations programme; and (iv) the creation of follow-up institutions to carry out the recommended reforms and monitor programmes.[63] Of these general types of recommendation, those related to reparations (as well as follow-up institutions) provide for another opportunity to further emphasise social justice issues.

Like truth commissions, reparations have also been viewed as transitional justice processes that are ripe with potential to address social justice concerns.[64] They are also seen as victim-focused and victim-friendly.[65] And while it is outside the scope of this chapter to go into reparation processes as such, when a truth commission has the ability to recommend or even award reparations, it offers yet another avenue where truth commissions can modestly affect social justice. Uprimmy contends that the recommendations or awards can attempt to harmonise the reparation with poverty-reduction policies or other development initiatives.[66] This can be done by focusing on a specific selection of beneficiaries or though more collective reparation awards. The Moroccan truth commission, for instance, approved US$85 million to be distributed to 16,000 individuals and recommended the creation of communal reparation programmes.[67] An institutional mechanism was established to manage the implementation of this communal programme.[68] It was meant for regions that experienced gross violations, suffered exclusion and lacked development opportunities, and included over a dozen projects involving, amongst other things, handicrafts, environmental tourism, well-digging and goat-breeding.[69]

Importantly, however, most reparations are rarely, if ever, satisfactorily handled by governments. There is little political will to implement reparations in transitional justice processes and in practice it seldom occurs.[70] This is the case

63 Bakiner, *supra* note 18, at 20.

64 Sandoval, *supra* note 12, at 169–170.

65 R. Carranza, 'The Right to Reparation in Situations of Poverty', International Center for Transitional Justice Briefing, New York, September 2009, at 4.

66 R. Uprimmy, 'Transformative Reparations of Massive Gross Human Rights Violations: Between Corrective and Distributive Ideas' (2009) 27 *Netherlands Quarterly of Human Rights* 635, at 643.

67 Morocco, Justice and Reconciliation Commission, National Commission for Truth, Justice, and Reconciliation, Summary of Final Report, December 2005; ICTJ, The Rabat Report, The Concept and Challenges of Collective Reparations, 12–14 February 2009, https://www.ictj.org/sites/default/files/ICTJ-Morocco-Reparations-Report-2009-English.pdf.

68 The truth commission still faced strong criticism for failing to deal with communities in Western Sahara, which was one of the areas hardest hit during the reign of King Hassan II.

69 See Remix Biens Communs, Community Reparation in Morocco, Characters of Community Reparation in Morocco, referencing table by Ruben Carranza, 'Comparing community reparations in Morocco, Peru, and Indonesia', 2009, http://wiki.remixthecommons.org/index.php?title=Community_Reparation_in_Morocco.

70 Waldorf, *supra* note 14, at 177.

even when there are good intentions, as with the Mauritius truth commission, which was set up to investigate and repay injustices of the past caused by colonialism and which ultimately touched on a wide variety of social justice issues,[71] but where very few of the 300 recommendations were implemented. In East Timor, despite the fact that the CAVR truth commission report documented ESC rights violation in detail and dealt with a number of social justice issues, when it came to reparations, the limitations became clear. It defined those victims deserving of reparations as those who had suffered civil and political rights violations due to 'feasibility and needs-based prioritization'.[72]

Financial constraints are the most often-cited reason for non-implementation of recommendations, particularly with reparation recommendations.[73] Yet when the political will is there, implementation of the recommendations can take place. Aciru references Argentina, Chile, Brazil, Morocco, Ghana, Sierra Leone and South Africa as some more positive examples,[74] though financial limitations still played a significant role in circumscribing impact. Therefore, the importance of political support cannot be overstated. It affects everything from communication of truth commission findings to following through on its recommendations.

As noted by Allen, a truth commission may very well be the 'embodiment of an unprincipled, political compromise'.[75] And while the intent and competing interests in the creation of the truth commission may not matter as such,[76] the political will to disseminate the findings and seriously consider and implement the recommendations matters a great deal. It is vital that truth commissions communicate their findings to a wider public, as well as to relevant political actors. Argentina and Chile have been recognised for their wide dissemination of the final reports of their truth commissions, whereas Liberia and Kenya have been seen as lacking in this regard.[77] If decision-makers and/or civil society actors reject or fail to endorse and mobilise around a truth commission's findings and recommendations, the influence of the commission will be minimal.[78] For example, according to Bakiner, the truth commission in Nepal, which had numerous criticisms levelled against it,[79] had little direct or indirect political

---

71 See Mauritius, Report of the Truth and Justice Commission, Volume I, November 2011.

72 Truth and Reconciliation in Timor-Leste Commission for Reparation, 'Chega! Final Report: Recommendations Part 11', at 40–41. For a criticism of this prioritisation, see UN Secretary-General, *Questions of the realisation in all countries of economic, social and cultural rights* 2007, A/HRC/4/L.9, para. 42.

73 Aciru, *supra* note 20, at 75.

74 Ibid, at 75.

75 Allen, *supra* note 3, at 321.

76 Ibid, at 322.

77 Aciru, *supra* note 20, at 75.

78 Bakiner, *supra* note 18, at 15.

79 Pasipanodya, *supra* note 17, at 392.

(and, by implication, social justice) impact: reparation recommendations were not implemented, there was no immediate publication of its final report, no official endorsement of its findings and no immediate creation of follow-up institutions.[80] In Kenya, the initial lack of civil society support for the government's second attempt at a truth commission, largely doomed any potential impact.[81] By the time prominent civil society organisations began to lobby the government to formally adopt the truth commission's report and create an implementation plan as required by law, it was clear that little political support existed.[82]

It is often the geo-political situation that dictates how much political support may be forthcoming. The bilateral Indonesia–Timor-Leste Commission of Truth and Friendship, established in 2005 after the CAVR, is a clear example where geo-political factors hampered any implementation of the truth commission's findings.[83] This commission, like the CAVR, documented important findings about the causes of the conflict and made recommendations for forward-looking, collective reparations and more permanent human rights institutions. In spite of this, because East Timor is heavily dependent upon Indonesia's assistance in achieving socio-economic development and other objectives such as membership in the Association of Southeast Asian Nations (ASEAN),[84] there was less emphasis placed on implementation than on the process itself. This lack of implementation must be seen in light of the context of geopolitical 'vulnerability and dependence'.[85] The truth commissions of El Salvador, Sierra Leone and Kenya were the only ones that stipulated that the recommendations would be binding, and even in these unusual situations the politicians still maintained a great deal of discretion on whether and what types of reforms to adopt.[86] The commissions are therefore vulnerable to the political will of their specific contexts.[87]

---

80 Bakiner, *supra* note 18, at 18. Fifteen other truth commissions in his study did produce some direct political impact.

81 L.K. Bosire and G. Lynch, 'Kenya's Search for Truth and Justice: The Role of Civil Society' (2014) 8 *International Journal of Transitional Justice* 256, at 258.

82 Human Rights Watch, '"I Just Sit and Wait to Die": Reparations for Survivors of Kenya's 2007–2008 Post-Election Sexual Violence', 2016, at 16–17, https://www.hrw.org/sites/default/files/report_pdf/kenya0216_web.pdf; B. Momanyi, 'Kenyan Authorities Urged to Implement TJRC Report', Institute for War and Peace Reporting, 16 August 2013, https://iwpr.net/global-voices/kenyan-authorities-urged-implement-human-rights-report.

83 Strating, *supra* note 39, at 233; Truth, Justice, and Reconciliation Commission, 'Turning Pebbles (Human Rights Watch)' (2011) VII *Academic and Civil Society Analysis* 16, at 77, https://digitalcommons.law.seattleu.edu/tjrc-academic/16.

84 Strating, *supra* note 39, at 235.

85 Ibid, at 242.

86 Bakiner, *supra* note 18, at 20; in the case of Kenya, the Kenyan parliament never formally adopted the report as required by law, though the government has set up a (limited) reparations fund for victims and issued public apologies to victims of historical human rights violations as recommended by the TJRC. See Human Rights Watch, *supra* note 82, at 81–82.

87 Robinson, *supra* note 57, at 39.

## 3. MODESTY IS A VIRTUE

Have truth commissions delivered on substantial social justice change? The answer is: not really. Truth commission processes have only included social justice aims to the extent that they could be easily adapted to do so.[88] The general toolkit provided by truth commissions is inadequate 'for pursing socioeconomic and structural outcomes transformative justice necessitates'.[89] There are inherent weaknesses attached to truth commission processes. One of them is the fact that they are meant to be temporary institutions or processes. Their lifespans rarely extend more than a few years. This results in the fact that their recommendations can be easily ignored by politicians with little repercussion.[90]

Truth commissions should not be expected to deliver on the reduction of structural inequality or a decline in poverty levels. They are simply not equipped to do so, particularly because of the highly fragmented and politically tense environments in which they operate.[91] To see truth commissions as a real means to deliver on the promise of social justice amounts to what Allen describes as 'wishful thinking (or at least, not very thoughtful wishing)'.[92] In order to address socio-economic issues, structural violence, social justice more generally, a diverse range of actors and processes are required, including, but stretching far beyond, transitional justice. Other tools and processes specifically designed to address poverty, inequality, and corruption are far better positioned, usually because they are linked with more permanent state structures.

Lofty goals raise lofty expectations, and it does a disservice to those victims and victim communities if false expectations are raised.[93] Yet a more modest question might produce a more nuanced answer. Have truth commissions been able to shed light on important social justice issues and have they contributed to struggles for greater social justice? The answer to these questions is yes. These modest contributions to social justice and goals of transformation should be praised without elevating truth commissions to the level of emancipator for all societal problems.

There have been positive steps taken to recognise social justice within truth commission structures, processes and outcomes. Truth commissions can contribute to social justice discourse by including ESC rights within their remits and by investigating root causes of conflict, structural inequality and marginalisation. They can prioritise the social justice needs and concerns of victims in their reports. They can ensure that victims have a strong and

---

88 Evans, *supra* note 13, at 4.

89 Ibid, at 2 and 7.

90 Waldorf, *supra* note 14, at 176–177.

91 Schmid, *supra* note 58, at 17; Aciru, *supra* note 20, at 74.

92 Allen, *supra* note 3, at 317.

93 Sandoval, *supra* note 12, at 168 and 184.

recognisable voice when participating. They can identify appropriate (and permanent) forums to tackle social justice-related issues.[94] In their final reports, these commissions can make specific recommendations for the establishment of permanent bodies to facilitate change or the drafting of national strategies aimed at specific social justice concerns. Their reports should not necessarily be seen as conclusive but should rather be seen as a first step in opening up spaces for new narratives and further investigations. In addition, truth commissions 'can be seen as a facilitating agent for the mobilisation of "non-conventional resources" such as social awareness, collective memory, solidarity, dedication and commitment'.[95] Though it is disputable whether such a claim can be made,[96] it is useful to look at the potential contribution of truth commissions to various types of change.

Sandoval looks at three forms of social change that transitional justice processes contribute to – ordinary, structural and fundamental – noting that it is important to understand 'whether, when and why' the three types of change are possible.[97] Ordinary social change concerns everyday changes that reflect dominant ideologies. These can be legal reforms that do not disrupt dominant ways of thinking or structures. Structural change is more complex. It seems as though a fundamental change has occurred (she gives the example of constitutional changes or the changes after the South African truth commission), but in reality, the dominant ideology, or a lighter version of it, remains the same. Finally, fundamental social change takes place when various structural changes provide the opportunities for new ideologies and values to flourish. These new values must be 'respected, endorsed, adopted, and articulated' by different political actors and parts of society so that they can ultimately change the social, economic and political conditions that contributed to the conflict or abuse.[98]

It is necessary for the structural changes to work in combination in order to affect meaningful fundamental change. If the work of truth commissions is going to make a larger, more significant impact on social justice, it must be seen as part of a larger whole. Though not looking at social justice *per se*, this view aligns with findings from Olsen, Payne and Reiter, which found that when used alone, truth commissions may have a negative effect on democracy and human rights, but when used in combination with other measures can yield more positive effects.[99]

Comprehensive strategies, including transitional justice processes like truth commissions and development initiatives, must complement one another.

---

94 Robinson, *supra* note 57, at 40. She gives the example of Kenya's truth commission. See Truth, Justice and Reconciliation Commission Final Report, Volume 2b, May 2013, at v.

95 Verwoerd, *supra* note 40, at 135.

96 Allen, *supra* note 3, at 333; see also Bakiner, *supra* note 18, at 8.

97 See Sandoval, *supra* note 12.

98 Ibid, at 182–183.

99 Olsen, Payne and Reiter, *supra* note 18, at 153–154.

Holistic strategies likes those being pursued in Colombia, with truth, accountability, reparation and larger legal and policy reforms taking place, serve as an example. Truth commissions have been referred to as 'stepping stones', whereby they provide a bridge away from injustice and towards democracy and development.[100] Yet they are not the only stepping stones on the pathway towards social justice. They are one small (temporary) stone, hopefully surrounded by more permanent stones. As a single policy instrument,[101] truth commissions will inherently always play a modest role, in part because of their temporary nature and in part because of their weak political leverage.

Given the fact that transitional justice, as a field, may have its limitations, specific processes, such as truth commissions, should prioritise working with other post-conflict responses to deliver on calls for social justice. Duthie argues that transitional justice measures should be designed and implemented so that they are 'development sensitive'.[102] If development work refers to the aim of 'improving the standard of living for all people in poor countries',[103] then a development-sensitive approach would require key stakeholders to be aware of what links may exist, and pursuing cooperation when beneficial and avoiding such links when engaging with such issues would hinder development work. Cooperation, when mutually beneficial, is particularly important given the scarcity of resources and competing needs of post-conflict societies.

One idea put forward has been to better link or coordinate between reparation programmes and asset-recovery initiatives.[104] For example, the Kenyan truth commission recommended this in its final report, although it was not taken up by parliament.[105] In addition, the World Bank has recently made efforts to link its anti-corruption efforts with transitional justice processes and rule of law reforms.[106] Moreover, in the Philippines, $680 million recovered from Swiss bank accounts belonging to the former dictator Marcos has been used to finance reparation programmes for victims of gross human rights violations. It is estimated that approximately 8,000 victims will receive $1,000 each, together

---

[100] Verwoerd, *supra* note 40, at 117.

[101] Ibid, at 119.

[102] See R. Duthie, 'Toward a Development-Sensitive Approach to Transitional Justice' (2008) 2 *International Journal of Transitional Justice* 292.

[103] See G. Junne and W. Verkoren, 'The Challenge of Postconflict Development', in G. Junne and W. Verkoren (eds.), *Postconflict Development: Meeting New Challenges*, Lynne Rienner Press, Boulder CO, 2005.

[104] Carranza, *supra* note 6, at 318; K. Andrieu, 'Dealing with a "New" Grievance: Should Anticorruption Be Part of the Transitional Justice Agenda?' (2012) 11 *Journal of Human Rights* 549.

[105] Kenya, Truth, Justice and Reconciliation Commission Final Report, Volume 4, 2013, at 87.

[106] World Bank, 'New Directions in Justice Reform: A Companion Piece to the Updated Strategy and Implementation Plan on Strengthening Governance, Tackling Corruption, Doc. 70640, May 2012, http://documents.worldbank.org/curated/en/928641468338516754/pdf/706400REPLACEM0Justice0Reform0Final.pdf; Carranza, *supra* note 6, at 319.

with a letter of apology from the Marcos family.[107] Likewise, in Peru, a fund was established to use the recovered assets of Fujimori, totalling over $90 million, for both anti-corruption and transitional justice measures, including reparations.[108]

This idea, therefore, is appealing – but questions remain. Would the funds only benefit those individuals labelled as 'victims', or should they be used for development more generally? Should collective reparative measures be taken, such as the creation of community education or health centres, or should payment be specific for individual victims? The lines between reparative justice and humanitarian and development aid begin to blur, which could lead to a diminishing of the reparative justice aspects of the process.[109] There is a complex relationship between collective reparations and development.[110] It is important to keep reparations and development initiatives 'conceptually distinct'.[111] Much, of course, will depend upon the specific circumstances of the country and feelings of victimhood as experienced by the population. Truth commissions need to be aware of the drawbacks of overlapping these conceptually different processes too much. Reparations should be aimed at addressing past abuses, even if they also aim at transforming future lives. They should not be used in place of existing state obligations to fulfil ESC rights or development goals.

The benefits of truth commissions focusing on issues that overlap with development, such as socio-economic harms, may not be easily measured. However, they could play a role in bringing attention to these types of violations, thereby contributing to the goals of development and possibly shaping future development policy.[112] As noted by Junne and Verkoren, post-conflict development work is not just about rebuilding but about transforming societies by restructuring society.[113] However, it is questionable whether such links would be transformative enough for some scholars, who question the foundations of existing transitional justice processes. These liberal and neoliberal foundations are often the same ones facilitating the need for development work. And if transitional processes seek to avoid destabilising already unstable societies, then it must be asked whether transformative actions will only promote additional unrest and tension.

In addition to a development-sensitive approach, a community-based approach has also been put forward as a way of making the work of truth commissions more relevant.[114] A community-based approach to truth-telling

107 Andrieu, *supra* note 104.
108 Carranza, *supra* note 6, at 324.
109 Robinson, *supra* note 57, at 43.
110 Schmid, *supra* note 58, at 18.
111 Duthie, *supra* note 102, at 299.
112 Ibid, at 302.
113 Junne and Verkoren, *supra* note 103, at 6.
114 Aciru, *supra* note 20, at 79.

would give 'decision-making over the design, remit, conduct, character, and outcomes of the "truth-telling" process' to a community.[115] Grassroots-led processes and outcomes could help ensure that social justice concerns have a central place within the processes. Moreover, they could ensure that truth commissions do not become 'truth-obscuring' processes when specific communities or narratives are left out of the truth-telling process. Yet this approach may not affect the change needed at the institutional and political level. Community-based approaches are important but they should not overlook the necessity of engaging with elite decision-makers at the policy-changing level.

## 4. CONCLUSION

Roht-Arriaza has argued that broadening the scope of 'transitional justice to encompass the building of a just as well as peaceful society may make the effort so broad as to become meaningless'.[116] While the efforts of truth commissions to deliver on social justice are far from meaningless, the transformative potential of truth commissions to bring about greater social justice is limited. Even when truth commissions are extending into the realm of development or looking at a broader set of human rights violations, this should not be seen as 'synonymous with transformative justice' or with delivering on social justice.[117] Rather it shows that truth commissions have a restricted capacity to respond to all social justice needs, but that they are well placed to make a modest discursive contribution to a greater whole. Bringing social justice concerns within the ambit of truth commissions is therefore not wishful thinking; much can be and has been done. However, in order to better understand the contribution of truth commissions to the broader transitional justice process, more thoughtful wishing may be in order.

115 P. Lundy and M. McGovern, 'Whose Justice? Rethinking Transitional Justice from the Bottom Up' (2008) 35 *Journal of Law and Society* 265, at 271; UNHCR, *A Community-based Approach in UNHCR Operations*, 2008.

116 N. Roht-Arriaza, 'The New Landscape of Transitional Justice', in N. Roht-Arriaza and J. Mariezcurrena (eds.), *Transitional Justice in the Twenty-First Century*, Cambridge University Press, Cambridge, 2006, at 2.

117 Sandoval, *supra* note 12, at 175.

# TRANSITIONING TOWARD DIGNITY

Erin Daly



## 1. INTRODUCTION

While each country experiences conflict differently, develops unique mechanisms of transitional justice, and structures and empowers its truth commissions to suit its particular needs and capacities, the endpoints are often similar: at least in their public commitments, countries invariably aspire to craft an inclusive society in which all citizens are engaged for the betterment of the individuals and communities that comprise the nation. This, it is presumed, will end violence and avoid its recurrence, and bring about lasting peace. These are, without a doubt, broad and ambitious goals, indicating deep transformations in statecraft, in the social fabric, and even in the psychology of the people. Thus, there is a link between how people feel about their society, how they engage in it, and the political and social spaces that both produce and result from that engagement. Human dignity, which has both individual psychological dimensions and relational social dimensions, links the personal and the political aims of transitional justice.

Often, the architects of transitional justice establish truth commissions for the stated purpose of moving toward the fulfilment of these goals. Truth commissions do not have the jurisdictional authority or the resources to accomplish any of these goals on their own, but they can galvanise institutions of the state and civil society to take action. They cannot draft constitutions and laws, but they can develop the framework for legal reform, identify the fundamental values that legal reform should embody, and identify the essential terms that legal reform should adopt. They typically do not have the authority to pay reparations, but they can identify the goals of a reparations programme and insist on its realisation according to a set timeframe. They cannot write a new curriculum, but they can frame the essential factual and historical accounts in a way that respects all legitimate perspectives and they can articulate the fundamental lessons of human rights to be inculcated. They cannot, on their own, define citizenship and nationhood, but they can reflect and embody the equal value of each person that demands respect for all. Truth commissions, then, have little power actually to make change, but they wield significant power to articulate the terms of debate and to create the framework in which social and political change will take place. They do this in their processes by showing respect for all and in their reports by careful description of the harms of the conflict and delineation of the recommended remedies.

The question then becomes: what can truth commissions do to maximise their effectiveness, even if their major contribution is to galvanise others to do the work of justice and reconciliation, based on the foundation of human dignity?

The argument here is that human dignity is the axis around which truth commissions revolve and ultimately on which their legacies rest. A truth commission that does not contribute to the promotion and protection of human dignity cannot be said to be successful or effective. The argument is further made that truth commissions are most likely to leave a lasting legacy if they are explicit and emphatic in their embrace of human dignity as their term of reference.

Dignity is embedded in the ethos of transitional justice and should therefore play a more central and clearly defined role in its implementation. Most truth commission processes and outcomes mention human dignity, but few give it the attention it deserves and they therefore fail to take full advantage of its promise. This chapter argues that the legacies of truth commissions, as the signature institutions of transitional justice, can be enhanced if they are more explicit in adopting the language of human dignity.

This chapter proceeds in three stages. First, by considering both international and domestic transitions, the argument is made that human dignity is and has been the animating value of transitional justice. Second, the chapter shows how truth commissions so far do incorporate the rough idea of human dignity in their processes and outcomes. Third, the chapter argues that explicitly and thoughtfully absorbing the lessons of human dignity would enhance the legacies and increase the effectiveness of truth commissions; the third section also shows exactly how this might work with respect to some of the most salient outcomes of truth commissions – amnesties, apologies and the consolidation of democracy.

## 2. TRANSITIONS TOWARD DIGNITY

### 2.1. THE ROLE OF DIGNITY IN GLOBAL TRANSITIONAL JUSTICE

Most accounts of transitional justice are domestic affairs, focusing on how a country reinvents itself after political violence.[1] But perhaps the most significant moment of transition to occur in the modern world, if not human history, is the coming together of 51 countries in the aftermath of the Second World War to form the United Nations. With a Charter whose preamble states that 'We the Peoples of the United Nations, Determined to save succeeding generations from the scourge of war, which twice in our lifetime has brought untold sorrow to mankind, and to reaffirm faith in fundamental human rights, in the dignity and worth of the human person, in the equal rights of men and women and of nations large and small',[2] this transformative institution not only aimed at quelling warfare but sought to lay the foundation for a new, global ethic that would be based on nothing less than the equal dignity of every human being. Explicitly articulated in the initial paragraphs of the Charter of the United Nations, this ethical touchstone for the new world was then quickly reinforced in the UN's first significant accomplishment (and perhaps still its greatest legacy), the Universal Declaration of Human Rights (UDHR). The Declaration's Preamble took the seminal idea of the Charter and rendered it in to law: 'Whereas recognition of the inherent dignity and of the equal and inalienable rights of all members of the human family is the foundation of freedom, justice and peace in the world', and later:

> Whereas the peoples of the United Nations have in the Charter reaffirmed their faith in fundamental human rights, in the dignity and worth of the human person and in the equal rights of men and women and have determined to promote social progress and better standards of life in larger freedom, … Now, Therefore The General Assembly proclaims This Universal Declaration of Human Rights as a common standard of achievement for all peoples and all nations …[3]

1 Political violence is the catch-all phrase I will use to denote all manner of political and social trauma, from an acute situation like a coup, a civil war or genocide to chronic conditions like apartheid and colonialism.

2 United Nations, *Charter of the United Nations*, 24 October 1945, 1 UNTS XVI, http://www.refworld.org/docid/3ae6b3930.html, Preamble.

3 UN General Assembly, *Universal Declaration of Human Rights*, 10 December 1948, 217 A (III), http://www.refworld.org/docid/3ae6b3712c.html, Preamble.

And to reinforce the point, the very first Article of the Declaration announces that 'All human beings are born free and equal in dignity and rights. They are endowed with reason and conscience and should act towards one another in a spirit of brotherhood.'[4] Where the Charter identified the recognition of human dignity as a global aspiration, the Declaration for the first time associated the principle of human dignity with the legal regime of rights.

These two innovations were designed not only to help the world transition from war to peace, but to transform the world from one in which a holocaust could happen to one in which it could not. Human dignity was the essential epiphany of this moment of global transitional justice. More precisely, the two global instruments represent several interdependent insights about the nature of humanity and the nature of the world that still resonate and define the global understanding of dignity today, both as an ethical concept and as a legal right that governments are bound to respect.

First, the idea of dignity embodies the recognition that every 'member of the human family' is entitled to respect from all others simply by virtue of being born human. It applies to all humans and it applies only to humans. There may be reason to wonder whether animals, ecosystems, corporations and other non-humans have dignity, but the dignity that comes to us through international law is immanent in the human person. It puts people of all genders, religions, ethnicities, ages, abilities and all other differences on the same playing field. It may, in fact, be the single thing that unifies us when all else differentiates and divides us. It is what all humans have in common.

The second insight is the decision to incorporate the first insight in a legal document – that is, the fact that every human being has dignity is not only a philosophical observation but a tenet at the foundation of human rights law, and even of the rule of law itself. Indeed, the foundation of the post-Second World War transformation was from one in which human dignity was an option to be invoked at will (yes in the case of the abolition of slavery, no in the case of colonialism) to one in which it could never be denied. One quality of human dignity is that once it is recognised, it cannot be unrecognised; once it is known, it cannot be un-known.

Third, the basis for human dignity is the human capacity for reason and morality. It is the capacity for self-conscious planning, which can manifest itself in the right to design one's own life plan.[5] This, in other words, is the capacity for creation and, to put it in Arendtian terms,[6] the capacity for recreation, rebirth, to build anew out of the ashes of the old. As such, it is the animating feature – the life force – of transitional and transformative justice.

4 Ibid, Article I.

5 Constitutional Court of Colombia, Sentencia T-088/08, at 3.5.5.

6 H. Arendt, *The Human Condition*, University of Chicago Press, Chicago, 1998.

Fourth, the UDHR articulation of human dignity is relational and, while it establishes a right that every individual can claim against a government, it also imposes an obligation on every human being to respect the dignity of every other. It reminds us that human beings exist only in community. One's dignity is a matter of relations with others, and one asserts one's dignity against others. This is embodied in the African concept of *ubuntu*,[7] but it also is inherent in the very concept of dignity as articulated in global international law. As such, the exclusion, marginalisation, humiliation and violence that are the marks of political violence also violate this aspect of dignity.

The simple phrases of the two foundational documents of the United Nations embody lessons to be applied to transitional justice throughout the world. Heeding those lessons will make today's truth commissions more effective in advancing their stated objectives, almost all of which rest on a foundation of the recognition of human dignity.

## 2.2. DIGNITY IN DOMESTIC CONSTITUTIONS

Among the first things that nations do when establishing the post-conflict order is to adopt a new or radically revised constitution. This helps to establish the values of the new dispensation and to entrench the institutional framework of governance. Often, new constitutions are adopted by referendum, to embody the democratic values of the new regime. One illustration of the spread of the awareness of human dignity – and one of the most notable manifestations of the impact of the UDHR – is the absorption of human dignity in constitutions in all regions of the world today. More than three quarters of the world's constitutions recognise the right to human dignity[8] – whether as a fundamental value, an inviolable right, a right associated with certain segments of society (women, the elderly), with certain interests (torture and capital punishment, education) or other values (privacy, equality) or some combination of these. In some constitutions, it represents the very purpose of the state.[9] Associated with these

7 'Ubuntu, generally translated as "humaneness", expresses itself metaphorically in umuntu ngumuntu ngabantu – "people are people through other people". In the words of Constitutional Court Justice Makgoro: "Its spirit emphasises respect for human dignity, marking a shift from confrontation to conciliation."' *Truth and Reconciliation Commission of South Africa Report*. Cape Town: Truth and Reconciliation Commission, 1999, Volume 1, at 127, quoting *S v Makwanyane and another* 1995 (3) SA 391, at paras. 307–308.

8 See *National Constitutions with Dignity Provisions*, available at the Dignity Rights Project website: https://docs.google.com/spreadsheets/d/1Tn8w8hJ7HOly-HY9rkUEPjyOAIdCfaUw2X3a594RDA8/edit#gid=0.

9 See Constitution of Peru, Title I, Chapter 1, Article 1: 'The defense of the human person and respect for his dignity are the supreme purpose of the society and the State.' See also e.g. Constitution of Plurinational State of Bolivia, Part I, Title I, Chapter II, Article 9.

texts, we are seeing an ever-growing body of constitutional jurisprudence that spans civil and political rights (information, association, speech, participation) and social and economic rights (housing, health, environment).

While this range across time and space might seem dizzying and infinitely diverse, the understandings of dignity coalesce around a very simple idea: that every human being has inherent moral worth that must be respected, and that every human being has equal worth. It is as if each person who has ever been or will ever be born has a coin at birth, one that can never be lost or extinguished (though it can, of course, be bruised).[10] Insofar as dignity entails the equal worth of all members of the human family, it is both substantive (worth) and qualitative (equal); it is different from each in that it necessarily entails both. It is thus not just about liberty or about equality, but about what happens at the intersection of liberty and equality.[11]

Echoing the principles implicit in the UDHR's recognition of human dignity, the worth of the human being is manifest in several domains. First, human worth means that the integrity of one's physical body must be respected: violence, including sexual violence, as a form of political oppression cannot be tolerated in a society that respects human dignity. (Hence, constitutions often associate dignity with criminal justice, the prohibition on torture, rape and even medical experimentation). Second, a society that respects dignity protects each person's moral agency – that is, his or her capacity to make decisions for and act for him/herself.[12] This prohibits the objectification of any human being, the use of one human being to suit the purposes or accomplish the aims of another.[13] The anti-objectification principle reveals dignity's integral connection with the concept of equality: the reason that no person can serve as the means to another's ends is that each person's worth is the same as every other person's. No one has more or less agency than any other so no one is entitled to assert his or her will over any other. This operates collectively as well, limiting what a majority can do to a minority. Third, the notion of civic or participatory dignity expands outward from the human capacity to engage with others on an equal basis and to create or re-create the terms on which one's bodily integrity and moral agency are to be protected; that is, participatory dignity is self-determination on a social scale. As it gives rise to self-government, it is the basis for democracy.

10 E. Daly, *Dignity Rights: Courts, Constitutions, and the Worth of the Human Person*, University of Pennsylvania Press, Philadelphia, 2015, at 14.

11 *Obergefell v. Hodges*, 576 U.S. ___, 135 S. Ct. 2584 (2015).

12 See e.g. *Air Transport Security* case, Bundesverfassungsgericht (BVerfG), 15 February 2006, 1 BvR 357/05, http://www. bverfg.de/entscheidungen/rs20060215_1bvr035705.html. See also *Indiana v Edwards*, 554 U.S. 164 (2008) (Scalia, J. dissenting) ('the dignity at issue is the supreme human dignity of being master of one's fate rather than a ward of the State – the dignity of individual choice').

13 BVerfG, 15 February 2006, *supra* note 12, at paras. 119–121.

And, fourth, dignity is way of life: Latin American countries protect *la vida digna*, while India and its neighbours interpret the right to life as the right to live with dignity, and the social states of Europe guarantee education, minimum pension, health care and so on to ensure that every citizen lives a dignified life.

These conditions constitute the essential minimal conditions for transitional justice. The recognition of equal concern and respect for all enables the development of an inclusive society. The consequential yet independent prohibition on violations of physical integrity makes violence intolerable and therefore is the ethos necessary to guarantee non-repetition of violence. The parallel prohibition on emotional and psychological violence precludes oppression, marginalisation, humiliation, and disenfranchisement. And without the assurance that each person lives with dignity, participation in democratic governance and in civil society are nearly impossible. The legacy of truth commissions thus rests on a foundation of the recognition of human dignity.

## 2.3. THE PASTS AND THE FUTURES OF DIGNITY

This understanding of human dignity, which insists on the capacity for iterative, and perhaps endless, self-creation, applies with similar vigour on a larger scale to nations in moments of transition. Self-determination refers equally to individual control over one's life and to the control that a people has over its community or nation; transitional justice, then, represents the moment in a nation's history when it self-consciously re-creates itself and determines its future course on the basis of a new foundational order. Hence South Africa's commitment to the restoration of 'human and civil dignity',[14] as articulated in the law creating the truth commission.

Dignity thus has the potential energy to drive not only transitional justice, but also societal transformation. In an early South African Constitutional Court case, Justice O'Regan drew a direct line with dignity from the past to the future:

> Apartheid was a denial of a common humanity. Black people were refused respect and dignity and thereby the dignity of all South Africans was diminished. The new Constitution rejects this past and affirms the equal worth of all South Africans. Thus recognition and protection of human dignity is the touchstone of the new political order and is fundamental to the new Constitution.[15]

This same impulse can be seen throughout the world: a tremendous variety of crimes and atrocities have given rise to transitional justice efforts, but, to a

---

14 Promotion of National Unity and Reconciliation Act, No. 34 of 1995.

15 *S v Makwanyane and another* 1995 (3) SA 391, at para. 329, cited in South African Truth Commission Report, *supra* note 7, Volume 1, at 126.

great extent, the common theme can be characterised as deprivations of human dignity. The violence of political crime is not just to the body but to the spirit of self-identity and autonomy – the desire to reduce another to a mere body, to crush the will, to eliminate not only the capacity to live, but the desire, the hope or the will to live. The rhetoric of dehumanisation, the policies of instrumentalisation and objectification, the denial of the individual in the collective (explicit in the extreme in instances of ethnic cleansing and genocide) are all essentially denials of the humanity of the other, and thus denials of the respect every person is owed by virtue of having been born a member of the human family. It is a deprivation of the capacity to decide for oneself the circumstances of one's life. Indeed, the essential harm of any inequality or discrimination to the point of oppression is the denial of human dignity. As former South African Constitutional Court judge Laurie Ackermann has said of apartheid: 'what lay at the heart of apartheid pathology … was the extensive and sustained attempt to deny to the majority of the South African population the right of self-identification and self-determination.' Similarly, the South African Truth and Reconciliation Commission Final Report described apartheid in part a system that was itself 'evil, inhumane and degrading … amongst its many crimes, perhaps its greatest was the power to humiliate, to denigrate and to remove the self-confidence, self-esteem and dignity of its millions of victims.'[16]

Political crimes are fundamentally crimes of indignity.[17] This is true in the systemic, quotidian experience of the decades-long policy of apartheid, and it is true in the acute violence of war. As the Liberian Truth and Reconciliation Report explained: 'During the Liberian civil wars, fighters committed wide-ranging violations of international humanitarian law. Statement givers reported massacres, rape as a weapon of war, torture, summary executions, collective punishments, violence to life, health, and mental well-being, as well as innumerable threats and outrages upon personal dignity.'[18] Outrages upon personal dignity are the catch-all form of political violence against the human person.[19]

---

16 South African Truth Commission Report, *supra* note 7, Volume 1, at 34. See also para. 3 of Security Council Resolution 392 (19 June 1976) and Security Council Resolution 473 (13 June 1980), affirming that 'apartheid is a crime against the conscience and dignity of mankind'.

17 'The public victim hearings vividly portrayed the fact that not only were international or domestic laws broken, not only was there a disrespect of human rights in the abstract, but the very dignity and 'personhood' of individual human beings were centrally violated': 1 South African Truth Commission Report, *supra* note 7, at 128.

18 The Advocates for Human Rights, *A House with Two Rooms: Final Report of the Truth and Reconciliation Commission of Liberia Diaspora Project*, DRI Press, St. Paul MN, 2009, at 10.

19 See also *Synoptic Overview of HRVIC Report: Conclusions and Recommendations Presented to President, Commander-In-Chief of the Armed Forces of the Federal Republic of Nigeria Chief Olusegun Obasanjo GCFR, Submitted by Human Rights Violations Investigation Commission,*

It thus stands to reason that transitional justice is typically designed to reject the past abuses of dignity and to pivot toward a new dispensation on the basis of respect for human dignity. This can be seen in constitutionalism[20] and exists in the mechanisms and institutions of transitional justice themselves. In many parts of the world, dignity has become not only the very purpose of transitional moments – the reasons why transitions must take place, the meaning of the new dispensation that will take the place of the old – but it is also inherent in the notion of transition itself. As the Indonesia–Timorese truth commission said:

> In today's era of globalization, taking full advantage of the freedom that we have attained, our peoples endeavour to build a solid foundation for a future of peace; a future where human dignity and social justice are the guiding force of transformation. Peace, however, is a process and has to be built. The pillars of peace are democracy, sustainable development and respect for human rights.[21]

That is, to build a new society on a solid foundation of peace and social justice, it is necessary to commit to the recognition of human dignity as a foundational value and, to ensure its implementation, as a right that can be claimed. To better understand the relationship of human dignity to transitional justice in general, we will explore its role in the archetypical institutions of transitional justice – truth and reconciliation commissions – and examine how truth commissions leave legacies of dignity.

## 3. THE ARCHITECTURE AND OPERATIONS OF TRUTH AND RECONCILIATION COMMISSIONS

For South African jurist Laurie Ackermann, dignity is the term or criterion of reference of South African constitutionalism, and it may very well be the term of reference for truth commissions around the world. In respect of what do we seek truth? Why do we reconcile? The ultimate goals of transitional justice all derive from a principle of human dignity.

Its resonance in the ideal of reconciliation was evident in South Africa, for instance, where the Act creating the truth commission established as one of the commission's goals 'the restoration of the human and civil dignity of victims of

---

May 2002, at 3: 'This personal accumulation of wealth led to the decay of our society. Public and private morality reached its nadir; and the casualties included human dignity, human rights and our basic freedoms. We also experienced institutional and structural decay.'

20 Constitution of the Republic of South Africa (10 December 1996), section 10, http://www.refworld.org/docid/3ae6b5de4.html.

21 *Per Memoriam ad Spem. Final Report of the Commission of Truth and Friendship Indonesia–Timor-Leste*, Terms of Reference, Preamble, paras. 1 and 3, at 173.

gross human rights violations through testimony and recommendations to the President concerning reparations for victims.'[22] Thus, the South African truth commission set as its fundamental goal the restoration of both the sense of human dignity to which all people everywhere are entitled just by virtue of being human and also the civil dignity that persons can exercise in a political community with others; these represent the right of self-determination individually and collectively. It aimed to achieve these goals both in how it operated – testimony to elucidate the truth about apartheid – and in its product, in the recommendations it would make to the president for all forms of reparation. The truth commission's legacy of dignity would result from both the process and outcome.

Liberia's truth commission also foregrounded the concept of human dignity in its final report. The report quoted liberally from provisions of international law that emphasise human dignity and in an extensive coda detailing international human rights and humanitarian law norms, it highlighted the recognition of dignity, drawing a direct line from the fundamental values of the community of nations to the humanity of the Liberian people themselves.[23]

In the body of the report itself, the Liberian commission devoted an entire section to 'Personal Liberty and Dignity', which considers the 'Right to Life', the 'Prohibition of Torture and Inhuman & Degrading Treatment' and the 'Prohibition of Slavery' all in terms of human dignity.

The commission, throughout its extensive report, also made many other references to the protection of human dignity in various contexts, including insisting for instance that prisoners live in conditions compatible with human dignity.[24] The Liberian commission also emphasised the importance of education to the protection and promotion of human dignity: 'The Government of Liberia should recognize that everyone has the right to education, which is to be directed to the "full development of the human personality and the sense of its dignity, and shall strengthen the respect for human rights and fundamental freedoms"'.[25] This explicit reference can be thought to strengthen the Liberian truth commission's legacy in galvanising dignity-based educational reform.

But these are the exceptions. Most commission reports mention dignity fleetingly and marginally. It is thus worth exploring how truth commissions might enhance their impacts by being more explicit about the relationship between dignity and the post-transition society in terms of reconciliation and truth. In other words, advancing human dignity should be an explicit value, and not an unstated undercurrent or an incidental by-product of truth commissions.

---

22 Promotion of National Unity and Reconciliation Act, No. 34 of 1995, §3(c), preamble; see also 1 South Africa Truth Commission Report, *supra* note 7, at 57.

23 *A House with Two Rooms*, *supra* note 18.

24 Ibid, at 440.

25 Ibid, at 459, quoting International Covenant on Economic, Social and Cultural Rights, Article 13(1).

## 3.1. THE THEORY OF RECONCILIATION

Perhaps the most perplexing question of all in the study of truth commissions concerns the true meaning of reconciliation. As Jeremy Sarkin and I have written elsewhere, '[r]econciliation may mean quite different things in different societies at different times.'[26] At its core, however, reconciliation must at some level be about joining together two or more on the basis of equality and mutual recognition. Reconciliation cannot work if the parties continue to believe in one's superiority over the other, nor can it work where one party denies the humanity or the value of the other. It thus both demands and reflects the fact of human dignity, understood as inherent equal worth. Indeed, the purpose of a reconciliation commission is to enable people on all sides to live together without committing further acts of violence, and violence can only be quelled when people recognise each other's common humanity.

This can be particularly challenging in the aftermath of atrocities, where perpetrators have committed acts of unimaginable violence, where victims and survivors have endured unspeakable pain. And yet, the call to reconciliation stands firm, even in these most painful situations. The central insight of those who first advanced the aspiration of reconciliation was that no one is beyond the pale.[27] No acts are so monstrous that, in the end, the humanity of the perpetrators can be denied. As a practical matter, the commitment to an ethos of human dignity, then, provides perpetrators a way to get back into the fold, to return to society as an equal member worthy of respect as a citizen, if not as a friend. In this sense, it can be the lifeline that perpetrators can hold on to as they try to accept the terms of the new dispensation: they may be punished, they may be reviled, but their dignity as a human being will be respected and that may be enough.

Every country that has adopted a meaningful truth and reconciliation process as a mechanism of transitional justice has transitioned toward a constitutional democracy. Therefore, even beyond establishing a lasting peace between persons or partisans, reconciliation embodies a commitment to include members from all sides of the conflict in the new society; when that society is a democracy, it reflects a commitment to include every person in the *demos* – the polity that makes up the sovereignty. Dignity is essential here, too, because a *demos* assumes the equality of its members – that no single voice is louder than any other, that no vote counts more than any other. Thus, a truth commission

---

26 E. Daly and J. Sarkin, *Reconciliation in Divided Societies: Finding Common Ground*, University of Pennsylvania Press, Philadelphia, 2007, at 34.

27 Reconciliation 'does not require that perpetrators of the grossest human rights abuses be embraced like brothers and sisters, but neither does it allow a society to deem them so monstrous that they are beyond the human pale': Daly and Sarkin, *supra* note 26, at 152.

can advance a legacy of reconciliation by insisting on the human dignity of all members of the polity, so that every person is respected as a fellow human being and admitted into the new society on an equal footing. This is acknowledgement and acceptance; it is not necessarily forgiveness or absolution.

## 3.2. THE PRACTICE OF TRUTH

Transitional justice is built on the assumption that one cannot move forward into a stable and fair dispensation unless the truths of the past are known, accepted and (at least to some extent) undeniable.

The South African truth commission was explicit about the role of dignity in the public hearings and then in its dignity-restoration mandate:

> It is particularly important to emphasise that establishing the truth could not be divorced from the affirmation of the dignity of human beings. Thus, not only the actual outcome or findings of an investigation counted. The process whereby the truth was reached was itself important because it was through this process that the essential norms of social relations between people were reflected. It was, furthermore, through dialogue and respect that a means of promoting transparency, democracy and participation in society was suggested as a basis for affirming human dignity and integrity.[28]

In South Africa, truth was explicitly the vehicle by which dignity would be restored. In consequence, 'the Commission embarked on the road of seeking to restore the dignity of victims through extensive statement taking and public hearings.'[29]

The Chilean process also made this clear:

> It is also true, as the decree states, that only the truth will make it possible to restore the dignity of the victims in the public mind, allow their relatives and mourners to honour them properly, and in some measure make it possible to make amends for the damage done.[30]

---

28 South African Truth Commission Report, *supra* note 7, Volume 1, at 114.

29 South African Truth Commission Report, *supra* note 7, Volume 1, at 78.

30 *Report of the Chilean National Commission on Truth and Reconciliation*, at 20, https://www.usip.org/sites/default/files/resources/collections/truth_commissions/Chile90-Report/Chile90-Report.pdf (originally published: University of Notre Dame Press, Notre Dame IN, 1993). See also ibid, at 24.
It must be noted that, at least in Chile, 'dignity' has both a positive and a nefarious meaning. For instance, Colonia Dignidad was a site used for detention and torture: see Report at 639–642 et seq. However, according to the Chilean Truth Commission Report (at 100), on 11 March 1974, the military junta published a Declaration of Principles of the Government of Chile, in which it declared (among many other things) that '[t]he human being has natural rights that are prior to and higher than the state', and that hence the state 'must be at the

The most successful truth commissions have been humble about their ability to announce the truth. They approach their task of creating a historical record in multiple dimensions, understanding that truths vary depending on the perspective and – if they value the principle of human dignity – they understand that each perspective has value that must be respected. Thus, recognising human dignity imposes on truth commissions an obligation to take seriously and respect the truths of each side.

The very act of telling one's own story can also manifest the restoration of dignity.[31] As the Kenyan law establishing the Truth, Justice and Reconciliation Commission indicated, the objectives of the commission were to

> promote peace, justice, national unity, healing, and reconciliation among the people of Kenya by … (among other things) … investigating into the whereabouts of victims and restoring the human and civil dignity of such victims by granting them an opportunity to relate their own accounts of the violations of which they are victims, and by recommending reparations measures in respect of them.[32]

This is true both because putting one's story into an official repository validates one's sense of reality, and thereby vindicates one's dignity, but also because the very act of telling – in one's own way, in one's own language, and in one's own good time – is a way of reclaiming one's dignity. One Chilean witness was explicit about this: 'For us this is a very painful but very important moment. It's the first time we've been able to speak. We have to speak of this situation with dignity and not keep hiding.'[33] To leave a legacy of dignity among the victims, truth commissions must rigorously respect and nurture dignity, both in how they solicit the narratives and in recording and manifesting them in commission reports and all other memorialisations.

service of the person rather than the reverse'. According to the Report, the document further stated that 'Chile has always lived under a legal framework … that has ever reflected the deep esteem Chileans feel for the spiritual dignity of the human person, and consequently for his or her fundamental rights. It is in this respect for human rights, more than in its tradition of the popular origins and constitutional succession of governments, in which the essence and core of Chilean democracy are to be found.' In addition to this, however, dignity was also used by the Catholic community in the spirit of reconstruction: as recounted in the Commission report (at 991), '[o]n April 1, 1987, Pope John Paul arrived in Chile on an official visit. He took part in mass gatherings in Santiago and in various parts of the country, offering a message of peace, love, and commitment to respect for the dignity of the person, which was broadcast widely on the media and was very moving for many people.' See also uses of dignity in statements of bishops, at 976–977.

31 'Making a statement to the Commission brought relief to some. The experience itself helped to break an emotional silence, started the process of integrating experiences that had been repressed or shut out for years, alleviated feelings of shame and, in an atmosphere of acceptance, began to restore dignity and self-respect.' 1 South African Truth Commission Report, *supra* note 7, at 367.

32 Kenyan Truth, Justice and Reconciliation Commission Bill, 2008, Part II, §5(o).

33 Chilean Truth Commission Report, *supra* note 30, at 1021.

Here, of course, sensitivity is necessary as well. To fully respect the dignity of each participant in the transitional justice process, the truth commission must attend to a number of issues that might otherwise have the effect of silencing or excluding some truths,[34] particularly because of the serious risk of re-traumatisation for the victims. For example, it is easy for truth commissions to meet, on common ground, those members of society who are most like them, but to truly respect the dignity of all, they must meet on the same terms of camaraderie and comfort members of the society who are least like them – they must meet in settings where all are comfortable, speak in languages that are natural for everyone, and ask questions and listen to responses in an attitude of respect for the equal worth of each interlocutor. This has many pragmatic implications: the location and architecture of the room; the location and style of seating; the time allocated for the telling of each person's story; the interventions of commissions, supporters, opponents and others; the skill and training of translators; the availability of post-testimony support; and so on.

All of these are equally important because insensitivity in any one could have the effect of silencing the truth and denying human dignity, thereby diminishing the impact of the truth commissions.

## 4. THE LEGACIES OF TRUTH AND RECONCILIATION COMMISSIONS

Truth and reconciliation commissions have a broad range of ambitions, which can include securing acknowledgement, apology, forgiveness or remorse; galvanising an amnesty process; prompting the establishment of memory sites such as memorials or museums; ordering or recommending reparations to individuals or communities; and issuing reports that describe or evaluate the truths of the past in order to lay the foundation for an understanding in the future. In combination, these actions can set the groundwork for a lasting peace by articulating the basis for guarantees of non-repetition, and even for the consolidation of democracy. Thus, at their best, truth commissions aim not only

34 'In addition, an extraordinary number of operational considerations had to be taken into account when hosting the hearings. An important concern of the Human Rights Violations Committee was to ensure that the human and civil dignity of victims was restored by granting them an opportunity to relate their own accounts of violations (as emphasized in section 3(1)(c) of the Act). It was, therefore, incumbent on the Human Rights Violations Committee to make sure that the environment at the hearing was conducive to achieving these objectives.' 1 South African Truth Commission Report, *supra* note 7, at 283. And '[s]ensitivity to such aspects was part of the commitment of the Commission to provide a service that was victim-friendly, culturally appropriate and respectful of the dignity of witnesses.' Ibid, at 290.

to help the nation pivot from war to peace but to transform the society from one in which differences were resolved by violence to one in which they are resolved by dialogue and negotiation, from one in which dignity was violated to one in which it is respected. This section considers the role of dignity in the securing of several specific remedies often associated with truth commissions and then considers the relationship between human dignity and the broader legacy of consolidation of democracy.

Although most truth commission reports mention dignity, few have focused on the importance of building a foundation based on human dignity, or have elucidated the relationship between human dignity and the other aspects of the truth commission legacy. It may be supposed, however, that the impacts of truth commissions would be advanced if they are intentional and explicit about the role that human dignity plays in the processes of transitional justice. This would frame the transitional justice work of the other institutions of government and help guide them on their paths.

## 4.1. ACKNOWLEDGEMENT

The most basic element of any reconciliation project is for people on all sides to acknowledge each other, to recognise each other as human beings. It is the first, and sometimes the last, thing that victims ask for from perpetrators: just look me in the eye and acknowledge me. See me as a person, just like you.

Acknowledging the other is directly connected to the recognition of human dignity. To acknowledge a person is to accept their humanity, their fundamental equality with oneself. One report of a meeting between mining company officials and Aboriginal elders in Australia began only after one participant said 'we're both grandfathers'.[35] The recognition of equal worth – you're a grandfather and I am too, and that means something – made discussion between equals possible. Acknowledgement of the other as equally human – that is, equal in human dignity – removes the possibility of diminishing another and in fact it renders othering impossible. The recognition of another person's equal worth does not require love or friendship but simply requires us to admit (literally?) everyone on an equal basis.

Even the acknowledgement of an event or a fact is related to the recognition of another's dignity. As the South African truth commission report explained:

> Acknowledgement refers to placing information that is (or becomes) known on public, national record. It is not merely the actual knowledge about past human rights

35 Recounted in Daly and Sarkin, *supra* note 26, at 185.

> violations that counts; often the basic facts about what happened are already known, at least by those who were affected. What is critical is that these facts be fully and publicly acknowledged. Acknowledgement is an affirmation that a person's pain is real and worthy of attention. It is thus central to the restoration of the dignity of victims.[36]

Acknowledgement is central to the restoration of another's dignity and therefore lies at the foundation of all other forms of justice.

For acknowledgement to be effective as part of the foundation of the new dispensation, it must be shared through educational programmes that reinforce human dignity. This can secure the truth commission's legacy into the future. As the Chilean commission said, 'we believe that the topic of human rights and of respect for each person's dignity must be incorporated into formal education, and that symbolic measures aimed at promoting these values must be adopted.'[37] The Chilean commission also recommended public human rights education: 'Carrying out a number of cultural activities on National Human Rights Day emphasizing the values of democracy, tolerance, and respect for human rights, as well as the essential dignity of the human person-all of these aimed at reconciling Chileans and bringing them together.'[38]

In some countries, education need not be formal for the truth commission to leave a legacy of dignity. The Mauritius commission recommended training in handicrafts (including home economics and leadership), which in all fields should be 'aimed at boosting up the progress of the persons and the community [and thus] would be of the utmost importance and restore the dignity and confidence of the Agaleans.'[39] The Mauritius commission also recognised other educational mechanisms of social transformation that would promote the dignity of the people:

> There are different coconut fields with different names. Their delimitation, with their proper names, will be a practical exercise in pedagogy to teach the History of Agalega to all the population, particularly young students. Names of streets and avenues should also be marked. This measure will reinstate the dignity of the people: from Camp Noir to Avenue, from hut to bungalow.[40]

Acknowledgement in all forms can constitute a lasting legacy that recognises and advances human dignity.

---

[36] South African Truth Commission Report, *supra* note 7, Volume 1, at 114.

[37] Chilean Truth Commission Report, *supra* note 30, at 1076.

[38] Ibid, at 1111.

[39] *Report of the Truth and Justice Committee of Mauritius*, Volume 1, at para. 257(b), https://www.usip.org/sites/default/files/ROL/TJC_Vol1.pdf.

[40] Ibid, at para 145(vi).

## 4.2. AMNESTY

Amnesty is slightly more complicated than mere acknowledgement because it involves giving something of value to someone who has not earned it. Amnesties are often viewed as giveaways to perpetrators that can seriously thwart a reconciliation process by fomenting a culture of impunity and by making plain the failure of the rule of law.[41] However, if carefully designed and managed, they reinforce the values of inclusion and acceptance based on truth. They can thereby advance the dignity interests of both sides. Thus, the challenge of amnesty programmes is to ensure that the benefit to society or to the victims outweighs the benefit to the perpetrators. The key, then, is to ensure that the terms of the amnesty programme at least restore the dignity of the victims. This not only provides an indispensable and immeasurable benefit to the victims; it also contributes to the consolidation of democracy and the ends of social justice by bringing both the victims and perpetrators, with human and civic dignity restored, into the fold of society.

In Timor-Leste, the truth-for-amnesty bargain was explicitly tied to the restoration of human dignity: 'The Terms of Reference … specify measures the Commission may recommend "to heal wounds of the past, rehabilitate and restore human dignity" [which includes, inter alia] "Recommend[ing] amnesty for those involved in human rights violations who cooperate fully in revealing the truth."'[42] As the report explained:

> The two important issues stressed in the Terms of Reference [in pt. 14] are (1) the purpose of giving amnesty recommendations is related to the Commission's goal of achieving reconciliation, that is, to heal wounds of the past and restore human dignity; and (2) amnesty recommendations shall be considered only when the alleged perpetrators meet the criteria encompassed in the term 'full cooperation.'[43]

The South African model chose to rest amnesty not on remorse or forgiveness but on truth, judging that the latter would ultimately be more valuable to society and more likely to contribute to the restoration of survivors' dignity. Indeed, to demand remorse might be a violation of the perpetrators' dignity, while demanding forgiveness might violate the dignity of the victims. It was understood that truth would be seriously compromised if the perpetrators were not induced to engage in the proceedings, and amnesty was the most effective inducement. Indeed, the restoration of dignity flowing from the elucidation of

---

41 See Sarkin's amnesty chapter in this volume.

42 *Per Memoriam ad Spem*, *supra* note 21, at 15.

43 Ibid.

the truth was deemed so valuable that it challenged 'the popular perception that amnesty exists only for the sake of perpetrators'.[44]

## 4.3. A LEGACY OF DEMOCRACY

The greatest potential legacy of a truth commission is to instil a lasting peace in which democracy can flourish.[45] Here, dignity's dual nature as both an individual attribute and a collective experience is critical. By touching each person, a truth commission can help to restore individual dignity of a damaged population and can leave an obvious legacy of social transformation. In the political domain, a truth commission can leave a democratic legacy by valuing the participatory dignity of each person. The truth commission can be the crucible in which these elements of individual human and participatory dignity can coalesce into a more just and inclusive democratic society.[46]

Dignity is tied to democracy in a variety of ways.[47] First, dignity is the source of rights: human dignity is what allows people to come together and determine not only their own individual life courses but their collective life courses as well. Again, the South African case is illustrative:

> A principal task of the Commission was 'restoring the human and civil dignity of victims'. The work of the Commission as a whole, together with the specific contributions of its three committees, underlined the need to restore the dignity of all South Africans. In the process, the sons and daughters of South Africa would begin to feel truly 'at home'.[48]

Second, dignity is the means for engaging rights: dignity is how we participate in democracy. Exercising democratic rights including the right to information, to speech, to participation and to association are manifestations of human dignity.

44 South African Truth Commission Report, *supra* note 7, Volume 1, at 128. The Report explained: 'Their greater understanding of events helped restore dignity and dispel the lies they were told about "criminals", "terrorists" or "informers". This challenges the popular perception that amnesty exists only for the sake of perpetrators.' Ibid. For a detailed analysis of the South African amnesty process, see J. Sarkin, *Carrots and Sticks: The TC and the South African Amnesty Process*, Intersentia, Antwerp, 2004.

45 Daly and Sarkin, *supra* note 26, at 220–222.

46 'Human rights violations lead to the loss of human dignity; establishing the truth is a powerful step toward restoring dignity. Restorative justice focuses on all parties involved in a conflict and seeks to reintegrate them into an inclusive society.' Chega! Final Report of the Commission for Reception, Truth and Reconciliation in East Timor (CAVR), at 294, https://etan.org/news/2006/cavr.htm.

47 For an elaboration on the relationship between human dignity and democracy, see Daly, *supra* note 10, at 130–160.

48 1 South African Truth Commission Report, *supra* note 7, at 125.

Third, it is the endgame: enhancing the dignity of all may be seen as the very purpose of democracy. As the Salvadoran commission wrote, 'Respect for human rights, which are the raison d'etre of the [fundamental] principles and the basis of a society organized to serve people, all of whom are vested with equal freedom and dignity.'[49]

While many truth commissions have referred to the relationship between democracy and dignity, few have explored it in depth and fewer still have identified it explicitly as part of their intended legacy – even though in almost all cases, it is. Rather, the commissions have, for the most part, simply averred that the two are intertwined and interdependent as if the string that connects consolidation of democracy with human dignity were nothing more, or less, than an instance of national intuition. But some commissions have tried to interrogate the relationship between human dignity and democracy, which can enhance the impacts that truth commissions have in laying the foundations for democracy. Again, the Salvadoran commission wrote in its report:

> The consolidation of the supremacy of civilian authority in Salvadorian society and the necessary subordination of the armed forces to it stem directly from the democratic concept of the rule of law, the primordial value of the dignity of the human person and, hence full respect for his rights.[50]

The Moroccan Justice and Reconciliation Commission articulated the dependence of the project of democratisation on the restoration of human dignity in terms of citizenship.

> Thus, the Commission gave a priority to the rehabilitation of victims of gross human rights violations, through rehabilitation and reinsertion programs, efforts to restore their dignity, through communal reparations empowering the society at both the local and national levels towards participating in the ongoing democratization of the country, to restore trust in a state of institutions and the rule of law, and to ensure their effective participation by way of a sense of citizenship that fosters social justice and the belief in a truly modern democratic society.[51]

In Morocco, truth was an essential element of this transformative agenda, not only because it helped to restore the dignity of the witness or survivor, but because it restored their 'sense of citizenship'. On a social level, it contributed

---

49 *From Madness to Hope: the 12-year war in El Salvador: Report of the Commission on the Truth for El Salvador*, at 174, https://www.usip.org/sites/default/files/file/ElSalvador-Report.pdf.

50 Ibid, at 174.

51 Kingdom of Morocco, National Commission for Truth, Justice, and Reconciliation, *Summary of the Final Report*, at 30, http://www.ccdh.org.ma/sites/default/files/documents/rapport_final_mar_eng-3.pdf.

'to the society's understanding of past events and [helps the nation] pursue its efforts to foster human rights as one of the main bases for national solidarity and social cohesiveness'. This, the commission stated, is essential to 'create the genuine conditions to overcome tension, mistrust and despair within the society and to avert the inclination to settle conflicts through violence'.[52] The psychological informs the political because political stability and inclusiveness can only thrive when individual dignity is secure.

Some truth commissions have focused on particular aspects of democratic consolidation. For instance, focusing on conflict resolution, the South African truth commission recognised that 'a culture of human rights and democracy does require respect for our common human dignity and shared citizenship, as well as the peaceful handling of unavoidable conflicts'.[53] Instantiating commitment to rule of law, the Chilean commission said:

> If the judiciary is to be a powerful protector of human rights there must be judges and lawyers firmly committed to the rights of persons and to the permanent values underlying those rights, primarily the principles of the dignity of the human being and of the rule of law.[54]

Even international peace may require the respect not only of national dignity but even of human dignity, as the commissioners of the Timor-Leste–Indonesia commission recognised:

> The leadership of the two nations realize that a common understanding about what occurred in East Timor in 1999, as well as learning lessons from these events, are of the utmost importance in the efforts to establish strong and beneficial relations between the two states and to restore human dignity.[55]

The intended twin legacies of the truth commission were to establish strong international bonds while at the same time restoring human dignity. Although it was not expressly stated, it may be inferred that the latter was a prerequisite for the former.

Truth commissions can, in their reports and public statements, frame and explain the relationship between dignity and democracy and provide a grammar for implementing a dignity-based democratic system; this, in turn, can help guide the work of the government in advancing democratic institutions and opportunities and galvanise the population to demand both democracy with dignity.

---

52 Ibid, at 30.

53 1 South African Truth Commission Report, *supra* note 7, at 108.

54 Chilean Truth Commission Report, *supra* note 30, at 1084.

55 *Per Memoriam ad Spem*, *supra* note 21, at 14.

## 5. CONCLUSION

Although it seems impossible to determine with precision the role of dignity in the legacy of truth commissions on a global scale, it is reasonable to posit that attention to human and or civic dignity in the transitional process has at least contributed to a transformation toward democracy and that the nations whose transitional processes have focused on human dignity are more prone to consolidation of democracy. The claim is not that dignity-infused truth commission processes necessarily produce a legacy of democracy, but rather that countries that infuse their truth commission processes with dignity discourse – that is, with the recognition of the worth and value of each person and with a commitment that each person is equal in his or her humanity to every other – are more likely to also respect democracy – the system of governance that embodies the idea of the equal worth of each person. Thus, the truth commission reports that have most explicitly focused on dignity are in countries that have tended toward the consolidation of democracy. In Africa, for instance, according to the Democracy Index, Mauritius ranks first, with South Africa fourth, Liberia fourteenth and Kenya seventeenth (out of 44 sub-Saharan nations).[56] Chile – the country with by far the highest level of focus on human dignity in its commission report – ranks third out of 24 countries in Latin America and the Caribbean on the Democracy Index.[57] The claim is not causal but it may at least be correlative.

Indeed, in Chile, human dignity served an explicitly transformative purpose, as a bridge toward what the Chilean commission called the 'common life' of the people:

> Furthermore, the whole of Chilean society must respond to the challenge of reparation. Such a process must move toward acknowledging the truth of what has happened, restoring the moral dignity of the victims, and achieving a better quality of life for those families most directly affected. Only in this fashion will we be able to develop a more just form of common life that will enable us to look with hope toward the future.[58]

In Chile, as elsewhere, dignity is a bridge between the past and the present, marking transitional time. It can bridge physical gaps, too, as between people who are connected by what unites them rather than distancing themselves because of the superficial differences they see. So, too, can it bridge institutions of governance, suggesting a common language that all parts of government and civil society can use to communicate. In this sense, it can contribute to the consolidation of democracy by including all in the demos and providing a way

56 Economist Intelligence Unit, *Democracy Index 2018*, (2019), at 28, http://www.eiu.com/topic/democracy-index.
57 Ibid, at 20.
58 Chilean Truth Commission Report, *supra* note 30, at 1057.

for people to talk to and with each other. If truth and reconciliation commissions are designed to excavate the truth in order to foster reconciliation and ultimately create a new society, the concept of human dignity – a psychological, civic and moral dignity – should be part of the process at each step to ensure a long-lasting and deeply transformative legacy of a common life.

# TOWARDS AN UNDERSTANDING OF HOW TRUTH COMMISSIONS CAN USE THEIR AMNESTY POWERS TO ENHANCE THEIR IMPACT AND LEGACY

Jeremy SARKIN*



## 1. INTRODUCTION

Truth commissions play vital roles in a variety of societies seeking to deal with past violence.[1] However, the extent or limitations of what that role is remains disputed.[2] There has been a chorus of voices questioning the efficacy of these

* My thanks to Robert Grant and Tessa Assies for their assistance with this chapter and for the helpful comments from Louise Mallinder and the anonymous reviewers.

1 P.B. HAYNER, *Unspeakable Truths: Transitional Justice and the Challenge of Truth Commissions*, New York: Routledge, second edition, 2011.

2 D. MENDELOFF, 'Truth-Seeking, Truth-Telling, and Post-Conflict Peacebuilding: Curb the Enthusiasm?' (2004) 6 *International Studies Review* 355. See also T.D. OLSEN, L.A. PAYNE,

truth commissions in achieving their goals, and whether or not human rights issues in post-conflict societies have been resolved, or at least improved, by such processes.[3] The frequency with which truth commissions are utilised,[4] with over 50 cases (and possibly more than 100 if a wider definition of truth commission is used) taking place in such societies does seem to exemplify the fact that truth commissions do hold at least some value.[5]

Borer claims that truth commissions have 25 or 26 distinct goals.[6] Primary amongst these perceived goals, however, is that of truth-gathering, hence their name.[7] Truth, as will be discussed, needs to be obtained from a variety of sources, including from perpetrators.[8] Torne in this regard has argued that another function of truth commissions is to establish the identities of perpetrators.[9] However, this is not always the case. Where truth commissions are intended to be the start of a process that later leads to prosecutions, they are sometimes prevented from disclosing names. In some of those cases, the truth commission also chooses to publish few, if any, names. Truth commissions do report in more general terms about institutional responsibility. They seek to clear the muddy waters of the past.[10] They attempt to clarify the national narrative of such societies, and to establish a set of facts as a basis of the truth about the history and evolution of a given conflict, in order to devise a new and more acceptable national narrative.[11] Whilst truth-gathering is unquestionably of great value and importance, the issue of accountability is more complex. The emergence of truth can open the door for accountability to come to the fore.[12] However, many have argued that truth commissions in fact decrease the possibility of achieving

---

and A.G. Reiter, *Transitional Justice in Balance: Comparing Processes, Weighing Efficacy*, United States Institute of Peace Press, Washington D.C., 2010.

3 See generally R.G. Teitel, 'Human Rights in Transition: Transitional Justice Genealogy' (2003) 16 *Harvard Human Rights Journal* 69.

4 R. May, '"Truth" and Truth Commissions in Latin America' (2013) 21(2) *Investigación y Desarrollo* 494.

5 B.A. Leebaw, 'The Irreconcilable Goals of Transitional Justice' (2008) 30 *Human Rights Quarterly* 95.

6 T.A. Borer, 'Truth Telling as a Peace-Building Activity: A Theoretical Overview', in T.A. Borer (ed.), *Telling the Truths: Truth Telling and Peace Building in Post-Conflict Societies*, University of Notre Dame Press, Note Dame IN, 2006, at 26.

7 G. Dancy, H. Kim and E. Wiebelhaus-Brahm, 'The Turn to Truth: Trends in Truth Commission Experimentation' (2010) 9 *Journal of Human Rights* 45.

8 J. Sarkin, *Carrots and Sticks: The TRC and the South African Amnesty Process*, Intersentia, Antwerp, 2004.

9 C.F. Torne, 'Truth Commissions and the Accountability Relationships They Generate: A New Framework to Evaluate Their Impact' (2015) 3(2) *Asian Journal of Peacebuilding* 233, at 236.

10 E. Wiebelhaus-Brahm, *Truth Commissions and Transitional Societies*, Routledge, New York, 2010.

11 M. Minow, 'Making History or Making Peace: When Prosecutions Should Give Way to Truth Commissions and Peace Negotiations' (2008) 7(2) *Journal of Human Rights* 180.

12 R.G. Teitel, *Transitional Justice*, Oxford University Press, New York, 2000.

accountability and justice in post-conflict societies.[13] Thus, there is a view that truth commissions are, at times, replacements for retributive justice.[14] Truth, it is argued, is sometimes traded off for accountability, and the opportunity for retribution or criminal charges is lost. Yet this may be too simplistic. Recent research suggests that truth commissions are most likely to improve the human rights situation of a transitional society when they accompany some form of trial (and the potential therein for amnesty to be granted).[15]

The importance of establishing the whole and complete truth[16] for the sake of victims' rights[17] is strongly held as an international principle, and is now established as a human right.[18] Truth commissions are vital cogs in this process.[19] They often provide the best mechanism by which the needs of victims for truth can be addressed.[20] However, obtaining this truth is dependent on the efficacy of a truth commission, and the methods practised by it.[21] It is also dependent on the financial and human capital resources given to the process.[22] Those are critically important to effectively collecting the truth.

In this context, the issue of amnesty needs to be evaluated. The way truth commission amnesty processes have worked is examined in this chapter to understand what the impact of a truth commission using amnesty was in different truth commission settings around the world. While some of the truth commission models examined in this chapter can be examined formally as to whether or not they properly comply with the various definitions of what constitutes a truth commission, the aim is to touch on all models that had amnesty powers. Crucially, all the other truth commissions that have been

---

13 See generally D.P. Forsythe, 'Transitional Justice: Criminal Courts and Alternatives', in D.P. Forsythe, *Human Rights in International Relations*, Cambridge University Press, Cambridge, 2012.

14 E. Daly and J. Sarkin, *Reconciliation in Divided Societies. Finding Common Ground*, University of Pennsylvania Press, Philadelphia, 2007.

15 T.D. Olsen, L.A. Payne, A.G. Reiter and E. Wiebelhaus-Brahm, 'When Truth Commissions Improve Human Rights' (2010) 4 *International Journal of Transitional Justice* 457.

16 T. Kelsall, 'Truth, Lies, Ritual: Preliminary Reflections on the Truth and Reconciliation Commission in Sierra Leone' (2005) 27 *Human Rights Quarterly* 361.

17 S. Karstedt, 'From Absence to Presence, from Silence to Voice: Victims in International and Transitional Justice since the Nuremberg Trials' (2010) 17 *International Review of Victimology* 9.

18 P. Naftali, 'Crafting a "Right to Truth" in International Law: Converging Mobilizations, Diverging Agendas?' (2016) 13 *Champ pénal/Penal field* (online).

19 R.I. Rotberg and D. Thompson (eds.), *Truth v. Justice: The Morality of Truth Commissions*, Princeton University Press, Princeton NJ, 2000.

20 T.G. Phelps, *Shattered Voices: Language, Violence, and the Work of Truth Commissions*, University of Pennsylvania Press, Philadelphia, 2004.

21 B. Hamber, *Transforming Societies after Political Violence: Truth, Reconciliation, and Mental Health*, Springer, Dordrecht, 2009.

22 E. Daly, 'Truth Skepticism: An Inquiry into the Value of Truth in Times of Transition' (2008) 2 *International Journal of Transitional Justice* 23, at 23–24.

established since the South African Truth and Reconciliation Commission (TRC), that had amnesty powers, have merely been able to recommend whether or not perpetrators who have cooperated with them should be given amnesty by the government.[23] However, even where truth commissions have not been given amnesty powers, they have often been able to offer use immunity for testimony (i.e. a privilege against self-incrimination where criminal prosecution remains a possibility).

This chapter therefore examines the legacy and impact of truth commissions in as far as how they have used amnesty powers, if they had an amnesty mandate, to achieve their goals, if they had such provisions. In analysing the range of mandates and powers of different truth commissions around the world, it aims to establish that having the power to directly grant amnesty makes truth commissions more impactful, and more likely of achieving a greater legacy in the country concerned. This is because truth commissions, if they have an amnesty power – specifically to grant rather than to recommend amnesty – seem achieve much more in terms of revealing the past, bringing truth to victims, and creating a clearer narrative of what occurred during periods of conflict. This is the case because, though not always specifically articulated, a function of truth commissions is to gain truth from all sources, including perpetrators. While perpetrator testimony and cooperation is not usually achieved to any large degree, the ability of a truth commission to draw the truth out of perpetrators should be a factor in evaluating their success.

Using the South African truth commission model, which granted amnesty, as a benchmark, this chapter contrasts the effectiveness of that truth commission amnesty process with those that only had the power to recommend amnesty, in such countries as Grenada, Timor-Leste, Indonesia–Timor-Leste, Liberia, Kenya, and the Republic of Korea. These truth commission amnesty processes are examined, as these are the only truth commissions that have had the power to recommend amnesty to determine the effect and impact of the amnesty process on the truth commission's role and legacy. There are a few such institutions that were to have such powers, but did not complete their mandates for a variety of reasons. These institutions are briefly mentioned at the end of the chapter for completeness.

All the truth commissions dealt with in the chapter had their own methodologies regarding amnesty, with diverse circumstances dictating how, when and why amnesty would be recommended.

The major focus of the chapter is therefore whether the impact and legacy of a truth commission with amnesty powers is different depending on whether a truth commission grants amnesty directly to perpetrators or recommends it

---

23 Amnesty International, 'Commissioning Justice: Truth Commissions and Criminal Justice', 26 April 2010, at 5, https://www.amnesty.org/en/documents/pol30/004/2010/en/.

to government. The argument is that giving truth commissions only the power to recommend amnesty, rather than the power to grant amnesty directly to perpetrators, has a negative impact on the likelihood of perpetrators coming forward and participating in these processes. This in turn negatively affects the truth commission's impact on truth recovery and therefore on its legacy. The power to recommend amnesty does have some limited effect and seems to be better, from the standpoint of drawing in perpetrators, compared to truth commissions that have no amnesty powers at all. That issue is not however taken up in this chapter. The goal of this chapter is rather to evaluate the successes and failures of each of the various truth commission models that had some type of amnesty provision, to see how to enhance the possibility of success for future truth commissions that utilise amnesties. It is argued that if truth commissions have the authority to use amnesties, particularly to grant such dispensations directly, and if they do so in ways that achieve greater perpetrator cooperation, their impact and legacy will be enhanced. A critical issue is that the way a truth commission uses its provisions, either to grant or recommend amnesty, makes a significant difference to the success of that process, the impact it achieves and therefore its legacy.

## 2. UNDERSTANDING AMNESTY

Generally, amnesty is a tool by which countries coming out of a conflict attempt to achieve various goals, including promoting unity, peace and stability[24] and for truth recovery.[25] The issue of amnesty is so important that 186 countries mention amnesty in their constitutions.[26] Many hundreds of amnesties have been dispensed around the world over the last few decades.[27] Amnesty, however, is strongly disavowed today by some, specifically for serious international crimes. The United Nations has taken this up and ensures that peace agreements and other processes do not violate such a position. However, many states still rely on a provision in international law that that permits, and in fact requires, nations to provide amnesty to individuals at the end of internal armed conflicts. While there is ongoing debate in some quarters, particularly among those who

---

24 M. Freeman, *Truth Commissions and Procedural Fairness*, Cambridge University Press, New York, 2006.

25 H. Cobban, *Amnesty After Atrocity?: Healing Nations After Genocide and War Crimes*, Paradigm, Boulder CO, 2007.

26 N. Vasuki, 'Transitional Justice Practice: Looking Back, Moving Forward', research report of Impunity Watch, May 2016, at 11.

27 L. Mallinder, 'Amnesties' Challenge to the Accountability Norm? Interpreting Regional and International Trends in Amnesty Enactment', in L.A. Payne and F. Lessa (eds.), *Amnesty in the Age of Human Rights Accountability: Comparative and International Perspectives*, Cambridge University Press, Cambridge, 2012, at 79.

advocate for amnesties, about what Article 6(5) of Protocol II to the Geneva Conventions of 1949 means and whether it ought to be relied on and used, the reality is that the breadth of the use of amnesty seemingly reflects that, for some, amnesties remain a very viable tool.

In spite of being often frowned upon, amnesties remain common even for serious international crimes.[28] Several studies show how usual amnesty processes are.[29] In just 2016, a number of states adopted amnesties for various crimes, including Colombia,[30] Iraq, the Philippines, Tunisia,[31] Ukraine,[32] Uzbekistan and Venezuela (although later rejected by the courts).[33] Many others adopted amnesties for tax and other non-political crimes. Thus, amnesties still continue to be extensively used as a tool by states.[34]

One definition of amnesty that is used, which has its limitations, is: 'the granting of a reduction or a complete exemption from punishment, to quash a pending case, and to prevent execution of a judgment that has already been passed, and involves an undefined number of cases as opposed to an individual pardon.'[35] While generally useful as far as what amnesty is, this definition is somewhat problematic as (1) it conflates amnesties with pardons for more than one person and (2) amnesties are sometimes granted to a defined number of cases. A better definition is: 'an extraordinary legal measure whose primary function is to remove the prospect and consequences of criminal liability for designated individuals or classes of persons in respect of designated types of offenses irrespective of whether the persons concerned have been tried for such offenses in a court of law.'[36] Where amnesty is granted to perpetrators of serious human rights violations, as opposed to amnesty for those who

---

28 See further on the legal issues J.C. Portilla, 'Evolving 21st Century Constraints Under International Law' (2014) 38 *The Fletcher Forum of World Affairs* 169.

29 See for example on the extensive use of amnesty in Latin America countries, R. Boed, 'The Effect of a Domestic Amnesty on the Ability of Foreign States to Prosecute Alleged Perpetrators of Serious Human Rights Violations' (2000) 33 *Cornell International Law Journal* 297.

30 R. Urueña, 'Playing With Fire: International Criminal Law, Transitional Justice, and the Implementation of the Colombian Peace Agreement' (2016) 110 *AJIL Unbound* 364.

31 Tunisia's Legislative Decree n° 2011-1.

32 Ukraine's 2014 amnesty was for participants in the protests. The amnesty proposed in the Minsk process has yet to be implemented.

33 L. Koerner, 'Venezuela: Supreme Court Rejects "Amnesty" Bill, Maduro Sets Up Truth Commission', *Green Left Weekly*, 17 April 2016.

34 L.A. Payne, F. Lessa, and G. Pereira, 'Overcoming Barriers to Justice in the Age of Human Rights Accountability' (2015) 37 *Human Rights Quarterly* 728.

35 K. Marxen, 'The Legal Limitations of Amnesty', in M.R. Rwelamira and G. Werle (eds.), *Confronting Past Injustices – Approaches to Amnesty, Punishment, Reparation and Restitution in South Africa and Germany*, Butterworth Press, Durban, 1996, at 34.

36 M. Freeman, *Necessary Evils: Amnesties and the Search for Justice*, Cambridge University Press, Cambridge, 2009, at 13.

were unjustly imprisoned, draft evaders or refugees, opinion is divided as to whether it is a useful tool for reconciling society,[37] or is in fact a method for perpetrators to avoid accountability.[38] It is therefore vital to distinguish between the different approaches to amnesty that exist, and how they have been applied across the world.[39]

There are different types of amnesty, including blanket amnesty, limited amnesty and conditional amnesty.[40] Blanket amnesty gives amnesty to all perpetrators for all crimes committed. The term 'blanket amnesty' is somewhat problematic, as very few amnesties really fit with how this term is usually understood. Most amnesties are limited in some way (e.g. covering only conflict-related offences or offences before or after certain dates; many otherwise broad amnesties nonetheless exclude a small number of offences). Thus, it may be preferable to use the term 'broad, unconditional amnesty' rather than the term 'blanket amnesty'. By contrast, limited amnesty covers particular crimes, certain people and/or a specific time period.

Conditional amnesty, on the other hand, demands that perpetrators fulfil a certain set of criteria before they can be granted or recommended for amnesty.[41] However, some processes contain conditions that need to occur post-amnesty. These conditions need to be fulfilled if offenders want to retain amnesty. The advantage gained by using this system is that amnesty can be an exchange for truth or handing in weapons or some other condition. In this way, one benefit of the justice system can still be applied to a person gaining amnesty – their crimes are revealed to the public. Thus, such a system can assist in exposing the truth. Something tangible and valuable, both to victims and to the wider public, is gained in exchange for amnesty. Conditional amnesty should therefore be the preferred method for those who value accountability and do not want to allow perpetrators to gain amnesty without any type of recompense. Gaining the truth about how and why crimes were committed is vital for a peace-creation process in transitional societies.[42] Thus, a conditional amnesty seems best suited if amnesty is to be given anyway and as a way to enhance truth recovery. This methodology ensures that people who need information, closure, transparency and trust in the new systems they are investing in are

37 Daly and Sarkin, *supra* note 14.

38 Payne and Lessa, *supra* note 27.

39 L. Mallinder, *Amnesty, Human Rights and Political Transitions: Bridging the Peace and Justice Divide*, Bloomsbury Publishing, London, 2008, at 154.

40 K. Allan, 'Prosecution and Peace: A Role for Amnesty Before the ICC?' (2011) 39 *Denver Journal of International Law and Policy* 239, at 242.

41 J. Sarkin, 'How Conditional Amnesties Can Assist Transitional Societies in Delivering on the Right to the Truth: Are Such Processes Compatible With International Law?' (2017) 6(2) *International Human Rights Law Review* 1.

42 P. Arthur, 'How "Transitions" Reshaped Human Rights: A Conceptual History of Transitional Justice' (2009) 31 *Human Rights Quarterly* 321.

aided in their endeavours to do so. Whilst all amnesties should be based on a trade-off for useful information, broad (blanket) or limited amnesties do not have the same capability as conditional amnesties to provide accountability or to achieve truth.[43] It is important to note that it is entirely possible to have a limited amnesty that is conditioned on disclosure of truth, as was the case, for example, of the Community Reconciliation Process in Timor-Leste, discussed later.

Although questions remain about whether the victims or the perpetrators benefit the most from it, a conditional amnesty is a viable truth-gathering tool and should be used as such. Such amnesties also are about accountability. Perpetrators have their names made public, and a discussion is held around the crimes that they have committed in the public sphere. This is the first step in holding perpetrators accountable, whilst the fact that they have to provide real, useful and verifiable information opens the door to having the truth become widely known.

Conditional amnesty, as I have previously argued,[44] must have both a tangible carrot, but also a stick.[45] For it to be effective, governments need to work to establish a system in which perpetrators who do not come forward of their own accord will be prosecuted. For this to occur, the prosecution authority must be credible and viable. It must have the political will required to commit to and persevere with the prosecutions in an effective manner. It must show perpetrators that they will not get away with their crimes if they do not come forward themselves. While this could be a problem as far as sequencing is concerned in practice – as prosecutions are usually expected to happen after a truth commission – some prosecutions could be started before, or while, the truth seeking institution does its work. This would not have to be many cases, only a variety of well-selected ones, particularly those where guilty pleas or plea bargains could be achieved or where the evidence was overwhelming. In this way, it is made clear to perpetrators that their interests are best served by coming forward and applying for amnesty.

For such a process to be successful, there are a variety of features that are necessary to ensure perpetrators participate if their motivation is purely personal. This may even be the case if institutional reasons rather than personal ones motivate them. Whilst it is possible that some perpetrators will come forward of their own accord, perhaps out of a sense of remorse or duty, it is important to have a secondary layer to the system to ensure that they come forward.

---

43 J. Sarkin, 'Truth Recovery From Conditional Amnesty Processes: Benefits And Constraints', in N. Adler (ed.), *Understanding the Age of Transitional Justice: Crimes, Courts, Commissions, and Chronicling*, Rutgers University Press, New Brunswick NJ, 2018.

44 Sarkin, *supra* note 41.

45 Sarkin, *supra* note 8.

A vital object that such processes ought to deal with, and therefore ensuring mechanisms comply with, is to make sure that, as far as possible, perpetrators who apply for amnesty tell nothing but the whole truth. However, the truth can be understood in a broad or narrow sense. It could be solely the facts about the direct commission of a crime, or it could be broader discussions of the institutional context in which the crimes took place. For truth recovery, both are necessary, but the emphasis at times is put on one or the other. Regardless, there needs to be a system that encourages those who apply for amnesty to give as much truthful information as possible. Perjury needs to be strongly discouraged, with harsh consequences for those who attempt to evade the real goal of the system – truth discovery – by not telling the whole truth about their involvement in crimes within the truth commission's mandate. While there are usually penalties for perjury in criminal law, other mechanisms could be used, including the removal of any grant of amnesty, as well as publication of these outcomes. There ought therefore to be more processes to deter people from not telling the truth. Conditional amnesty best serves this purpose by having a clause in all applications for amnesty that clearly states that deceitfulness will be punished severely, and that amnesty offers will be withdrawn if it is found that a perpetrator was not telling the (material or substantial) truth.

The question often arises in this context about what truth revelation is. Is it 100 per cent of the truth, even where the details are complicated and happened a long time ago, or is it a lesser amount? What happens if the applicant cannot remember all the details? What happens if the majority of the truth is revealed, but one fact is not disclosed? Obviously, it is difficult to make specific rules concerning such matters, but using concepts such as 'material', 'significant' or 'substantial' to ensure that the full facts emerge is critical. The context and reasons for an omission is important. If it is done negligently, rather than purposefully, that may be a reason why such a lapse should not be considered material. The decisions on such matters do however need to be taken on a case-by-case basis. However, as is discussed later, for such matters to even be known about, it is important to have investigations that support or contradict what perpetrators testify to. Such enquiries are essential at the time of the applications. An investigation has to occur before a decision is made on the merits of the application. The quality of such an investigation cannot be in doubt, otherwise there is a greater potential for the truth to be suppressed and at times for lies to be told.

The third important step to ensuring that conditional amnesty works suitably is that it needs to be easy to apply for amnesty. Perpetrators must be able to receive clear information about how the process works, whether their application will be eligible and if it is likely that they will receive amnesty. They must also be able to clearly understand how the process works. Thus, the process should be clear and transparent, and the authorities should follow a practical, well-thought-out process with which it will not be difficult to comply. Doubts about whether or not an applicant will get amnesty will be a reason why potential applicants do not apply.

A fourth condition ought to be that some appropriate implementation body, for example a truth commission, is established that is allowed to operate independently and is appropriately resourced to enable it to administer the amnesty process quickly, consistently and fairly.

Various nations have successfully used conditional amnesties, although not usually through truth commissions. For example, tens of thousands of Vietnam draft dodgers received amnesty in the 1970s in the USA after they pledged allegiance to that country and worked for two years in the public sector.[46] Armenia also enacted a conditional amnesty in 2004 for draft dodgers, who had to pay a fine to gain amnesty; 5,000 people benefitted from this process.[47]

None of the examples above concerning conditional amnesties involved more than a cursory element of truth revelation (and none involved truth-telling), and the crime for which people received amnesty was pretty minor compared to the crimes examined by truth commissions.

## 3. THE NATURE OF AMNESTY IN TRUTH COMMISSION PROCESSES

The role that amnesties can play in truth commissions suffers from a chronic lack of research. Much of the research is focused on international law issues and whether amnesties are legitimate and legal.[48] However, more work is needed to look at how amnesties, if used pragmatically, enhance perpetrator cooperation and therefore impact, specifically as far as truth recovery is concerned. However, enhancing offender involvement in truth commission processes can also assist reconciliation. Conditional amnesties involving truth commissions also enhance accountability, as often few perpetrators are prosecuted or go through vetting or lustration processes. However, perpetrator involvement can have other possible benefits that enhance impact and legacy, such as increasing notions of transparency and democratic accountability.

Most of the discussion – generally speaking academic – around truth commissions and amnesty centres on the South African experience. The TRC

46 Y. Bui and J.L. Jordan, 'Amnesty and Pardon', in *The Encyclopaedia of Criminology and Criminal Justice*, Wiley, London, 2014.

47 'Armenia Again Extends Conditional Amnesty For Draft Evaders, *Asbarez.com*, 8 December 2010, http://asbarez.com/89931/armenia-again-extends-conditional-amnesty-for-draft-evaders/.

48 M. Pensky, 'Amnesty on Trial: Impunity, Accountability, and the Norms of International Law' (2008) 1 *Ethics & Global Politics* 1, at 8–11.

process in that country was unique, as the commission was given the ability to directly grant amnesty. The South African TRC has therefore become the benchmark for such discussion. Since then, amnesty has sometimes been a part of a number of truth commission processes in a range of countries when truth commissions have been granted the authority to recommend that amnesty be granted. However, the authority to actually grant the amnesty has been vested in the state, which simply considers the viewpoint of the truth commission. All the countries where a truth commission has had the power to recommend amnesty are examined in this chapter. Although some states attempted to model their truth commissions on the South African one, they were not able to replicate that commission, as they were barred by their mandates from granting amnesty directly. There are also a few truth commissions that had amnesty powers but which did not, or have not, completed their mandate; they are briefly mentioned at the end of the chapter for completeness.

It is clear that one of the major benefits to truth commissions, when they have and use amnesties, insofar as they involve those who committed the abuses, is learning more about the past. Truth recovery is, however, not the only benefit, as noted, since the participation of perpetrators can have benefits for democratisation, building a human rights culture and notions of accountability, as well as potentially contributing to social cohesion, nation-building and reconciliation. The role of truth commissions specifically in terms of enhancing truth recovery is however crucial. This is because they often learn too little truth about the past[49] because the information of offenders is not usually obtained. This limits the truth commissions' impact and legacy. Part of the reason for a lack of truth gathering generally is that most of what is learned through the process comes from victims. Victims typically have very little knowledge, as they usually only know about a specific incident in which they, or a family member, were victimised. In some cases, however, it may be that no one knows about a specific incident. There are crimes or violations that are committed that leave no victims alive to give information about what occurred. Thus, for example, where disappearances have occurred, the relatives of the disappeared person, or others besides the perpetrators know very little about what occurred. Thus, disappearances are one of the crimes where using an amnesty or some other form of leniency may be particularly useful.

Thus, generally speaking, victims know very little about atrocities that were carried out. They only usually know what actually happened in that episode, not why it was done, who ordered it, or even necessarily who carried out the orders. As a result, most truth commissions have the aim to find 'who did

49 A. Chapman and P. Ball, 'The Truth of Truth Commissions: Comparative Lessons from Haiti, South Africa, and Guatemala' (2001) 23 *Human Rights Quarterly* 1.

what to whom, when, where, and occasionally why'.[50] Victim testimony does not fill in the vast knowledge gaps that exist. It is extremely difficult to piece together a larger picture of an oppressive regime or sequence of events from these types of testimonies. Beyond the series of abusive incidents that make up the brutal tactics of these regimes, there are larger questions to be asked – who supplied arms, ammunition, economic support or covert military help to these regimes, as well as what the chain of command was for establishing and then executing oppressive strategies.

These questions can only be answered with the cooperation of perpetrators.[51] Despite the examination and research components attached to truth commissions, information about the broad strategies of the state, as well as the chain of command for the execution of human rights abuses, are often purposefully hidden or badly recorded. To gain this truth, perpetrators need to provide the other side of the story by coming forward and revealing those details.[52] Herein lies the problem; perpetrators rarely come forward without an incentive. They may do so sometimes, for a range of reasons including for political motives, but generally they fear that there will be legal repercussions if they reveal what they know. This is particularly true where their identities are unknown, their crimes hidden, and their position within the oppressive regime has been kept a secret. In those circumstances, there is very little reason why they should risk their freedom and quality of life after the transition to peace.

The question then becomes how to bring these perpetrators forward. This has been a difficult issue for all truth commission processes held in the recent past. If legal repercussions act as the stick, the most effective way to supplement that system is to also offer a carrot. Subpoenas and publically naming names during such processes, as occurred in a number of processes discussed below, are ways to incentivise offenders to testify in the absence of amnesty. Sometimes, in spite of using these tools as a means to prod perpetrators to cooperate, they still do not do so. However, at times these types of strategies that have been adopted by some processes have borne fruit, and perpetrators have provided information and have been willing to testify publically, even in the absence of a formal amnesty or specific assurances other than the limited benefits of use immunity.

---

50 C.E. Loyle and C. Davenport, 'Transitional Injustice: Subverting Justice in Transition and Postconflict Societies' (2015) 15(1) *Journal of Human Rights* 126.

51 L. Waldorf, 'Ex-Combatants and Truth Commissions', in A. Patel, P. De Greiff and L. Waldorf (eds.), *Disarming the Past: Transitional Justice and Ex-Combatants*, Social Science Research Council, New York, 2009.

52 C. Lawther, '"The Cast of the Past": Truth Commissions and the Making and Marginalization of Identity' (2017) *Ethnopolitics* 113.

Thus, this chapter argues that a system of conditional amnesty can be a most effective carrot, and that truth commissions need to be able to offer that amnesty, without the involvement or restrictions placed on them by government interference. If perpetrators believe that politics is at play in such processes, they will be loath to apply. If the truth commission can make such amnesty decisions alone, without being overtly influenced by the state or political parties, and there is no system to review or overturn such decisions, perpetrators will usually be more willing to enter such a process. Truth commissions, therefore, need to clearly illustrate the value of applying for amnesty to the perpetrators, or they will resist the process, as they will fear the possible ramifications for their liberty. For the carrot to work, perpetrators need to have faith in the system. They need to believe that their confessions will have a positive outcome for them. If not, they will not agree to give testimony. In this regard, Bisset writes that:

> If perpetrators suspect that there is a possibility that amnesty will be refused and that their disclosures might then be used to further investigations or employed against them in subsequent trials they will be less likely to participate, thereby limiting the prospects for reconciliation.[53]

While the comment is correct as far as perpetrator perceptions are concerned, it seemingly conflates two distinct tools: amnesty and use immunity/privilege against self-incrimination. The latter concepts commonly form part of truth commission mandates, with or without amnesty. The critical issue is that whether information given by a perpetrator as a part of an amnesty application can be used for other purposes depends on what the truth commission's rules are. It depends on whether the law forbids information given to the truth commission from being used against that person if the application is not granted. However, the issue is not as much about what the rules or the law says, but rather about what offenders' perception or understanding is of what will happen to the information they have provided. It is important to note that even with use immunity, perpetrators that reveal themselves already increase the possibility of investigation and prosecution. While the actual testimony cannot be used in a trial, it can be used to undertake further investigations that may reveal independent evidence about the crime. Critically, the most important issue is the perception of the potential amnesty applicant about the process and the likelihood of a positive outcome, than the reality of legal liability.

Crucially, the conflation of amnesty and use immunity issues is extremely common on the part of those who go through these processes. This is usually

---

53 A. Bisset, 'The Privilege Against Self-Incrimination in Truth Commission-Administered Accountability Initiatives' (2017) 30(1) *Leiden Journal of International Law* 173.

because of their lack of legal knowledge and often their lack of access to legal advice. This is usually because in many parts of the world where truth commissions have been established perpetrators have few resources to get legal assistance. That is not always the case – as, for example, in South Africa (that model will be examined in the next section of this chapter), where state agents who applied for amnesty had legal assistance paid for by the state and therefore had greater knowledge about how the information they provided could not be used against them if they were unsuccessful in their quest for amnesty. However, the overwhelming majority of South African amnesty applicants did not have any legal assistance, and in fact many of them were not literate and had no idea about the distinction between amnesty and use immunity and how the law operated. Thus, even though there is a distinction in law, often those who may want to apply for amnesty do not know about that distinction. Further, even if they have been told about the law, they may fear that the effect of their application is to put them in the public eye, which may mean that they became a target of an investigation or prosecution that would not have happened had they remained silent.

These types of lack of knowledge and misconceptions about the law and the legal process give rise to a number of problems for truth commissions. A fundamental one is the double-edged sword of getting perpetrators to come forward, whilst also trying to ensure that those who do come forward tell the truth to a satisfactory standard.[54] Truth commissions are usually established to gain a comprehensive body of knowledge about the past, because many believe that, in order for a peaceful and stable democracy to develop, people must be well informed about the past,[55] and able to bring accountability to perpetrators, in whatever form that may take.[56] However, placing the hopes for a united society and an accurate, truthful historical record on the shoulders of perpetrators who are at risk of legally injuring themselves is often a vain hope. For that reason, as noted earlier, some truth commissions are given powers to subpoena alleged perpetrators. A subpoena can give certain legal guarantees to those involved, such as, if contained in the legislation, that any information obtained cannot be brought up against the testifier at a later trial. The problem with relying on subpoenas is the fact that truth commissions hardly use them if they are given such powers. Part of the reason for this, at least in some countries, is that the truth commission has to rely on the local justice

54 N. Pierce, 'Picking up the Pieces: Truth and Justice in Sierra Leone' (2008) 6 *New Zealand Journal of Public and International Law* 117, at 120.

55 G. Fiddler, 'Using a Conditional Amnesty and Truth And Reconciliation Commission as a Transitional Justice Mechanism in Syria' (2015) 47 *The George Washington Institute of International Law Review* 893, at 917.

56 M. Popkin, *Truth Without Justice*, Pennsylvania State Press, Philadelphia, 2000, at 80.

system to enforce the subpoena, and that is not always reliable. Subpoenas are also used more often against high-level perpetrators, usually officials who gave the order but were not present when the crime was committed, and as such they do not know much about the specific details of what occurred. Subpoenas also usually lead to an evidentiary hearing, which is often closed and not open to the public. Perpetrators are not there voluntarily, and do not speak in positive or favourable ways. Thus, these types of processes do not contribute to reconciliation and other benefits of voluntary participation.

Another mechanism for obtaining information from perpetrators is by vetting and lustration systems. These processes demand that people give information in order to keep their jobs, with the threat of being fired, or not being rehired, if they do not cooperate and provide the information they have. Thus, the threat of legal action has been used in a variety of ways to coerce suspected perpetrators into coming forward of their own accord. In Sierra Leone, while the TRC issued only six subpoenas, it was the threat of being subpoenaed that motivated more perpetrators to cooperate. The Liberian TRC simply published the names of those suspected to have been involved, hoping that public and legal pressure would ensure their cooperation.

Amnesty is often viewed, simply by the nature of the word, as a mechanism to reduce accountability, and to allow perpetrators to escape liability or accountability.[57] As a result, sometimes the word amnesty is not used, but rather other words, such as immunity. The use of different words has occurred in a variety of places without solving the problem that perpetrators and others do not really understand what the process itself is and what the effects for them are. They usually simply understand the broad point that they will not be prosecuted in the future. Thus, a variety of terms have been used not always to describe or connote different legal processes or results. In Timor-Leste, for example, the truth commission was entitled to recommend immunity to the courts and the Prosecutor-General's office.[58] This process was geared toward having the affected communities play a hand in the justice and reconciliation efforts.[59] Interestingly, in Timor-Leste – the only truth commission discussed that had, in some way, the ability to grant 'amnesty', with the concurrence of other institutions – relatively large numbers of perpetrators applied for amnesty, but many still did not apply; some were not in the country, while others did not know about

57 J. Gavron, 'Amnesties in the Light of Developments in International Law and the Establishment of the International Criminal Court' (2002) 51 *International and Comparative Law Quarterly* 91, at 107–108.

58 Timor-Leste CAVR Report Chega Part 9, at paras. 3–4.

59 P. Burgess, 'Justice and Reconciliation in East Timor: The Relationship between the Commission for Reception, Truth and Reconciliation and the Courts' (2004) 15 *Criminal Law Forum* 135.

the process or how to apply. Regardless, the process was able to attract many more offenders to apply for amnesty than in a number of other countries where the truth commission simply recommended amnesty, for a variety of reasons, as will be discussed later. More offenders applied for amnesty because there was a Special Court that drove low-level offenders, to (wrongfully) fear prosecutions. Those prosecutions were actually aimed at high-level perpetrators. The process was also seen to be credible, and perpetrators who were still in the country knew that they were well known and thus ought to apply for amnesty.

## 4. THE SOUTH AFRICAN TRC AS A BENCHMARK

The South African TRC is one of the most studied truth commissions of the many such institutions that have been created over the last 50 years. Part of the reason for this is because it stands alone as having had the power to grant amnesty. It was a landmark case that revolutionised the way in which truth was bargained for. As a result, many later truth commissions began to implement a system that would offer conditional amnesty in exchange for truth. Although the South African case was unique in that it allowed the TRC to make the decision about whether to grant amnesty in an independent fashion, the popularisation of conditional amnesty began at this point.

The amnesty granted in that context was largely positively viewed as being well instituted in a political sense. However, there have been negative comments, particularly about the effects and impact of that amnesty. Thus, in 2006, when South Africa presented its report to the United Nations Committee against Torture, the committee found:

> While noting with appreciation the remarkable work of the Truth and Reconciliation Commission and its role in the peaceful transition in the State party, the Committee notes that de facto impunity persists regarding persons responsible for acts of torture during apartheid.[60]

This statement could be read in various ways, including as a criticism of the amnesty process and that there was impunity for those who committed torture. Thus, the Committee against Torture seemingly praises the work of the truth commission but notes the issue of impunity for certain crimes. It is important to note that in South Africa after the beginning of democracy – which intersects with the work of the truth commission – levels of crime

---

[60] UN Committee against Torture, Conclusions and Recommendations: South Africa, 7 December 2006, UN Doc. CAT/C/ZAF/CO/1, at para. 18.

rose significantly. South Africa was then, and still is today, unable to deal with that increasing problem. Certainly, de facto impunity occurs where the state fails to investigate and prosecute, as occurred in South Africa for apartheid-era crimes. Thus, the failure to follow up with prosecutions for those who did not apply for amnesty or had their applications rejected can also be considered to fall within what the Committee against Torture meant when it noted that de facto impunity persists. What is true is that, generally speaking, amnesties can promote impunity, and often do unless managed carefully. This is because impunity is a problem that occurs in many transitional and post-conflict states. It can have major negative ramifications, including on the possibility of repetition of abuses at some time in future, which remains very common in such states.

In the South African case, there are also, however, some who remain unconvinced as to the TRC's legitimacy and legality.[61] One of the big questions was whether it was acceptable for the TRC to offer amnesty for the most serious of crimes, including international ones.[62] These types of questions are raised for all amnesties and need to be dealt with.

However, the process of creating the TRC and its amnesty provisions helped it to overcome some of the criticisms that are levelled against amnesties in general. Most importantly, the process was agreed upon democratically, and it was enacted via a vote in the South African Parliament in 1994.[63] The issue of an amnesty was agreed during the settlement negotiations between the apartheid regime and the liberation movements.[64] Amnesty was to be given if the truth was told about crimes that were committed with a political motive.[65] An Amnesty Committee (one of three committees within the TRC) was set up to administer the process. The makeup of the Amnesty Committee, which was panelled initially only by sitting judges, did manage to draw in applications for amnesty. The fact that those selected as members of the Amnesty Committee were already Supreme Court judges lent credibility to the process, and some perpetrators, especially from the security forces, came forward as a result. While some of those people, particularly in the security forces, felt that they could not trust the TRC as a whole, they seemed to have more trust in the Amnesty Committee which was generally separate from the rest of the institution.[66]

---

61 M. Mamdani, 'Amnesty or Impunity? A Preliminary Critique of the Report of the Truth and Reconciliation Commission of South Africa (TRC)', in M. Du Plessis and S. Peté (eds.), *Repairing the Past? International Perspectives on Reparations for Gross Human Rights Abuses*, Intersentia, Antwerp, 2007.

62 Mallinder, *supra* note 39.

63 South Africa Promotion of National Unity and Reconciliation Act 1995.

64 J. Clark, 'Reconciliation Via Truth? A Study of South Africa's TRC' (2012) 11 *Journal of Human Rights* 189.

65 Sarkin, *supra* note 8.

66 Ibid.

As far as its work was concerned, the Amnesty Committee attempted to be as unbiased and depoliticised as possible, with the judges supposedly stringently applying the law. However, political considerations did affect the decision-making process, at least as far as some cases are concerned, including one concerning the son of TRC Chairperson Archbishop Desmond Tutu. Another concerned the refusal of amnesty to the killers of ANC leader Chris Hani on the basis of a supposed lack of full disclosure.[67] Such types of decisions had different impacts. The Tutu decision undermined the legitimacy of the process for some, while the refusal of amnesty to the Hani killers was seen to have a positive effect for others. Granting amnesty to some at the beginning of the amnesty process (for example, to police captain Brian Mitchell for his involvement, in support of the Inkatha Freedom Party against the United Democratic Front, in the killing of 11 people in the 1988 Trust Feed massacre) was meant to induce more people, particularly in the security services, to apply for amnesty. However, the effect of the Mitchell amnesty decision was undermined by the acquittal of the former Minister of Defence Magnus Malan, as well as other senior security force personnel and others, around the same time (at the end of 1996) in the courts. Those acquittals drove a narrative that perpetrators had little to worry about because the state did not have the resources or the capacity to successfully prosecute such cases. Some argue that as a result of the outcome of that case, fewer people applied for amnesty. It is possible, however, that the conviction of police colonel Eugene de Kock in October 1996 for 89 politically motivated crimes drove some people to apply for amnesty. The broad point is, however, that one or two cases, can severely impact the process as a whole. While the acquittal of the Minister of Defence and his co-accused and the de Kock conviction, both in the ordinary courts, were of course separate from the amnesty process, and thus are not examples of the political nature of that process, they are examples of how outside developments can affect the legitimacy and effectiveness of such a process. Regardless, all these cases, both amnesty decisions and court ones, can affect how a process is viewed and can affect its legacy.

The numbers of applications for amnesty in the South African TRC process are difficult to fully comprehend. While 7,000 applications were received, approximately 4,500 were dismissed as being ineligible simply on the basis of their application documents, largely because the applicants (the majority) were deemed not to have had a political motivation for carrying out the offence they perpetrated.[68] For these 4,500 applicants, no hearings

---

67 J. Sarkin, 'An Evaluation of the South African Amnesty Process', in A. Chapman and H. van der Merwe (eds.), *Truth and Reconciliation: Did the TRC Deliver*, University of Pennsylvania Press, Philadelphia, 2008.

68 Truth and Reconciliation Commission of South Africa, *Final Report*, 29 October 1998, 5 volumes, Juta & Co., Cape Town, 1998.

were held.[69] Problematically, the overwhelming majority of those applicants were in prison at the time they applied for amnesty and had no access to legal assistance. In total, of all the applicants for amnesty (over 7,000), only 1,167 people were granted it. However, this number cannot be assumed to be in any way representative of those who ought to have applied for amnesty, as it is unknown how many people should have applied. Part of the reason is that it is not possible to verify the full extent of the crimes that were committed in enforcing apartheid.[70] It must also be remembered that many of the people who applied for and were granted amnesty had actually fought against the apartheid regime, on the side of the liberation movements. The data indicates that a majority of amnesty applicants were in fact black, and were not from the security forces or elements of the white government that ordered many of the atrocities.[71] Thus, a range of external issues affected the truth commission and played a role in the extent of applications and therefore the type of information that was obtained. The legacy of the amnesty process was therefore deeply impacted.

Because the prosecuting authority set up by the new government seemed to lack the political will or capacity to prosecute perpetrators who did not come forward, many of those who had committed abuses seemingly did not apply for amnesty. The acquittal of former Minster of Defence Magnus Malan and his more than 20 co-accused a few weeks before the deadline for amnesty applications was read by potential applicants as a sign that the state did not have the commitment to take up such cases or did not have the skills and resources to do so. This was offset to some degree by the conviction of Colonel de Kock. However, the public disputes between the prosecutors, investigators and others in these cases was also seen as sign that there was a lack of coordination and synchronised response. The failure of the prosecuting authority to act as the stick, where the carrot of amnesty was being offered, meant that many perpetrators did not see applying for amnesty as necessary. They seemed to believe that they would not be called to answer for what they had done. With that assumption, to give themselves up voluntarily was viewed by at least some as unnecessarily risky. That was mitigated to some extent by the conviction in the de Kock case, as that brought to the fore that amnesty might be needed by some, but to what extent is unknown.

There are two important questions from an impact and legacy point of view for the South African TRC. Firstly, did more truth come out than would have been the case without the conditional amnesty provision? Secondly, if so, was that extra truth gained because the TRC was allowed to grant amnesty on its own, without the state review that occurred in later processes,

---

69 Sarkin, *supra* note 8.

70 R. Bhargava, 'Restoring Decency to Barbaric Societies', in Rotberg and Thompson, *supra* note 19, at 65 note 35.

71 Sarkin, *supra* note 67.

where the truth commission could only recommend amnesty? Regarding the first question, it does seem clear that more truth was gained, as a number of perpetrators came forward with information, giving answers to old questions. This was the case despite the extremely complex legal criteria that had to be met before amnesty was granted. The complicated provisions of the law and the uncertainty about how the Amnesty Committee was going to interpret those legal requirements burdened the process.

As far as how much truth emerged, the present author has noted in his book on the TRC's amnesty process that more truth was learnt about the structural system that capacitated the human rights violations and that '[m]uch was learnt … about particular events'.[72] Importantly, the TRC noted that 'disinformation about the past that had been accepted as truth by some members of society lost much of its credibility'.[73] Priscilla Hayner also notes in regard to that amnesty process that: 'it seems clear that significant and detailed information emerged from the amnesty process that contributed to the broader goal of revealing the truth'.[74] New truth did emerge as a result of the amnesty process. While some of the amnesty applications provided information not previously known, others helped to corroborate information about which there had previously been uncertainty. This was the case even though there is evidence that some perpetrators designed and coordinated their stories so as to ensure their amnesty was granted.[75] While some perpetrators conspired together to create the most innocuous version of events, much more truth was gained from perpetrators than could have been established by dealing only with victim testimony.

However, much remained untold. There were many conspicuous gaps in the information disclosed. Very little information about sexual and gender-based violence or crimes committed outside the country during the South African Defence Force's involvement in regional conflicts or in attacks on the liberation movements. Some political parties, like the Inkatha Freedom Party, forbade their members from participating in the process to get amnesty, even though hundreds of them were in prison for the perpetration of politically motivated crimes. Interestingly, several of the total number of applicants received 'partial amnesty' – in other words, they were granted amnesty for the crimes they disclosed, but denied amnesty for other crimes, for a range of reasons, including non-full disclosure.

72 Sarkin, *supra* note 8, at 272.
73 South African TRC Report, *supra* note 68, Volume 1, at 111.
74 Hayner, *supra* note 1, at 30.
75 Sarkin, *supra* note 8, at 275.

When it comes to whether the process was successful or had sufficient impact, the issue is partly about how much new information was obtained and partly about how much information was confirmed. On the basis of the amount of new information received and new corroborating information, then of course the South African amnesty succeeded. But to some extent that can be seen to be a thin measure of success. A better measure of impact and success is the quality and significance of what was revealed, weighed against the cost of receiving it (i.e. the effect and legacy of having an amnesty for the country as a whole, specifically looking towards the future). As far as the quality and significance of what was revealed is concerned, the application forms and the transcripts of amnesty hearings provide substantial important information both on the processes behind the atrocities and on the details of what actually occurred. While a few additional names of those who committed such deeds were revealed, more was exposed about why the deeds were carried out, the context in which they were ordered and the way in which they were carried out. But the purpose, as determined by the way the hearings were conducted, was not really to gain the minutiae of the information. The application forms and the hearings aimed to determine whether the requirements in the law to grant amnesty had been met.

The answer to the second question (whether more truth was learnt because of the way the process was set up) is more complex. There is a view that the makeup of the Amnesty Committee – and particularly that at least one of the first five Committee members came from the Afrikaner community and other members were sitting Supreme Court judges who were widely public respected, at least in the white community – meant that at least some perpetrators from the security force sector had more faith that the system would treat them fairly. It seems that some of them were drawn into the process because they believed in the process at least to some degree, but also because the best lawyers gave them legal advice that was paid for by the state. The fact that people came forward who may not otherwise have been identified seems to indicate that at least some saw a benefit in using the mechanisms employed by the South African TRC. That said, certainly some came forward because they were likely to be named by others who were making such applications. Thus, issues of trust, legitimacy and perceptions of fairness were critical issues.

However, it must be understood that the full merits of the South African process as a model to be used elsewhere cannot be fully appreciated, as no other country has applied the South African model. 'It is therefore hard to know how transferable it is. As a result, it is difficult to judge the mechanism comparatively. There have been some processes, as will be described below, that took aspects of the South African model, but none that have applied it specifically, with the power to grant amnesty directly.

## 5. THE POWER TO RECOMMEND CASES FOR AMNESTY

The political climate in a post-conflict society is often difficult to navigate. A new government has to juggle a range of issues, including their desire for prolonged peace, their need to consolidate their own position, and the demands for justice. A vital question is how to deal with the past and whether or not to give amnesty. Often amnesty is given to allow the transition to occur and be maintained. This is never an easy decision, as there are many possible difficulties that result. One of the issues that arises is whether a state should decide to have an amnesty process and, if so, what the procedure ought to be. Related to that, if the amnesty is to be conditional, there is the question of who should make the decisions about who is granted amnesty.

In this regard, governments have been unwilling to give up having the final say over amnesty cases ever since the South African process. New governments have wanted to control the outcome of truth commissions for their own political benefit. The South African model is at least in part responsible for this distrust that governments have towards giving truth commissions amnesty powers. They fear that the model reflects what a lack of control over such a process means, and how some people who ought not to have got amnesty did, and vice versa. As a consequence, other countries do not want to replicate the South African model. Allowing a truth commission independence, but at the same time wanting to control the outcome of an amnesty process, are incongruous. States battle politically to find the right balance between these competing concerns. In fact, the issue of independence of truth commissions, and institutions in a state in general, is a massive problem for states. They want these bodies to appear to be independent, but in actual fact they want to control them. As a result, many states that have created truth commissions have only given them the power to recommend amnesty. Governments, or prosecutors, then review those recommendations and take the final decision as to who should then be granted amnesty. However, the politics of whom the government selects are problematic, particularly in various societies that have suffered human rights abuses. Often the government is composed of one side of the conflict, and therefore is unlikely to be trusted by the other side. Sometimes there may be a government of national unity, but one of the parties controls the justice department, where amnesty decisions are usually made. Thus, uncertainty remains a major concern for perpetrators who may wish to enter such a process.

In this contest between political actors in their quest to control these processes and their outcomes, one of the major obstacles regarding truth commissions has been the inability of these institutions to entice perpetrators to come forward. This is due to a number of factors, first and foremost the fear of a low likelihood of obtaining amnesty. Other factors that have made perpetrators reluctant to confess include the difficult criteria that must be fulfilled in order to be recommended for amnesty and the inability of governments to prosecute perpetrators.

This chapter will now examine some of those different truth commission models to reveal that truth commissions with the power to recommend amnesty have been less effective than the South African system at bringing both truth and accountability to the victims and the general public in their respective countries. Mention is also made in places as to how these processes have allowed such amnesty processes to enhance reconciliation, social cohesion and nation-building. This is done to determine how truth commissions can enhance their impact and their legacies using amnesty processes.

## 6. TRUTH COMMISSION AMNESTY PROCESSES AROUND THE WORLD

### 6.1. GRENADA

The Grenadian Truth and Reconciliation Commission was established on 4 September 2001 under the terms of the Commission of Inquiry Act, Ch 58 of the Revised Laws of Grenada 1990.[76] It was mandated to investigate violations committed between 1976 and 1991.[77] This truth commission was given the power '[t]o recommend indemnity to various persons who give what is considered to be truthful evidence at the enquiry'.[78] This was interpreted to mean that those who came forward would be 'favourably considered for the grant of amnesty or exemption from prosecution'.[79] The Grenadian process saw very few perpetrators come forward, as amnesty was not guaranteed or even likely in the view of perpetrators. The TRC report found that:

> It is the belief and understanding of the Commission that there are persons who might have made themselves available to appear before it and testify if they could have been given assurance of protection against prosecution; and that there were persons who appeared before the Commission and did give evidence, but were inhibited from

76 Grenada, Truth and Reconciliation Commission, 'Terms of Reference of the Truth and Reconciliation Commission', in *Report on Certain Political Events which Occurred in Grenada 1976–1991*, 28 March 2006.

77 J.O. McCalpin, 'Written into Amnesia? The Truth and Reconciliation Commission of Grenada' (2013) 62(3/4) *Social and Economic Studies* 113.

78 Grenada Truth and Reconciliation Commission, *supra* note 76.

79 Ibid, at Volume 1, Part 7.

> speaking 'the truth, the whole truth and nothing but the truth' for fear of playing into the hands of the prosecuting authorities.[80]

This seems to indicate that people did not believe that they would stand a chance at being given amnesty by the government, and therefore did not apply. Thus, their lack of faith in the system prevented them from entering it in the first place. Therefore, the process did not benefit from as much truth recovery as it could have. This obviously affects its impact. The Grenadian process needs to be contrasted with the South African case, where some people viewed the process to be fair, and their chances of achieving a favourable outcome as good. They were more willing to participate. Thus, the body that grants amnesty needs to be trusted. Furthermore, having to convince two bodies – first the truth commission and then the government – is seemingly problematic. This reduces the trust and certainty that perpetrators seek. Therefore, they are less likely to cooperate, which then reduces the ability of the process to have greater impact.

## 6.2. TIMOR-LESTE

Timor-Leste's truth commission (formally known as the Commission for Reception, Truth and Reconciliation (CAVR))[81] illustrates again that without some guarantee of amnesty (although in this case called immunity), perpetrators are less likely to turn out. This is because perpetrators tend to stay away without some legal safety net. This affects the ability of the process to have increased impact.

The CAVR[82] set out to 'inquire into human rights violations committed on all sides, between April 1974 and October 1999, and facilitate community reconciliation with justice for those who committed less serious offenses'. In the first three years, the CAVR did not get any perpetrator testimony, while receiving 7,000 victim testimonies. A series of obstacles impeded the CAVR's ability to entice perpetrators to come forward.

Under section 32 of the United Nations Transitional Administration in East Timor (UNTAET) regulation setting up the truth commission, the commission had the authority to issue a community reconciliation agreement (CRP) to offenders. The agreement had to be supported, however, by the Office of the Prosecutor-General (OPG) and the courts. If this occurred, and provided

---

80 Ibid.

81 J. Roosa, 'How Does a Truth Commission Find Out What the Truth Is? The case of East Timor's CAVR' (2008) 80(4) *Pacific Affairs* 569.

82 See generally M. Hirst and A. Linnarsson, 'Children and the Commission for Reception, Truth and Reconciliation in Timor-Leste', Innocenti Working Paper No. 7, UNICEF Innocenti Research Centre, Florence, 2010.

that the offender adhered to the conditions of the community reconciliation process (CRP), they received immunity. Thus, it could be argued that this process granted conditional amnesty rather than recommended it. However, before exemption from prosecution was given, the OPG had to examine the merits of the case and endorse it for the CRP. Only then could it be sent to a court for approval. Thus, the CAVR did not in fact grant amnesty, but rather recommended it.

As far as the process was concerned, over 1,300 people applied and provided information about what they had done. However, their reasons for doing so must be understood in the context of what was happening in terms of holding offenders accountable. Thus, the number of applicants was due to the fact that there was a strong drive to prosecute offenders, albeit those that were high-level perpetrators. Shortly after the violence, in fact by the next year (2000), UNTAET established the Special Panels of the Dili District Court. This was seen to be an indication that the government and the UN were determined to prosecute offenders. This quick action and deemed commitment was a result of United Nations Security Council adopting Resolution 1272, which demanded that the people responsible for the violence and destruction in Timor-Leste be brought to justice. This indicated to perpetrators that they would be held accountable if they were in the country. The fact that the Special Courts were already functional by December 2001 was a further incentive for perpetrators to come forward in the hope of receiving amnesty. While it is true that the Special Courts operated against higher-level offenders and the CRP against lower-level ones, that distinction was largely unknown to offenders, at least initially. Who the Special Court was going to specifically target was unclear, and there was thus a general fear amongst perpetrators who remained in Timor-Leste, rather than fleeing to Indonesia, that they were in legal jeopardy.

However, a number of obstacles still existed in the process. Firstly, a large number of people had fled the country, and were not present to participate in the process and give testimony.[83] Secondly, while the CRP aimed to be 'a cheaper, faster, less complicated process', it did not always go as planned.[84] The process was flawed, as the regulations about how people could be considered eligible constantly changed, with differing definitions of what a 'serious' crime was. There were issues about CRP's functionality, mainly in that it was a complex process that was difficult to understand or to follow through with. The application process was complicated and required a written report about

83 PIERCE, *supra* note 54.

84 P. BURGESS, 'East Timor's Community Reconciliation Process', in N. ROHT-ARRIAZA and J. MARIEZCURRENA (eds.), *Transitional Justice in the Twenty-First Century: Beyond Truth versus Justice*, Cambridge University Press, Cambridge, 2006, at 184.

applicants' political involvement,[85] an oral report and a recommendation from the OPG in order for a person to be eligible for the CRP. There was clearly a large knowledge gap. The majority of people in the 1,371 cases that went to the CRP had no legal representation, and were under the impression that they were being guaranteed amnesty.

In the end, over 90 per cent of cases were granted immunity after being agreed to by the OPG and the courts. The process was closer to a conditional amnesty, with the truth being provided about the violations of the past, giving closure to victims and their families,[86] whilst still holding perpetrators accountable in some sense. Thus, the process drew significant participation that positively impacted its outcome. However, approximately 3,000 offenders did not participate, for a variety of reasons, including, seemingly, a lack of awareness of it before the closing date for applications.[87]

As far as the impact of the process as a whole is concerned, McAuliffe and Burgess find that the CRP was very successful, but more in terms of reconciliation efforts.[88] Pigou has argued that its legacy is that the CRP unquestionably added to social cohesion and that it relieved animosities in various parts of the country.[89] However, it is argued that this process is context-specific, and that it is not possible to learn much for other places from this model.[90]

## 6.3. INDONESIA–TIMOR-LESTE

Established in 2005, the Indonesia–Timor-Leste Commission on Truth and Friendship (CTF) was established as a cooperative process between the two countries to deal with the past in Timor-Leste. It could be argued, however, that the CTF was not a genuine truth commission, as it focused only on one event: the referendum of 1999. However, it could be argued that the violence during the referendum was not one event but many events over a period of time, and thus this institution does qualify as a truth commission.[91] Nevertheless, one of its functions was to 'recommend amnesty for those involved in human rights violations who cooperate fully in revealing the truth'.[92] Even though

85 P. McAuliffe, 'East Timor's Community Reconciliation Process as a Model for Legal Pluralism in Criminal Justice' (2008) *Social Justice & Global Development Journal* (online), at 9.

86 Ibid, at 10.

87 Burgess, *supra* note 84, at 196.

88 McAuliffe, *supra* note 85, at 10; and Burgess, *supra* note 84, at 176.

89 P. Pigou, 'The Community Reconciliation Process of the Commission for Reception, Truth and Reconciliation', UN Development Programme, 2004, at 84.

90 Burgess, *supra* note 84, at 176.

91 See the introduction to the book on this issue.

92 UNTAET Regulation No. 2001/10, 3 July 2001, UN Doc. UNTAET/REG/2001/10, section 14(c)(i)–(iv).

part of the process was held in Indonesia, and perpetrators were 'protected' by Indonesian sovereignty, they did not avail of the proffered amnesty. In the end, only 62 people gave testimony at the hearings. It seems as though almost none of them were perpetrators, indicating that the CTF was unable to incentivise perpetrators to come forward. In the end, no applications were recommended for amnesty.[93]

This was likely as a result of the stringent conditions set for an application to receive amnesty. Specifically, perpetrators had to provide useful information that helped to uncover the truth before they could be considered. Applicants were therefore being asked to risk a lot by coming forward, as they would have to give much incriminating evidence, without knowing whether it would be considered enough to warrant amnesty. The risk was evidently too high for the vast majority, and this resulted in a very low turn out of perpetrators. Again, the lack of perpetrators making applications can be attributed to a lack of certainty about whether having both the commission and the state involved in determining whether amnesty ought to be granted made the outcome of the process seem too unpredictable for perpetrators.

Moreover, the incentive to come forward did not exist very strongly for most perpetrators, as there was little threat of prosecutions. As the hearings were held in Indonesia, where there was little risk of prosecution, coming forward was an unnecessary risk. Thus, the CTF provided neither carrot nor stick, and was ineffective at gathering truth from perpetrators, and ultimately promoting accountability. Generally, the impact of the CTF was limited. Its provisions were not that useful in obtaining much new information about what occurred. It may have had some impact on issues of reconciliation between the two countries, but its legacy is, broadly speaking, limited.

## 6.4. LIBERIA

Liberia's TRC is an interesting case, wherein it was possible for amnesty to be recommended in the event that perpetrators testified and showed remorse. This was contained in the Act setting up the TRC, which provided for:

> amnesty under terms and conditions established by the TC upon application of individual persons making full disclosures of their wrongs and thereby expressing remorse for their acts and/or omissions, whether as an accomplice or a perpetrator, provided that amnesty or exoneration shall not apply to violations of international law and crimes against humanity in conformity with international laws and standards.[94]

93 Indonesia–Timor-Leste, Commission on Truth and Friendship, *Per Memoriam ad Spem* (Through Memory to Hope) 2008, at aviii.

94 Act to Establish the Truth and Reconciliation Commission (TRC) of Liberia, National Transitional Legislative Assembly, 12 May 2005, Article VII, §26(g).

Widely seen to be similar to the South African TRC, the Liberian system was different in a variety of key ways. Firstly, it could only recommend amnesty.[95] Secondly, it did not allow serious international crimes to be considered for amnesty, as was allowed in the South African case.[96] Thirdly, perpetrators were required to show remorse in order to qualify for amnesty, unlike in South Africa.

To try and get more people to come forward, the Liberians used the coercive tactic of using testimony provided beforehand to compile a list of names of people suspected of being involved in the violence that it then released.[97] This was done in the hope that potential prosecutions or shame would compel these people to testify and thereby be able to gain amnesty if they met the criteria of being recommended by the truth commission.[98] The initially publically released list contained 198 names.[99] This process was different, however, to the amnesty given to children and to the perpetrators of non-serious crimes.[100]

The truth commission received 20,000 statements and 800 testimonies, but only recommended 38 amnesties.[101] This suggests that very few perpetrators actually came forward, considering the scale of the violence witnessed in the country. Had more people been named, and if a range of other tools been used to incentivise offenders to participate, more truth would have emerged, as more perpetrators would have been likely to cooperate with the truth commission.

Thus, whilst the truth commission could recommend amnesty, very few perpetrators came forward, and even fewer testified. The critical issue is that those who were publically named came forward in greater numbers. Thus, for offenders to participate, they need to be incentivised to participate. There are various ways this can be achieved, such as having their names announced publically or on lists of persons who are subject to investigations.

---

95 O. Ojielo, 'Critical Lessons in Post-Conflict Security in Africa: The Case of Liberia's Truth and Reconciliation Commission', Occasional Paper 1, Institute for Justice and Reconciliation, 2010.

96 R. de la Cruz Gitau, '"God Willing, I Will Be Back": Gauging the Truth and Reconciliation Commission's Capacity to Deter Economic Crimes in Liberia' (2008) 17(4) *African Security Review* 64.

97 Amnesty International, 'Liberia: Will those investigated by the Truth and Reconciliation Commission ever be prosecuted?', Public Statement, AI Index: AFR 34/010/2008, 5 December 2008, https://www.amnesty.org/download/Documents/52000/afr340102008en.pdf.

98 Ibid.

99 Ibid.

100 Republic of Liberia, Truth and Reconciliation Commission, Final Report, 1 July 2009, Volume 2: Consolidated Final Report, at 8.

101 See A. Weah, 'Hopes and Uncertainties: Liberia's Journey to End Impunity' (2012) 6 *International Journal of Transitional Justice* 331.

## 6.5. KENYA

After more than 1,300 people died in an explosion of ethnically fuelled political violence in Kenya in 2007, the Truth Justice and Reconciliation Commission (TJRC) was established by Kenya's Parliament.[102] It was established to investigate not only the violence at that time, but all such cases since 1963. The TJRC aimed to create a more comprehensive history of these violations. It was therefore driven to obtain the truth about human rights violations of the previous four decades. In this way, the country attempted to build on the post-electoral-violence peace process as an opportunity to reshape the national dialogue and understanding of previous violence.

Amnesty could be recommended by the TJRC if a perpetrator came forward with information that could expose the truth about the country's violent history of human rights abuses.[103] In terms of the law, the TJRC was so restricted in its amnesty powers that in its final report it was noted that very little could realistically be achieved as only a small portion of perpetrators were willing to risk coming forward. In fact, the TJRC did not end up using its power to recommend amnesty at all.[104] The TJRC stated that because it could only recommend amnesty, little would come out of that process. Another limitation was that the Kenyan legislation also made clear that amnesty could not be recommended for something that qualified as a gross violation of human rights. The commissioners also found the criteria as to when and how amnesty was to be granted very problematic. Therefore, the amnesty recommendation system in the Kenyan context was viewed by the TJRC as entirely unhelpful in gaining more truth about the past injustices suffered in the country.[105] It could, however, be argued that the perpetuation of the same leadership (Kenyatta/Ruto), albeit on a reconciliatory footing,[106] stopped many perpetrators coming forward since there was a background threat that revealing the chain of command for the violence might have exposed the top rungs of the government. In other words, the truth commission did not take place under a new government or with a clean slate. It is important to note in this context that there are numerous allegations of witness killings and intimidations that took place when the ICC launched its investigations to deal with the same events.

---

102 Truth, Justice and Reconciliation Act 6 of 2008, 28 November 2008.

103 Ibid, Section 34.

104 Kenya, Truth, Justice and Reconciliation Commission, *Final Report*, 2013, http://digitalcommons.law.seattleu.edu/tjrc/1, 2013.

105 Ibid, Volume 1, at §125.

106 See generally T.O. Hansen, 'Transitional Justice in Kenya – An Assessment of the Accountability Process in Light of Domestic Politics and Security Concerns' (2011) 42 *California Western International Law Journal* 1.

Problematically, the TJRC copied the South African truth commission provisions in many respects. It had many of the limitations that held back the South African system from achieving more of its goals, such as the extremely complex legal criteria to be eligible for amnesty. The TJRC seemingly learned very few lessons from the amnesty failures of the truth commissions that came before it. Not only did it limit itself by reapplying some of the legal restrictions that had damaged the South African truth commission, but the TJRC also did not allow its truth commission to directly grant amnesty. As a result, very few perpetrators who may have had valuable information came forward. It has been argued that the 'powers of the Kenyan Commission were so severely limited that they were unavailable as a tool for the Commission to use to entice perpetrator testimony or foster reconciliation'.[107] Thus, the Kenyan process indicates that the amnesty tool had limited impact. It did not play much of a role in truth-finding or in attempts to promote reconciliation. The legacy of the TJRC could have been enhanced if this had worked, but the problems in the process probably meant that even a successful use of its amnesty provisions could not have saved it and its legacy.

## 6.6. REPUBLIC OF KOREA

Korea has had several experiences with truth commissions since 1996. Nearly 20 truth commissions[108] have been created to establish national unity and a comprehensive understanding of the country's complex history. The largest and most broadly mandated[109] of these was the 2005 Truth and Reconciliation Commission of Korea (TCK).[110] This process investigated the extent of human rights abuses from 1910 to 1993.

As far as amnesty is concerned, the TCK was permitted to recommend to the president immunity for any person 'who obtains or submits critical materials for clearing up the truth in the investigation'.[111] However, the amnesty recommendation system was not enough to tempt perpetrators into coming

---

107 R. Slye, 'Putting the J into the truth commission: Kenya's Truth Commission', in M. Swart and K. Van Marle (eds.), *Twenty Years On: Other Ways of Being and the South African Truth and Reconciliation Commission*, Brill, Leiden (forthcoming).

108 T.U. Baik, 'Fairness in Transitional Justice Initiatives: The Case of South Korea' (2012) 19 *Buffalo Human Rights Law Review* 169, at 170.

109 A. Wolman, 'Looking Back While Moving Forward: The Evolution of Truth Commissions in Korea' (2012) 14(3) *Asian-Pacific Law & Policy Journal* 27.

110 United States Institute of Peace, 'Framework Act on Clearing Up Past Incidents for Truth and Reconciliation', enacted by Law No. 7542, 31 May 2005.

111 Republic of Korea, Truth and Reconciliation Commission, *Truth and Reconciliation Activities of the Past Three Years*, 2009, at 123.

forward to provide their information. They seemingly did not believe that they needed amnesty and did not trust that, if they participated, they would eventually get amnesty. In this regard, Dong-Choon Kim has stated: 'few veterans have been willing to come forward'.[112] The fact that 'the TCK rarely issued an order compelling a person to appear before it and never penalized anyone for refusing to appear before it'[113] meant that very little new truth was unveiled as a result of this process. Clearly, a process that simply recommends amnesty is not decisive in convincing perpetrators to come forward and share their information with the truth commission. Thus, this Korean process did not see much being contributed by its amnesty provisions. It had limited impact and its legacy is seen to be imperfect.

## 6.7. OTHER TRUTH COMMISSION AMNESTY PROCESSES

Around the world, a series of other truth commissions have also battled with the complex question of how to use amnesty as a means to elicit truth from perpetrators. These truth commission amnesty process designs are not, however, that helpful: for a range of reasons they have not been implemented or completed because their mandates were either not established or because the processes were halted and they never completed their work.

The Democratic Republic of the Congo (DRC) has witnessed fractious and consistent violence since colonial times, but its intensity has increased in recent times. In 2003, the DRC included a truth commission in its transitional constitution,[114] which resulted from the Inter-Congolese Dialogue peace process. This truth commission was set up to 'establish truth and to promote peace, justice, reparation, forgiveness and reconciliation for sustaining national unity'[115] in relation to violence occurring from July 2003 to February 2007. To complete its work, the truth commission was allowed to recommend amnesty,[116] but ultimately made no such recommendations. Sometime later, another truth commission was set up and argued that it should have the ability to grant amnesty directly, conceding that the ability to recommend only rendered the powers of the truth commission extremely limited.[117]

---

112 K. Dong-Choon, 'Korea's Truth and Reconciliation Commission: An Overview and Assessment' (2012) 19 *Buffalo Human Rights Law Review* 97, at 107.

113 Ibid.

114 Articles 154–160 of the DRC's Transitional Constitution.

115 O. Wa Kambala and T. Savage, 'Decayed, Decimated, Usurped and Inadequate: the Challenge of Finding Justice through Formal Mechanisms in the DR Congo', in I. Aertsen et al. (eds.), *Restoring Justice after Large-Scale Violent Conflicts: Kosovo, DR Congo and the Israeli-Palestinian Case*, Willan Publishing, Devon, 2008, at 346.

116 DRC, Loi No. /04/018 du juillet 30 2004 portant sur l'organisation, attributions et fonctionnement de la Commission de Vérité et Réconciliation, Article 8g.

117 Ibid.

In Nepal, the most recent process to deal with the past has focused on the armed conflict between the Communist Party of Nepal (Maoist) and the government that occurred from 1996 to 2006. A previous truth commission process, the Commission of Inquiry to Locate the Persons Disappeared during the Panchayat Period, occurred between 1990 and 1991. Amnesty proved very controversial in the process of establishing the latest truth commission. Civil society opposed amnesty, but the government has consistently favoured such a measure. In fact, early drafts of the legislation included provisions that would empower the truth commission to recommend amnesty.[118] Section 26(1) of the Commission on Investigation of Disappeared Persons, Truth and Reconciliation Act (2014) provided that the truth commission could recommend amnesty to the government; it could also recommend that action be taken against those not given amnesty.[119] However, the Nepalese Supreme Court struck down the amnesty provisions as incompatible with their constitution. The process is still underway, but uncertainty around it has driven away many potential applicants for amnesty. What the amnesty process will look like and what the results will be will only be ascertained when the process has been completed.

In Burundi, processes to deal with the past have been elusive. There was meant to have been a truth commission process since 2003, as agreed to in the 2000 Arusha Peace accords. The truth commission that was designed contains an amnesty provision. The institution aimed to provide insight into the human rights violations, such as murder, torture and enforced disappearances, that occurred from 1962 to 2008.[120] That process has taken many years to get off the ground.[121] The controversial truth commission was finally established in 2014 with a four-year mandate. How its amnesty process will work remains to be seen.

The final place where there is to be some relationship between a truth commission and amnesty is in Colombia. This process is just starting, following the 2016 peace agreement between the government and FARC.[122]

---

118 International Center for Transitional Justice and the Kofi Annan Foundation, 'Challenging the Conventional: Can Truth Commissions Strengthen Peace Processes?', 2016, at 76–77, https://www.ictj.org/publication/challenging-conventional-can-truth-commissions-strengthen-peace-processes.

119 Section 13(e), Commission on Investigation of Disappeared Persons, Truth and Reconciliation Act (2014).

120 S. Vanderginste, 'Bypassing the Prohibition of Amnesty for Human Rights Crimes under International Law: Lessons Learned from the Burundi Peace Process' (2012) 29(2) *Netherlands Quarterly of Human Rights* 189.

121 S. Vandeginste, 'Burundi's Truth and Reconciliation Commission: How to Shed Light on the Past while Standing in the Dark Shadow of Politics?' (2012) 6 *International Journal of Transitional Justice* 355.

122 Final Agreement to End the Conflict and Establish a Stable and Long-lasting Peace, Colombian Government–FARC, 24 November 2016, http://especiales.presidencia.gov.co/Documents/20170620-dejacion-armas/acuerdos/acuerdo-final-ingles.pdf.

The agreement creates a Comprehensive System of Truth, Justice, Reparation and Non-Repetition, which includes amnesty and pardon. Also to be established is a Commission for the Identification of the Truth, Coexistence and Non-Repetition.[123] The commission will not grant amnesty,[124] but will have the power to compel testimony that cannot be used against the person who testifies. Conditional amnesty-granting powers will be in the hands of the Special Jurisdiction for Peace (SJP), but how this will work is unclear. Applicants who confess to having committed politically motivated crimes will be given 'special treatment' by the SJP if they tell the truth, acknowledge responsibility, participate in reparations and deliver guarantees of non-repetition.[125] The law says they will have 'effective restrictions on freedoms and rights',[126] but how that will work has not been defined.

Thus, as can be seen from this section, a further number of truth commissions were to have been involved in amnesties. However, for a number of reasons, these institutions were never activated, are still working, or are still in the pipeline. The critical issue is that truth commissions are continually being given some type of amnesty power, but today always to recommend amnesty and not to grant it directly to perpetrators, as was the case with the South African truth and reconciliation commission. This type of amnesty process, which recommends amnesty only, does not seem to achieve much and does not enhance truth commission impact as it is seemingly less trusted, and therefore fewer potential applicants make use of it. Thus, if there is a desire to increase truth commission impact and legacy, then they ought to be given the power to directly grant amnesty. However, much needs to be done by both the truth commission and the other institutions of the state to ensure that perpetrators believe they need amnesty and do in fact apply for it.

## 7. CONCLUSION

Truth commissions are undoubtedly valuable tools, especially in post-conflict societies. They can even be used as a mechanism through which to end conflict. The role that amnesty provisions play in truth commissions is, however, heavily contested. Whilst some view them as controversial and not in line with international law (and often domestic law), this chapter has argued that, without

123 J. Bustamante-Reyes, 'Colombia's Path to Peace' (2017) 42(1) *New Zealand International Review* 14.

124 I.M. Ortiz Acosta, 'Seeking Truth in Colombia: Perspectives on a Truth Commission' (2017) 2 *Razón Crítica* 21.

125 Colombia, Proyecto de ley Estatutaria de la Administración de Justicia en la Jurisdicción Especial para la Paz, Bill No. 8/2017.

126 C. Josi, 'Accountability in the Colombian Peace Agreement: Are the Proposed Sanctions Contrary to Colombia's International Obligations' (2016) 46 *Southwestern Law Review* 401.

the promise of amnesty, a truth commission is unlikely to lead to perpetrator accountability in which the culprit participates voluntarily or the provision of more truth that the country can use to build a foundation of unity and trust. Crucially, from a truth point of view, whilst victim testimony is valuable and should be heard, it is perpetrator testimony that has much to offer to elucidate the past.[127] That testimony can give broad insights into the way the system ran, but crucially for victims can also give many glimpses into the events that occurred, which often remain hidden. This allows for closure for both victims and perpetrators, and the opportunity for the truth to be known by the wider public. This can have impact on a range of other issues in that society as it moves forward in its quest to be more democratic and more human rights-friendly.

However, the way in which an amnesty process is set up and dispensed is vital to the success or failure of truth commissions' achievement of their goals, and this chapter has shown through a series of examples how a badly designed amnesty process may nullify any positive effects a truth commission may have.

Giving amnesty is vital to bringing perpetrators to the table. Without legal protection, their motivation to come forward and admit their roles in the horrors of the past is slim. As has been illustrated in all the examples of countries where truth commissions did not manage to tempt a large number of applicants, many perpetrators stay away and take their chances with the legal system. In South Africa's case, however, when amnesty was put on the table, there was to some degree a larger inflow of applicants, and additional truth was uncovered because some applicants were wooed into the process and believed that they would have a good chance of getting amnesty if they applied. This process was also helpful for reasons of political stability. It contributed, though not on its own, to national reconciliation, social cohesion and nation-building. Whilst there are clearly problems with the South African TRC model, all the other truth commissions against which it has been used as a yardstick have failed to make the same kind of truth-seeking gains that were present in South Africa. Being limited to only recommending amnesty cuts off the capability of truth commissions. They struggle to attract applicants, as people fear the repercussions of participation. People do not trust having to go through two institutions, one of which is a government that may be likely to grant (or not grant) amnesties based on political affiliation or other political factors. People desire some reassurance, and will not risk their freedom or reputation without a legal safety net. Although South Africa is an isolated case, this chapter argues that the promise of amnesty granted directly by a

---

[127] N.V. Nwogu, 'When and Why it Started: Deconstructing Victim-Centered Truth Commissions in the Context of Ethnicity-Based Conflict' (2010) 4 *International Journal of Transitional Justice* 275.

truth commission attracted a far higher number of applicants. Only one body needed to be convinced of a perpetrator's eligibility for amnesty, and that truth commission had no overtly political leaning, and so was perceived by applicants as being more trustworthy. There are, however, contextual factors: in some states there may be more trust in government than in others, and the type of transition (or the fact that there has not been a transition) may play an important role, as in Kenya.

Generally speaking, for potential amnesty applicants to actually apply, the process must be accessible, easy to understand and trusted. Clearly, people will be more willing to engage with a one-stop process that they have faith in. As previously noted, every country is different, and it would be foolish to create blanket policies. There are, however, general lessons to be learnt from how previous processes worked. Conditional amnesties can be tailored to each situation so as to get the most out of each truth commission, both by gaining truth, and by bringing to account those who have committed crimes in the past.

Even if a state will not allow a truth commission to grant amnesty, there is an argument to be made that at the very least the truth commission should be able to give immunity from the use of the information provided against the applicant. In this way a truth commission will be able to perform its truth-recovery function to full effect, as people might hopefully be more tempted to confess their crimes with some mild form of immunity as a protection.[128]

Finally, it is important to note that many things outside the purview and control of a truth commission affect the impact and legacy of that truth commission, especially as regards amnesty. Thus, how the prosecution services act, how many cases are brought, when those cases occur, if they lead to convictions, whether the crime rate climbs, the political environment, etc., are all important issues that impact how the truth commission is viewed. The perceptions that exist may change over time, and thus an institution's legacy may not remain static.

128 Bisset, *supra* note 53.

# TRUTH COMMISSIONS IN NON-TRANSITIONAL CONTEXTS

## Implications for Their Impact and Legacy

Eric WIEBELHAUS-BRAHM



## 1. INTRODUCTION

In the 21st century, it is commonly accepted that states have a legal and normative obligation to provide the truth about histories of violence and repression; truth commissions are often suggested as a means of fulfilling this obligation.[1] Truth commissions came to prominence as a result of their use as part of transitions from military rule to democracy in Latin America and from apartheid to inclusive democracy in South Africa. The global attention

[1] E. WIEBELHAUS-BRAHM, 'Truth Commissions', in W.A. SCHABAS and N. BERNAZ (eds.), *Routledge Handbook of International Criminal Law*, Routledge, New York, 2011; M.B.J. HIRSCH, 'Ideational Change and the Emergence of the International Norm of Truth and Reconciliation Commissions' (2014) 20 *European Journal of International Relations* 810; M.B.J. HIRSCH, 'Agents of Truth and Justice: Truth Commissions and the Transitional Justice Epistemic Community', in D. CHANDLER and V. HEINS (eds.), *Rethinking Ethical Foreign Policy: Pitfalls, Possibilities and Paradoxes*, Routledge, New York, 2007, at 184–205.

paid to the South African Truth and Reconciliation Commission (TRC), in particular, popularised this form of transitional justice. The truth commission model gained favour at least in part because it appealed to a variety of audiences. For perpetrators and those who feared that criminal accountability would be destabilising, truth commissions were less threatening. For many victims and activists, by contrast, truth commissions represented some measure of justice. As such, truth commissions seemed to provide a useful compromise, addressing past abuses in some fashion during attempted democratic transitions.[2] In fact, in the wake of the South African TRC, truth commissions came to be seen by many as valuable in their own right, in that they could provide a valuable contribution to social and psychological repair, as well as the (re)construction of more democratic political institutions after political transitions.[3]

As the truth commission model gained greater visibility and more adherents, it has also been increasingly utilised in a variety of other contexts. First, truth commissions have been employed in war-to-peace transitions. Even further, the model has sometimes been applied to contexts where little to no real political change has occurred at all. This chapter distinguishes three non-transitional contexts in which truth commissions have been employed with growing frequency.[4] First, truth commissions are sometimes created by governments after they have decisively defeated an armed threat. Second, firmly entrenched authoritarian regimes have sometimes created truth commissions to achieve policy goals. Finally, truth commissions have sometimes been set up in well-established democracies in order to address historical wrongs that occurred in previous generations. One may quibble about whether these different types of investigative commissions belong in the same category.[5] However, often in policy and academic debates, these types of investigations are lumped together for the purposes of theory building and hypothesis testing.

Appreciating the different circumstances under which truth commissions are established is also important for debates about assessing the impact of transitional justice mechanisms, something about which scholars, activists, policy-makers and affected communities are increasingly concerned. Too often these policies have been promoted based upon 'faith' rather than sound empirical evidence.[6] Examining the effects of truth commissions, in particular,

---

2 E. Skaar, 'Truth Commissions, Trials – or Nothing? Policy Options in Democratic Transitions' (1999) 20 *Third World Quarterly* 1109.

3 Hirsch, 'Ideational Change', *supra* note 1.

4 This is not meant to be an exhaustive list of non-transitional contexts, but rather to highlight three that have been appearing with growing frequency.

5 E. Brahm, 'What Is a Truth Commission and Why Does It Matter?' (2009) 3 *Peace and Conflict Review* 1.

6 O.N.T. Thoms, J. Ron and R. Paris, 'State-Level Effects of Transitional Justice: What Do We Know?' (2010) 4 *International Journal of Transitional Justice* 1.

has attracted considerable attention.[7] The overarching goal is to place the promotion of justice policies on more sound empirical footing in order to generate more realistic expectations among victims and the wider public in general. Yet a host of methodological and conceptual challenges have beset the effort to evaluate the contributions of truth commissions, as well as other transitional justice processes.[8] Moreover, it is often overlooked that expectations about truth commissions were largely developed in the context of democratic transitions.

This chapter examines the reasons why truth commissions have emerged in these other kinds of contexts and the ways in which truth commission expectations might need to be altered in these different environments. First, it examines the circumstances in which truth commissions are created. Second, it reviews prevailing expectations about the impact of truth commissions, noting that there is usually an assumption that they are created in transitional contexts, where social, political, and economic institutions are undergoing significant upheaval. Third, it explores how truth commissions often differ when they are employed in contexts where little to no transformation is taking place. Specifically, it examines truth commissions that have been created in post-conflict scenarios, such as in Sri Lanka, where the government decisively defeated an armed threat, so there is no real political transition. It also considers Bahrain and Morocco, where firmly entrenched authoritarian regimes created truth commissions to address histories of human rights violations. In addition, cases such as Canada's TRC and the Maine-Wabanaki TRC represent examples of the model being utilised in well-established democracies in order to address historical wrongs. The chapter concludes by reflecting upon the conceptual and empirical consequences with respect to setting expectations as to the legacies of

---

7 T.D. Olsen et al., 'When Truth Commissions Improve Human Rights' (2010) 4 *International Journal of Transitional Justice* 457; E. Wiebelhaus-Brahm, *Truth Commissions and Transitional Societies: The Impact on Human Rights and Democracy*, Routledge, New York, 2010; O. Bakiner, *Truth Commissions: Memory, Power, and Legitimacy*, University of Pennsylvania Press, Philadelphia, 2016; A. Ferrara, *Assessing the Long-Term Impact of Truth Commissions: The Chilean Truth and Reconciliation Commission in Historical Perspective*, Routledge, New York, 2014; L.K. Taylor and A. Dukalskis, 'Old Truths and New Politics: Does Truth Commission "Publicness" Impact Democratization?' (2012) 49 *Journal of Peace Research* 671; H. van der Merwe and A.R. Chapman (eds.), *Truth and Reconciliation in South Africa: Did the TRC Deliver?*, University of Pennsylvania Press, Philadelphia, 2008.

8 D. Mendeloff, 'Truth-Seeking, Truth-Telling and Post-Conflict Peacebuilding: Curb the Enthusiasm?' (2004) 6 *International Studies Review* 355; B. Stewart and E. Wiebelhaus-Brahm, 'The Quantitative Turn in Transitional Justice Research: What Have We Learned About Impact?' (2017) 1 *Transitional Justice Review* 97; E. Brahm, 'Uncovering the Truth: Examining Truth Commission Success and Impact' (2007) 8 *International Studies Perspectives* 16; H. van der Merwe, V. Baxter and A.R. Chapman (eds.), *Assessing the Impact of Transitional Justice: Challenges for Empirical Research*, United States Institute of Peace Press, Washington D.C., 2009.

truth commissions in such contexts. The creation of these bodies are at least in part a consequence of a global truth commission norm. While these examples might be dismissed as costless, cynical attempts to exploit a global truth-seeking norm, the public nature of these bodies ensures that they draw the world's attention to a government's response to a truth commission's work.

## 2. WHEN ARE TRUTH COMMISSIONS CREATED?

The circumstances under which truth commissions are likely to be established have evolved markedly over time. Truth commissions were originally primarily seen in the midst of attempted democratic transitions. In this context, they were largely promoted as a compromise solution for new, fragile governments seeking to balance demands for accountability against threats of violence and instability by perpetrators with the ability to protect themselves from punishment.[9] By the beginning of the 21st century, however, a growing epistemic community of experts reframed perceptions of truth commissions 'from being merely a weaker compromising alternative for judicial justice to becoming an option infused with its own intrinsic and elevated values and goals.'[10] More generally, during this period, transitional justice measures were increasingly being utilised outside of what Dustin Sharp calls paradigmatic transitions to liberal democracy. In particular, truth commissions were used with growing frequency as conflict resolution measures in peacebuilding contexts.[11] He suggests we reconceptualise transitional justice as the pursuit of justice as part of a transition to positive peace. Adopting such an understanding of transitions opens up the possibility of viewing the contexts examined in this chapter as transitional. Of the research that does examine truth commissions outside of liberal political transitions, most focus on those created as part of negotiated settlements to intra-state conflict. The other contexts examined here have garnered little attention. My goal in this chapter is to probe the motivations behind and the legacies of truth commissions in a sampling of these underexplored situations.

Why has this expansion of truth commissions to more types of contexts occurred? Several explanations present themselves that might shed light on the motivations of the creators of the truth commissions explored in this chapter. One explanation suggests political manipulation to advance actors' agendas. Sharp implicitly argues that truth commissions are created to contribute to a

---

9 J. Elster, 'Coming to Terms with the Past. A Framework for the Study of Justice in the Transition to Democracy' (1998) 39 *Archives Europeennes de Sociologie* 7; Skaar, *supra* note 2.

10 Hirsch, 'Agents of Truth and Justice', *supra* note 1, at 186.

11 D.N. Sharp, 'Emancipating Transitional Justice from the Bonds of the Paradigmatic Transition' (2015) 9 *International Journal of Transitional Justice* 150.

positive peace.[12] However, a growing body of research explores political elites' attempts to 'hijack' justice to advance their own political power.[13] Stable regimes, authoritarian or democratic, may create truth commissions because they believe them to be strategically useful. Truth commissions may also be created with growing frequency because of a normative consensus that they are beneficial and appropriate. Arguably, a global truth commission norm exists that is rooted in

> [a] practical consensus that … TRCs may achieve multiple and important psychological, political, and legal goals, including many of the goals of criminal prosecutions. A second, normative consensus that emerged was that finding truth is in itself a form of justice … Finally, in light of the TRCs' broader practicality and elevated moral value, TRCs increasingly came to be seen as distinct from trials and as a complementary rather than an alternative tool for dealing with the past.[14]

Michal Ben-Josef Hirsch gives much of the credit for the development of a truth commission norm to the South African TRC. Specifically, she credits such features as its quasi-legal powers, transparency, publicity, and the pursuit of reconciliation and healing as being key to propelling the development of a truth commission norm.[15] The logic of consequences and appropriateness explanations may not be mutually exclusive. As Sharp argues, governments of any stripe may find that 'the law and legalism associated with transitional justice serve[s] to obfuscate the very real power dynamics and contested political choices'.[16] Thus, the secure governments that have created the truth commissions explored in this chapter are complying with – perhaps seeking to exploit – global norms. They are also doing so in an environment in which there is a lack of clear evidence as to how the impact and legacy of truth commissions can be maximised.

## 3. WHAT KIND OF IMPACTS CAN WE EXPECT FROM TRUTH COMMISSIONS?

Clarifying the effects of truth commissions has been an abiding interest for scholars and practitioners for well over a decade.[17] Some argue that one should distinguish assessments of the success of truth commissions – meaning whether

---

12 Ibid.

13 J. Subotić, *Hijacked Justice: Dealing with the Past in the Balkans*, Cornell University Press, Ithaca, 2009; C.E. Loyle and C. Davenport, 'Transitional Injustice: Subverting Justice in Transition and Post-Conflict Societies' (2016) 15 *Journal of Human Rights* 126.

14 Hirsch, 'Ideational Change', *supra* note 1, at 818.

15 Ibid, at 817–818.

16 Sharp, *supra* note 11, at 156.

17 Bakiner, *supra* note 7; Wiebelhaus-Brahm, *supra* note 7; Olsen et al., *supra* note 7; Mendeloff, *supra* note 8.

they accomplished what they were mandated to do – from the impact of truth commissions, which would be the effects of truth commission investigations, hearings and reports on individuals and society in the country in question.[18] In fact, as truth commissions have gone from a second-best solution to being seen as an important exercise in their own right, as Jeremy Sarkin's introduction to this volume examines in greater depth; a broad range of cause–effect relationships have been identified with respect to truth commissions.[19]

Nonetheless, there is no consensus in the empirical literature as to whether and how truth commissions might bring about these ends. As Hayner puts it, 'many comfortable assumptions have been restated over and again in untested assertions by otherwise astute and careful writers, thinkers, and political leaders ... Some of the most oft-repeated statements, and those that we perhaps most wish to be true, are due careful scrutiny.'[20] In fact, many of the alleged cause–effect relationships suffer from conceptual weaknesses and pose formidable empirical challenges.[21] Although some observers argue that the varied claims made about the effects of truth commissions might more appropriately be viewed as moral aspirations rather than empirically testable hypotheses,[22] as noted, many academics, policy-makers, activists and victims have accepted these arguments and have adjusted their expectations accordingly.

Although it remains contested whether truth commissions have measurable effects on individuals and societies and, if so, whether that effect is positive or negative, there is, at least implicitly, relative consensus on the causal mechanisms through which these effects might be realised. First, the 'publicness' of truth commissions has been connected with their impact.[23] Several truth commissions have held public hearings. Although historically sub-Saharan African commissions have been more likely to conduct public hearings, the attention given to South Africa's TRC – its hearings in particular – has contributed to

---

18 Brahm, *supra* note 8.

19 P.B. Hayner, *Unspeakable Truths: Confronting State Terror and Atrocity*, Routledge, New York, 2001, at Chapter 3; A.R. Chapman, 'Coming to Terms with the Past: Truth, Justice, and Reconciliation' (paper presented at the TRC: Commissioning the Past conference, 6 November 1999), at 94; T.A. Borer, 'Truth Telling as a Peace-Building Activity: A Theoretical Overview', in T.A. Borer (ed.), *Telling the Truths: Truth Telling and Peace Building in Post-Conflict Societies*, University of Notre Dame Press, South Bend, 2006, at 26.

20 Hayner, *supra* note 19, at 6.

21 For a discussion of some of the issues involved, see Brahm, *supra* note 8; E. Lutz, 'Transitional Justice: Lessons Learned and the Road Ahead', in N. Roht-Arriaza and J. Mariezcurrena (eds.), *Transitional Justice in the Twenty-First Century: Beyond Truth Versus Justice*, Cambridge University Press, New York, 2006; Mendeloff, *supra* note 8; Brahm, *supra* note 5; Stewart and Wiebelhaus-Brahm, *supra* note 8; Thoms, Ron and Paris, *supra* note 6.

22 J. Allen, 'Balancing Justice and Social Unity: Political Theory and the Idea of a Truth and Reconciliation Commission' (1999) 49 *University of Toronto Law Journal* 315, at 316–317; M. Ignatieff, 'Articles of Faith' (1996) 25 *Index on Censorship* 113, at 110.

23 Taylor and Dukalskis, *supra* note 7.

the spread of the practice globally.[24] Although we lack systematic evidence, it also appears to be increasingly common for truth commission hearings to be broadcast nationwide in the affected country on radio and television. Even when hearings have not been public, media engagement and the publication of the truth commission's final report potentially bring the investigation into the national conversation. Second, the final report may prompt change by revealing new information about past abuses, promoting new narratives about the past, and, through its recommendations, prompting reforms to laws and institutions. Through these means, truth commissions have the *potential* to contribute to changes in norms, behaviours, rules and structures in society.

What about less ideal circumstances? Governments may suppress truth commission reports. In addition, in their design and/or operation, commission investigations may appear to be manipulated for political purposes. In addition, lack of access to media and illiteracy may impede the impact of truth commissions. Depending on circumstances, these negatives can be countered to some extent. Domestic opposition groups and civil society, as well as the international community, may pressure the government to take truth commission investigations and reports more seriously. Reports might be leaked when governments seek to suppress them, as happened with Nigeria's Human Rights Violations Investigation Commission for instance. In Sierra Leone, international donors funded children's and youth versions of the TRC's final report that used a graphic novel style, among other things, to try to make the findings more accessible to a broader audience. It is unclear, though, whether these factors can overcome a genuine lack of political will to make the truth commission process meaningful.

Furthermore, we do not know whether prevailing expectations about commission impact are appropriate for the circumstances in which truth commissions are being created with greater frequency. Expectations about truth commission impact are at least implicitly predicated on truth commissions being established in transitional contexts where the fluidity of conditions increase the possibility of more substantial political, legal and social change. Increasingly, however, truth commissions are being established in non-transitional contexts where, for a variety of reasons, the absence of democratisation or peace accords may constrain the degree of change that is possible. By drawing on a range of empirical examples, the next section explores whether and how we might need to adjust our expectations for the impact of truth commissions in these non-transitional contexts.

---

24 G. Dancy, H. Kim and E. Wiebelhaus-Brahm, 'The Turn to Truth: Trends in Truth Commission Experimentation' (2010) *Journal of Human Rights* 45, at 47. For a discussion of the pros and cons of public hearings, see P.B. Hayner, *Unspeakable Truths: Transitional Justice and the Challenge of Truth Commissions*, 2nd edn, Routledge, New York, 2011, at 218–220.

## 4. EXPLORING TRUTH COMMISSIONS IN NON-TRANSITIONAL CONTEXTS

This section briefly examines some of the growing number of cases in which truth commissions have been established outside of transitional circumstances. Adapted from Onur Bakiner's survey of truth commission cases,[25] Table 1 summarises the truth commission cases that were not created in the immediate aftermath of a democratisation process or a negotiated transition from civil war. Most of these commissions are what Cath Collins calls post-transitional, meaning that opportunities arose to address lingering justice demands long after political transitions.[26] They are the product of a more extended transitional process. In the 21st century, though, truth commissions have also been employed in countries where political change has been minimal at best. Governments, for example, have sometimes created truth commissions after successfully defeating rebel groups. In Sri Lanka, for example, the Rajapaksa government created the Lessons Learnt Commission after defeating the Tamil Tigers on the battlefield. Elsewhere, stable authoritarian regimes have created truth commissions to investigate histories of human rights abuses. Monarchies in Morocco and Bahrain, for example, have utilised the truth commission model. Finally, truth commissions have sometimes emerged in well-established, white settler democracies with histories of racial oppression. The chapter considers examples from the United States and Canada.

This section briefly examines these cases and reviews the empirical evidence for the effects of these truth commissions on their respective societies. It is not my intention to argue that all of these cases are directly comparable with each other. These examples have been created by national and subnational governments. Moreover, it should be clearly noted that these cases have not been randomly selected. Rather, my intention is to present a series of what Eckstein called *heuristic* case studies. He defined heuristic case studies as those 'deliberately used to stimulate the imagination towards discerning important general problems and possible theoretical solutions.'[27] Indeed, cases were selected partially based upon the fact that there has been a significant amount written in order to show how these different contexts might influence the impact they have had on the respective societies. A central argument of the chapter is that these bodies are the product of an emergent global truth commission norm. The conclusion reflects upon what these cases reveal about the global and national legacies of

25 Bakiner, *supra* note 7.

26 C. Collins, *Post-Transitional Justice: Human Rights Trials in Chile and El Salvador*, Penn State University Press, Pennsylvania, 2010.

27 H. Eckstein, 'Case Study and Theory in Political Science', in F.I. Greenstein and N.W. Polsby (eds.), *Handbook of Political Science*, Addison-Wesley Publishing Co., Reading, Mass., 1975, at 104.

truth commissions and how our theoretical expectations should be adjusted when truth commissions are established in these non-transitional contexts.

**Table 1. Non-transitional truth commissions**

| Country | Name of Commission | Years of Operation | Context of Commission |
|---|---|---|---|
| **Uruguay** | Peace Commission | 2000–2003 | Post-transition |
| **South Korea** | Presidential Truth Commission on Suspicious Deaths of the Republic of Korea | 2000–2004 | Post-transition |
| **Panama** | Panama Truth Commission | 2001–2002 | Post-transition |
| **Grenada** | Truth and Reconciliation Commission | 2001–2004 | Post-transition |
| **Ghana** | National Reconciliation Commission | 2002–2004 | Post-transition |
| **Chile** | National Commission on Political Imprisonment and Torture | 2003–2004 | Post-transition |
| **Morocco** | Equity and Reconciliation Commission | 2004–2006 | Authoritarian |
| **Paraguay** | Truth and Justice Commission | 2004–2008 | Post-transition |
| **South Korea** | Truth and Reconciliation Commission, Republic of Korea | 2005–2010 | Post-transition |
| **Ecuador** | Truth Commission | 2007–2010 | Post-transition |
| **Mauritius** | Truth and Justice Commission | 2009–2013 | Settler-Colonial |
| **Solomon Islands** | Truth and Reconciliation Commission | 2009–2013 | Post-transition |
| **Canada** | Truth and Reconciliation Commission of Canada | 2009–2015 | Settler-Colonial |
| **Sri Lanka** | Lessons Learnt and Reconciliation Commission | 2010–2011 | Government victory |
| **Brazil** | Truth Commission | 2011–2014 | Post-transition |
| **Bahrain** | Bahrain Independent Commission of Inquiry | 2011 | Authoritarian |
| **Maine (USA)** | Maine Wabanaki-State Child Welfare TRC | 2013–2015 | Settler-Colonial |

Source: Adapted from O. Bakiner, *Truth Commissions: Memory, Power, and Legitimacy*, University of Pennsylvania Press, Philadelphia, 2016.

## 4.1. FOLLOWING REBEL DEFEAT

In May 2010, Sri Lankan President Mahinda Rajapaksa established the Lessons Learnt and Reconciliation Commission (LLRC) to investigate human rights violations that happened between the breakdown of the government's ceasefire with the Liberation Tigers of Tamil Eelam (LTTE) in 2002 and the end of the civil war in 2009. The war, which varied in intensity over its 26 years, came to a bloody conclusion as the government launched a massive final assault on the LTTE. With the government victorious, it was in a strong position to dictate the way in which the past was dealt with. In such circumstances, the conventional wisdom is that the government would either ignore violations or focus on atrocities committed by the LTTE. Nonetheless, the government faced significant international pressure to address reports that government forces were particularly brutal and targeted civilians in the war's final months.[28] The UN estimates that nearly 40,000 died in the final five months of the conflict.[29] The timing of the LLRC seemed designed to head off a UN Panel of Experts that was established to investigate atrocities.[30] The selection of a truth commission also reflected Sri Lanka's own history and the global prominence of the truth commission model.[31]

Rajapaksa's government was firmly in control of the LLRC, and it seems to have been clearly designed to produce a government-friendly truth. Its mandate avoided addressing the root causes of the conflict. The eight commissioners, who were appointed by Rajapaksa, included no opposition figures. Despite its inauspicious beginnings, the LLRC proved to be more credible than appeared likely at the outset. In total, the commission conducted 57 public sessions and undertook field visits to over 40 locations to collect evidence and testimony.[32] It visited certain battle zones in Sri Lanka's north and east in order to clarify details of the civil war's final months. To encourage participation, the commission gave witnesses a variety of options for submitting their testimonies, including orally, by camera, by mail, or through a third party.[33] Critics charged that the LLRC was

---

28 M. Ganguly, 'Sri Lanka's Hollow Victory', Human Rights Watch, New York, 2009, http://www.hrw.org/news/2009/08/26/sri-lanka-s-hollow-victory.

29 Office of the United Nations Secretary General, *Report of the General-Secretary's Panel of Experts on Accountability in Sri Lanka*, United Nations, New York, 2011, http://www.un.org/News/dh/infocus/Sri_Lanka/POE_Report_Full.pdf.

30 Anonymous, 'Against the Grain: Pursuing a Transitional Justice Agenda in Postwar Sri Lanka' (2011) 5 *International Journal of Transitional Justice* 31, at 31.

31 In 1994, Sri Lankan President Chandrika Bandaranaike Kumaratunga established three Commissions of Inquiry into the Involuntary Removal or Disappearance of Persons to investigate human rights violations earlier in the conflict. See Hayner, *supra* note 24, at 247–248. As discussed below, the Sri Lankan government made frequent reference to the South African TRC model as it tried to stave off international pressure for criminal accountability.

32 Lessons Learnt and Reconciliation Commission, *Report of the Commission of Inquiry on Lessons Learnt and Reconciliation*, November 2011, http://slembassyusa.org/downloads/LLRC-REPORT.pdf.

33 L. Wickramasinghe, 'The Lessons Learnt and Reconciliation Commission (LLRC) Concludes Its Work', Sri Lankan Ministry of External Affairs, http://www.mea.gov.lk/index.php/media/news-archive/3146-the-lessons-learnt-and-reconciliation-commission-llrc-concludes-its-work-the-final-report-will-be-handed-over-to-the-president-on-20-november.

selective in the incidences it investigated, and that thousands of witnesses refused to come forward out of fear for their safety.[34] Nonetheless, more than 6,000 submissions were made to the commission. To be sure, the LLRC's portrayal of the conflict largely conformed to the government's narrative, namely that the LTTE was primarily responsible for atrocities. Despite this, the LLRC produced many recommendations that were intended to promote peace. For example, it called upon the state to address the needs of families of missing persons, displaced persons, child soldiers and detainees. In addition, it recommended that the government compensate victims. It also urged the government to promote minority rights, implement power sharing for minorities and devolve some power to the regions. For its part, the government was slow to implement the recommendations, suggesting it was more interested in the appearance rather than the substance of transitional justice. Repression of Tamil activists remained high under Rajapaksa. To date, mostly LTTE fighters have been prosecuted for civil war atrocities. Only a handful of government agents have been convicted. Nonetheless, the LLRC ensured continued international attention on the need to provide genuine accountability for past abuses.

International pressure to enact LLRC recommendations and to pursue accountability and reparations has been more persistent in Sri Lanka. In the wake of continued international pressure, in 2012, the government created a 'national action plan' that, among other things, included a pledge to implement the LLRC's recommendations.[35] In the years since, the international community, both individual states and collectively through the UN Human Rights Council, have kept continued pressure on the Sri Lankan government to address the past, the attention partially sustained by the commitments made in creating the LLRC. The Human Rights Council has repeatedly rejected the Sri Lankan government's claims that it has sufficiently addressed civil war-era atrocities. In early 2014, UN High Commissioner for Human Rights Navi Pillay released a report documenting war crimes committed during the civil war.[36] She called upon the international community to create its own inquiry since the government had failed to do so.[37] In a desperate attempt to stave off the report's release, Rajapaksa's government pledged to establish a new, South African-style Truth

---

34 Anonymous, *supra* note 30, at 53.

35 A. Keenan, 'Sri Lanka: Time for Action, Not Action Plans', *The Interpreter*, 26 September 2012, https://www.lowyinstitute.org/the-interpreter/sri-lanka-time-action-not-action-plans.

36 United Nations High Commissioner for Human Rights, *Promoting Reconciliation and Accountability in Sri Lanka*, United Nations, New York, 2014.

37 D. Nelson, 'Sri Lanka Rejects UN War Crimes Probe as More Bodies Found in Mass Grave', *The Telegraph*, 25 February 2014, http://www.telegraph.co.uk/news/worldnews/asia/srilanka/10660548/Sri-Lanka-rejects-UN-war-crimes-probe-as-more-bodies-found-in-mass-grave.html.

and Reconciliation Commission to address the past.[38] Ultimately, the Human Rights Council voted to launch an international investigation of war crimes.[39]

In the end, Rajapaksa's intransigence cost him political power. The growing international isolation led Maithripala Sirisena and others in the ruling party to split off and ultimately defeat Rajapaksa in the 2015 elections. Sirisena's rhetorical acceptance of transitional justice won his administration some breathing space. By 2017, however, the international community had again grown impatient with the lack of action, and pressure has again resumed to follow through on the pledges Sirisena had made.[40]

This case exemplifies the complicated global legacy of truth commissions. The Sri Lankan government and its critics seem to share a view of truth commissions as weak substitutes for prosecution. Creating the LLRC was the Rajapaksa government's attempt to alleviate pressure in a relatively costless manner. The commission found no evidence of a systematic plan to commit atrocities. The government also largely ignored the LLRC's recommendation. As the victor, it rejected measures that would likely have promoted human rights, democracy, and reconciliation, among other things, in Sri Lanka. For their part, critics are unsatisfied without accountability for government forces. The shared logic is consistent with a view of truth commissions as compromise solutions that provide the veneer of justice without threatening those in power.

Nonetheless, even as a flawed institution, the LLRC has helped keep the world's attention on atrocities committed during the war. The recommendations were surprisingly credible, which made avoiding them politically costly. Having been established, the LLRC's final report provided a rallying point for domestic and international actors' continued demands. While the LLRC's impact has been modest to date, it has arguably helped maintain international attention on past abuses longer than might otherwise have been the case.

## 4.2. FIRMLY ENTRENCHED AUTOCRACIES

Not only have governments that have successfully quelled armed rebellion used the truth commission model, so too have authoritarian regimes facing little threat to their survival. Under different circumstances, Morocco's King Mohammed VI and Bahrain's King Hamad bin Isa Al Khalifa have each established commissions to address human rights violations in their respective kingdoms.

38 G. Dominguez, *supra* note 29.

39 United Nations High Commissioner for Human Rights, *Report of the OHCHR Investigation on Sri Lanka*, United Nations, New York, 2015.

40 A. Keenan, 'Sri Lanka's Transition to Nowhere', International Crisis Group, 16 May 2017, https://www.crisisgroup.org/asia/south-asia/sri-lanka/286-sri-lanka-s-transition-nowhere.

Activists in both countries had actually been advocating for a truth commission to investigate histories of human rights violations since the monarchs had come to power at the turn of the century.[41] This section will briefly describe each before comparing their impact.

### *4.2.1. Morocco's Equity and Reconciliation Commission*

When King Mohammed VI came to Morocco's throne in 2004, he sought to distinguish himself from his father's rule. King Hassan II's 40-year rule was known as the 'Years of Lead' for the brutal repression of dissent that characterised his government.[42] Mohammed sought to plot a new course on human rights, including creating the Equity and Reconciliation Commission (IER) to investigate violations committed under his father.[43] The IER was mandated to investigate human rights violations by government forces, specifically forced disappearances and arbitrary detention, which occurred between 1956 and 1999. It was supposed to educate the public about the past, as well as promote victim healing and reconciliation, at least partly through coming up with a compensation scheme for victims. Overall, the IER provided medical and psychological care for victims, recommended monetary compensation for almost 10,000 individuals, and called upon the government to compensate and reinstate nearly 2,000 individuals who had lost their jobs for political reasons.

While the IER was clearly intended to establish the new king as a modern, progressive monarch, the commission itself earned praise from many quarters. To be sure, the commission was criticised for avoiding Western Sahara and human rights violations under Mohammed VI. The mandate's focus on a narrow set of human rights abuses left a far from complete picture of Morocco's human rights problems.[44] However, the government also provided the IER with an ample budget, and appointed a set of commissioners who were well respected in the human rights field. In addition, the commission held seven public hearings across the country and organised several roundtable discussions on Morocco's future political, legal, economic and cultural development, all of which were

---

41 E. Fakhro, 'Truth and Fact-Finding in the Arab Monarchies', in C. Sriram (ed.), *Transitional Justice in the Middle East and North Africa*, Oxford University Press, New York, 2017, at 162.

42 F. Loudiy, *Transitional Justice and Human Rights in Morocco: Negotiating the Years of Lead* Routledge, New York, 2014.

43 King Hassan created the Advisory Council on Human Rights (CCDH) in 1990 and King Mohammed established the Independent Arbitration Commission (IAC), both which could be considered a sort of precursor to the IER. For more on the CCDH and IAC, see ibid.

44 BBC, 'Morocco Truth Panel Details Abuse', 2005, http://news.bbc.co.uk/1/hi/world/africa/4536258.stm; S. Faramarzi, 'Moroccan Truth Commission Questioned', *Yahoo News*, December 19, 2005, http://news.yahoo.com/s/ap/20051217/ap_on_re_af/morocco_truth_commission.

broadcast on television and radio. These programmes generated significant public discussion about human rights in Morocco.[45]

In late 2005, the IER's final report was made public. It attributed most of the disappearances to state security agents. While it reportedly gave a list of names to the government, the IER did not name names in its report.[46] Among the IER's recommendations, it called upon the government to investigate unresolved cases, establish a reparations programme for victims, direct economic development to regions most affected by human rights violations, decommission detention centres, reform the constitution to codify Moroccans' fundamental rights and freedoms, and engage in judicial and other institutional reforms to prevent future human rights abuses. King Mohammed VI pledged to implement the IER's recommendations.

Despite this, the government was criticised for responding slowly to the IER's recommendations.[47] The government did move quickly on reparations. Via the CCDH, the government has paid out US$85 million to over 16,000 affected persons.[48] Over the years, the government, the UN and civil society groups have often disagreed on progress on implementation. In early 2010, a government official asserted that all IER recommendations were either implemented or in the process of being implemented.[49] The UN Working Group on Enforced or Involuntary Disappearances and Amnesty International, among others, present a more pessimistic picture.[50] Elham Fakhro summarises the IER's contribution thus:

> In revealing a narrative of past abuses, distributing reparations, and outlining structural recommendations for change, the IER succeeded in fulfilling the terms of

---

45 K. Times, 'Emotional Moments at Morocco's Rights Commission Hearings', February 4, 2005, cited in V. Opgenhaffen and M. Freeman, *Transitional Justice in Morocco: A Progress Report*, New York, International Center for Transitional Justice, 2005, https://www.ictj.org/sites/default/files/ICTJ-Morocco-Progress-Report-2005-English.pdf.

46 Fakhro, *supra* note 42, at 168.

47 J. Thorne, 'Morocco's Truth Commission Undermined by Government Lethargy, Rights Groups Say', *Associated Press*, July 17, 2006.

48 P. Hazan, 'IER: Truth without Punishment', *International Justice Tribune*, January 23, 2006. The European Commission also financed a significant portion of the community reparations scheme. See International Center for Transitional Justice, *The Rabat Report: The Concept and Challenges of Collective Reparations*, New York, International Center for Transitional Justice, 2009, https://www.ictj.org/sites/default/files/ICTJ-Morocco-Reparations-Report-2009-English.pdf.

49 Libération, 'Le Processus de Suivi Des Recommandations de l'IER S'est Achevé: 'C'est À l'Etat et À La Justice de Prendre Le Relais'', January 15, 2010, http://www.libe.ma/Le-processus-de-suivi-des-recommandations-de-l-IER-s-est-acheve-C-est-a-l-Etat-et-a-la-justice-de-prendre-le-relais_a8218.html.

50 United Nations Office of the High Commissioner for Human Rights, *UN Working Group on Enforced or Involuntary Disappearances Concludes Visit to Morocco*, June 26, 2009, http://www.ohchr.org/en/NewsEvents/Pages/DisplayNews.aspx?NewsID=9144&LangID=E; Amnesty International, *Broken Promises: The Equality and Reconciliation Commission and Its Follow-Up*, January 6, 2010, http://www.amnesty.org/library/info/MDE29/001/2010/en.

its mandate, and acting as a catalyst for reforms within mainland Morocco. Constraints within the commission's mandate, however, precluded the commission from assuming a broader role in generating accountability [and it] has done little to alter the structure of political authority in the state.[51]

### *4.2.2. Bahrain's Independent Commission of Inquiry*

Bahrain's truth commission experiment was prompted by the government's response to 2011 protests that were part of the so-called Arab Spring. The protests grew out of the longstanding grievances of Bahrain's Shia majority, many of whom view the ruling Sunni Al-Khalifa family as foreign occupiers.[52] Inspired by protestors in Cairo's Tahrir Square, Bahrainis began occupying Manama's Pearl Roundabout to demand genuine democracy on 14 February 2011. At one point, as many as 200,000 people – approximately 25% of Bahrain's adult population – were at the protest.[53] For the first couple of weeks, the government vacillated between repression and modest concessions. A government-staged counter-demonstration on 2 March led to an escalation of violence, which prompted Saudi Arabia and the United Arab Emirates to intervene on 14 March. As the Bahrain Independent Commission of Inquiry (BICI) later documented, 40 people died and many others were tortured during the crackdown.[54] Thousands of others were dismissed from their jobs, expelled from school or convicted by special National Security Courts for their participation in the demonstrations. Despite successfully quelling the protests, the government faced significant pressure to address the human rights violations that had occurred. The monarchy sought to respond to domestic and international criticism by establishing an independent investigation by foreign experts – BICI. The commission was established by royal decree on 29 June 2011.

Like Morocco, the Bahraini government created a highly credible commission. It invited prominent international legal experts to run BICI (M. Cherif Bassiouni, Sir Nigel Rodley, Philippe Kirsch, Badria Alawadhi and Mahnoush H. Arsanjani). Moreover, BICI's mandate was broad and robust. Commissioners had unfettered access to government files and officials, and were given discretion to use their budget as they saw fit. In approximately four months, BICI collected approximately 9,000 testimonies. They worked to be neutral in their approach, which some opposition figures took to be too

---

51 Fakhro, *supra* note 42, at 170.

52 G.E. Fuller and R.R. Francke, *Arab Shi'a: The Forgotten Muslims* Palgrave Macmillan, New York, 1999, at 119–154.

53 A. Humphreys, 'The Arab Awakening: A Bahraini Activist Struggles to Keep Protests Alive', *National Post*, December 21, 2011, http://news.nationalpost.com/2011/12/21/the-arab-awakening-a-bahraini-activist-struggles-to-keep-protests-alive/.

54 Bahrain Independent Commission of Inquiry, *Report of the Bahrain Independent Commission of Inquiry*, 2011, http://www.bici.org.bh/BICIreportEN.pdf.

pro-government.[55] In fact, after having unsuccessfully campaigned for a commission for years, opposition leaders were shocked by the speed with which BICI came about, so much so that many 'doubted the sincerity of the investigative efforts'.[56] Nonetheless, the BICI report was quite critical of the government's handling of the protests. It documented thousands of abuses. While it concluded that human rights abuses were not official policy, the report argued that the intimidation of protesters 'could not have happened without the knowledge of higher echelons of the command structure'.[57]

The government broadcast the presentation of BICI's final report, and the report itself was made public. Among its recommendations was a call to establish follow-up bodies to continue the investigation, prosecute those responsible for human rights abuses, and monitor the implementation of BICI recommendations. Furthermore, the commissioners urged the government to create human rights training programmes for the judicial system and the security sector, to undertake a review of laws to ensure compliance with international human rights standards, and to develop a national reconciliation and education programme to promote tolerance, human rights and the rule of law. At the ceremony, the king pledged to enact the commission's recommendations. In the years following, however, the government and Bassiouni publicly disagreed on several occasions over whether all of the recommendations had in fact been implemented.[58] For its part, the Shia opposition argues that BICI did not go far enough in examining the historical origins of the violence, nor was there sufficient accountability for those responsible for the abuses.[59] As of early 2018, the government continues to actively oppress Shias and pro-democracy activists.

---

55 A. Shehabi, 'Bahrain's Independent Commission of Inquiry: A Path to Justice or Political Shield', *Jadaliyya*, November 22, 2011, http://www.jadaliyya.com/pages/index/3244/bahrains-independent-commission-of-inquiry_a-path-.

56 Fakhro, *supra* note 42, at 176.

57 Bahrain Independent Commission of Inquiry, *Report of the Bahrain Independent Commission of Inquiry*, 2011, at 281, http://www.bici.org.bh/BICIreportEN.pdf.

58 '20 BICI Recommendations Implemented', *Gulf Daily News*, 23 February 2012, http://www.biciactions.bh/wps/portal/BICI/%21ut/p/c5/04_SB8K8xLLM9MSSzPy8xBz9CP0os3gLAxNHQ093A3eLMEc/dl3/d3/L2dJQSEvUUt3QS9ZQnZ3LzZfT0FISUdHRzBHT0Q5OTBJUFA/index1f99.html?WCM_GLOBAL_CONTEXT=/wps/wcm/connect/egov+english+library/bici/media/news/news27; S. Singh Grewal, 'Rights Action Plan', *Gulf Digital News*, 26 February 2014, http://archives.gdnonline.com/NewsDetails.aspx?date=04/07/2015&storyid=371383; J. Lynch, 'Experts Call on Obama to Promote Bahrain Reform During Visit to Saudi Arabia', http://pomed.org/pomed/experts-call-on-president-obama-to-discuss-reform-in-bahrain-during-visit-to-saudi-arabia/?utm_source=Sailthru&utm_medium=email&utm_term=%2AMideast%20Brief&utm_campaign=Mideast%20Brief%203-11-14; 'New BICI Recommendation Implementation Report to Be Published', *Bahrain News Agency*, 23 November 2013, http://www.bna.bh/portal/en/news/589428.

59 A. Hammond, 'Bahrain Used "Excessive Force" in Crackdown: Inquiry', *Reuters*, November 23, 2011, http://www.reuters.com/article/2011/11/23/us-bahrain-violence-idUSTRE7AM0VB20111123; Fakhro, *supra* note 42 at 180.

### 4.2.3. *Comparative Thoughts*

In both cases, it is easy to be sceptical of the value of the commissions. The governments were firmly in control and, while limited liberalisation occurred, liberal democracy is not in the offing.[60] Moreover, as important Western allies in the Middle East, they faced little diplomatic pressure to address human rights violations. As such, it is somewhat surprising that each country established credible, well-financed truth commissions. As the years have gone by, the IER and BICI have largely vanished from public discussions. Nonetheless, their reports remain authoritative accounts of human rights violations. Furthermore, each commission prompted some positive change, both in terms of other transitional justice measures and legal and institutional reform. Finally, their recommendations remain a publicly available reform agenda that domestic and international activists can continue to use to put pressure on the state.

## 4.3. ADDRESSING COLONIAL WRONGS IN WELL-ESTABLISHED DEMOCRACIES

A final type of truth commission is those established by longstanding democratic societies to address the deep-seated legacies of historical wrongs. There certainly are precedents for truth commissions in established democracies.[61] This section focuses on commissions created to deal with the consequences of racial oppression in North America, specifically some legacies of colonialism.[62] The government of Canada and the American state of Maine have each established truth commissions to examine the historical treatment of indigenous persons, specifically the practice of separating indigenous children from their families and communities in order to assimilate them.

Canada's Truth and Reconciliation Commission was established to examine Indian residential schools, which were established to 'civilise' and assimilate First Nations children from the late 1860s until the 1990s. The government worked with several Christian churches to implement the programme,

60 One can only speculate as to whether these truth commissions could be interpreted as part of a transition to positive peace.

61 Hayner, *supra* note 24, at 17–19 and 298–299.

62 This section is not intended to provide a comprehensive overview of the use of truth commissions in established democracies. As Sarkin discusses in his introduction to this volume, definitions are contested and, therefore, there is a lack of consensus as to which investigative commissions actually are truth commissions. Depending upon one's definition, several other bodies may constitute other examples of truth commissions in this context, such as Australia's Stolen Children Inquiry (1997), the Oklahoma Commission to Study the Tulsa Race Riot of 1921 (2001), and the Greensboro Truth and Reconciliation Commission (2006).

which provided substandard education and exploited children for labour. An estimated 150,000 indigenous children attended residential schools. Aside from separating children from their families and attempting to deprive them of their culture, there were widespread reports of abuse in many schools. Victims formed the largest ever class action lawsuit, culminating in the 2007 Indian Residential Schools Settlement Agreement, which included the truth commission in addition to compensation and commemoration.

Maine's Wabanaki-State Child Welfare TRC was created for similar reasons. Wabanaki is an Algonquian word that refers to the collective identity of Algonquians living in Maine. Similar to Canada, Maine's policy was to remove children from indigenous communities to facilitate assimilation. Then, from the 1950s to the 1970s, state policy led to the removal of roughly 650 Wabanaki children for placement with non-Wabanaki families.[63] After years of negotiation between Wabanaki leaders and Maine officials, they reached agreement on the mandate for the commission in June 2012. The TRC was specifically tasked with creating a common narrative about Wabanaki children's historical engagement with the child welfare system, recommending reforms to the child welfare system, and promoting healing between Wabanaki and government officials.[64]

To date, we have little data on the effects of the TRC in Maine. In Canada, different sectors of society appear to have responded to these initiatives in very different ways. Indian residential school staff saw themselves as victims and were upset by how the Canadian TRC constructed its history. Many Indigenous and allied settler Canadians were upset by the Harper government's refusal to acknowledge the genocidal nature of the system,[65] but the subsequent Trudeau government seems to be taking its obligations more seriously.

There are also questions about the broader society's engagement with the respective truth commission processes. Given the fact that indigenous populations in Canada and the US make up a small proportion of the population, one of the challenges for these types of truth commissions is to engage the broader population. The TRC estimated that about 155,000 visitors attended its public events.[66] However, De Costa documents the

63 E. Bjorum, '"Those Are Our People and That's Our Family": Wabanaki Perspectives on Child Welfare Practice in Their Communities' (2014) 8 *Journal of Public Child Welfare* 279, at 282.

64 Maine Wabanaki-State Child Welfare Truth & Reconciliation Commission, *Beyond the Mandate: Continuing the Conversation: Report of the Maine Wabanaki-State Child Welfare Truth & Reconciliation Commission*, Maine Wabanaki-State Child Welfare Truth & Reconciliation Commission, Hermon, 2015.

65 R. Niezen, *Truth and Indignation: Canada's Truth and Reconciliation Commission on Indian Residential Schools*, 2nd edn, University of Toronto Press, Toronto, 2017.

66 Truth and Reconciliation Commission, *Honouring the Truth, Reconciling for the Future: Summary of the Final Report of the Truth and Reconciliation Commission of Canada*, McGill-Queens University Press, Montreal, 2015, at 25, http://www.myrobust.com/websites/trcinstitution/File/Reports/Executive_Summary_English_Web.pdf.

TRC's failure to reach a broader audience.[67] Most TRC activities occurred in First Nations communities, though seven national events were held in major cities and the closing event took place in Ottawa. Later in its work, the commission also introduced 'education days' that enabled approximately 15,000 students to learn more about this history.[68] The TRC engaged local and national media, and many testimonies were streamed online. Yet most of the individuals who attended events were government officials, academics, documentarians and others there for professional reasons. Nonetheless, a 2016 survey found a substantial increase in awareness among non-Aboriginal Canadians of the historical wrongs and current disparities facing Aboriginal Peoples compared to a benchmark study conducted in 2008.[69] Although few could recall any of the TRC's Calls to Action, more than 40 per cent reported reading or hearing something about the TRC.

More generally, the Canadian TRC focused on only one element of the ongoing structural violence being carried out by the settler-colonial state. The TRC went beyond schools to address colonial violence more generally. However, its contribution to reconciliation will likely depend upon whether it prompts a greater engagement with how colonial violence exists in the present.[70] The current Trudeau government has opened up discussion about settler-colonial violence. It speaks of reconciliation, and has even taken some concrete steps. However, measures of recognition and reconciliation have largely reinforced the status quo. Discussions remain rooted in the same discourse that justified genocidal violence, which suggests genuine decolonisation will not result.[71]

---

67 R. de Costa, 'Discursive Institutions in Non-Transitional Societies: The Truth and Reconciliation Commission of Canada' (2017) 38 *International Political Science Review* 185, at 190–195.

68 Truth and Reconciliation Commission, *Canada's Residential Schools: Reconciliation. The Final Report of the Truth and Reconciliation Commission of Canada*, McGill-Queens University Press, Montreal, 2015, at 128, http://www.myrobust.com/websites/trcinstitution/File/Reports/Volume_6_Reconciliation_English_Web.pdf.

69 The Environics Institute (June 2016) 'Canadian Public Opinion on Aboriginal Peoples', https://www.environicsinstitute.org/docs/default-source/project-documents/public-opinion-about-aboriginal-issues-in-canada-2016/final-report.pdf?sfvrsn=30587aca_2.

70 R. Nagy, 'The Scope and Bounds of Transitional Justice and the Canadian Truth and Reconciliation Commission' (2013) 7 *International Journal of Transitional Justice* 52–73.

71 G. Coulthard, *White Masks, Red Skins: Rejecting the Colonial Politics of Recognition*, University of Minnesota Press, Minnesota, 2014; A. Woolford, 'Genocide, Affirmative Repair, and the British Columbia Treaty Process', in A.L. Hinton (ed.) *Transitional Justice: Global Mechanisms and Local Realities after Genocide and Mass Violence*, Rutgers University Press, New Brunswick, 2010.

## 5. CONCLUSION

Much of the impact we have come to expect of truth commissions is contingent upon the degree of publicness, their final reports, and the transitional context in which they typically operate. It seems likely that, all else being equal, the more truth commissions are in the public eye, the more they will spark societal reflection and discussion about the past. The consequence may be policy and normative change. Final reports are an important element here, particularly in that they generate a narrative about the past that shapes how it is remembered. Moreover, the recommendations articulated in truth commission reports may bring about change through their actual implementation or even contestation over their actual implementation. The conventional wisdom is that these effects are more likely in transitional contexts where opportunities for legal and institutional change are often greater and where prevailing norms and beliefs may be under greater scrutiny.

One global legacy of truth commissions has been their growing use in non-transitional contexts. The proliferation of truth commissions in an increasing variety of circumstances reflects differing perceptions among policy-makers and activists about the likely consequences of utilising this form of transitional justice. The relatively secure governments in each of these cases may have believed that engaging the global norm may placate demands for justice from domestic and international audiences. Local and global human rights activists, as well as some officials, by contrast, likely hoped that the commissions would be precursors to other justice measures like prosecution and reparations. Moreover, many have likely accepted the conventional wisdom that truth commissions empower victims by providing them with a voice and by acknowledging their suffering. The use of truth commissions, then, is at least partially the result of contrasting assumptions about what their effects will be.

What does the brief examination of the cases in this chapter suggest about how these mechanisms might differ in non-transitional contexts? First, the lack of fluidity that is often present in transitional contexts may constrain the amount of change that is possible. Democratic transitions and peace settlements usually introduce a significant redistribution of political power and may result in substantial legal, institutional and even constitutional change. Following government civil war victory or in stable regimes, whether authoritarian or democratic, institutional stasis is more likely. To be sure, as highlighted above, truth commissions have prompted change in what might be less fertile contexts. Nonetheless, change is more modest. Official public acknowledgement of past wrongs, reparations and human rights training, to cite a few examples, are important achievements and may promote healing, human rights and democracy in their respective societies. However, particularly given our reliance upon aggregate measures to assess impact, the effect is unlikely to be measurable.

Second, at least for authoritarian contexts and following government victory, international pressure appears important for determining the degree of impact truth commissions are likely to have. In these instances, perpetrators of human rights violations are firmly in control of politics. Nonetheless, significant gains are sometimes achieved. The Moroccan government made a major investment in reparations. Bahrain's monarchy permitted the publication of a report that was quite critical of its behaviour. In the absence of demands from the international community, it is hard to imagine these governments creating truth commissions, let alone acting upon any of their recommendations. Transitional governments, by contrast, are often vulnerable to international pressure as they seek recognition and support from the international community. As the cases reviewed show, international influence lasts only as long as international interest is sustained. As important Western allies in a geo-strategically critical region, Bahrain and Morocco have faced comparatively less pressure than Sri Lanka. For their part, established democracies are more immune to these pressures.

Finally, the level and intensity of domestic audience engagement in truth commissions seems to vary considerably between transitional and non-transitional contexts. During political transitions, victims and other civil society groups often see opportunities to shape the political agenda. Space has opened that may not have existed previously. Strategic actors may also recognise that the window of opportunity to create change may close quickly. The broader public, too, is often deeply engaged in politics as it anxiously awaits an uncertain future. For example, a weekly summary of the TRC's activities was one of the most popular TV programmes of late-1990s South Africa. Governments might feel more compelled to act upon a truth commission's findings in such a context. It is also more difficult for those who condone or are indifferent to past violence to avoid the issue.

In non-transitional contexts, by contrast, the space for debate and change is often much more limited. Constitutional reform, for example, has been challenging in the nominally democratic Sri Lanka; the monarchies have little incentive to change. What is remarkable, then, is that all three of these countries have made some reforms in response to truth commission recommendations. To varying degrees, truth commission processes may have helped to sustain or build civil society organisation around justice agendas. It is unclear how much attention the broader public in these societies have paid to the truth commissions. If attention is limited, is it due to a lack of interest or pessimism that anything would come of it? In established democracies, it also appears that building broader public interest in historical wrongs can be challenging. There is a lack of data regarding public interest in and attention to truth commissions in North America, though it appears to be primarily the victim community that has paid attention. While there may be healing value for those individuals, such endeavours appear less likely to bring about broader normative or institutional change.

In sum, the spread of truth commissions to non-transitional circumstances reflects a major global legacy of truth commissions. Stable, secure governments create truth commissions in part because of international norms that see them as useful for promoting peace, human rights and reconciliation, among other things. Whether these governments comply with the norm for strategic reasons or because they have internalised the norm is an open question. Regardless of motivations, truth commissions' national legacy will be determined by how much pressure governments face to act upon commission findings. Engagement by the domestic public and the international community in truth commission processes appears significant in shaping their long-term importance, because governments, even authoritarian ones, need to respond in some way to pressure. The extent to which broader and deeper public engagement with truth commission processes can be generated seems likely to magnify their impact in non-transitional contexts.

# SURROGACY AND RESISTANCE

## Evolving Patterns in Unofficial Truth Commissions and Truth Projects

Pádraig McAuliffe



## 1. INTRODUCTION

One of the most notable trends in contemporary transitional justice is the near-ubiquity of unofficial truth projects (UTPs) in post-conflict and post-authoritarian states. These are complex and idiosyncratic processes that serve multiple social purposes. The nature of these projects depends on the motivations for pursuing 'truth' and the political realities that contextualise them. Some of these UTPs mimic official truth commissions in terms of organisational practice (investigators, hearings, national reports) and state-wide coverage, like Guatemala's Recovery of Historical Memory project (*Recuperación de la Memoria Historia*, REMHI). Others, by contrast, are micro-scale and *sui generis*, like the memorial in a family compound honouring family members killed in anti-communist massacres in mid-1960s Indonesia.[1] Some projects are primarily conscious attempts to recover historical memory (e.g. the Kosovar Memory Book and Bosnian Book of the Dead), while for others historical recovery is a by-product of other reconciliatory activities that nevertheless coalesce into

1 L. Dwyer, 'Building a Monument: Intimate Politics of "Reconciliation" in Post-1965 Bali', in A.L. Hinton (ed.), *Transitional Justice: Global Mechanisms and Local Realities After Genocide*, Rutgers University Press, New Brunswick, 2011, at 227–248.

memory production (e.g. the Sarajevo Women's Court). Some projects are extremely technical (the classic example being the Documentation Center of Cambodia's (DC-CAM) panoply of archival expertise, digitisation, outreach programmes and publications),[2] while others are essentially low-tech and haphazard (clandestine monuments in Rwanda and Burundi, for example). Sometimes victims are the primary motive actors, as in the archiving and oral history projects of Argentina's *Memoria Abierta*, whereas in other cases it has been their descendants (Spain's 'grandchildren generation' have taken the lead in recovering Spain's historical memory through exhumations).[3] Some employ traditional or indigenous methods (e.g. Guatemalan braid-weaving to commemorate abuses and atrocities),[4] while others embrace Facebook, Twitter and YouTube.[5]

The ubiquity of UTPs can be explained by a confluence of 'a globalized discourse of memory as redemptive on both personal and national levels',[6] the inevitability of grassroots attempts to remake national or local social worlds, and the resources and globalised expertise available to domestic civil society actors concerned with documenting or remembering the past. However, it is notable that few have tried to understand what they signify in terms of the legacy of truth commissions. To date, only one work has really tried to do so, namely Louis Bickford's widely cited article in the *Human Rights Quarterly* in 2007.[7] In it, he examined the typical characteristics that define UTPs, illustrated these with reference to nine case studies and outlined the main differences between them and official truth commissions. He concluded that UTPs could enjoy one of three possible relationships with the state – as replacements for official truth commissions where they are politically or logistically unfeasible (pointing to the Brazilian *Nunca Mais* and Uruguayan *Servicio Paz y Justicia* projects (SERPAJ)), as precursors to potential or expected state measures (e.g. the Iraq Memory Project), or as complementary to existing official measures (exemplified by REMHI's work in the shadow of the state's *Comisión para el Esclarecimiento Histórico*).[8]

2 M. Caswell, 'Khmer Rouge Archives: Accountability, Truth, and Memory in Cambodia' (2010) 10 *Archival Science* 25.

3 F. Ferrandiz and A. Baer, 'Digital Memory: The Visual Recording of Mass Grave Exhumations in Contemporary Spain' (2008) 9 *Forum: Qualitative Social Research* 1, at 9.

4 L. Arriaza and N. Roht-Arriaza, 'Weaving a Braid of Histories: Local Post-armed Conflict Initiatives in Guatemala', in R. Shaw and L. Waldorf with P. Hazan (eds.), *Localizing Transitional Justice: Interventions and Priorities After Mass Violence*, Stanford University Press, Stanford, 2010, at 205.

5 See for example A. Kurze, '#WarCrimes #PostConflictJustice #Balkans: Youth, Performance Activism and the Politics of Memory' (2016) 10 *International Journal of Transitional Justice* 451, at 463.

6 R. Shaw, 'Memory Frictions: Localizing the Truth and Reconciliation Commission in Sierra Leone' (2007) 1 *International Journal of Transitional Justice* 183, at 185.

7 L. Bickford, 'Unofficial Truth Projects' (2007) 29 *Human Rights Quarterly* 994.

8 Ibid, at 1005.

Bickford's study was extremely valuable. It arrived at a time when transitional justice scholars recognised the pressing need for a better understanding of localised and/or civil society-based truth seeking processes operating independently of the state.[9] It was unclear at the time 'whether the establishment of UTPs is a developing trend in transitional justice, or a cluster of isolated cases.'[10] At the time Bickford wrote his piece, there were relatively few studies of how community-based organisations, NGOs and victims' groups adopted strategies to document memories or collect evidence on past abuses. Evaluation of transitional justice and its components was 'in its infancy'.[11] In the intervening dozen years, scholarship on transitional justice generally and UTPs particularly has improved significantly, both in quality and quantity. The arrival of the *International Journal of Transitional Justice* in the same year has provided a venue for these types of site-specific or field-based studies by anthropologists, archivists, exhumers and memory experts, which are referred to throughout this chapter. This has been complemented by parallel work on the ethnography of commemorative sites[12] and globalised memorial culture.[13] These draw attention to issues like the need for space for conflicting stories and exclusion of forgotten voices that fitted with emerging trends in critical transitional justice scholarship (more on which anon). Qualitative studies on macro-level truth projects based on repeated collection of primary data, panel surveys and population surveys, as well as quantitative and mixed-method analyses premised on hypothesis-based testing, have become more normal in the field since Bickford's article.[14]

As a result, the metrics by which UTPs might be judged have shifted. While for Bickford actual, official truth commissions were an apt benchmark by which to judge their procedures and efficacy, UTPs now fall to be considered in a more critical, more self-reflexive scholarly and policy-making environment

---

9 As argued in L. Arriaza and N. Roht-Arriaza, 'Social Reconstruction as a Local Process' (2008) 2 *International Journal of Transitional Justice* 152.

10 G. Dancy, H. Kim and E. Wiebelhaus-Brahm, 'The Turn to Truth: Trends in Truth Commission Experimentation' (2010) 9 *Journal of Human Rights* 45, at 59.

11 B. Hamber, L. Sevchenko and E. Naidu, 'Utopian Dreams or Practical Possibilities? The Challenges of Evaluating the Impact of Memorialization in Societies in Transition' (2010) 4 *International Journal of Transitional Justice* 397, at 399.

12 An excellent recent example is C. Levey, *Fragile Memory, Shifting Impunity: Commemoration and Contestation in Post-Dictatorship Argentina and Uruguay*, Peter Lang, New York, 2016.

13 B. Misztal, 'Collective Memory in a Global Age: Learning How and What to Remember' (2010) 58 *Current Sociology* 24.

14 See e.g. J. Gibson, 'Does Truth Lead to Reconciliation? Testing the Causal Assumptions of the South African Truth and Reconciliation Process' (2004) 48 *American Journal of Political Science* 201; E. Wiebelhaus-Brahm, *Truth Commissions and Transitional Societies: The Impact on Human Rights and Democracy*, Routledge, London, 2010; T. Olsen, L. Payne and A. Reiter, *Transitional Justice in Balance: Comparing Processes, Weighing Efficacy*, United States Institute of Peace Press, Washington D.C., 2010.

where top-down/international/elite-driven justice is contrasted unfavourably with bottom-up/local/everyday justice processes.[15] Whereas once, the official authorisation of the state conferred legitimacy on the work of truth commissions, questions of agency, exclusion and socio-economic structures are increasingly addressed on the broader transitional justice agenda that call into question the centrality of the state, international expertise and liberal transitional justice scripts that foreground particular narratives about past violence. Amidst a sense that transitional justice amounted to a global project that reflected North–South political and economic inequalities,[16] critics of transitional justice began to argue that the strongly universalist and normative demands of the international community for 'accountability' and 'truth' elevated the legal and restorative aspects of justice over crucial (re)distributive needs.[17] Scholars increasingly highlight the disconnection between secular, statist, donor-driven transitional justice and local realities, as well as the problematic power relations at work in the construction of victim voices through its institutions.[18] The elite-led and instrumentalised nature of official memory projects 'continue to deny the agency of victims, perpetuating the disempowerment that victimhood represents'.[19] The tendency now is to theorise the (potential) effect of these unofficial approaches to truth-telling not by reference to official state-based truth and reconciliation commissions, but rather in terms of their effect on everyday life in localities reconstructing their sense of security.[20]

This more critical discourse fed into a series of assumptions about how bottom-up, grassroots and non-state transitional justice activities would work. Bickford argued that UTPs took one of two guises – a bottom-up model that could give meaningful effect to national or local visions of truth, on the one hand, or a viable alternative strategy to replicate standard formal truth processes where the state proves unwilling or unable to institute them, on the other.[21] These two guises manifested two distinct possibilities for transitional

---

15 M. O'Reilly, 'Peace and Justice through a Feminist Lens: Gender Justice and the Women's Court for the Former Yugoslavia' (2016) 10 *Journal of Intervention and Statebuilding* 419, at 421.

16 R. Nagy, 'Transitional Justice as Global Project: Critical Reflections' (2008) 29 *Third World Quarterly* 275.

17 R. Mani, *Beyond Retribution: Seeking Justice in the Shadows of War*, Polity, Cambridge, 2002.

18 K. McEvoy and K. McConnachie, 'Victims and Transitional Justice: Voice, Agency and Blame' (2013) 22 *Social & Legal Studies* 489, at 497.

19 S. Robins, 'Constructing Meaning from Disappearance: Local Memorialization of the Missing in Nepal' (paper presented at International Studies Association, San Diego, April 2012).

20 P. Riano Alcala and E. Baines, 'The Archive in the Witness: Documentation in Settings of Chronic Insecurity' (2011) 5 *International Journal of Transitional Justice* 412, at 433.

21 Bickford, *supra* note 7, at 995.

justice – the latter represented an 'embracing and reworking' of transitional justice processes at the intersection of the global and the local, while the former presented the possibility of 'avoiding, protesting against or rejecting' top-down prescriptions by formulating culturally specific responses.[22] This potentially resistant quality of UTPs excited observers disillusioned with the limitations of official truth commissions. It was assumed that projects divorced from state control and liberal-legalist teleologies could empower victims as drivers of the justice process, as opposed to marginalise them as passive recipients of externally derived justice blueprints. UTPs could give greater effect to those 'uncomfortable voices' that reject the legitimising narratives of statist transitional justice, particularly the idea that victim-led reconciliation could be produced via truth-telling.[23] Furthermore, community-based approaches to truth-telling would foster genuine agency, allowing victims and beneficiaries control over the design, remit and conduct of truth-telling, fostering creative adaptation and uniquely context-sensitive forms of memorialisation.[24] When asked in polls and surveys, survivor populations tend to prioritise socio-economic justice and material issues over the symbolic justice that supposedly therapeutic formal truth models accentuated.[25] There is an assumption that truth projects where citizens and communities are active participants facilitate 'the permanent ability to identify and analyse problems, formulate and plan solutions, mobilise resources and implement them, to gain control over the processes that affect the peoples' lives'.[26] It is further assumed that because spontaneous, unofficial forms of memorialisation are insider-driven, they can avoid formalisation and be all the better for it.[27] In short, the 'creative re-appropriations of the techniques and technologies of transitional justice' we see in UTPs would inherently and inevitably 'challenge the very state-bureaucratic model from which they were derived'.[28] In so doing, civil society truth processes could better address the difficult questions about how to construct plural and conflicting narratives that included diverse experiences.

---

22 These possibilities for transitional justice as a whole (and not merely UTPs) are outlined in P. Riano-Alcala and E. Baines, 'Editorial Note' (2012) *International Journal of Transitional Justice* 385, at 385.

23 C. Lawther, 'Transitional Justice and Truth Commissions', in C. Lawther, L. Moffett and D. Jacobs (eds.), *Research Handbook on Transitional Justice*, London, Routledge, 2017, at 348.

24 P. Lundy and M. McGovern, 'Whose Justice? Rethinking Transitional Justice from the Bottom Up' (2008) 35 *Journal of Law and Society* 265, at 271.

25 V. Pupavac, 'International Therapeutic Peace and Justice in Bosnia' (2004) 13 *Social & Legal Studies* 377, at 392.

26 Lundy and McGovern, *supra* note 24, at 280.

27 Arriaza and Roht-Arriaza, *supra* note 9, at 170.

28 J. Rubin, 'Transitional Justice against the State: Lessons from Spanish Civil Society-led Forensic Exhumations' (2014) 8 *International Journal of Transitional Justice* 99, at 101.

Unofficial truth-seeking projects would be well equipped to handle complexities of the grey areas where perpetrator, victim and bystander identities intermingle in a way state-based processes that force victims and perpetrators to play assigned roles have signally failed to do.[29] In the years since Bickford's article, a near-consensus has slowly crystallised that '[t]ruth-telling processes that are locally owned, created, and driven will be more effective at fostering the many objectives of more formalized truth commissions.'[30]

Though the nature of the phenomenon (the sheer diversity of UTPs) and the accessibility of empirical knowledge (the large number, geographical remoteness and lack of publicity regarding some UTPs) make this a difficult area to make definitive conclusions about them in terms of the legacy of truth commissions, study of field-based research, expert reports and NGO analysis makes clear that UTPs have a very mixed record in bearing these hopes out. What we see in a decade's worth of analysis after Bickford's initial scoping study is a somewhat ambivalent form of resistance that splits the difference between the idealised bottom-up model that could give meaningful effect to national or local visions of truth, on the one hand, and the more technocratic process of substituting for formal truth processes where the state proves unwilling or unable to institute them, on the other. We see a variety of truth-telling or truth-recording processes that function in deliberate contradistinction to state-level attempts to selectively shape meta-narratives over conflict or to institutionalise amnesia. However, many civil society and grassroots actors do this by replicating the formal, institutionalised technocratic and globally networked transitional justice critics assumed they would happily depart from *because* they lend legitimacy to this effort. Before making this argument, section 2 outlines the definitional issue at play in this chapter, i.e. what is meant by a UTP. Section 3 examines the perceived crisis of legitimacy in official truth commissions, and how UTPs were thought to avoid these problems. Sections 4 and 5 examine the dynamics of resistance and surrogacy that form the core of this chapter's argument. These sections illustrate how grassroots actors have adopted explicitly resistant approaches to state-controlled meta-narratives, but have done so by maintaining fidelity to the ideals that animated 'first-generation' official truth projects – the search for a (different) meta-narrative of conflict, technical proficiency and integration with other forms of transitional justice, even amidst creative adaptation. In effect, many UTPs operate as surrogates for official truth commissions, or at least as surrogates for the aspirations that guide them.

---

29 O. Simic and K. Daly, '"One Pair of Shoes, One Life": Steps Towards Accountability for Genocide in Srebrenica' (2011) 5 *International Journal of Transitional Justice* 477, at 480.

30 M. Sirleaf, 'The Truth About Truth Commissions: Why They Do Not Function Optimally in Post-Conflict Societies' (2013) 35 *Cardozo Law Review* 2263, at 2334.

## 2. DEFINING UNOFFICIAL TRUTH PROJECTS

It is notoriously difficult to define a truth commission, as evidenced by the wildly divergent tallies of them that studies have arrived at.[31] The same problems attach to UTPs and unofficial truth commissions. Unofficial truth commissions are somewhat straightforward insofar as some bodies adopt this precise nomenclature (e.g. the Greensboro Truth and Reconciliation Commission) and others obviously imitate official truth commissions (e.g. the aforementioned REMHI, *Nunca Mais* in Brazil, Uruguay's SERPAJ). These unofficial truth commissions occurred relatively early in the period where transitional justice became mainstreamed as a policy response. It is tempting to speculate that the greater frequency, mainstreaming and standardisation of official truth commissions have made unofficial bodies that mimic truth commissions less likely to be established because they are now less necessary to fulfil this remit. The concept of a UTP is more vague. To break it into its component parts, 'unofficial' is relatively clear-cut – it refers to truth or memory projects not established by government law or decree, by bodies themselves established by the government, or by international governance organisations like the United Nations or the Organization for Security and Co-Operation in Europe. Truth, though, as a concept somewhat confounded by postmodernism, can be understood as a record of events which, though never fully knowable, can be partially disclosed and verified. However, what distinguishes an analytically useful categorisation of truth project from other work relating to memory or history is more ambiguous and equivocal. UTPs are not necessarily bounded and clearly identifiable bodies apt for immediate analysis. Bickford primarily concentrated on initiatives oriented towards revealing the truth about past abuses that were created by civil society, and focused on two types of UTP – truth commission-like efforts that mimicked most attributes of official truth commissions, and projects that gathered documentation of past human rights abuses.[32] However he went on to admit he was only 'scratch[ing] the surface' in the area given the limited number of case studies and the narrow remit of comparison with official truth commissions.[33] Given the multiplicity of forms they adopt, the category of what might be a UTP is porous and fluid, and so the conceptual parameters of what is being explored in this chapter need to

---

31 33 are identified in O. Bakiner, *Truth Commissions: Memory, Power, and Legitimacy*, University of Pennsylvania Press, Pennsylvania, 2015, at 27–29; 40 are identified in P.B. Hayner, *Unspeakable Truths: Transitional Justice and the Challenge of Truth Commissions*, Routledge, London, 2010; while Olsen, Payne and Reiter, *supra* note 14, observe that 68 countries have utilised truth commissions (at 39).

32 Bickford, *supra* note 7, at 994–995.

33 Ibid, at 1026.

be set out, particularly bearing in mind that potential UTPs might not call themselves by this nomenclature or even identify primarily as such.

It is perhaps most instructive to understand UTPs by what they are not, by disaggregating them from what they functionally resemble. At what point is an exhumation, a monument, a work of art, a documentary archive or a public discussion of past trauma *just* an exhumation, a monument, a work of art, a documentary archive or a public discussion of past trauma, and at what point does it become a purposively different (even if complementary) truth *project*? It is instructive to take the example of publicly discursive ventures dealing with trauma. We are familiar with forms of public testimony that attempt to accord 'justice as recognition', those which acknowledge the pain and humiliation endured by victims of collective violence and reverse their symbolic devaluation through recapitulation of past events.[34] We are also familiar with inter- and intra-cultural exchange between individuals or groups 'digging' into the recent past, as well as memory-based dialogue and healing workshops for people of different backgrounds, that draw on an accounting of violent histories.[35] While these oral histories shed light about unknown facts or important controversies, it is necessary to distinguish between work that is primarily empowering of victims and/or reconciliatory that is representative of 'truthfulness' (the meaning attached to events by survivors) from that which records 'truth' (that which collates, clarifies and contextualises empirical facts).[36] UTPs collate individual histories in the service of creating a unified narrative or narratives, and so have greater epistemological authority than individual oral or written exchanges primarily designed to 'convey respect, recognition, compassion, contrition, and so forth'.[37] Discussion does not necessarily lead to remembering (and vice versa). To adopt Crocker's distinction, it is UTPs' primary concern for 'forensic' truth in the sense of fundamental details of the event (the whom, what, when, where and how), established through testimony, data, records and visuals related to the event, that define them as UTPs, even if they also record 'emotional truth' concerning physical and psychological impacts on survivors.[38] As such, UTPs can be defined as processes in which a search for forensic truth is a major focus, even where other truths or socially beneficial consequences are achieved. For example, the Sarajevo Women's Court allowed women to tell their stories of

34 F. Haldeman, 'Another Kind of Justice: Transitional Justice as Recognition' (2008) 4 *Cornell International Law Journal* 675.

35 See for example the workshops explored in A. Crosby and M. Brinton Lykes, 'Mayan Women Survivors Speak: The Gendered Relations of Truth Telling in Postwar Guatemala' (2011) 5 *International Journal of Transitional Justice* 456, at 466.

36 To draw on a distinction made in Riano Alcala and Baines, *supra* note 20, at 415.

37 M. Urban Walker, 'Truth Telling as Reparations' (2010) 41 *Metaphilosophy* 525, at 530.

38 D. Crocker, 'Reckoning With Past Wrongs: A Normative Framework' (1999) 13 *Ethics & International Affairs* 43, at 49.

experiencing violence as individuals, but the testimonies were filmed and were to be published in the form of a book.[39]

The exhumation of corpses might equate to a UTP or not, depending on context. The body can be a bearer of public truth (e.g. collectively, exhumations can provide explicit evidence of battlefield deaths or state executions), but it can more obviously be a private object of restoration or cultural closure ('the dichotomy between the body as evidence and the body as person').[40] In many cases, exhumations simply result in the return of remains to families for reburial, which may have the additional benefits of allowing those who survive the deceased to move on, particularly where cultural norms or psycho-spiritual beliefs establish mandatory rituals.[41] Practices that honour the dead, even where therapeutic, are not necessarily historical or epistemological. However, corpses can also play a role in the political life of transitional societies by revising the past and reorienting worlds of meaning towards the present.[42] In some states, exhumations and reburials have served explicitly politico-historical purposes. In Spain, organised civil society exhumations have been undertaken to spur discussions in the public sphere about the Franco era, consciously confronting a public silence that limited deliberation to distinct family circles.[43] Exhumation of clandestine mass graves of Quechua-speaking people of the south-central Andes revealed both patterns of extermination and a scale of mass death that had not been appreciated in Peru.[44] Particularly when re-burials are accompanied by monuments that include the names of the dead and year/month of death, they both create and ratify knowledge. In Guatemala,

> After civil patrollers from Xococ pulled down a first, modest memorial, village associations built a bigger, concrete memorial and inscribed it with the names of the murdered villagers, this time adding that they were 'killed by the civil patrollers from Xococ.' Similar murals exist in Comalapa and other towns of the Chimaltenango area. They often constitute the first community recognition of local history.[45]

---

39 J.N. Clark, 'Transitional Justice as Recognition: An Analysis of the Women's Court in Sarajevo' (2015) 10 *International Journal of Transitional Justice* 67.

40 I. Rojas-Perez, 'Inhabiting Unfinished Pasts: Law, Transitional Justice, and Mourning in Postwar Peru' (2013) 4 *Humanity: An International Journal of Human Rights, Humanitarianism, and Development* 149, at 155.

41 S. Eppel, '"Bones in the Forest" in Matabeleland, Zimbabwe: Exhumations as a Tool for Transformation' (2014) 8 *International Journal of Transitional Justice* 404, at 409–410.

42 K. Verdery, *The Political Lives of Dead Bodies: Reburial and Postsocialist Change*, Columbia University Press, New York, 2005.

43 F. Ferrandiz, 'Cries and Whispers: Exhuming and Narrating Defeat in Spain Today' (2008) 9 *Journal of Spanish Cultural Studies* 177.

44 Rojas-Perez, *supra* note 40, at 150–151.

45 Arriaza and Roht-Arriaza, *supra* note 9, at 167.

It is this conscious attempt to recover collective memory, in contrast to more individualised memory, that marks some exhumation processes as truth *projects* – 'the larger the public event and the more prominent the participants or initiators of memory are, the more it is also deemed to have impact on the macro level discourses of dealing with the past.'[46] One way of identifying UTPs is to determine a distinct role for the production of knowledge (documentation, pedagogy, publicity) outside of restorative activities, a preoccupation with producing authoritative and/or shared narratives of past violence over (but not opposed to) its healing. It is for this reason that documentation or archiving projects can be considered UTPs. Public art projects, novels, memoirs, theatre and film can be considered unofficial and certainly describe history and victim experience, but do not create (or intend to create) either collective memories or an authoritative historical narrative within which they are interpreted. As such, like Bickford, I do not consider them UTPs.[47] More controversially, I do not include the telling of stories by victims or perpetrators through indigenous or customary law like *nahe biti* in East Timor, *Fambul Tok* in Sierra Leone or *mato oput* in Uganda in my consideration of UTPs. Though victims testify and perpetrators confess, the social purpose is radically different to that of UTPs. To no doubt grossly generalise, they are typically instances of short-term social remembering (for the purposes of victim compensation and/or perpetrator re-integration) as a prelude to deliberately forgetting and moving on.[48] The real interest is affirming community values, not exploring or acknowledging general histories of violence that might in fact prove a barrier to such reintegration.

## 3. EMERGING CRITIQUE OF TRUTH COMMISSION LEGACIES

One can imagine how, depending on context, these UTPs could emerge as a surrogate for, or as an implicitly critical challenge to, truth commissions. They carry within them the potential to meet some, or all, of the practical and symbolic aspirations associated with truth commissions outlined by Popkin and Roht-Arriaza: creating an authoritative historical record of past abuses, redress

---

46 U. Kayser-Whade and S. Schell-Faucon, 'Transitional Justice and Civilian Conflict Transformation. Current Research, Future Questions', CCS Working Papers No. 10, 2009, at 33.

47 Bickford, *supra* note 7, at 1003.

48 This acknowledgment-to-oblivion model is distinct from the *chosen amnesia* or deliberate eclipsing of particular memories to facilitate rural life in Rwanda, as noted in S. Buckley-Zistel, 'Remembering to Forget: Chosen Amnesia as a Strategy for Local Coexistence in Post-Genocide Rwanda' (2006) 76 *Africa* 131.

to victims, proposals for reform, and establishing some accountability for perpetrators.[49] The goal of truth commissions to illustrate patterns of violence and to record hidden histories is obviously shared by UTPs.[50] It is clear too how they might serve additional, oft-bruited purposes of promoting reconciliation between antagonists and drawing the necessary 'bright line' between past, present and future.[51] Truth commissions might serve as the inspiration for UTPs insofar as they emphasise personal testimony and experience – 'moving beyond statistics to real people of blood, flesh and tears, a commission that gathers individual testimony can present human consequences of atrocities that are otherwise unfathomable and overwhelming'.[52] Just as truth commissions move from the relatively restricted goal of truth recovery to more totalising objectives like reconciliation and forgiveness after the South African model, NGOs responsible for UTPs publicly aspire to the wider 'creative consequences' so often claimed for them like macro-level reconciliation, peacebuilding and deterrence.[53] National-level UTPs like the Bosnian and Kosovar Books of the Dead or Cambodia's DC-CAM archive attempt to replicate the impact Bakiner observes in influencing leaders to publicly acknowledge human rights abusers and/or catalysing policy or institutional change.[54]

However, UTPs can also be seen to respond to some of the critiques that have attached themselves to truth commissions regarding both their processes and their impact. This is so particularly as we move from judging them by the standard, relatively circumscribed outputs like mandate fulfilment or report publication to more ambitious deliverables like changing countries or changing hearts. In terms of process, the very idea of establishing truth has been thrown into question. Thirty years of truth commissions have demonstrated that the promise to deliver a single, shared comprehensive vision of the past has proven illusory. Post-conflict and post-authoritarian societies are characterised by mutually incompatible truths – the record a truth commission propagates is often not regarded as legitimate or objective by certain groups in society. Because antagonistic communities remain segregated and because people 'expect a commission not to tell the truth, but to tell *their* truth', few commissions prove authoritative enough to preclude criticism of their processes or denial of

---

49 M. Popkin and N. Roht-Arriaza, 'Truth as Justice: Investigatory Commissions in Latin America' (1995) 20 *Law & Social Inquiry* 79.

50 Hayner, *supra* note 31, at 25.

51 E. Daly, 'Truth Skepticism: An Inquiry Into the Value of Truth in Times of Transition' (2008) 2 *International Journal of Transitional Justice* 23, at 23.

52 M. Minow, *Between Vengeance and Forgiveness: Facing History after Genocide and Mass Violence*, Beacon Press, Boston, 1998, at 76.

53 R. Teitel, *Transitional Justice*, Oxford University Press, New York, 2000, at 110.

54 O. Bakiner, 'Truth Commission Impact: An Assessment of How Commissions Influence Politics and Society' (2013) 8 *International Journal of Transitional Justice* 6.

their findings.[55] Public opinion about the South African truth and reconciliation commission, for example, broke down along black–white racial lines.[56] In Liberia, the recriminations and misrepresentations on the part of perpetrators at, and outside, the truth commission served as an obstacle to national healing and reconciliation, while more people than not found discussing the past 'too painful'.[57] It is for similar reasons that the belief that publicly relaying one's testimony could prove empowering or healing has proven chimerical. Though for some, working through the past has provided some psychological comfort through catharsis or through outing one's victimiser, these therapeutic models are increasingly coming under fire.[58] In particular, the risk of re-traumatisation of witnesses has prompted a re-think of what truth commissions should and can do – restorative justice for survivors seems beyond the capabilities of official truth bodies.[59] Critics now argue that the purported benefits of truth commissions for victims are based less on empirical fact than on speculative faith.[60]

Critiques premised on the insufficiency of truth built on pre-existing critiques of scale. National truth commissions are constrained by issues of resources, government support (see for example the consistent failure of governments to implement their recommendations),[61] timescales and mandate; but they are also constrained by issues of coverage, given that relatively few victims can participate and that people in remote areas could not engage at all. The monolithic truth essayed at the national level cannot take account of the myriad local micro-truths, particularly those in remote rural areas. As Lundy and McGovern argued, 'the tendency to exclude local communities as active participants in [national] transitional justice measures is a primary flaw, raising fundamental questions of legitimacy, local ownership, and participation.'[62] Field studies discovered that local communities found truth commissions to be overly Western and alien, expressing preferences for more culturally legitimate or familiar forms of memory.[63] The top-down nature of standardised national truth commissions left communities within the state feeling left out and disengaged.[64]

---

55 Daly, *supra* note 51, at 29, 37 and 38.

56 J. Sarkin and E. Daly, 'Too Many Questions, Too Few Answers: Reconciliation in Transitional Societies' (2003) 35 *Columbia Human Rights Law Review* 661, at 674.

57 Sirleaf, *supra* note 30, at 2322–2323.

58 See E.G. Pupavac, *supra* note 25.

59 A. Chapman and H. van der Merwe, *Truth and Reconciliation in South Africa: Did the TRC Deliver?*, University of Pennsylvania Press, Philadelphia, 2008, at 272.

60 D. Mendeloff, 'Truth-seeking, Truth-telling, and Postconflict Peacebuilding: Curb the Enthusiasm?' (2004) 6 *International Studies Review* 355.

61 See for example J. Langer, 'Are Truth Commissions Just Hot-Air Balloons? A Reality Check on the Impact of Truth Commission Recommendations' (2017) 29 *Desafíos* 177.

62 Lundy and McGovern, *supra* note 24, at 266.

63 Sirleaf, *supra* note 30, at 2323.

64 M. Aciru, 'Rethinking Post-Truth Commissions: Empowering Local Capacities to Shape Post-Truth Commissions Discourse' (2017) 11 *Human Rights & International Legal Discourse* 71, at 79.

This position corresponded with a broader critique that transitional justice was too technocratic, assuming that plannable goals could be effected in a linear cause–effect manner by a standard truth-telling toolkit.

Perhaps the main reason for the increasing dismay regarding national truth commissions was the fact that whatever truth they revealed represented the choices that an institutionalised, state-sponsored teller makes about what to prioritise and whom to listen to. The macro-historical role of truth commissions in documenting and acknowledging the crimes of previous regimes allows new governments to 'occupy the moral high ground' and so lends them legitimacy as they forge a shared historical memory.[65] There is a concern that top-down choices over *who* should narrate truth and *how* correspond more to the imperatives of nation-building than they do to the ordeal of trauma and victimhood.[66] Richard Wilson, notably, demonstrated how South African elites commandeered the concept of reconciliation as part of the process of nation-building, shaping simplistic binaries of victims and perpetrators and reifying the idea of the forgiving victim.[67] Theidon, observing the homogenised testimonial framework for victim experience in Peru, posited that the gap between national imperatives and local needs in relation to truth 'invites us to consider the extent to which "democratic transitions" and processes of "national reconciliation" may be little more than the reconfiguration of elites' pacts of domination or governability unless these national processes are articulated with social reconstruction at the local level.'[68] The more a truth process is driven by the state's interest in nation-building through remembrance, forgiveness or sanctioned memory, the less it is owned by the people.

UTPs have been proposed as a critical response to, and a means of avoiding, the problems of homogenised truths, local divisions, irrelevance, technocracy and state appropriation of victim experience. It is argued that the advantages of civil society-based truth projects over the standardised technocratic model of national truth commissions was that they could be 'rooted in local communities, creative, adapted to local culture and circumstance and responsive to local needs' – their greater legitimacy as a result should make them more 'satisfying' to victims and communities.[69] Civil society truth projects offer the potential not only to challenge the instrumentalisation of victim experience in pursuance of a dubious collective biography of the

65 Daly, *supra* note 51, at 39.

66 B. Hamber, *Transforming Societies after Political Violence: Truth, Reconciliation, and Mental Health*, Springer, Dordrecht, 2009, at 130.

67 R. Wilson, *The Politics of Truth and Reconciliation in South Africa: Legitimizing the Post-Apartheid State*, Cambridge University Press, New York, 2001.

68 K. Theidon, 'Justice in Transition: The Micropolitics of Reconciliation in Postwar Peru' (2006) 50 *Journal of Conflict Resolution* 433, at 455–456.

69 D. Androff, 'Can Civil Society Reclaim Truth? Results from a Community-based Truth and Reconciliation Commission' (2012) 6 *International Journal of Transitional Justice* 296, at 301.

state, but to avoid the simplifications of the macro-historical imperative, the technocratic impulse behind standardisation of truth projects and reliance on international templates. Experience over the last decade reveals mixed success in achieving these aspirations.

## 4. ASYMMETRICAL MEMORY: RESISTANCE IN UNOFFICIAL TRUTH PROJECTS

As Edkins notes, 'the form of political authority that the nation represents is intimately tied up with, and made possible by, the way in which it invokes its memories, and with what it remembers and why.'[70] Civil society-based truth projects that have emerged do so as forms of resistance to this selective presentation or management of memory by the state in ways that re-inscribe one-sided, complex or amnesiac histories. The examples examined in this chapter bear out the scholarly intuition that non-governmental truth projects, archives and documentation can often prove more trustworthy investigators and stewards of records, graves and testimony than the governments of the states they work in.

This is most obviously the case in those states where little or no transitional justice was ever genuinely pursued. In these states, NGOs have conspicuously opposed amnesiac tendencies of governments that lack the will or inclination to pursue meaningful accountability. Of course, NGOs are often involved in documenting violations and patterns of abuses as a prelude to later transitional justice (for example HREIB/ND-Burma created records for what they hoped would later be a series of trials or a truth commission in Myanmar),[71] but in genuinely post-transitional cases, there is usually less an intention to shape a hegemonic truth as there is to let sleeping dogs lie. For example, in Burundi, grassroots truth projects (e.g. collective commemorations by youth groups, memorials, documentation of massacres, unsystematic truth and reconciliation sessions between victims and perpetrators) have occurred in the shadow of a governmental reluctance to recognise or accredit any victims' associations or assist any memorialisation activities it cannot control.[72] The government claims that public testimony or exhumations are too emotive in a divided society and

---

70 J. Edkins, 'Remembering Relationality: Trauma, Time and Politics', in D. Bell (ed.), *Memory, Trauma and World Politics: Reflections on the Relationship between Past and Present*, Palgrave Macmillan, London, 2006, at 101.

71 L. Bickford et al., *Documenting Truth*, International Center for Transitional Justice, 2009, at 31.

72 B. Vanderlick and A. Batungwanayo, *Lieux de Memoire, Commemorative Initiatives and Memorials to Burundi's Conflicts: Invisible and Permanent Memories*, Impunity Watch, Utrecht, 2012, at 14 and 21–22.

would compromise work on their thus-far non-existent truth and reconciliation commission.[73] In Spain, similarly, civil society exhumations (with almost no state support) have foregrounded narratives of civil war terror and suffering that were ignored for decades, consciously and explicitly rejecting the national 'pact of oblivion' premised on the notion that revisiting the past would cause greater harm than good.[74] Going back almost as far, civil society actors in Japan, China and South Korea have consciously engaged as 'oppositional memory workers' in commemorative activities and related litigation to highlight the experiences of forgotten victims (most notably sex slaves) in Asia's long Second World War. In so doing, they complicate simplistic hero/victim dichotomies that underpin heretofore hegemonic national narratives.[75] Most UTPs are prompted by more recent concerns. In Afghanistan, the blanket parliamentary amnesty (2008) passed for crimes committed in its wars since the 1970s and the emphasis on combatant re-integration over any other form of justice spurred the Afghanistan Independent Human Rights Commission to create a Transitional Justice Coordination Group to establish a war victims' network. This, in turn, led to a Victims' Jirga for Justice where people from different regions described human rights violations committed at various junctures in the country's conflicts.[76]

However, it is more common to see UTPs spring up in states where some transitional justice has occurred. Here, civil society and grassroots truth projects consciously disavow the socio-political legitimation of/by the state, and instead 'tend to argue for "new" and "alternative" histories and counter-histories to the emerging "new" official history' that canalises potentially contradictory pluralisation of memory.[77] The Cambodian state has famously embarked on its trials of the Khmer Rouge leadership as its sole official form of accountability. Beyond this, it has opposed all forms of memorialisation, committing instead to 'dig a hole and bury the past in it', presenting a tightly controlled and self-exculpatory version of the last 40 years.[78] DC-CAM finds present-day public legitimacy in acting as a critical corrective to the view implicitly propagated at the Extraordinary Chambers that the Khmer Rouge era can be explained by a handful of malevolent rulers, as opposed to the more complex picture of

---

73 Ibid, at 30.

74 P. Aguilar and L. Payne, *Revealing New Truths about Spain's Violent Past: Perpetrators' Confessions and Victim Exhumations*, Palgrave Macmillan, London, 2016.

75 C. Soh and D. Connolly, 'Cosmopolitan Memories in East Asia: Revisiting and Reinventing the Second World War' (2014) 8 *International Journal of Transitional Justice* 383.

76 S. Kouvo and D. Mazoori, 'Reconciliation, Justice and Mobilization of War Victims in Afghanistan' (2011) 5 *International Journal of Transitional Justice* 492, at 498–500.

77 U. Kayser-Whande and S. Schell-Faucon, *Transitional Justice and Civilian Conflict Transformation: Current Research, Future Questions*, Centre for Conflict Studies, Marburg, 2008, at 34.

78 Caswell, *supra* note 2, at 38.

complicity that emerges in its own archives, including the possible culpability of ex-Khmer Rouge cadres like Prime Minister Hun Sen and his allies.[79] The Rwandan state, similarly, has dictated the meta-narrative surrounding the genocide through selective cooperation with the ICTR, domestic trials and the state-directed Gacaca process. The Kagame government has policed discussion about the genocide through criminal laws forbidding 'divisionism' and drawn distinct lines around which victims should be publicly commemorated. Survivors and their representatives have explicitly resisted state appropriations of their experiences by creating their own memorials, thereby partially re-shaping prevailing public representations of genocide memory:

> [S]urvivor engagement in the construction of genocide memorials is distinct from, and sometimes at odds with, the state impulse to employ memorials to consolidate its power. Survivors' intrinsic concerns are in tension with efforts to instrumentalize genocide memory.[80]

The miscellany of memorialisation projects in East Timor (mostly commemorating massacres) suggest that survivors there are resisting and transforming an official discourse of transitional justice and nation-building that valorises veterans who fought and the clandestine resistance during the Indonesian occupation, but implicitly deprecates the experiences of victims and glosses over internecine rivalries between the independence leadership. Though the official CAVR truth commission took a rounded view of survivor experiences over the *longue durée*, its discourse of innocent, passive victimhood actually contributed to the definition of victims in negative relation to veterans, which has had an impact on the distribution of welfare resources and public esteem.[81] As Kent puts it, 'some of these practices can be understood … as political struggles for recognition from the state by individuals and groups who perceive themselves to be excluded from the nationbuilding process.'[82] In similar ways, though falling outside what might be considered a UTP for the purposes of this chapter, a glut of prison memoirs and literature has emerged in Morocco as a form of resistance to the monarchy's stated attempt to 'turn the page definitely' on past abuses through its 2004–2006 Equity and Reconciliation Commission (*Instance Equité et Réconciliation*), given the ongoing occurrence of the sort of human rights abuses that characterised the Years of Lead.[83]

---

[79] Ibid, at 31.

[80] R. Ibreck, 'The Politics of Mourning: Survivor Contributions to Memorials in Post-genocide Rwanda' (2010) 3 *Memory Studies* 330, at 332–343.

[81] A. Rothchild, 'Victims Versus Veterans: Agency, Resistance and Legacies of Timor-Leste's Truth Commission' (2017) 11 *International Journal of Transitional Justice* 443.

[82] L. Kent, 'Local Memory Practices in East Timor: Disrupting Transitional Justice Narratives' (2011) 5 *International Journal of Transitional Justice* 434, at 455.

[83] N. Hachad, 'Narrating Tazmamart: Visceral Contestations of Morocco's Transitional Justice and Democracy' (2018) 23 *Journal of North African Studies* 208.

The need for civil society groups to complicate narratives of conflict through truth processes is as prevalent in societies with a free mass media as it is in less liberal states like East Timor or Cambodia. This is most apparent in the Balkans, where memorialisation processes have challenged the orthodoxy of nationalist, chauvinist and simplified narratives promoted by official attempts to manage memory. Though the Sarajevo-based Research and Documentation Center's painstaking Bosnian Book of the Dead project was motivated by the realisation that no concrete figures existed for national war dead, in finding 'only' just under 100,000 deaths it resisted the dominant Bosniak narratives that as many as 250,000 died in the war, and challenged the incorrect but prevailing assumption that civilian deaths were greater in number than military deaths.[84] Bosnian elites argued that these lower figures contradicted the reconciliatory politics of the new state and the status of Bosniaks as the war's biggest victims, but Nettelfield argues that the greater concern was the challenge the figures presented to the state's monopoly on truth that the ICTY did little to effectively challenge.[85] Civil society-based documentation of war crimes in Kosovo was an explicit form of resistance to the ethno-nationalist instrumentalisation of internationalised transitional justice and statist memory projects for identity consolidation by Kosovar Albanian and Serb leaderships. In particular, the leading Kosovar Albanian parties have (a) employed masculinised discourses of heroism to consolidate power, monopolising memory and (as in East Timor) implicitly deprecating the experience of civilian victims, and (b) established a research institute to concretise a one-sided history of Serbian victimisation of Kosovo.[86] The Kosovo Memory Book produced by the Humanitarian Law Centre Kosovo (a database that documents all or nearly all the human losses during the conflict in Kosovo in the period between 1998 and 2000) purposefully includes all forms of death, 'providing names and narratives for all casualties of the conflict rather than leaving them only as a number, which could become subject to ethno-political manipulation.'[87]

In these truth projects, we see a strongly resistant quality in the challenge to the state's monopoly on truth or historical narratives. What is notable about these UTPs, however, is the fact that they are not resistant to the mores, techniques and preoccupations that have characterised the standard truth commission models derived from the likes of Chile, South Africa and

---

84 L. Nettelfield, 'Research and Repercussions of Death Tolls: The Case of the Bosnian Book of the Dead', in P. Andreas and K. Greenhill (eds.), *Sex, Drugs, and Body Counts: The Politics of Numbers in Global Crime and Conflict*, Cornell University Press, New York, 2010, at 159.

85 Ibid, at 173.

86 G. Visoka, 'Arrested Truth: Transitional Justice and the Politics of Remembrance in Kosovo' (2016) 8 *Journal of Human Rights Practice* 62, 67–68 and 70.

87 Ibid, at 72.

Sierra Leone. This might prove surprising to some. The expectation is that once given the freedom to freely determine the scope and emphasis of their socio-historical inquiry, grassroots civil society organisations would pursue something radically different from these norms. Jeffery, Kent and Wallis, for example, expected that these bodies would 'subvert formal, internationally accepted justice processes' and that their projects might be 'at odds with global expectations'.[88] This is what critics of transitional justice expected resistance to look like. As Jones and Bernath somewhat sceptically note:

> Resistance is identified in behaviour deemed to be deviant vis-à-vis the predefined goals and activities of transitional justice processes ... A tendency to take transitional justice as the starting point means that resistance to it is framed and analysed as a counterpoint to the values and purposes that advocates ascribe to transitional justice processes.[89]

What we see above, however, is that resistance is framed not against transitional justice as a concept in the abstract, its institutions *qua* institutions or its internationalisation. Resistance is generally framed instead against governments whose amnesia or selectivity towards truth does not correspond to deeply felt popular desires for different truth(s). Particularistic defiance of governments is what characterises most UTPs, not generalised antipathy to the liberal-legalism of transitional justice. Civil society actors 'resist the government-controlled transitional justice process through making their own' – civil society resistance 'constitutes at the same time a claim for, and the enactment of, a higher degree of participation' in the conventional aspirations of transitional justice.[90] If anything, the traditionally 'conservative' teleology of truth commissions towards a different civil and political compact has been in evidence. We see this in two main areas. The first is the types of liberal (as opposed to transformative or revolutionary) politics espoused by those helming UTPs. The second is the fealty to the techniques, goals and internationalisation of truth commissions.

## 5. PAINTING INSIDE THE LINES: THE 'CONSERVATIVE' ORIENTATION OF UTPs

As noted earlier, critical approaches to transitional justice assume that the normative influence and donor-driven nature of transitional justice have

88 R. Jeffery, L. Kent and J. Wallis, 'Reconceiving the Roles of Religious Civil Society Organizations in Transitional Justice: Evidence from the Solomon Islands, Timor-Leste and Bougainville' (2017) 11 *International Journal of Transitional Justice* 378, at 384.

89 B. Jones and J. Bernath, 'Introduction: Resistance and Transitional Justice', in B. Jones and J. Bernath (eds.), *Resistance and Transitional Justice*, Routledge, London, 2017, at 5.

90 Ibid, at 152.

prioritised a narrow range of bodily integrity abuses and a liberalising political teleology that has blocked more emancipatory approaches that emphasise economic justice, inequalities and empowerment. This critique complements a broader expectation within studies of memory politics that the creation of bespoke spaces for articulating and recounting experiences of violence deprecated or muted by officially sanctioned narratives could fold 'into the broader demand for political recognition and a renegotiated citizenship from previously marginalised voices'.[91]

However, the rhetoric of transformation and revolution is consciously omitted in these projects. Civil society actors who operate UTPs do not want a radically different type of truth commission, but instead want meaningful effect given to what the standardised model of truth commission assumes is important – to determine the facts, root causes and societal consequences of past human rights violations, typically understood as deaths, massacres and gross bodily integrity abuses, in the face of their denial or obfuscation by their governments. Those civil society actors who operate UTPs privilege a form of empowerment where communal narratives and personal stories are resources. In states where dominant historical narratives known by most people within the state serve as a backdrop against which their own localised or sectional narratives are told, publicly propagating their own narratives creates meaning, memory and identity that are valued independently of any broader socio-economic transformation.[92] Beyond this inherent worth, in undemocratic states like Rwanda and Burundi, or dubiously democratic states like Kosovo and East Timor, these activities revive the liberal-legalist impulse to replace cultures of impunity with cultures of responsibility or rights that animated the first waves of transitional justice. In democratic states like Spain, South Korea and Croatia, 'democratic maturity can prove itself by absorbing complicated debates on the possible politics of memory, assuming their plurality, and accommodating demands that have significant, if not mass, social support' in respect of historical narratives.[93] Even those UTPs that depart most dramatically from the official truth commission model eschew wider social transformation. Youth activism over memory in the former Yugoslav states, for example, has been distinctly less reformist than earlier youth movement mobilisations, preferring performance activism over conventional social movement activities like protests; awareness-raising has trumped direct institutional change.[94] This is not to say that UTPs do not

---

91 V. Das and A. Kleinman, 'Introduction', in V. Das and A. Kleinman (eds.), *Remaking a World: Violence, Social Suffering, and Recovery*, University of California Press, Berkeley, 2001, at 3–4.

92 In making this argument, I draw on J. Rappaport, 'Empowerment Meets Narrative: Listening to Stories and Creating Settings' (1995) 23 *American Journal of Community Psychology* 795.

93 Ferrandiz, *supra* note 43, at 190.

94 Kurze, *supra* note 5, at 461.

respond to the needs of the marginalised. For example, the *Salón de Nunca Más* established by rural women in Granada was a conscious response to the marginalisation of peasant women by state transitional justice policy. However, the project was more about redressing imbalances in memorialisation and preserving memory of local victims as a means of cultivating non-violence and respect for human rights as goods in themselves than any broader attempt to catalyse structural change.[95] Far from addressing the deep-lying structural and economic inequalities that underlie mass social conflict, UTPs tend to reflect truth commissions' emphasis on changing individual and community behaviours through altering their self-perception.[96]

None of this means that survivor communities and the civil society organisations that represent them do not care about socio-economic justice or do not desire transformation. However, for all the hopes that UTPs would be 'proactive in social reconstruction',[97] most manifest a pragmatic acceptance that projects that deliberately eschew interaction with the state have an inherently limited ability to change the broader social structures they perpetuate. For example, while the Sarajevo Women's Court and Greensboro Truth and Reconciliation Commission consciously moved beyond the individual violations and specific events to explore the wider structural inequalities in Bosnia and North Carolina that formed the background for these abuses, their ability to 'trickle up' to achieve structural change in any meaningful way was negligible.[98] This highlights the limited impact unofficial status makes more likely – the absence of state sanction boosts the legitimacy of the UTP and its freedom to inquire broadly into socio-economic circumstances that cause conflict, but isolates them from any bureaucratic machinery outside the locality or civil society to address it. If we accept that UTPs can only emerge as an effective force for change as part of a wider agenda pursued by supportive national leaders, then the commendably adversarial politics many UTPs pursue may prove self-limiting. Dudai and Cohen's warning that civil society justice mechanisms are better understood as 'bottom-bottom' than 'bottom-up' on the basis that they may never 'break from their immediate circles and influence society's leadership' is apt.[99] None of the indicators of direct political impact of official truth commissions tested for by Bakiner – governmental endorsement,

95 G.R. Romero, 'Voices Around Us: Memory and Community Empowerment in Reconstruction Efforts in Colombia' (2012) 6 *International Journal of Transitional Justice* 547.

96 This critique is of truth commissions is made in C. Moon, 'Healing Past Violence: Traumatic Assumptions and Therapeutic Interventions in War and Reconciliation' (2009) 8 *Journal of Human Rights* 71, at 82.

97 Romero, *supra* note 95, at 555.

98 O'Reilly, *supra* note 15, at 430 and 432; Androff, *supra* note 69, at 305.

99 R. Dudai and H. Cohen, 'Dealing with the Past when the Conflict Is Still Present: Civil Society Truth-Seeking Initiatives in the Israeli-Palestinian Conflict', in Shaw and Waldorf with Hazan (eds.), *supra* note 4, at 251–252.

official publication, reparations programmes and follow-up institutions to guarantee reform[100] – flowed from their unofficial brethren like REMHI in Guatemala or SERPAJ in Uruguay.[101] Consequently, UTPs are justified by their proponents in language that mimics that of official truth commissions – 'discovery and dissemination of truth', 'counter[ing] the propaganda, misconceptions and myths', 'reduc[ing] deniability that victims were violated', 'breaking the silence',[102] 'bearing witness to the traumatic events'.[103] DC-CAM's archives have always been about fostering three elements its organisers see as essential to Cambodia's recovery – 'accountability, truth, and memory'.[104] Spain's exhumations are explicitly founded on the idea of recovering historical memory to renegotiate the original democratic transition pact on more genuinely liberal lines, which culminated in the Spanish parliament's unanimous condemnation of Franco's coup.[105] The traditional link to reconciliation has been apparent, as in Rwanda, for example:

> Some interviewees did not see it as a priority to win specific recognition for Tutsi victims, putting greater emphasis on the need to find ways to 'unite people' through remembrance. But the aims of gaining recognition for victims as Tutsis and of forging closer relations with other Rwandans were not generally seen as distinct or incompatible. There was a view that reconciliation, or at least peaceful coexistence, could only be accomplished by promoting the truth about the genocide: 'We need unity and reconciliation but not badly interpreted, founded on the meaning of the genocide'.[106]

Few would doubt that initiatives like exhumation projects in Spain and Guatemala, archival projects like DC-CAM or documentation projects like the Bosnian and Kosovar Books of the Dead represent departures from the truth commission model in a way that Guatemala's REMHI or Uruguay's SERPAJ do not. Few would doubt either that more localised memory projects like Colombia's *Salón del Nunca Más*, Guatemala's Houses of Memory, or East Timor and Burundi's scattered memorials do not represent a significant 'vernacularisation' of the ideas and practices that inspire official truth and memory processes with local norms and ways of being.[107] However, the hope

---

100 Bakiner, *supra* note 54, at 20.

101 M. Ballengee, 'The Critical Role of Non-Governmental Organizations in Transitional Justice: A Case Study of Guatemala' (1999) 4 *UCLA Journal International Law & Foreign Affairs* 477, at 496–497; and Bickford, *supra* note 7, at 1009.

102 Androff, *supra* note 69, at 296 and 298.

103 Ferrandiz and Baer, *supra* note 3, at 6.

104 Caswell, *supra* note 2, at 25 [abstract].

105 G. Blakely, 'Digging Up Spain's Past: Consequences of Truth and Reconciliation' (2005) 12 *Democratization* 44, at 44.

106 Ibreck, *supra* note 80, at 339.

107 S.E. Merry, *Human Rights and Gender Violence: Translating International Law into Local Justice*, University of Chicago Press, Chicago, 2009.

expressed by scholars that community-based approaches to truth-telling would catalyse those communities into innovating in relation to historical inquiry, or that values and ideas informing truth would be articulated within and by each community has been realised only ambiguously.[108] The fear that local dialogue processes would lose their value if 'programmed' or encouraged by international actors has not been realised at all.[109] Nor indeed have communities been empowered to define local problems and conceptualise distinct programmes to address them.[110] Though critics of truth commissions assume that practices of truth-telling would be locally or culturally specific and grounded in long-established community norms, the UTPs surveyed above are at all points shown to be creatively adapting, reinterpreting and applying not just the ideals and democratic principles originally developed for official truth commissions, but also many of the practices.

While scholarly advocates of UTPs have argued that fealty to the legal-oriented and technical discourse of state-based truth commissions on the part of a UTP would inevitably distance that project from victims and communities,[111] in practice they have been characterised by a willingness to embrace expertise and global standards of practice. For example, while the Sarajevo Women's Court was established to provide a feminist model of transitional justice in response to the exclusionary legalism of the ICTY, it ended up appropriating the language, symbols and rituals of law.[112] The civil society-based Regional Commissions for Establishing Facts About War Crimes and Other Gross Human Rights Violations on the Territory of the Former Yugoslavia (RECOM) has been assailed by critics for its state-centric logic and its legal-oriented and technical discourse.[113] Though they are guided by cultural-spiritual beliefs about burial, those Zimbabweans who conduct exhumations in the Matabeleland know that 'in order for the bones to "speak" ... the exhumations need to be done expertly so that events at the time of death can be established, as well as the identity of the deceased'.[114] DC-CAM abides by the highest international standards of archiving. Likewise, the Kosovo Memory Book adopted a stringently rigorous methodology for its database on the assumption that the more accurate and comprehensive its record of fatalities, the less the record can be questioned or denied.[115] Even the paradigmatically grassroots Guatemalan process of weaving braids to commemorate abuses and atrocities is systematised by trained

108 Lundy and McGovern, *supra* note 24, at 271 and 274.
109 Arriaza and Roht-Arriaza, *supra* note 9, at 170.
110 Lundy and McGovern, *supra* note 24, at 280.
111 A. Kurze, 'Democratizing Justice in the Post-conflict Balkans: The Dilemma of Domestic Human Rights Activists' (2012) 7 *CEU Political Science Journal* 242, at 245.
112 O'Reilly, *supra* note 15, at 429.
113 Kurze, *supra* note 111, at 244.
114 Eppel, *supra* note 41, at 406.
115 Visoka, *supra* note 86, at 73.

professionals who record the information collected through computerisation and video.[116]

Far from manifesting distinctly local or national worldviews about truth or memory, UTPs have drawn on globalised human rights and transitional justice discourses to articulate their aspirations. They also draw on global assistance for finance and expertise. Local memory practices and commemorations in East Timor, though drawing on traditional cultural practices, are supported by national and international NGOs.[117] Guatemalan historical research and oral history projects are co-produced by international 'outsiders' and domestic 'insiders'.[118] In Spain, those who exhume bodies capture the exhumations in mass media formats, consciously ensuring they are 'reabsorbed' into a globalised memorial culture.[119] Furthermore, a desire to link UTPs with other transitional justice is an under-appreciated characteristic that may surprise those who see them as a response to the shortcomings and biases of official transitional justice. Just as truth commissions in the likes of Argentina, Chad and Guatemala saw their findings later used for trials, many UTPs are animated by the hope they will contribute to future 'formal' or statist transitional justice. DC-CAM's archives are a primary source of evidence for the Khmer Rouge trials, and have always functioned as an 'informal surrogate' for the truth commission many Cambodians would like to see.[120] Likewise, the Iraqi Memory Foundation's compilation of 11 million pages of records on the Saddam Hussein regime has been used in Iraqi High Tribunal trials.[121] UTPs in north-west Colombia and northern Uganda are primarily concerned with acknowledging past abuses, but also amass evidence for future use in human rights and transitional justice processes.[122] The Tribunal of Conscience for Women Survivors of Sexual Violence in Guatemala was established in part to prepare the foundations for a 'paradigmatic' prosecution of sexual violence before the domestic courts.[123] Additionally, exhumations of clandestine graves in Guatemala are attended by figures from the public prosecutor's office or judges in the (oft-disappointed) expectation that prosecutions might follow.[124] The Sarajevo Women's Court mixed its explicitly restorative approach with demands for greater accountability at ongoing domestic and international tribunals.[125] One of the core objectives for the aforementioned RECOM was

---

116 Arriaza and Roht-Arriaza, *supra* note 4, at 213.
117 Kent, *supra* note 82, at 443.
118 Crosby and Brinton Lykes, *supra* note 35, at 459.
119 Ferrandiz and Baer, *supra* note 3, at 13.
120 Caswell, *supra* note 2, at 26 and 36.
121 Bickford et al., *supra* note 71, at 14.
122 Riano Alcala and Baines, *supra* note 20, at 430.
123 Crosby and Brinton Lykes, *supra* note 35, at 456.
124 Arriaza and Roht-Arriaza, *supra* note 9, at 166–167.
125 O'Reilly, *supra* note 15, at 429.

to catalyse leaders in the former Yugoslav states to establish an international truth commission.[126]

## 6. CONCLUSION

Over a decade ago, Shaw and Waldorf argued that 'although policymakers and scholars now routinely recognize the importance of adapting mechanisms of transitional justice to local circumstances, such adaptation tends to be conceptualized in ways that do not modify the foundational assumptions of transitional justice.'[127] Notwithstanding the undoubted variety we see in UTPs and the greater critical awareness of transitional justice's ideological blind spots, it remains difficult to argue that these innovations have significantly modified the foundational assumptions of truth commissions. The use of globalised discourse, expertise and language of transitional justice are not tactical appropriations of liberalism. Nor indeed can they be explained by the influence of international donations, though this does of course help. UTPs are premised on many of the same causal beliefs about memory's link to justice and truth's link to democratic citizenship that underpinned the classic Chilean, South African or Liberian truth commission models. They are less a rejection by civil society of the liberal-legalist basis of truth commissions than a demand that its members' historical experience be acknowledged in similarly credible fashion. Few would doubt that the civil society actors are concerned with issues of socio-economic justice. However, their non-official status places inherent limitations on their ability to meaningfully address such issues. Localised or non-state ownership of transitional justice allows civil society to act as 'active agents of change' as critics of truth commissions expect,[128] but that area of activity magnifies, as opposed to extends, the traditional scope and remit of truth commissions. Civil society truth projects strain against limitations imposed by their own governments, but in so doing mimic much of what truth commissions have traditionally aspired towards, even when eschewing that precise form. 'Making your own' form of truth is the dominant form of resistance we see in UTPs – it is through acting as a surrogate for failed or non-existent truth commissions that this becomes a reality.

---

126 Kurze, *supra* note 5, at 461.

127 R. Shaw and L. Waldorf, 'Introduction: Localizing Transitional Justice', in Shaw and Waldorf with Hazan (eds.), *supra* note 4, at 4.

128 Aciru, *supra* note 64, at 81.

# INDEX

Lightning Source UK Ltd.
Milton Keynes UK
UKHW051506230622
404866UK00005B/131